My name is Daisuke Ashihara. My goal is to create a manga that both first-time readers and returning fans will enjoy. Here's *World Trigger* volume 1.

—Daisuke Ashihara, 2013

Daisuke Ashihara began his manga career at the age of 27 when his manga *Room 303* won second place in the 75th Tezuka Awards. His first series, *Super Dog Rilienthal*, began serialization in *Weekly Shonen Jump* in 2009. *World Trigger* is his second serialized work in *Weekly Shonen Jump*. He is also the author of several shorter works, including the one-shots *Super Dog Rilienthal*, *Trigger Keeper* and *Elite Agent Jin*.

WORLD TRIGGER VOL. 1
SHONEN JUMP Manga Edition

STORY AND ART BY DAISUKE ASHIHARA

Translation/Lillian Olsen
Touch-Up Art & Lettering/Annaliese Christman
Design/Sam Elzway
Editor/Hope Donovan

Printed in the U.S.A.

Published by VIZ Media, LLC
P.O. Box 77010
San Francisco, CA 94107

10 9 8 7 6 5 4 3
First printing, October 2014
Third printing, December 2018

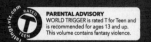

SHONEN JUMP MANGA EDITION

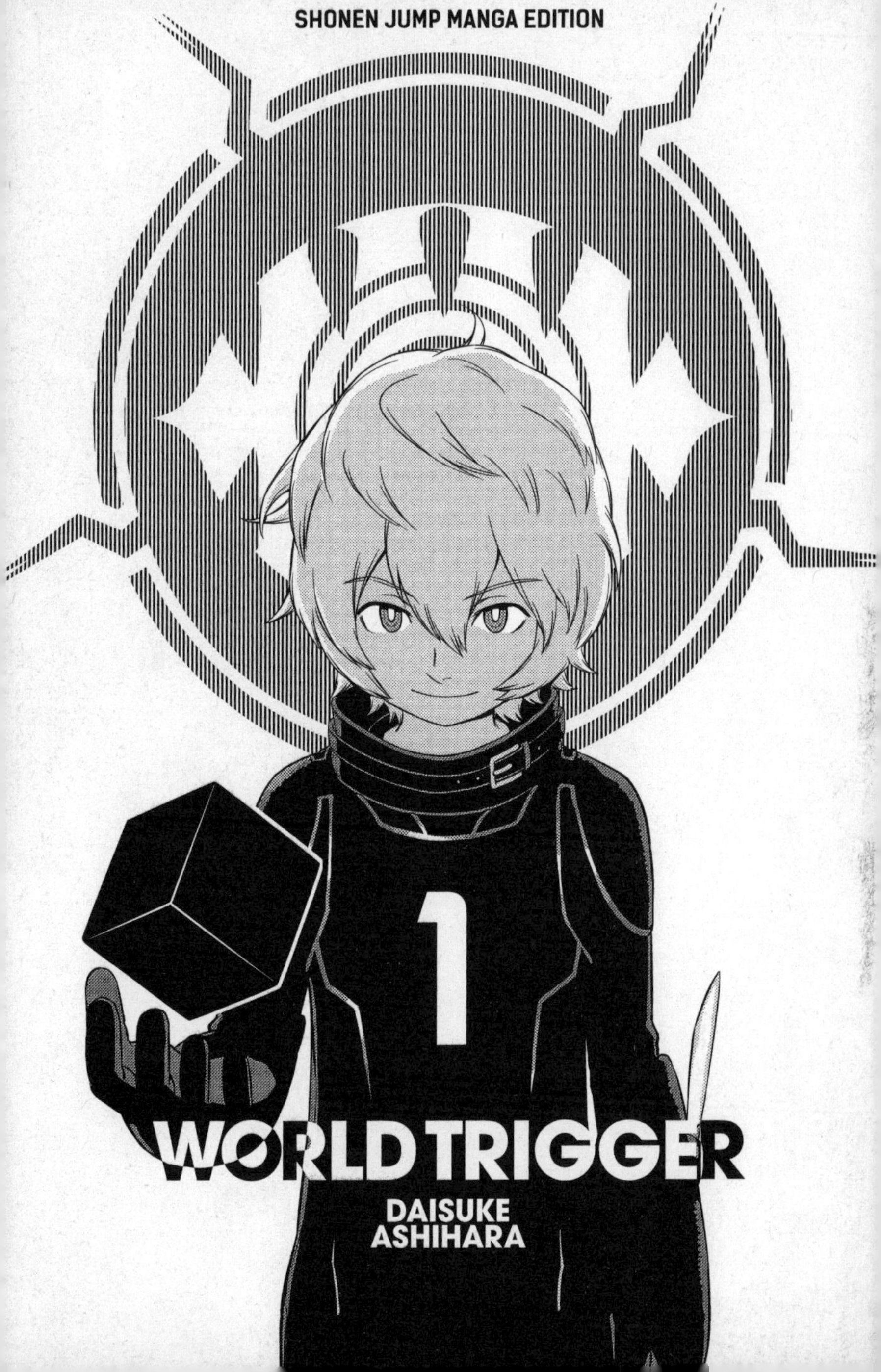
1

WORLD TRIGGER

DAISUKE
ASHIHARA

WORLD TRIGGER

CONTENTS

1

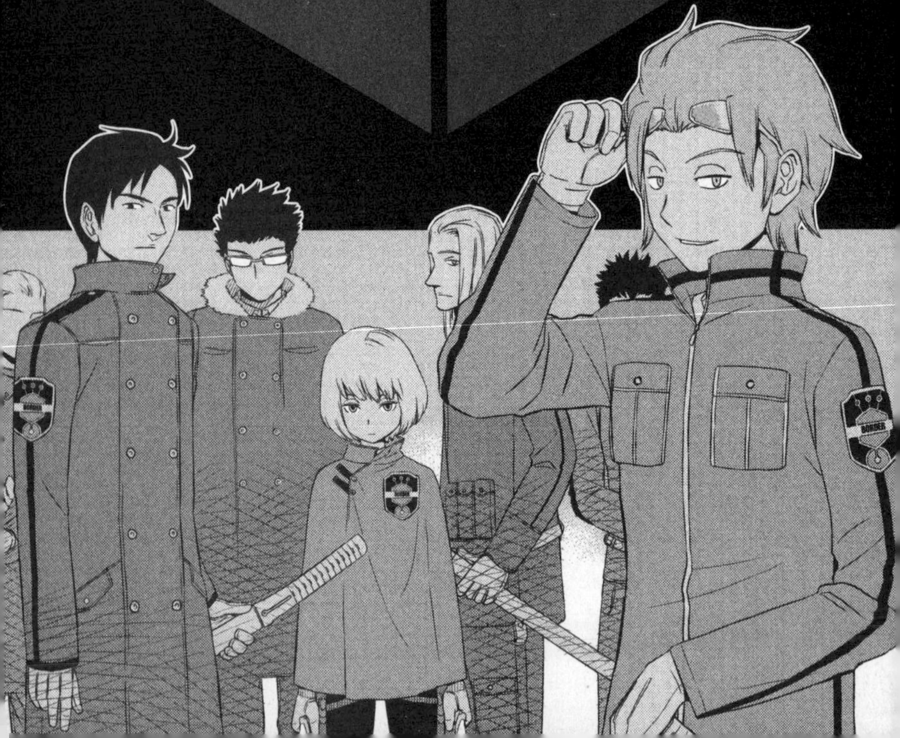

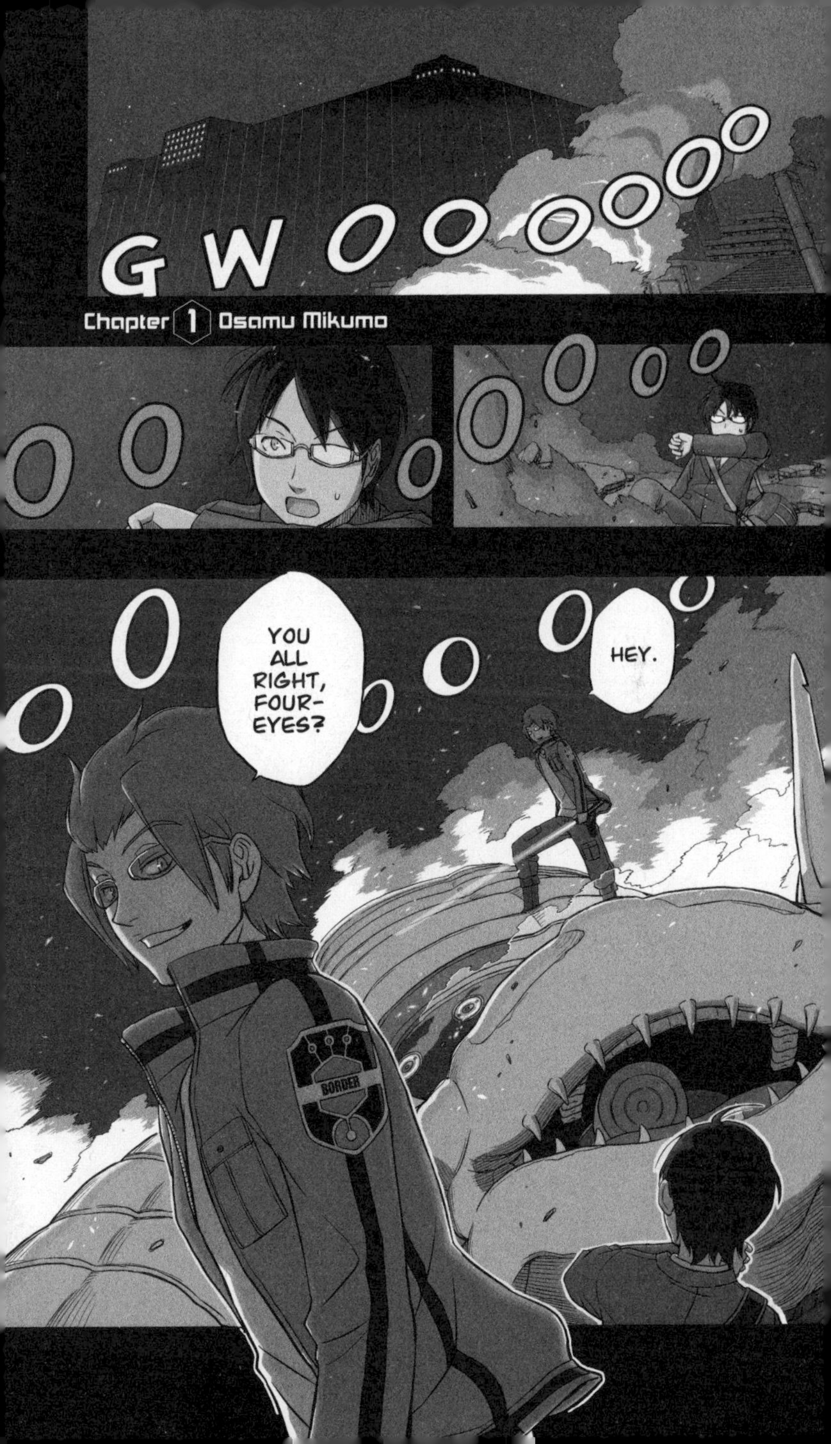
GWOOOOOOO
Chapter 1 Osamu Mikumo
OOOO
OOOO
HEY.
YOU ALL RIGHT, FOUR-EYES?
OOOOOO

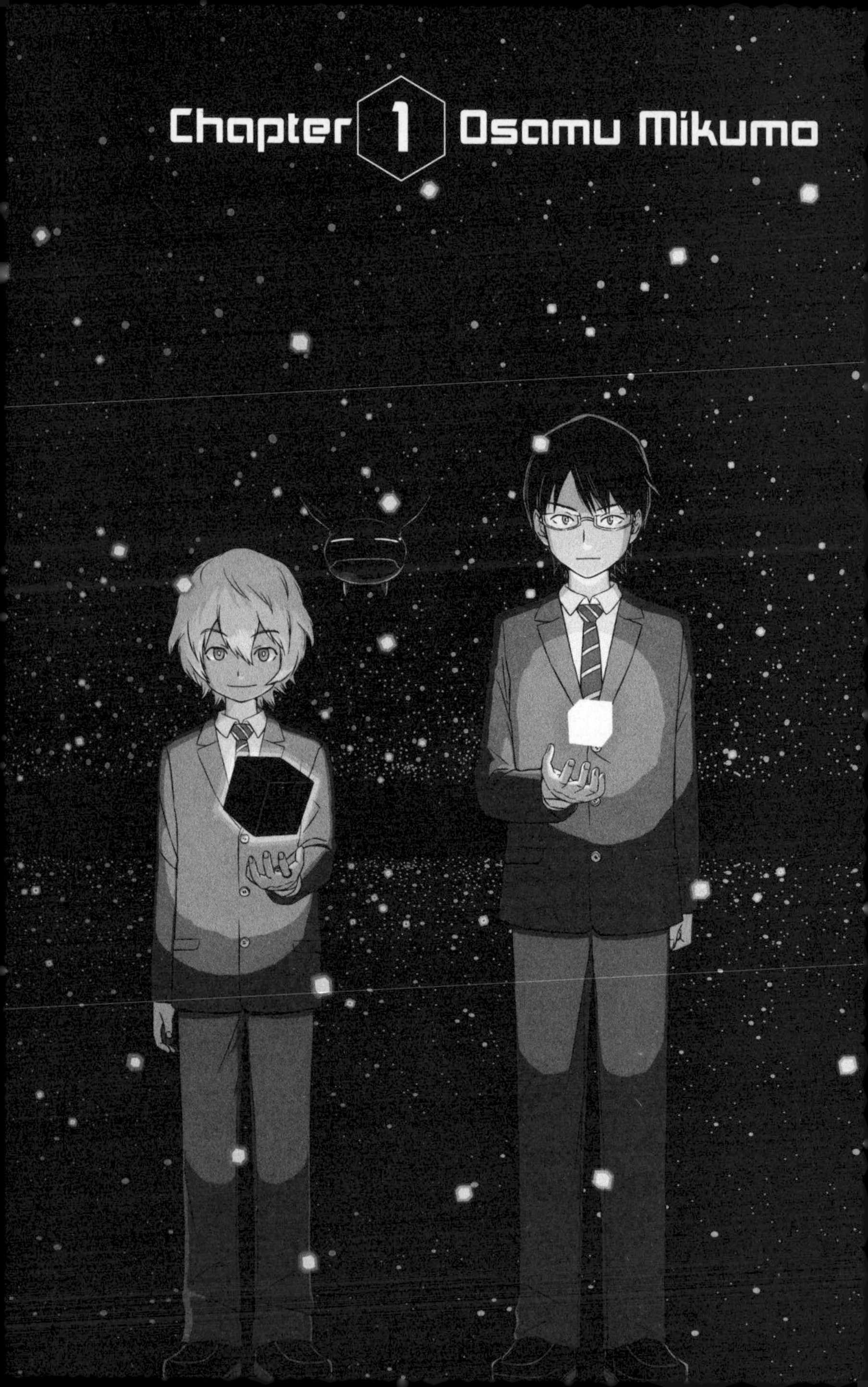
Chapter 1 Osamu Mikumo

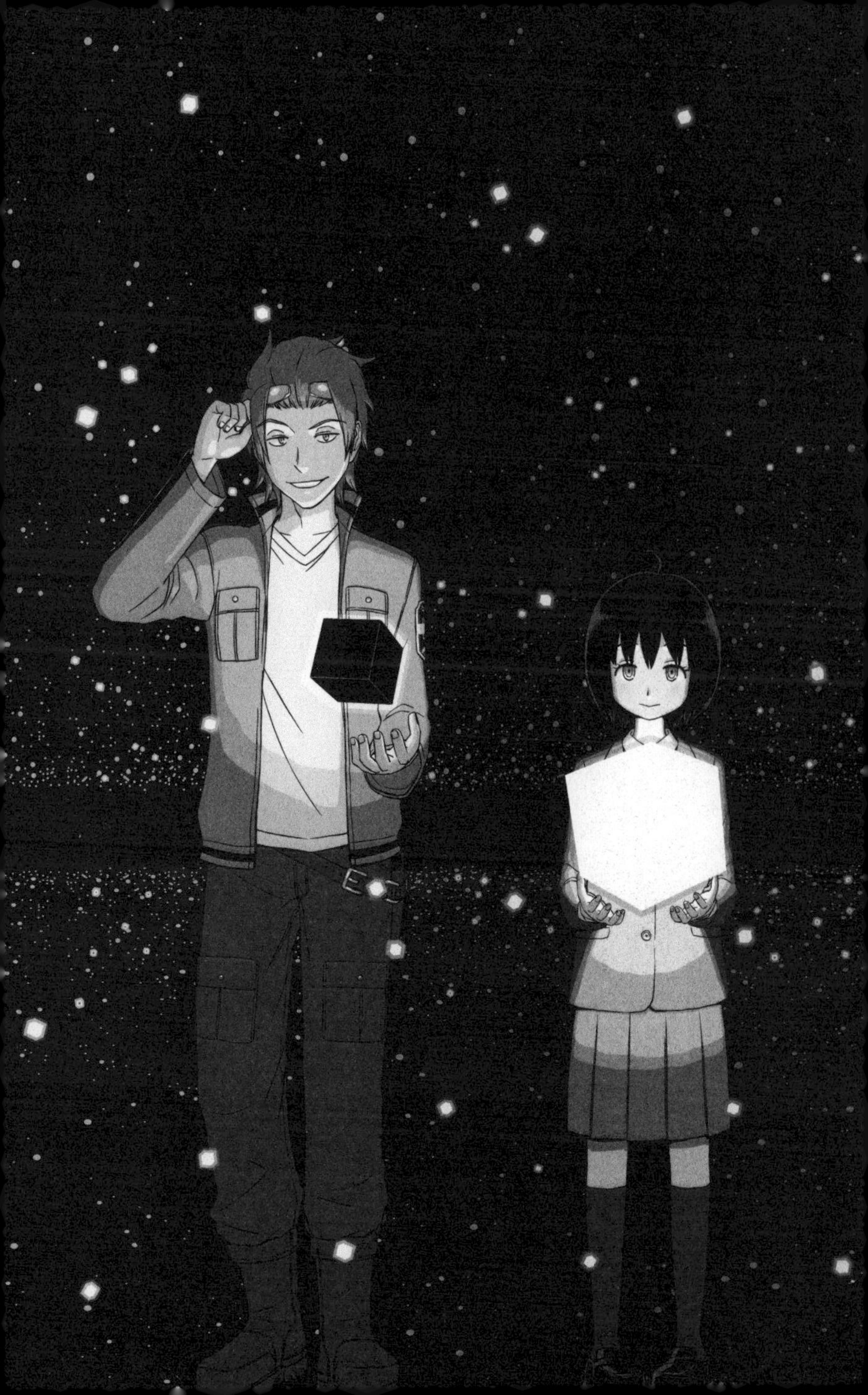

WORLD TRIGGER

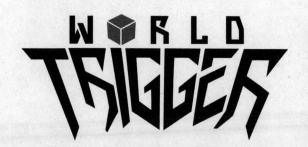

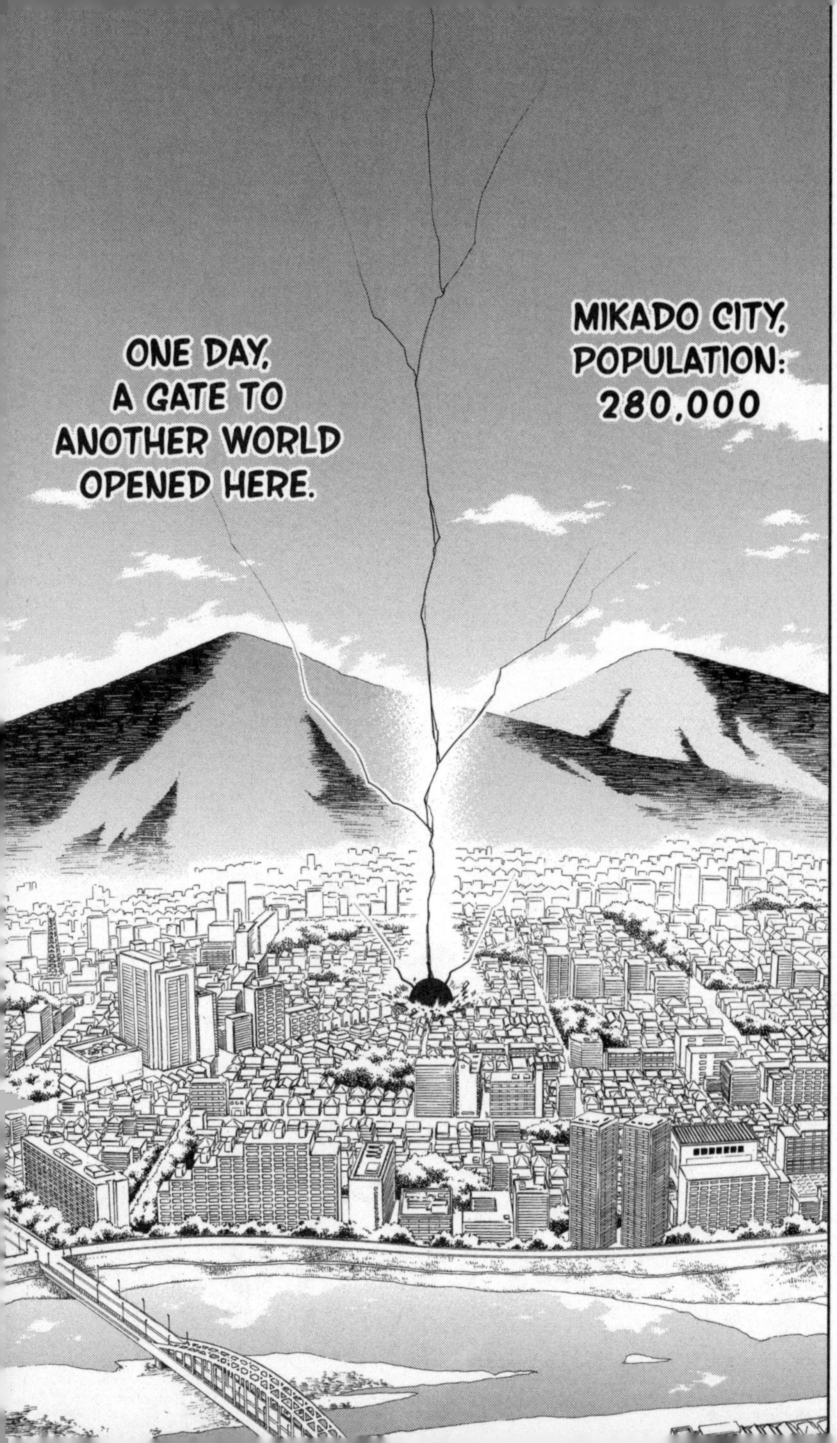
MIKADO CITY, POPULATION: 280,000
ONE DAY, A GATE TO ANOTHER WORLD OPENED HERE.

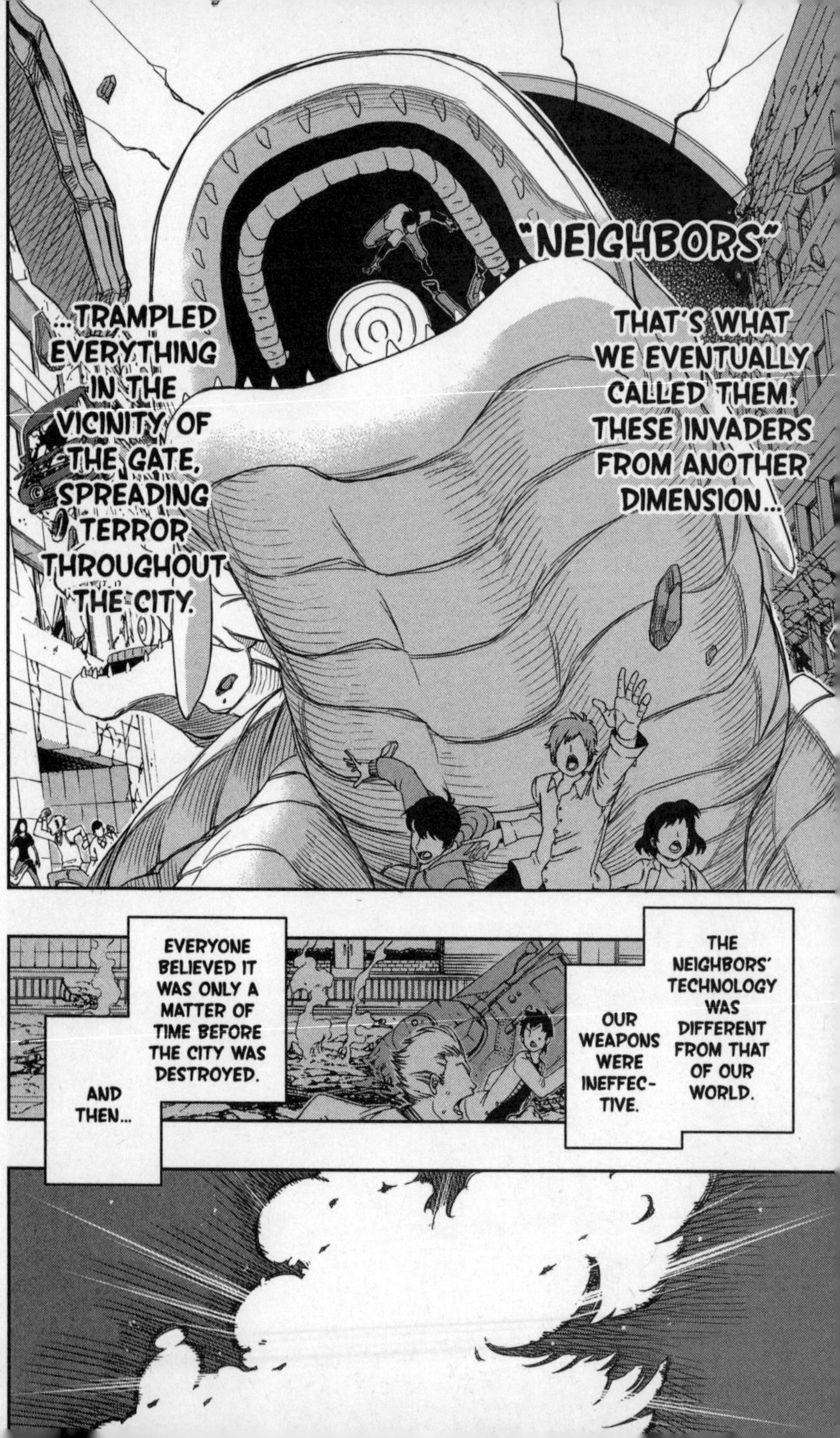
"NEIGHBORS"
THAT'S WHAT WE EVENTUALLY CALLED THEM. THESE INVADERS FROM ANOTHER DIMENSION...
...TRAMPLED EVERYTHING IN THE VICINITY OF THE GATE, SPREADING TERROR THROUGHOUT THE CITY.
THE NEIGHBORS' TECHNOLOGY WAS DIFFERENT FROM THAT OF OUR WORLD.
OUR WEAPONS WERE INEFFEC-TIVE.
EVERYONE BELIEVED IT WAS ONLY A MATTER OF TIME BEFORE THE CITY WAS DESTROYED.
AND THEN...

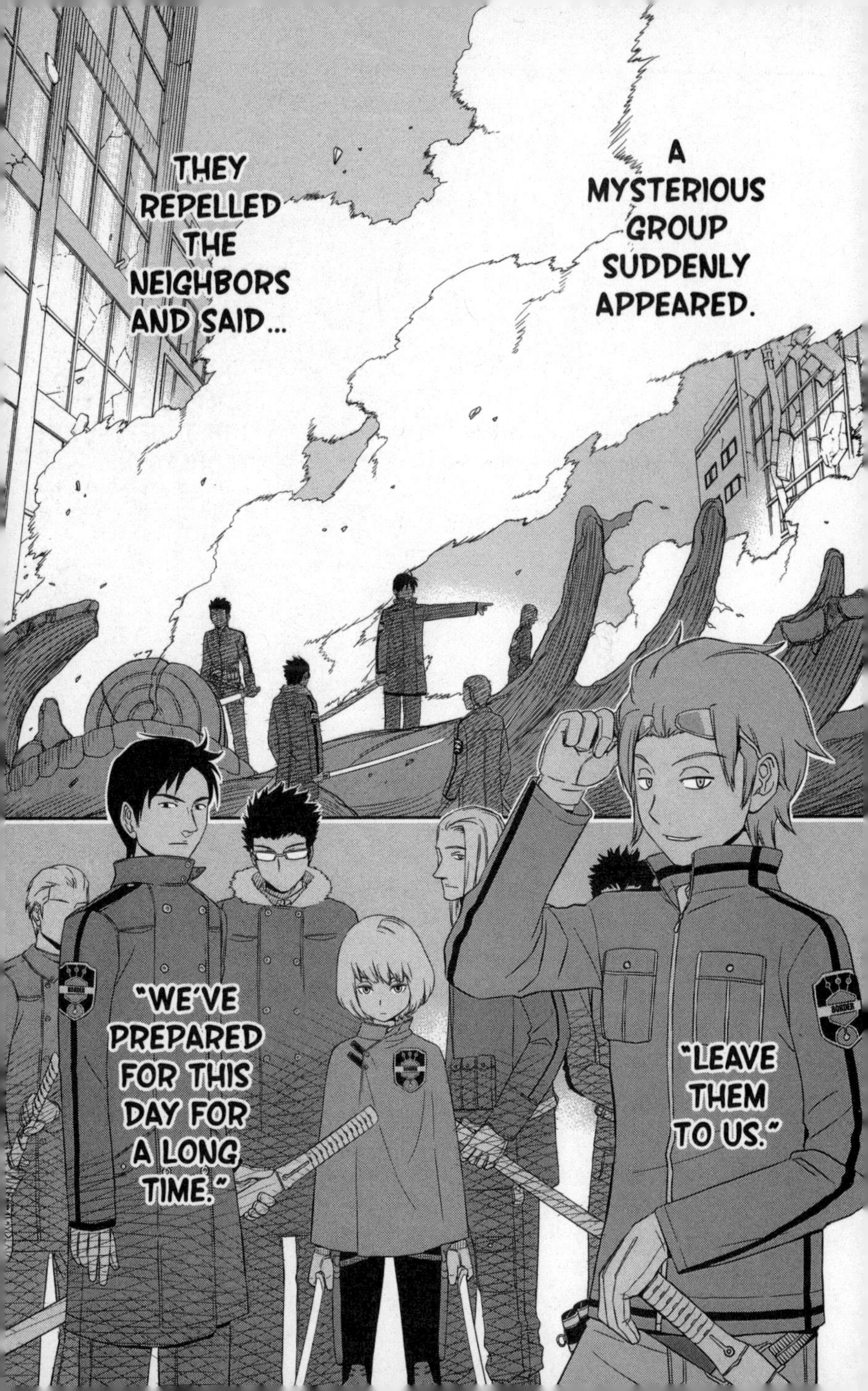
A MYSTERIOUS GROUP SUDDENLY APPEARED.
THEY REPELLED THE NEIGHBORS AND SAID...
"LEAVE THEM TO US."
"WE'VE PREPARED FOR THIS DAY FOR A LONG TIME."

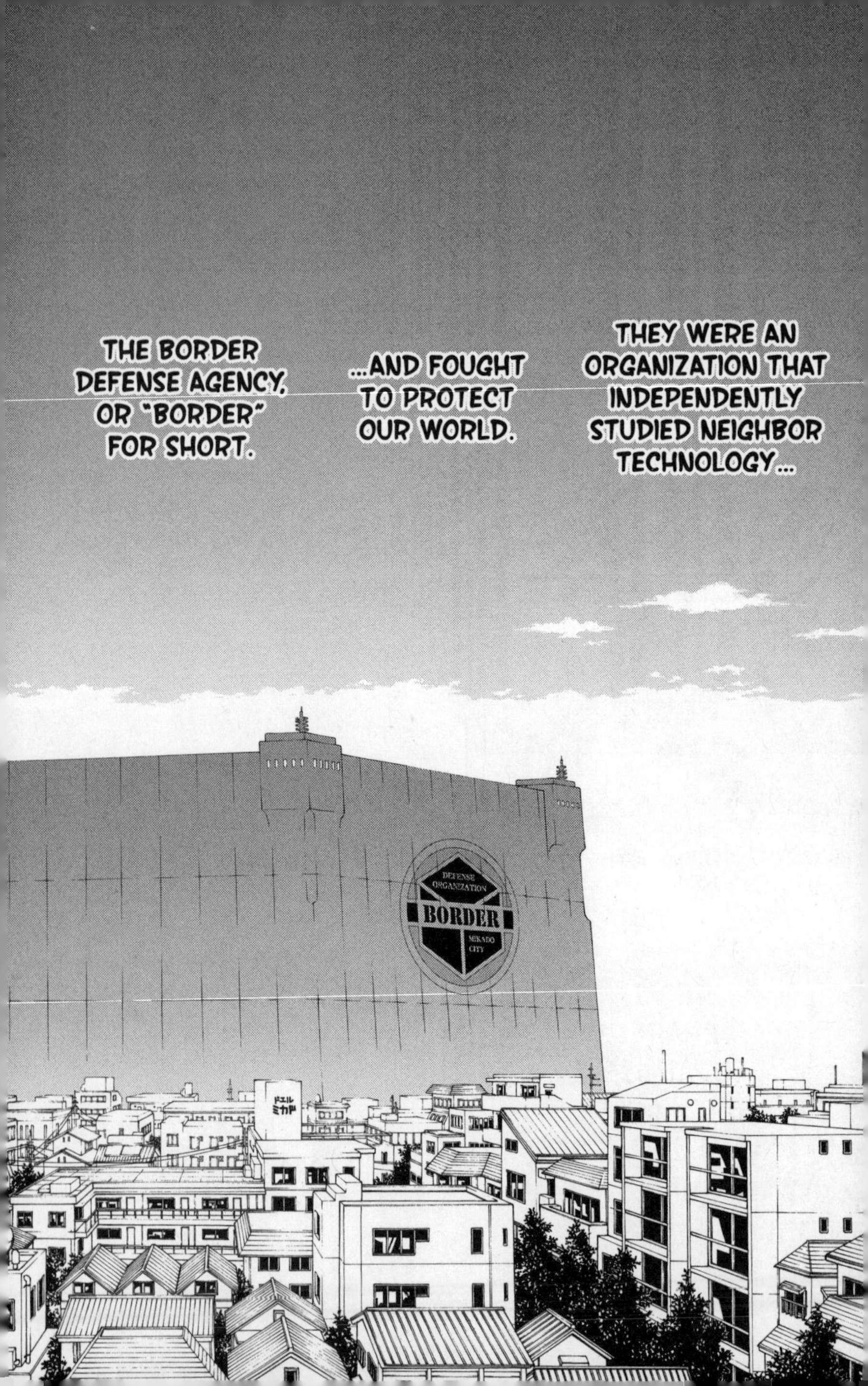
THEY WERE AN ORGANIZATION THAT INDEPENDENTLY STUDIED NEIGHBOR TECHNOLOGY...
...AND FOUGHT TO PROTECT OUR WORLD.
THE BORDER DEFENSE AGENCY. OR "BORDER" FOR SHORT.
DEFENSE ORGANIZATION
BORDER
MIKADO CITY

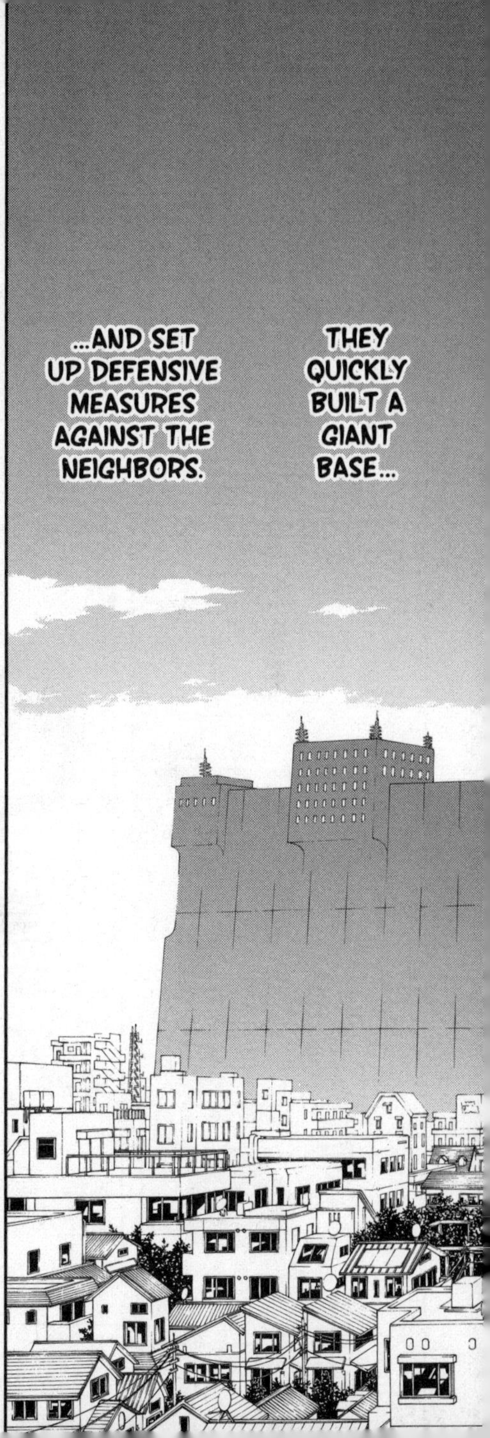
THEY QUICKLY BUILT A GIANT BASE...
...AND SET UP DEFENSIVE MEASURES AGAINST THE NEIGHBORS.

READ THIS WAY

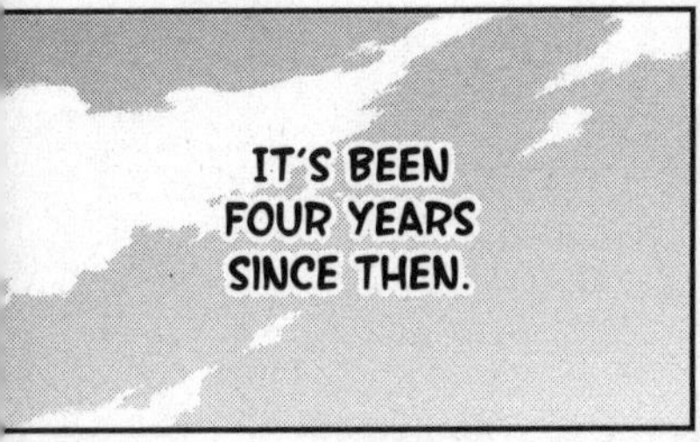
IT'S BEEN FOUR YEARS SINCE THEN.

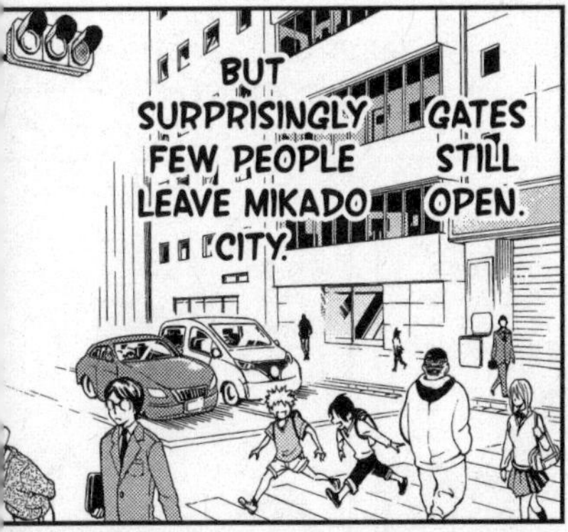
GATES STILL OPEN.
BUT SURPRISINGLY FEW PEOPLE LEAVE MIKADO CITY.

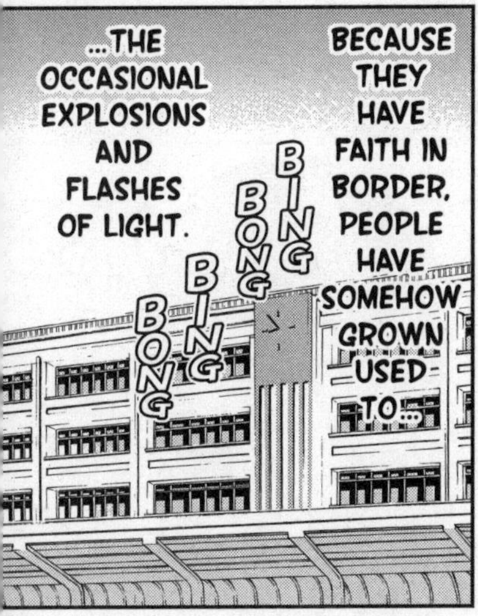
BECAUSE THEY HAVE FAITH IN BORDER, PEOPLE HAVE SOMEHOW GROWN USED TO...
BING
BONG
BING
BONG
...THE OCCASIONAL EXPLOSIONS AND FLASHES OF LIGHT.

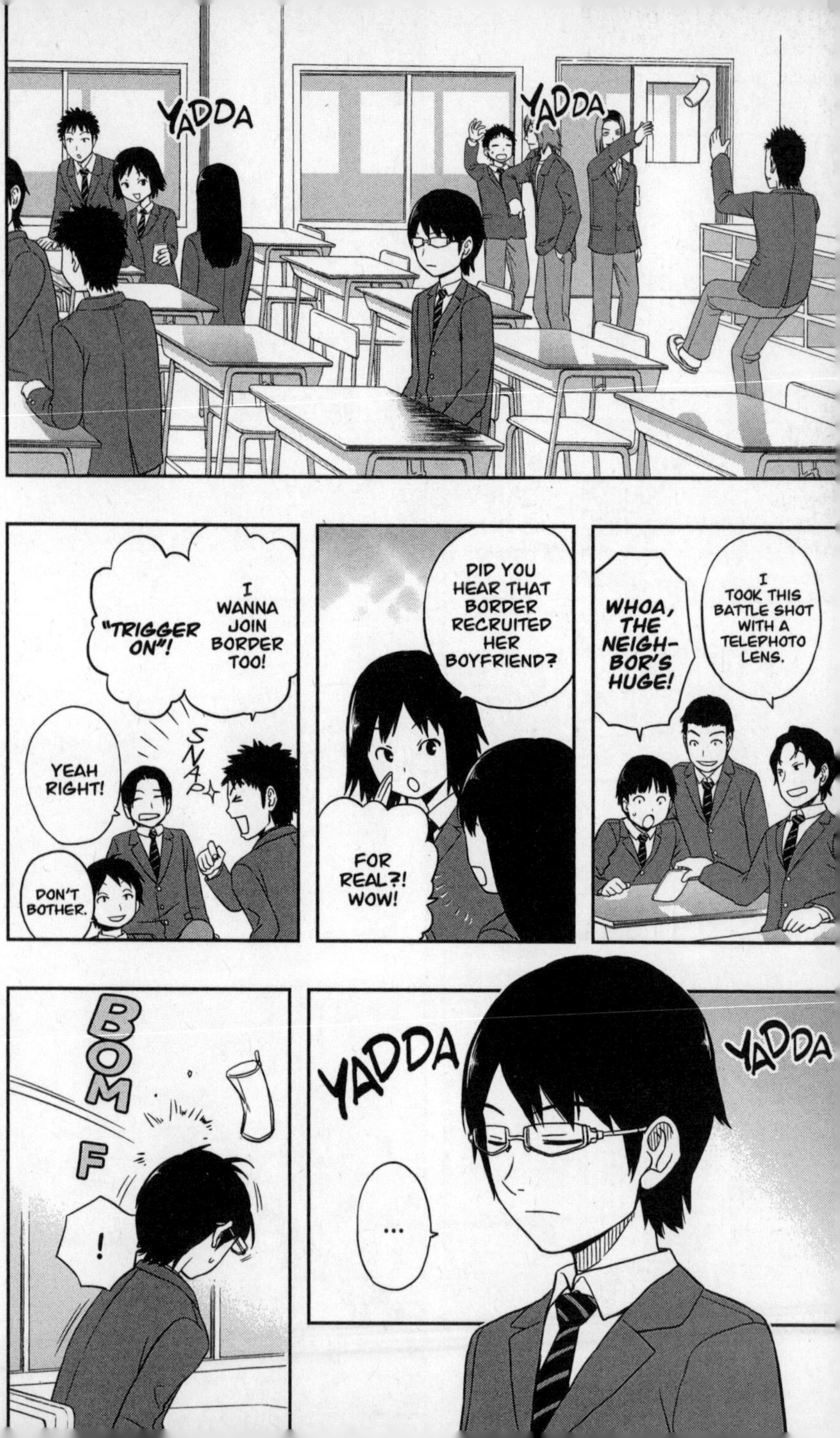
YADDA
YADDA
I TOOK THIS BATTLE SHOT WITH A TELEPHOTO LENS.
WHOA, THE NEIGHBOR'S HUGE!
DID YOU HEAR THAT BORDER RECRUITED HER BOYFRIEND?
FOR REAL?! WOW!
I WANNA JOIN BORDER TOO!
"TRIGGER ON"!
SNAP
YEAH RIGHT!
DON'T BOTHER.
YADDA
YADDA
...
BOMF
!

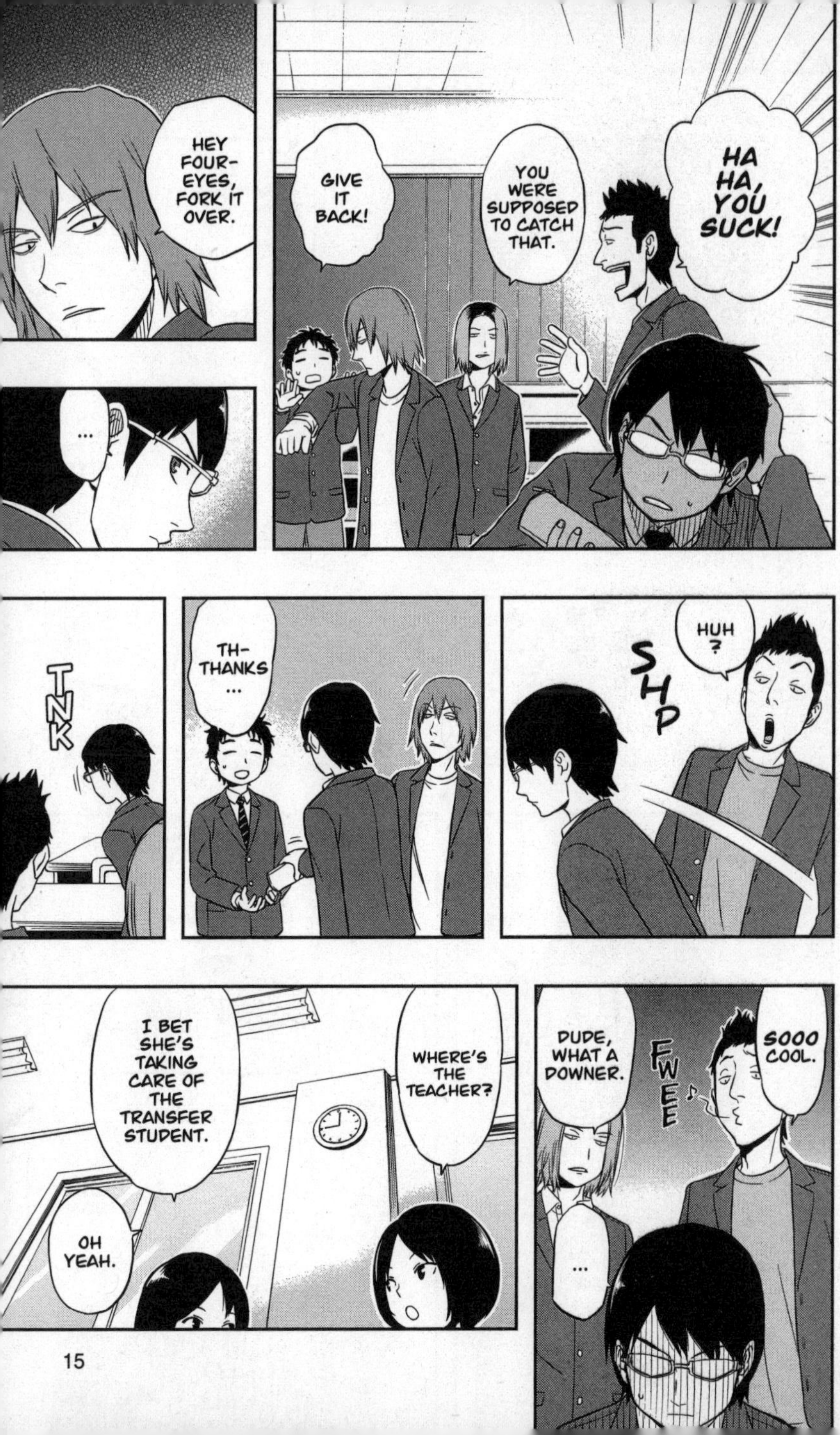
HA HA, YOU SUCK!
YOU WERE SUPPOSED TO CATCH THAT.
GIVE IT BACK!
HEY FOUR-EYES, FORK IT OVER.
...
HUH?
SHP
TH-THANKS...
TNK
SOOO COOL.
FWEE
DUDE, WHAT A DOWNER.
...
WHERE'S THE TEACHER?
I BET SHE'S TAKING CARE OF THE TRANSFER STUDENT.
OH YEAH.

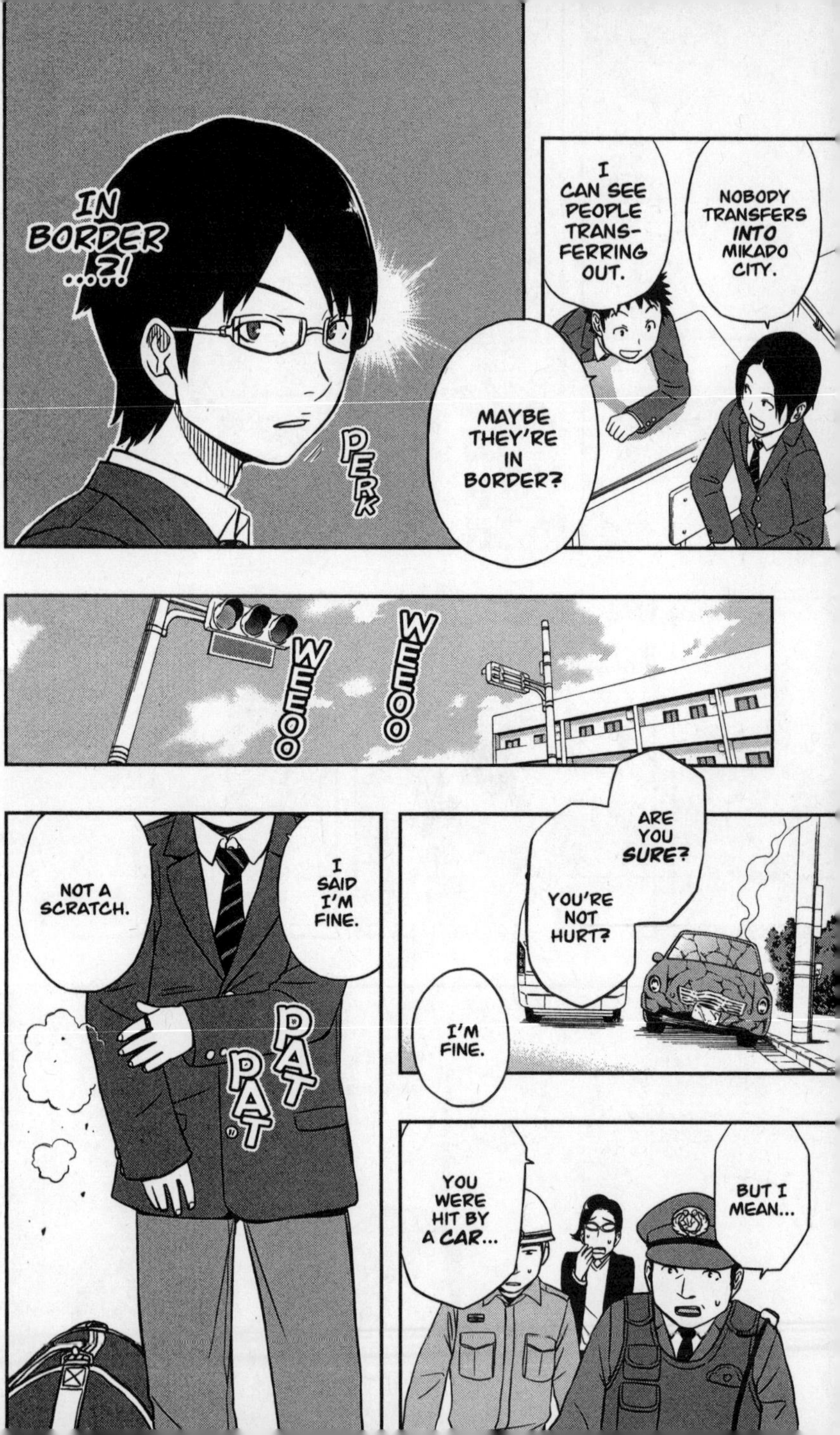
NOBODY TRANSFERS INTO MIKADO CITY.
I CAN SEE PEOPLE TRANS-FERRING OUT.
MAYBE THEY'RE IN BORDER?
IN BORDER ...?!
PERK
WEEOO
WEEOO
ARE YOU SURE?
YOU'RE NOT HURT?
I'M FINE.
BUT I MEAN...
YOU WERE HIT BY A CAR...
I SAID I'M FINE.
NOT A SCRATCH.
PAT
PAT

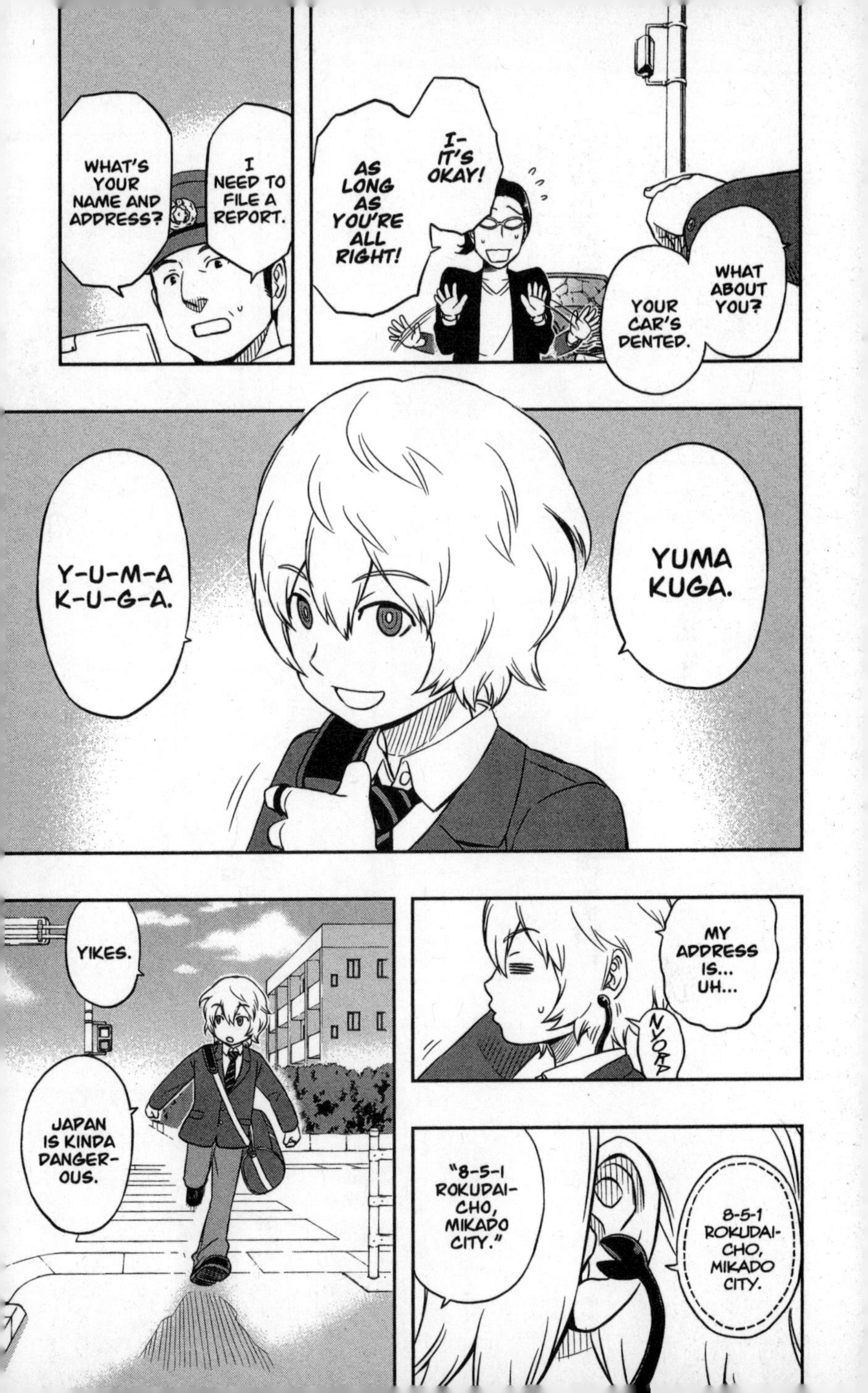
WHAT ABOUT YOU?
YOUR CAR'S DENTED.
I- IT'S OKAY!
AS LONG AS YOU'RE ALL RIGHT!
I NEED TO FILE A REPORT.
WHAT'S YOUR NAME AND ADDRESS?
YUMA KUGA.
Y-U-M-A K-U-G-A.
MY ADDRESS IS... UH...
NYORO
8-5-1 ROKUDAI-CHO, MIKADO CITY.
"8-5-1 ROKUDAI-CHO, MIKADO CITY."
YIKES.
JAPAN IS KINDA DANGER-OUS.

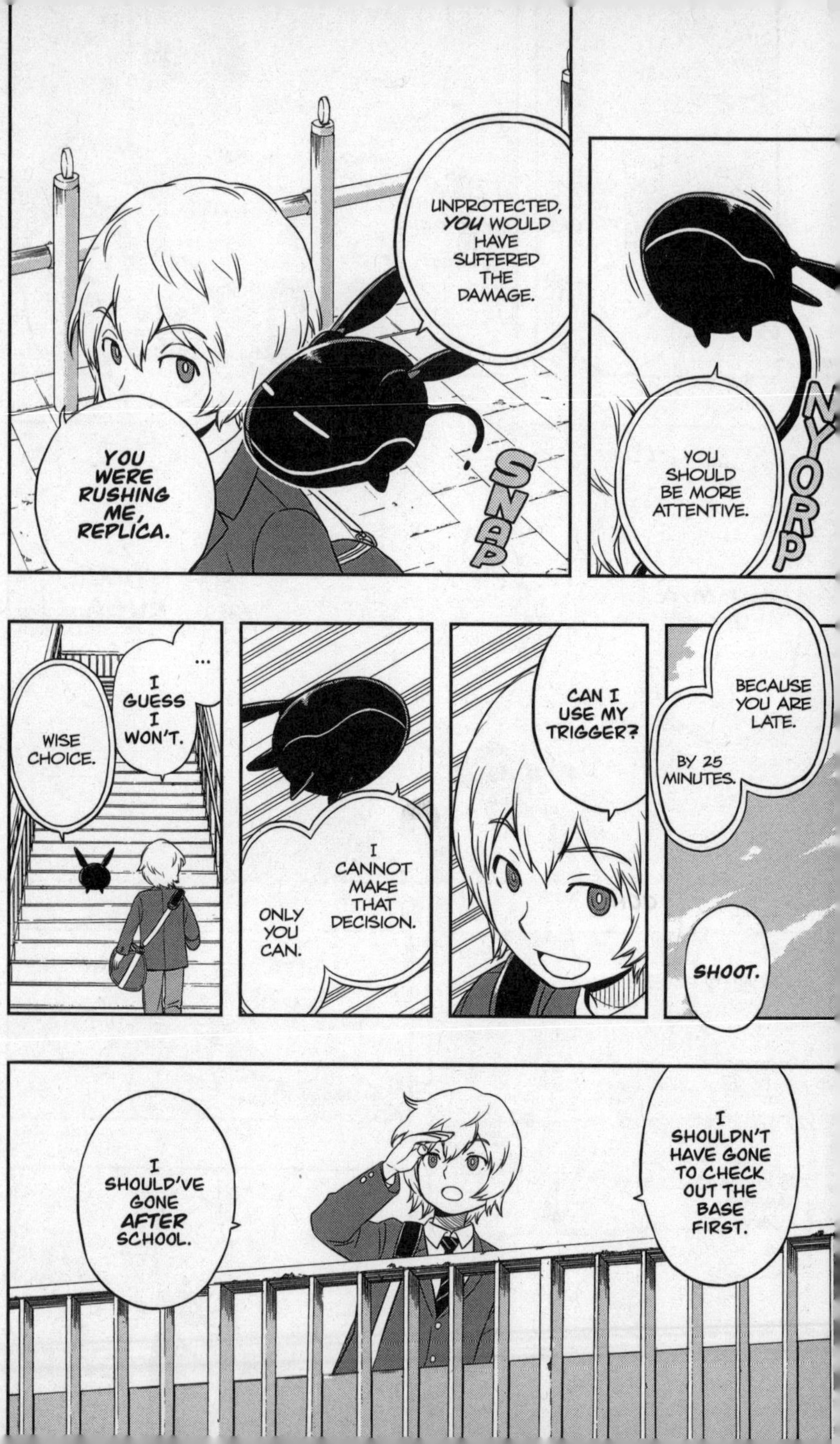
NYORP
YOU SHOULD BE MORE ATTENTIVE.
UNPROTECTED, YOU WOULD HAVE SUFFERED THE DAMAGE.
SNAP
YOU WERE RUSHING ME, REPLICA.
BECAUSE YOU ARE LATE.
BY 25 MINUTES.
SHOOT.
CAN I USE MY TRIGGER?
I CANNOT MAKE THAT DECISION.
ONLY YOU CAN.
... I GUESS I WON'T.
WISE CHOICE.
I SHOULDN'T HAVE GONE TO CHECK OUT THE BASE FIRST.
I SHOULD'VE GONE AFTER SCHOOL.

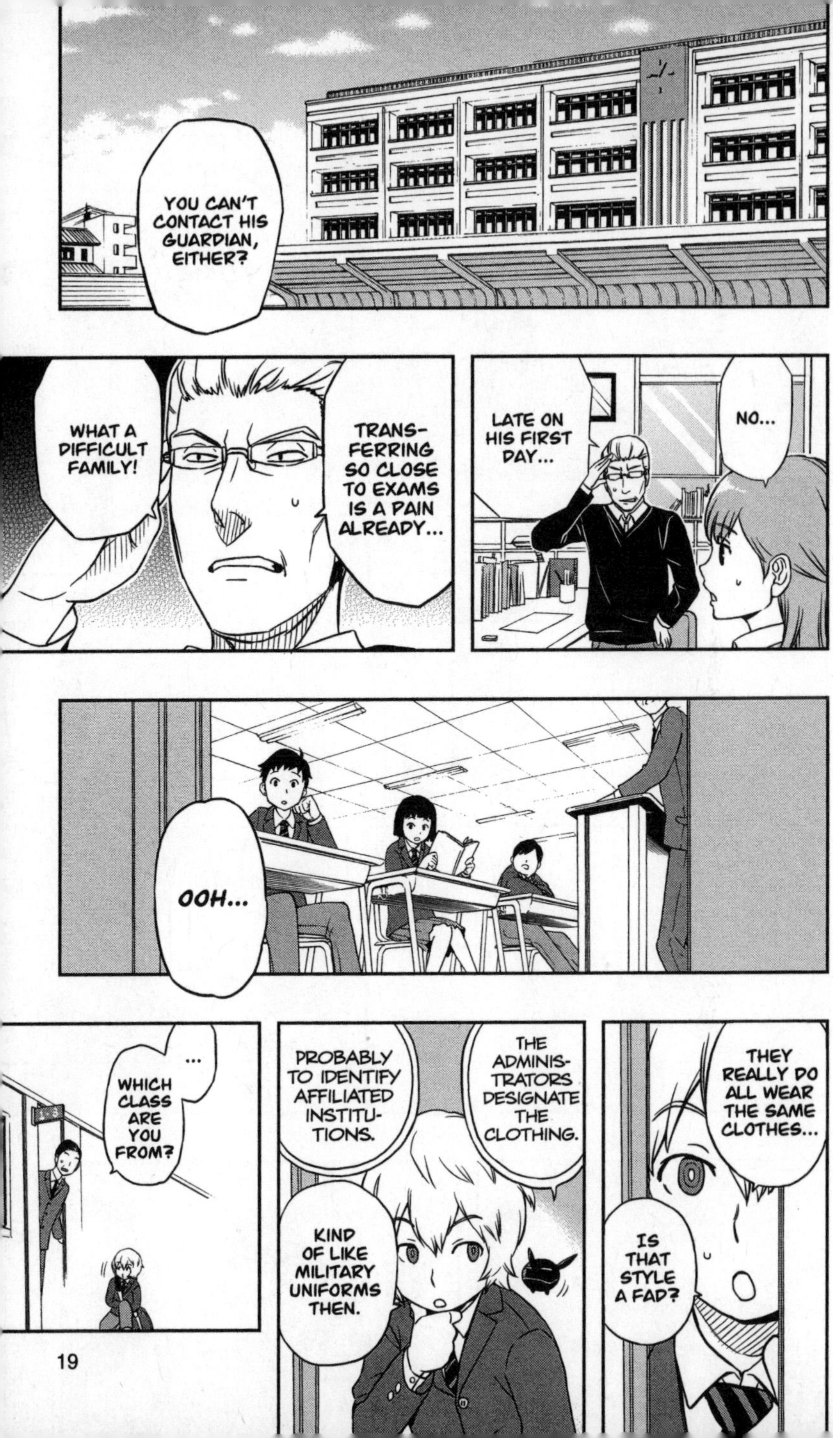
YOU CAN'T CONTACT HIS GUARDIAN, EITHER?
NO...
LATE ON HIS FIRST DAY...
TRANSFERRING SO CLOSE TO EXAMS IS A PAIN ALREADY...
WHAT A DIFFICULT FAMILY!
OOH...
THEY REALLY DO ALL WEAR THE SAME CLOTHES...
IS THAT STYLE A FAD?
THE ADMINISTRATORS DESIGNATE THE CLOTHING.
PROBABLY TO IDENTIFY AFFILIATED INSTITUTIONS.
KIND OF LIKE MILITARY UNIFORMS THEN.
...
WHICH CLASS ARE YOU FROM?

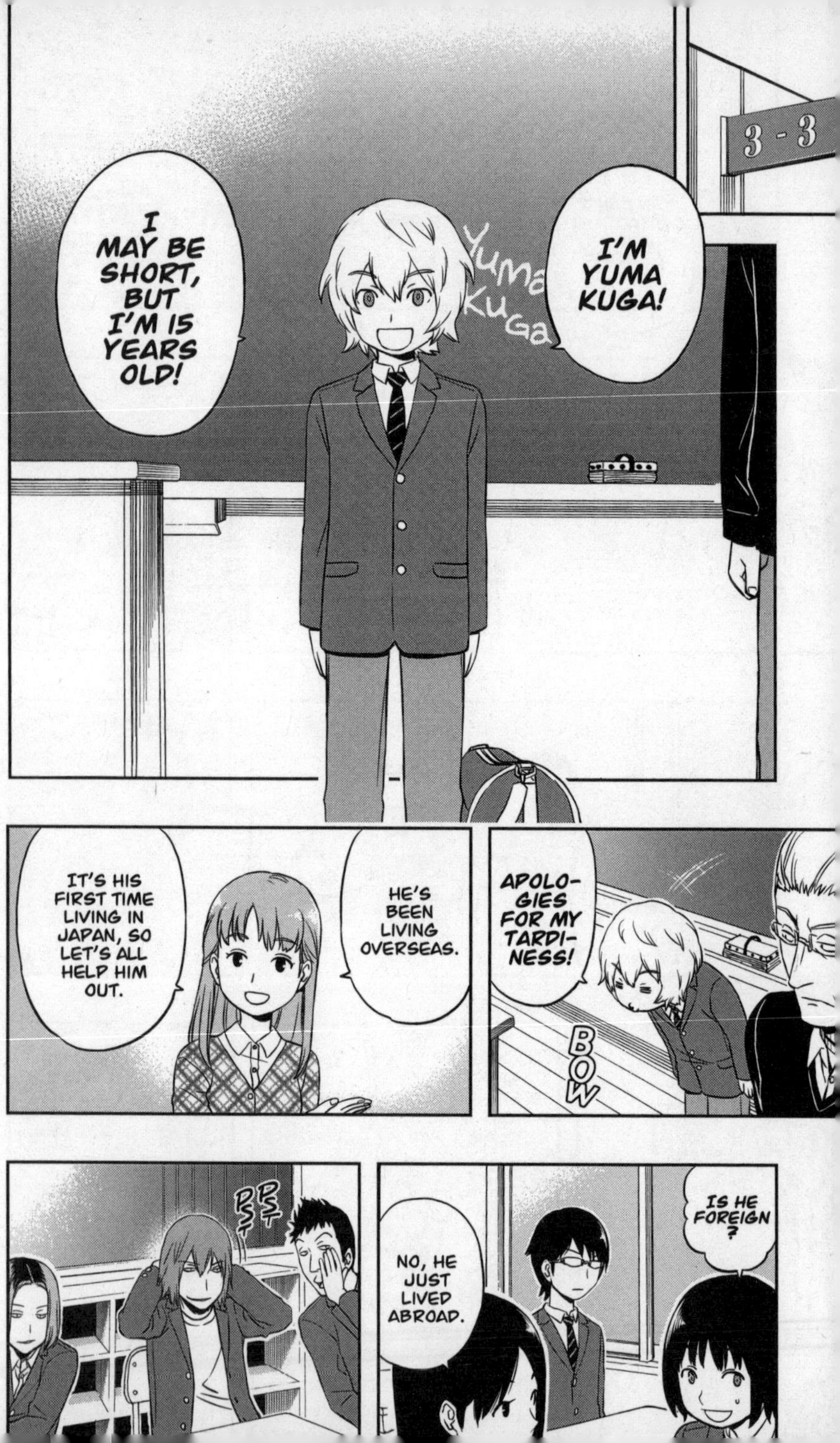
3-3
I'M YUMA KUGA!
Yuma Kuga
I MAY BE SHORT, BUT I'M 15 YEARS OLD!
APOLOGIES FOR MY TARDINESS!
BOW
HE'S BEEN LIVING OVERSEAS.
IT'S HIS FIRST TIME LIVING IN JAPAN, SO LET'S ALL HELP HIM OUT.
IS HE FOREIGN?
NO, HE JUST LIVED ABROAD.
PST PST

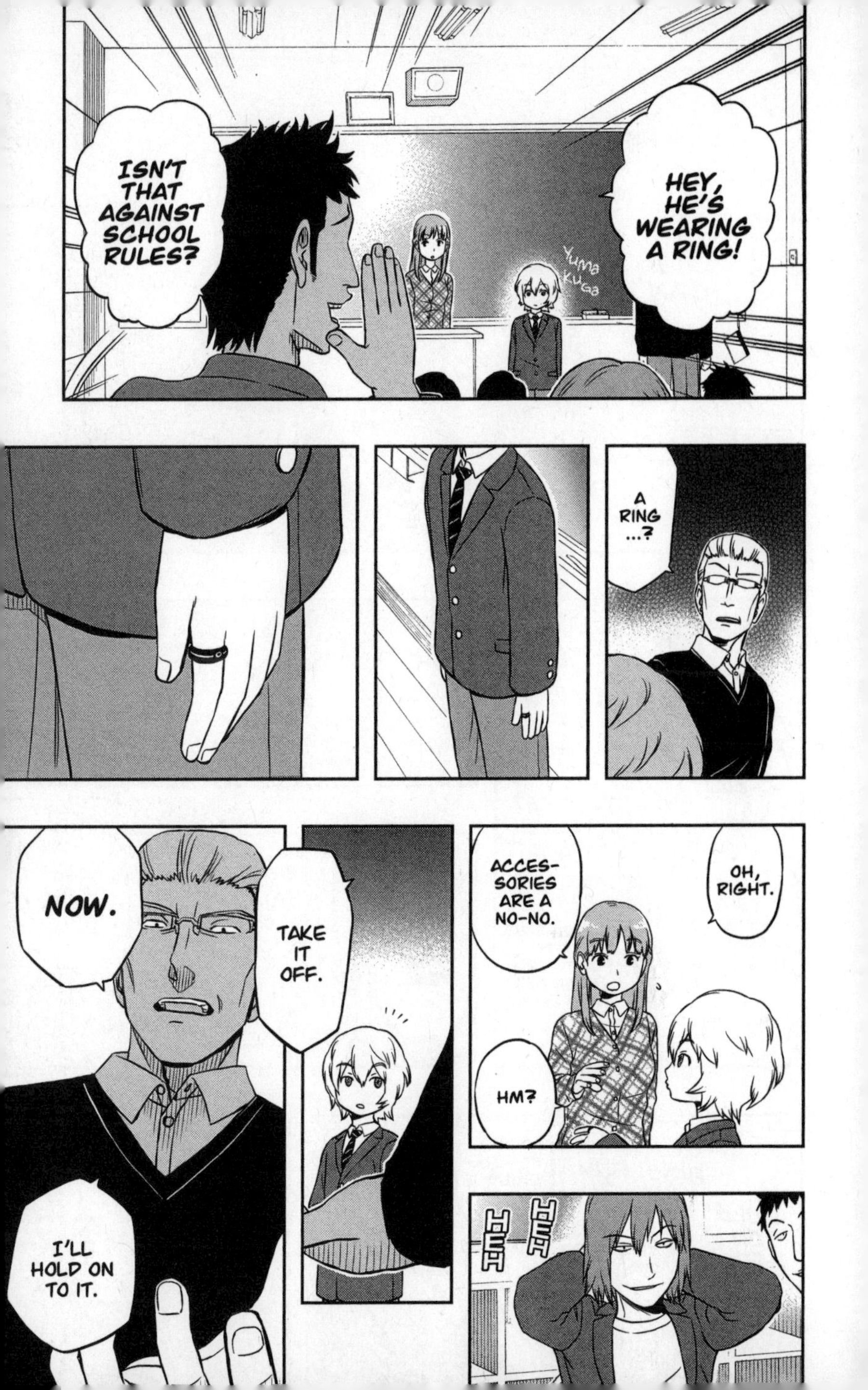
HEY, HE'S WEARING A RING!
Yuma Kuga
ISN'T THAT AGAINST SCHOOL RULES?
A RING ...?
OH, RIGHT.
ACCES-SORIES ARE A NO-NO.
HM?
HEH HEH
TAKE IT OFF.
NOW.
I'LL HOLD ON TO IT.

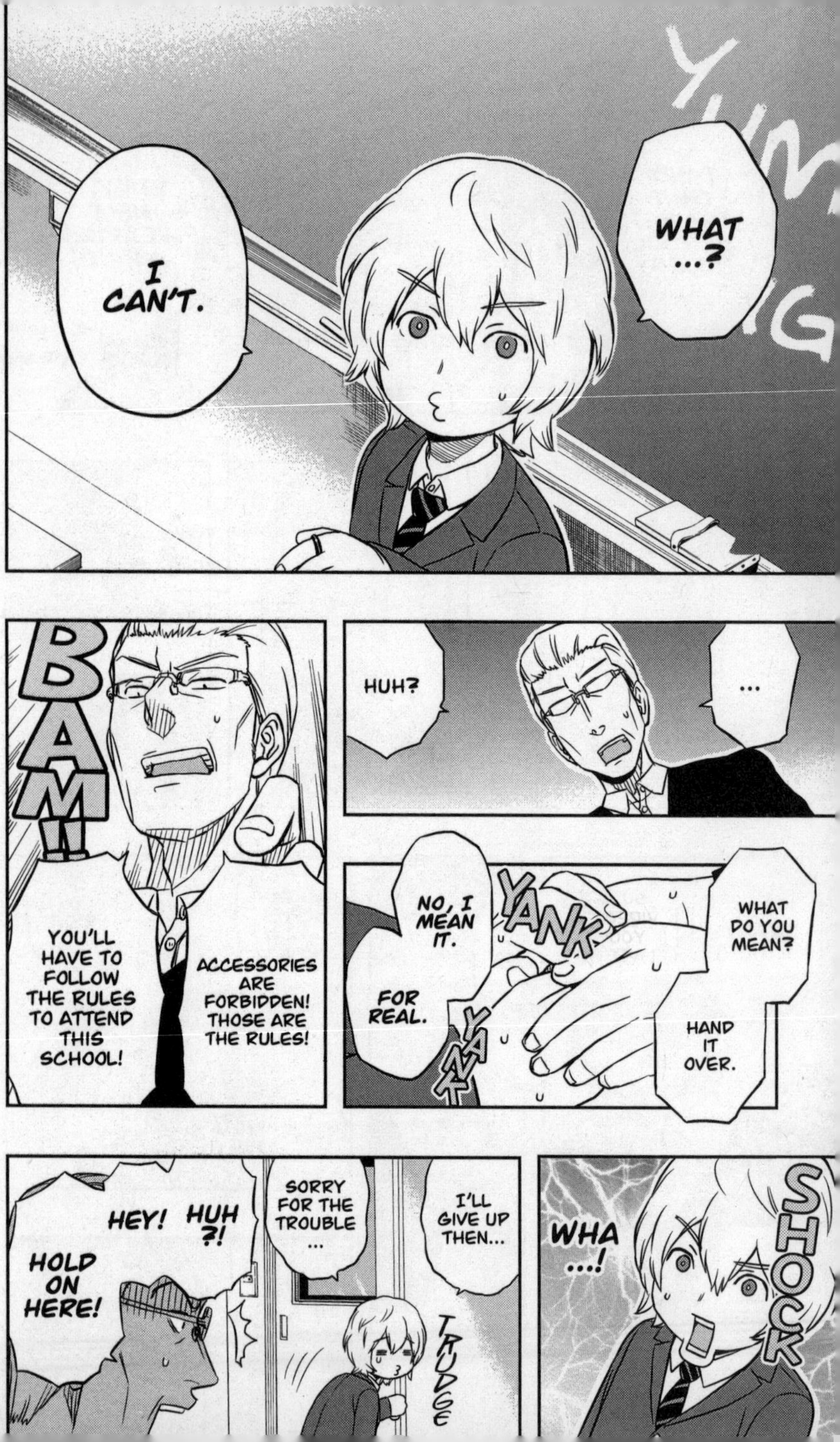
WHAT ...?
I CAN'T.
...
HUH?
WHAT DO YOU MEAN?
YANK
HAND IT OVER.
NO, I MEAN IT.
FOR REAL.
YANK
BAM!
ACCESSORIES ARE FORBIDDEN! THOSE ARE THE RULES!
YOU'LL HAVE TO FOLLOW THE RULES TO ATTEND THIS SCHOOL!
SHOCK
WHA ...!
I'LL GIVE UP THEN...
SORRY FOR THE TROUBLE ...
TRUDGE
HUH ?!
HEY!
HOLD ON HERE!

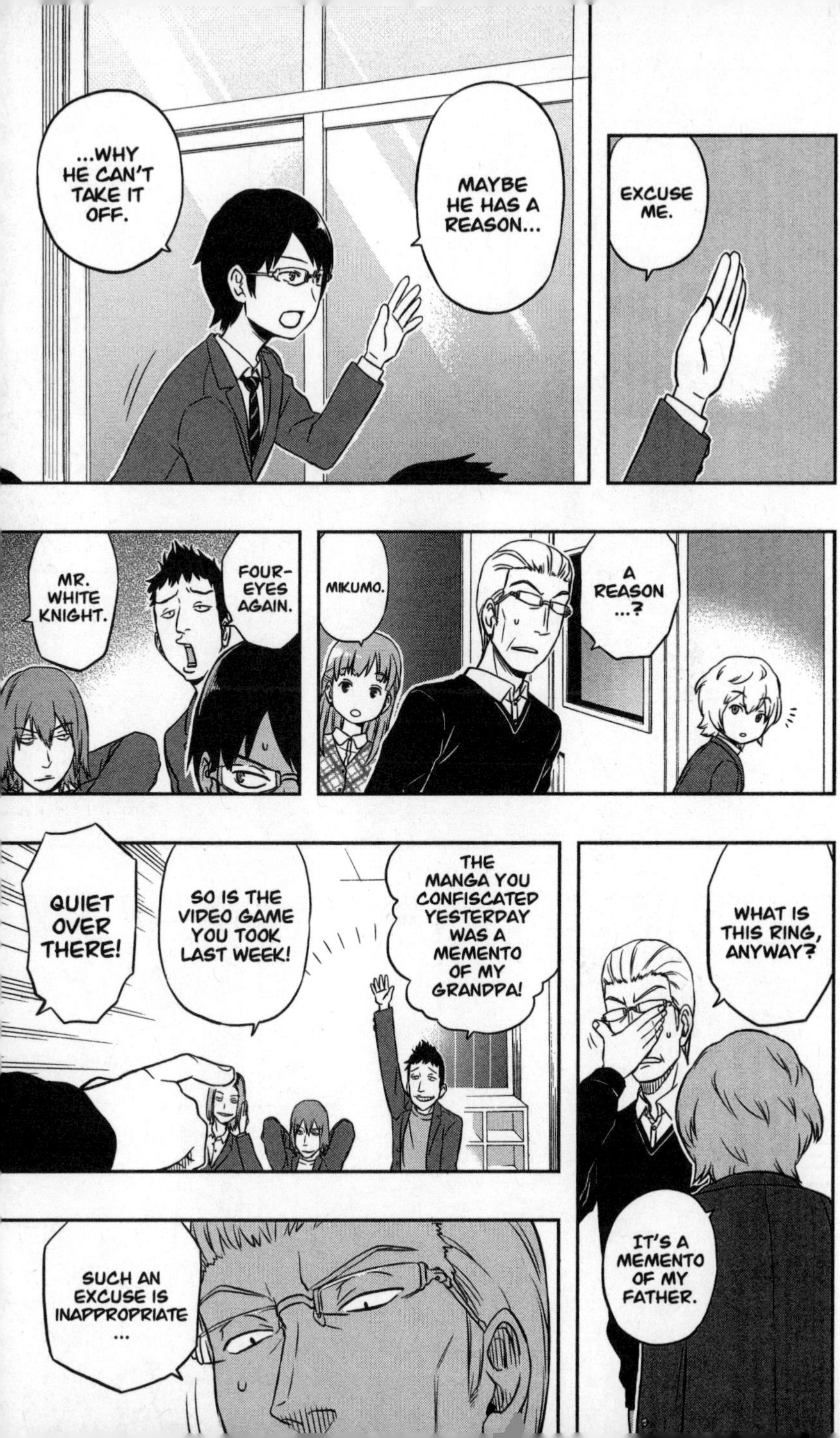
EXCUSE ME.
MAYBE HE HAS A REASON...
...WHY HE CAN'T TAKE IT OFF.
A REASON ...?
MIKUMO.
FOUR-EYES AGAIN.
MR. WHITE KNIGHT.
WHAT IS THIS RING, ANYWAY?
IT'S A MEMENTO OF MY FATHER.
THE MANGA YOU CONFISCATED YESTERDAY WAS A MEMENTO OF MY GRANDPA!
SO IS THE VIDEO GAME YOU TOOK LAST WEEK!
QUIET OVER THERE!
SUCH AN EXCUSE IS INAPPROPRIATE ...

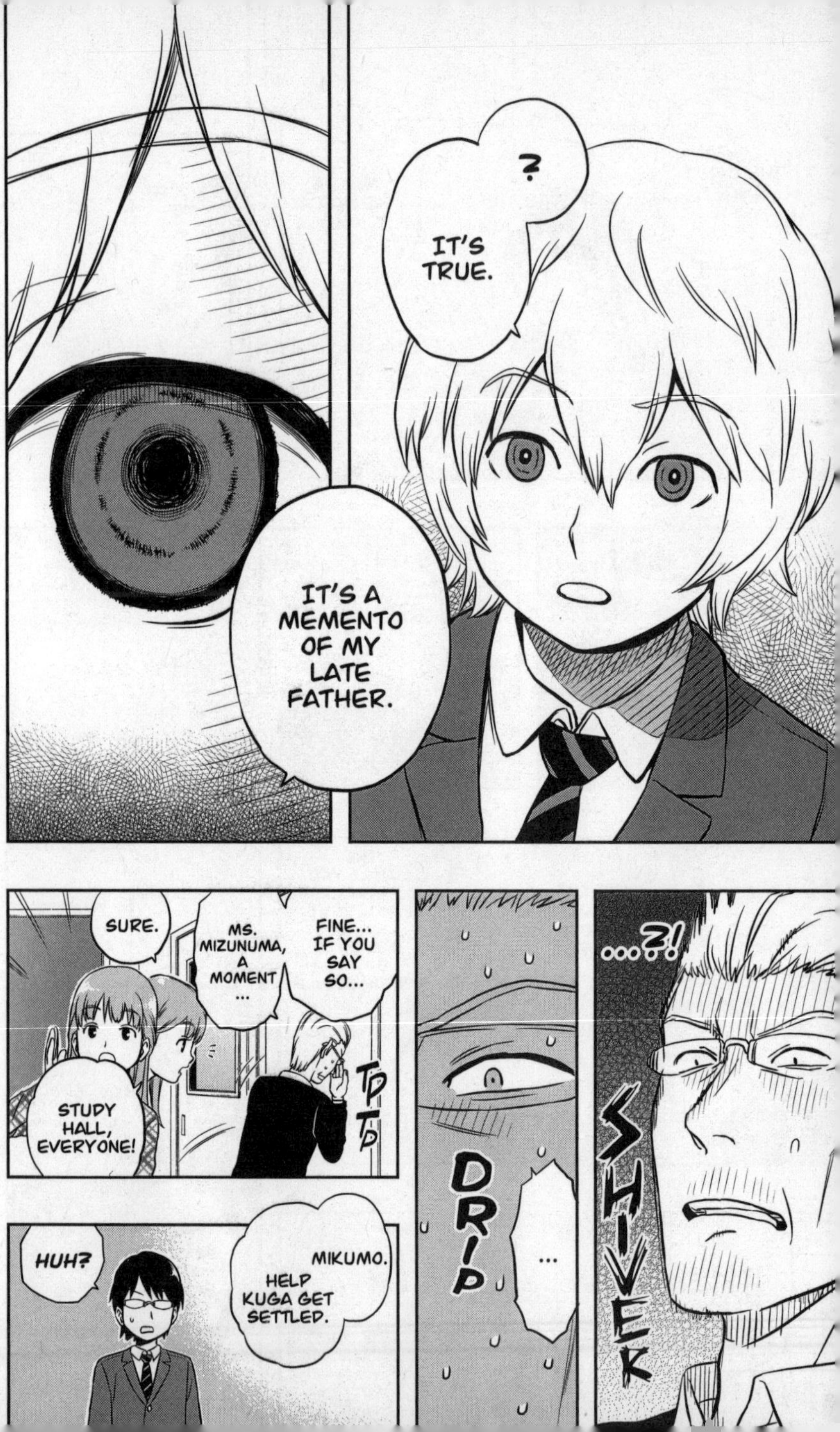
?
IT'S TRUE.
IT'S A MEMENTO OF MY LATE FATHER.
...?!
SHIVER
...
DRIP
FINE... IF YOU SAY SO...
MS. MIZUNUMA, A MOMENT ...
SURE.
TP TP
STUDY HALL, EVERYONE!
MIKUMO. HELP KUGA GET SETTLED.
HUH?

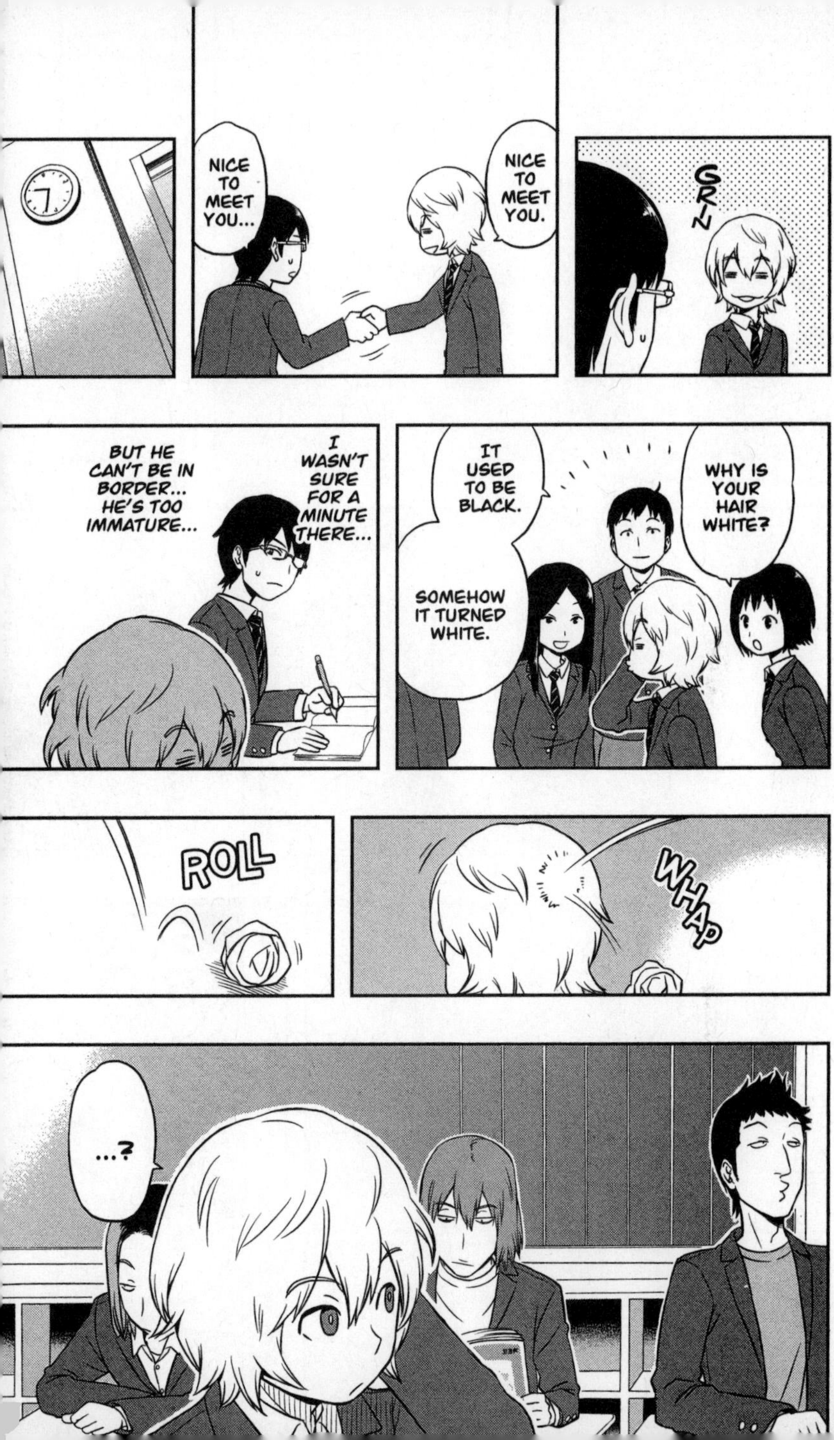
GRIN
NICE TO MEET YOU.
NICE TO MEET YOU...
WHY IS YOUR HAIR WHITE?
IT USED TO BE BLACK.
SOMEHOW IT TURNED WHITE.
I WASN'T SURE FOR A MINUTE THERE...
BUT HE CAN'T BE IN BORDER... HE'S TOO IMMATURE...
WHAP
ROLL
...?

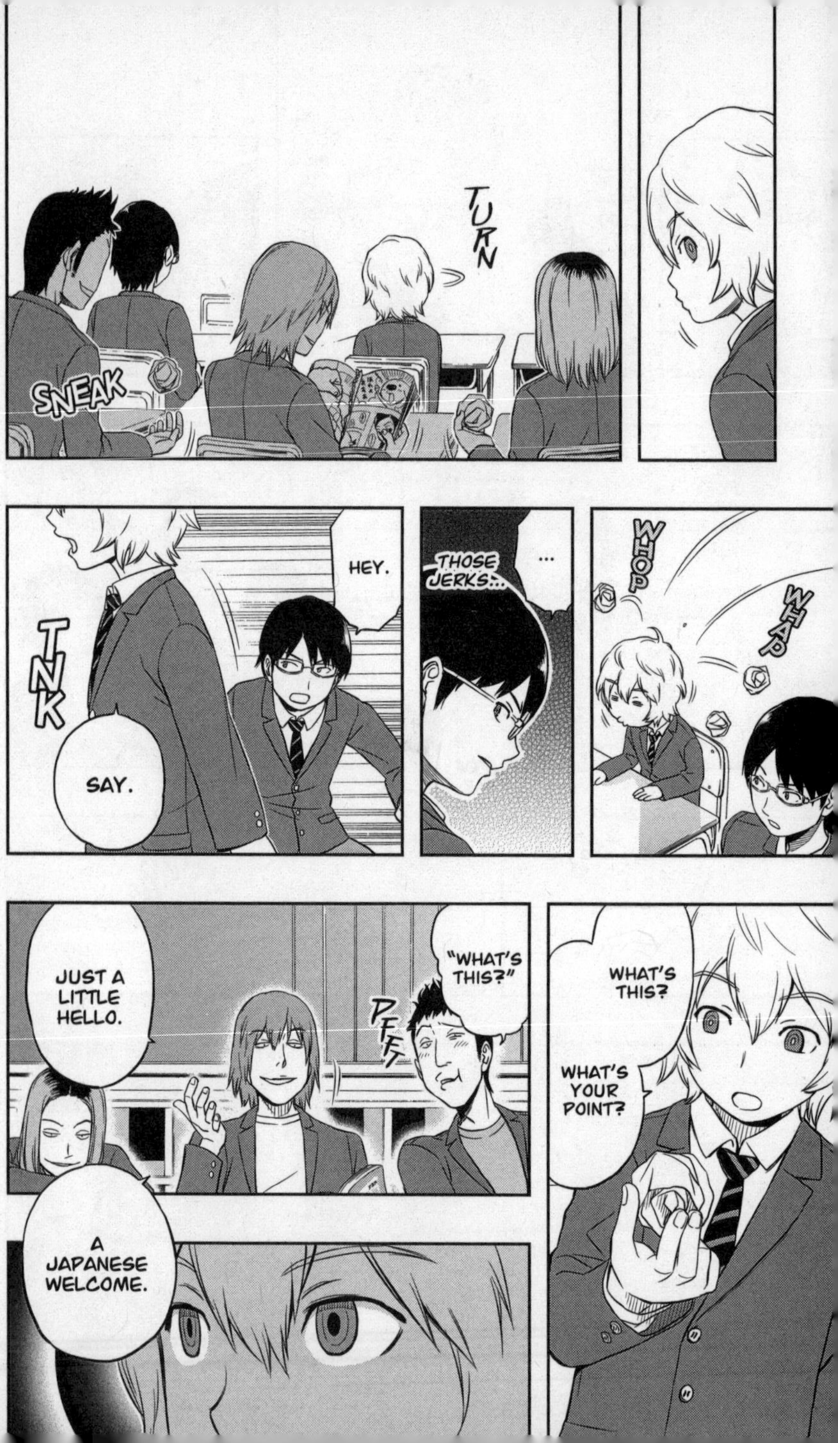
TURN
SNEAK
WHOP
WHAP
...
THOSE JERKS...
HEY.
TNK
SAY.
WHAT'S THIS?
WHAT'S YOUR POINT?
"WHAT'S THIS?"
PFFT
JUST A LITTLE HELLO.
A JAPANESE WELCOME.

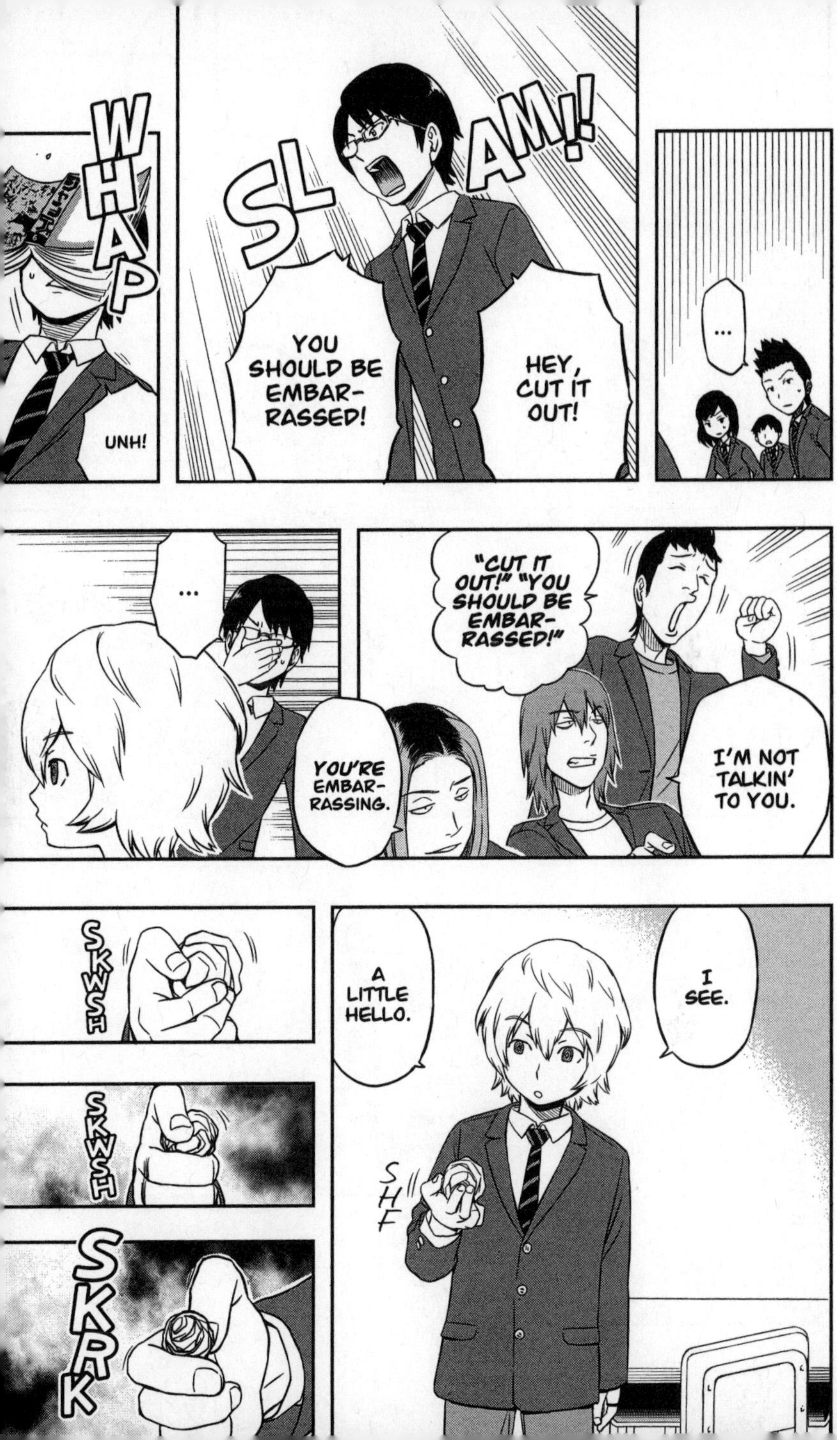
...
SLAM!!
HEY, CUT IT OUT!
YOU SHOULD BE EMBAR-RASSED!
WHAP
UNH!
"CUT IT OUT!" "YOU SHOULD BE EMBAR-RASSED!"
I'M NOT TALKIN' TO YOU.
YOU'RE EMBAR-RASSING.
...
I SEE.
A LITTLE HELLO.
SHF
SKWSH
SKWSH
SKRK

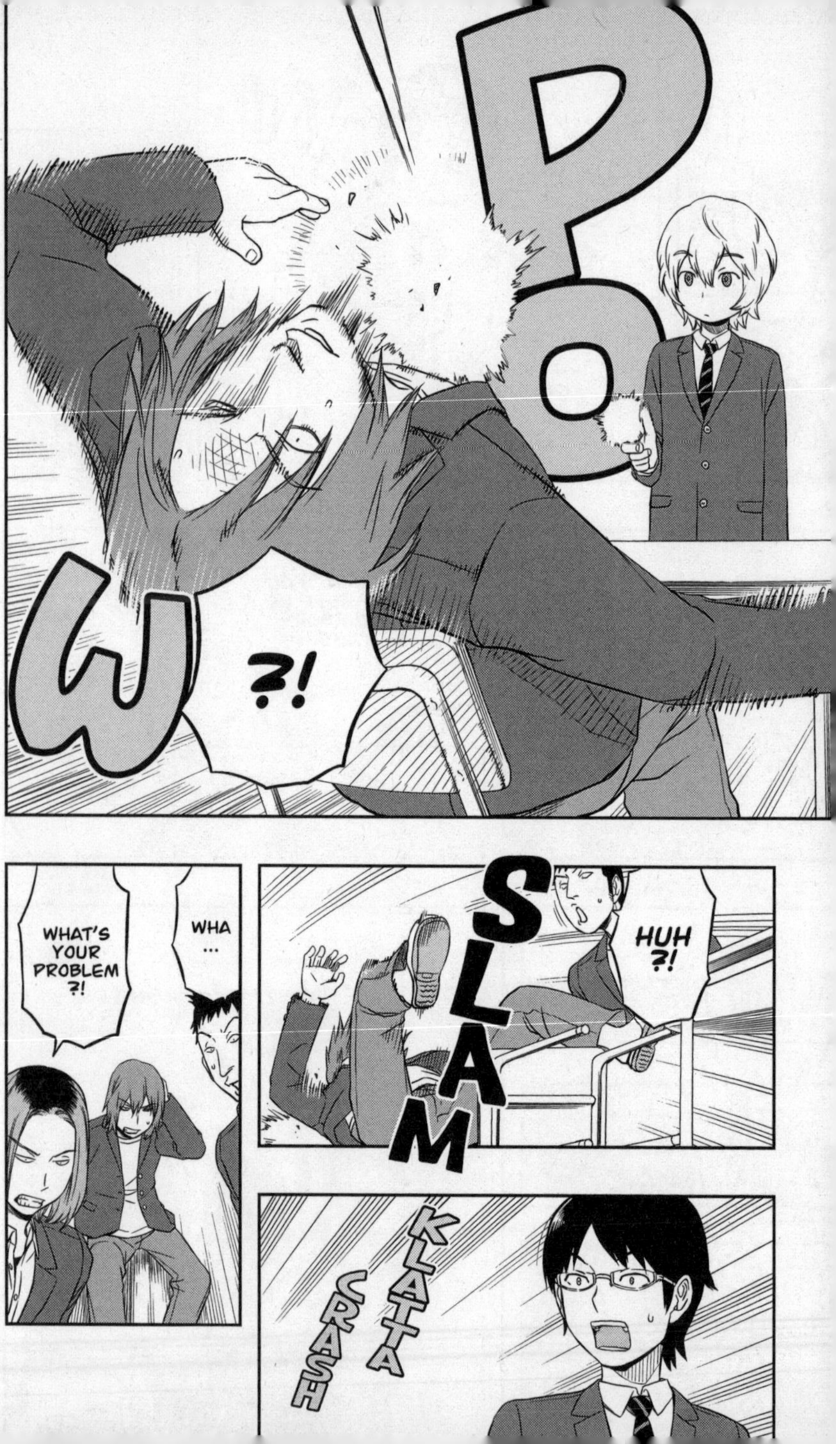
POW
?!
SLAM
HUH ?!
KLATTA
CRASH
WHA ...
WHAT'S YOUR PROBLEM ?!

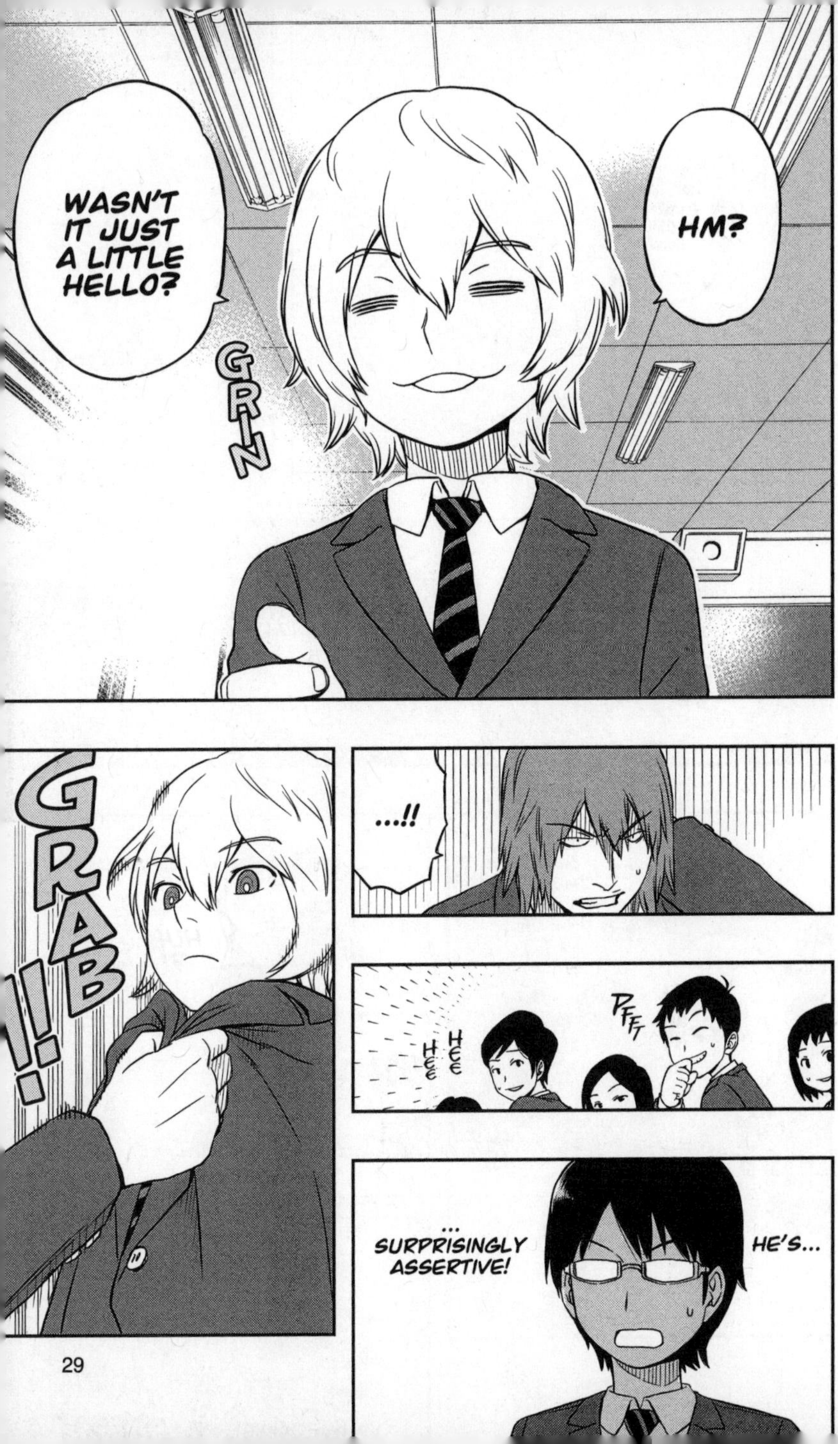
HM?
WASN'T IT JUST A LITTLE HELLO?
GRIN
...!!
HEE HEE
PFFT
HE'S...
... SURPRISINGLY ASSERTIVE!
GRAB!!

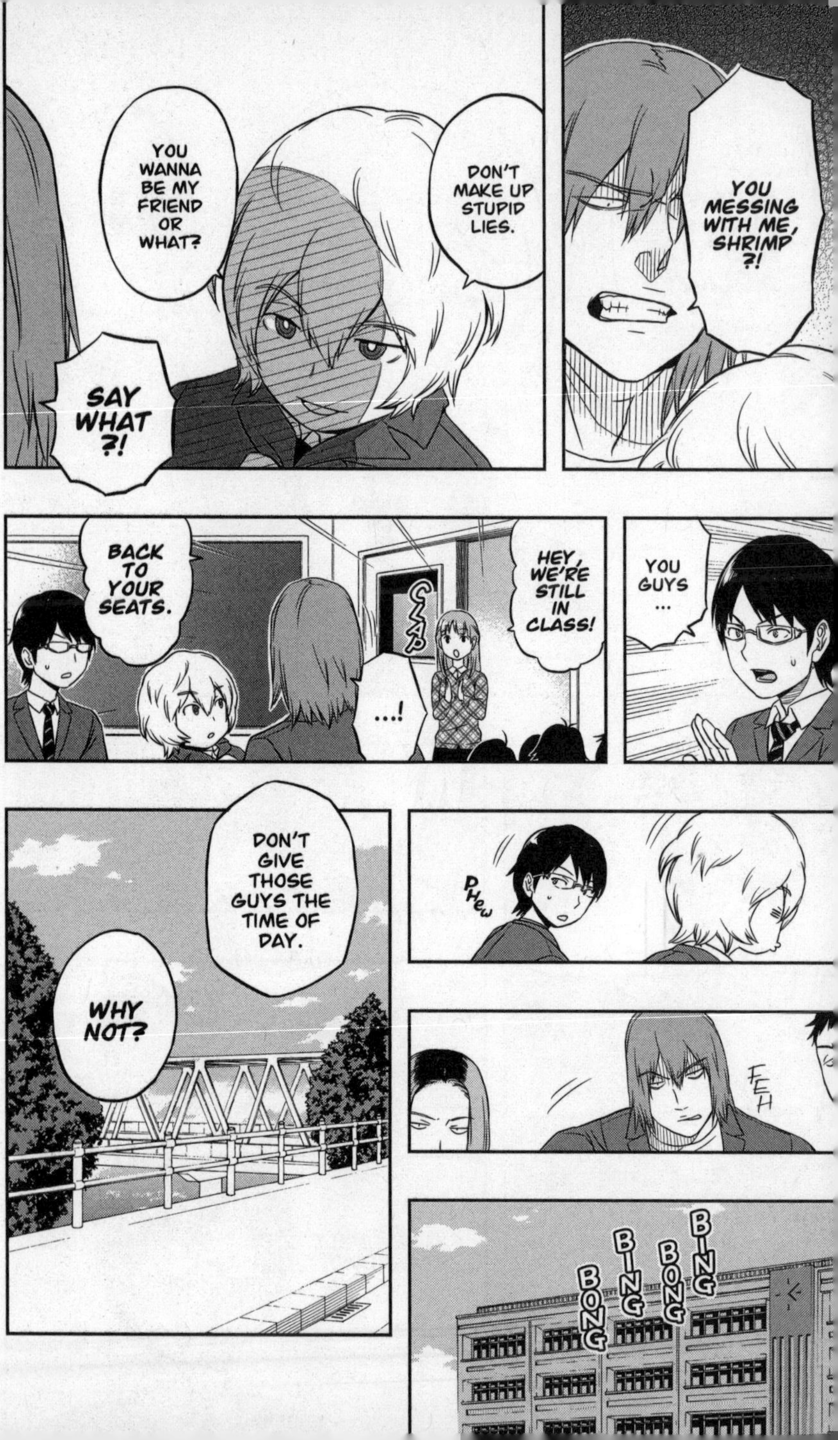
YOU MESSING WITH ME, SHRIMP?!
DON'T MAKE UP STUPID LIES.
YOU WANNA BE MY FRIEND OR WHAT?
SAY WHAT?!
YOU GUYS...
HEY, WE'RE STILL IN CLASS!
CLAP
...!
BACK TO YOUR SEATS.
Phew
FEH
BING BONG BING BONG
DON'T GIVE THOSE GUYS THE TIME OF DAY.
WHY NOT?

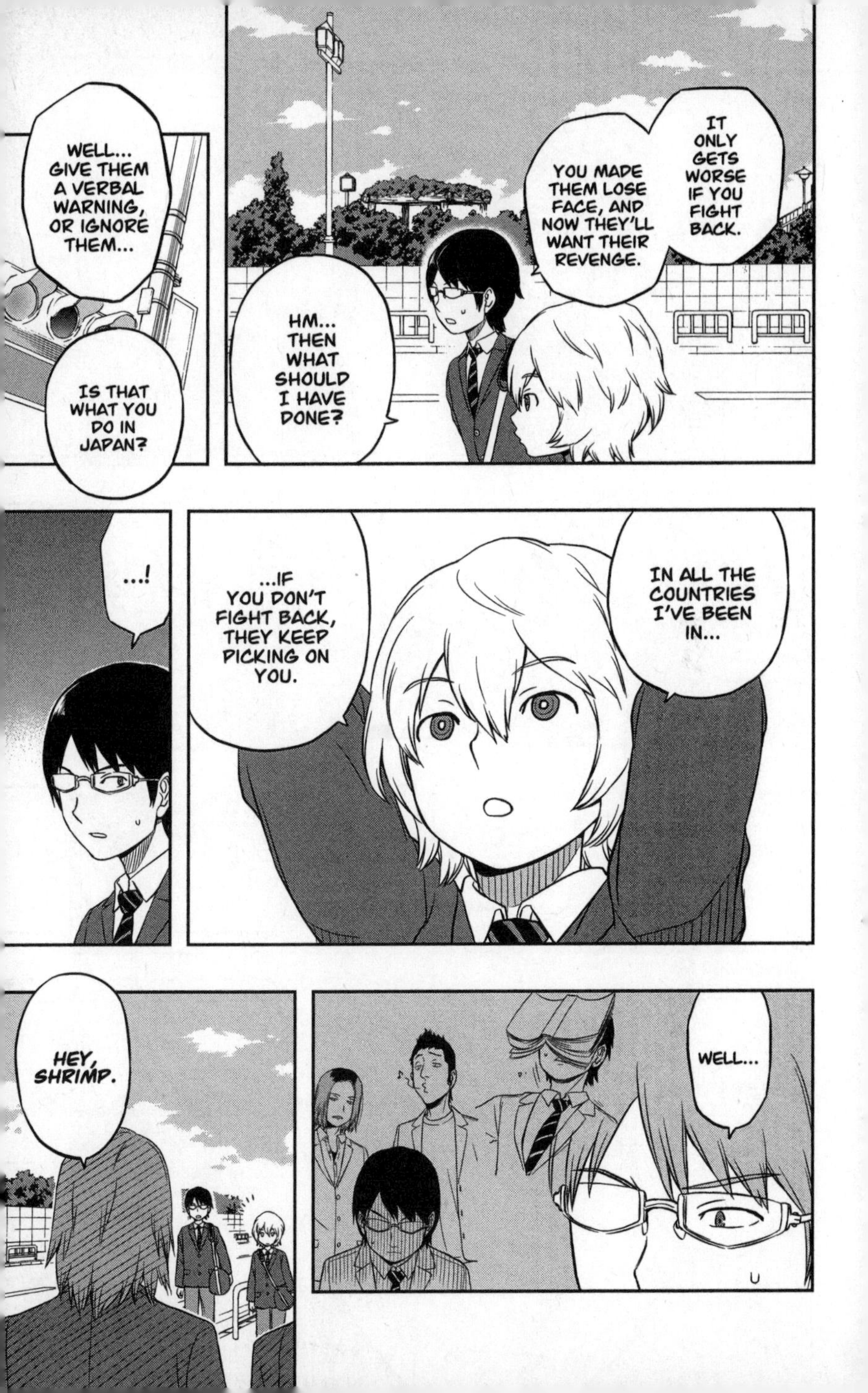
IT ONLY GETS WORSE IF YOU FIGHT BACK.
YOU MADE THEM LOSE FACE, AND NOW THEY'LL WANT THEIR REVENGE.
HM... THEN WHAT SHOULD I HAVE DONE?
WELL... GIVE THEM A VERBAL WARNING, OR IGNORE THEM...
IS THAT WHAT YOU DO IN JAPAN?
IN ALL THE COUNTRIES I'VE BEEN IN...
...IF YOU DON'T FIGHT BACK, THEY KEEP PICKING ON YOU.
...!
WELL...
HEY, SHRIMP.

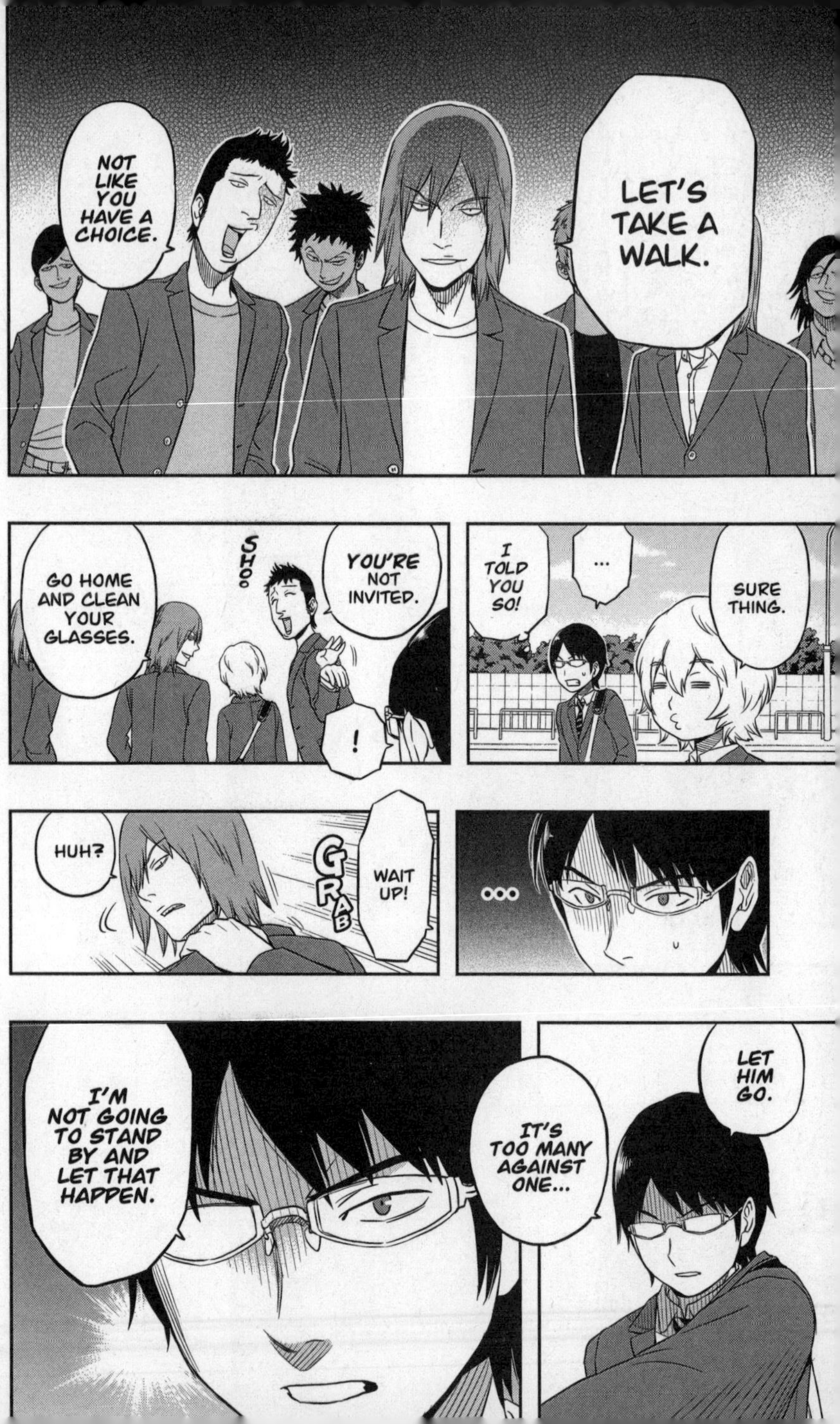
LET'S TAKE A WALK.
NOT LIKE YOU HAVE A CHOICE.
SURE THING.
...
I TOLD YOU SO!
YOU'RE NOT INVITED.
SHOO
GO HOME AND CLEAN YOUR GLASSES.
!
...
WAIT UP!
GRAB
HUH?
LET HIM GO.
IT'S TOO MANY AGAINST ONE...
I'M NOT GOING TO STAND BY AND LET THAT HAPPEN.

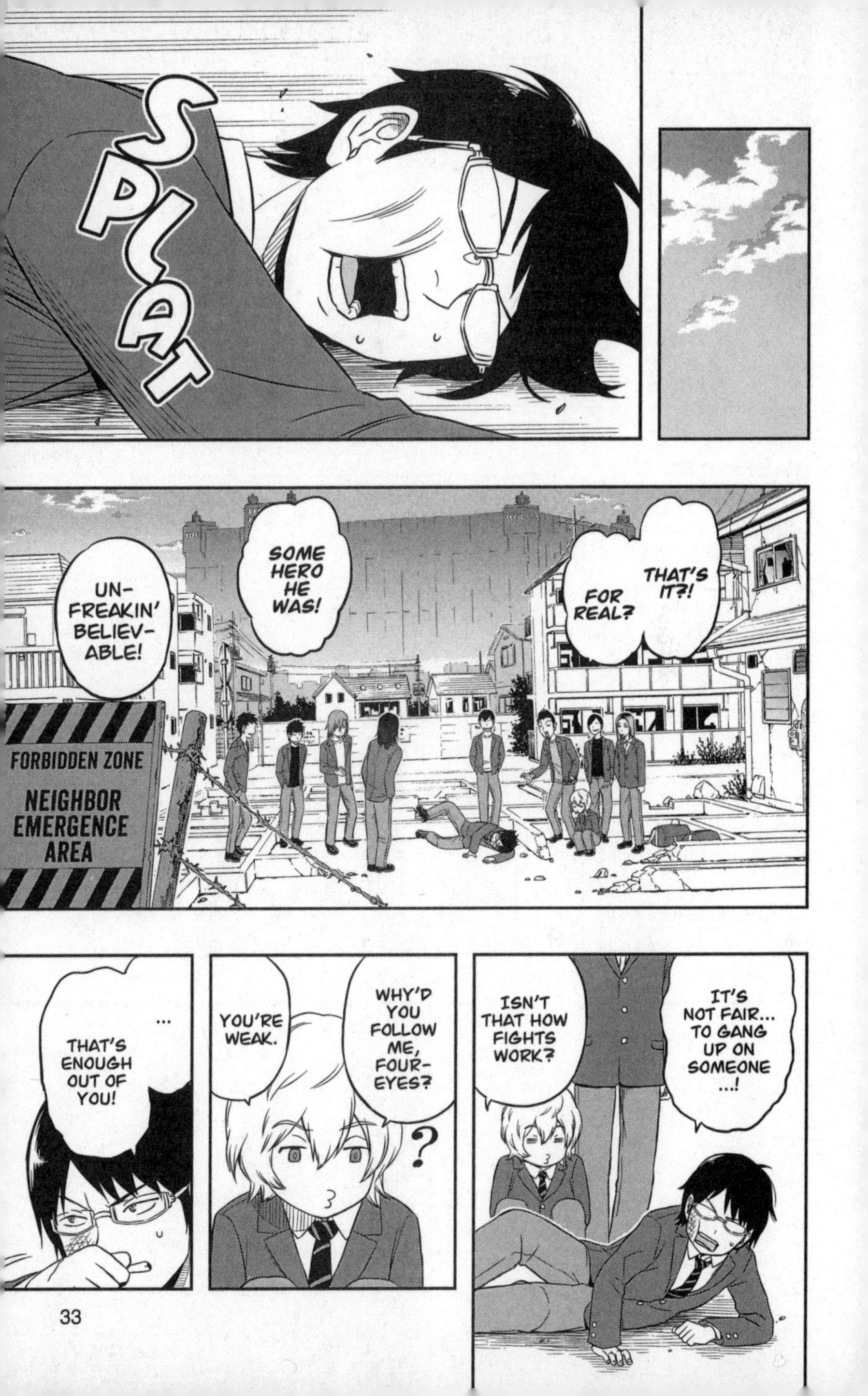
SPLAT
THAT'S IT?!
FOR REAL?
SOME HERO HE WAS!
UN-FREAKIN' BELIEVABLE!
FORBIDDEN ZONE
NEIGHBOR EMERGENCE AREA
IT'S NOT FAIR... TO GANG UP ON SOMEONE ...!
ISN'T THAT HOW FIGHTS WORK?
WHY'D YOU FOLLOW ME, FOUR-EYES?
YOU'RE WEAK.
?
...
THAT'S ENOUGH OUT OF YOU!

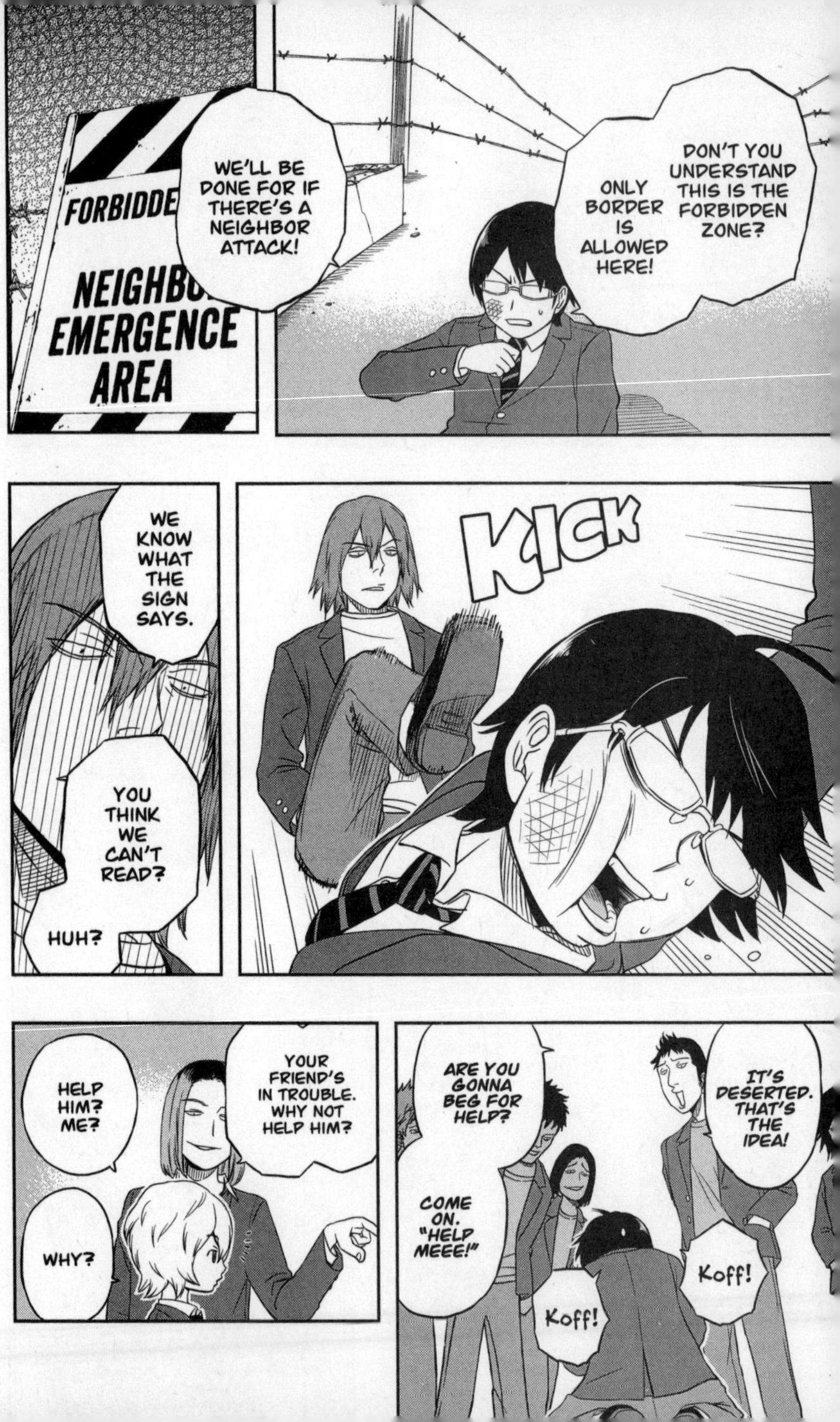
DON'T YOU UNDERSTAND THIS IS THE FORBIDDEN ZONE?
ONLY BORDER IS ALLOWED HERE!
WE'LL BE DONE FOR IF THERE'S A NEIGHBOR ATTACK!
FORBIDDE
NEIGHBO
EMERGENCE
AREA
KICK
WE KNOW WHAT THE SIGN SAYS.
YOU THINK WE CAN'T READ?
HUH?
IT'S DESERTED. THAT'S THE IDEA!
ARE YOU GONNA BEG FOR HELP?
COME ON. "HELP MEEE!"
Koff!
Koff!
YOUR FRIEND'S IN TROUBLE. WHY NOT HELP HIM?
HELP HIM? ME?
WHY?

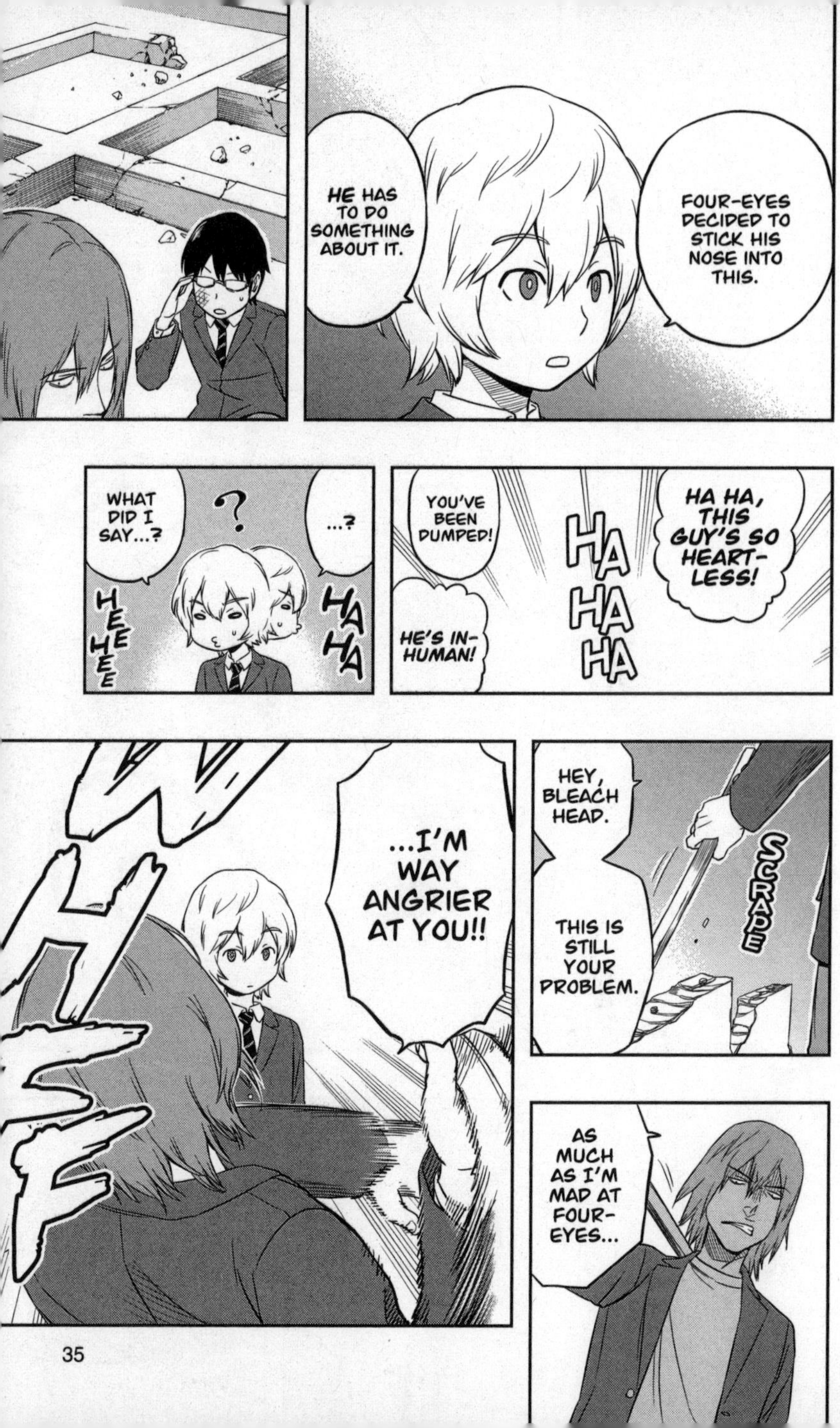
FOUR-EYES DECIDED TO STICK HIS NOSE INTO THIS.
HE HAS TO DO SOMETHING ABOUT IT.
HA HA, THIS GUY'S SO HEART-LESS!
HA HA HA
YOU'VE BEEN DUMPED!
HE'S IN-HUMAN!
...?
HA HA
?
WHAT DID I SAY...?
HEHEHEE
HEY, BLEACH HEAD.
SCRAPE
THIS IS STILL YOUR PROBLEM.
AS MUCH AS I'M MAD AT FOUR-EYES...
...I'M WAY ANGRIER AT YOU!!

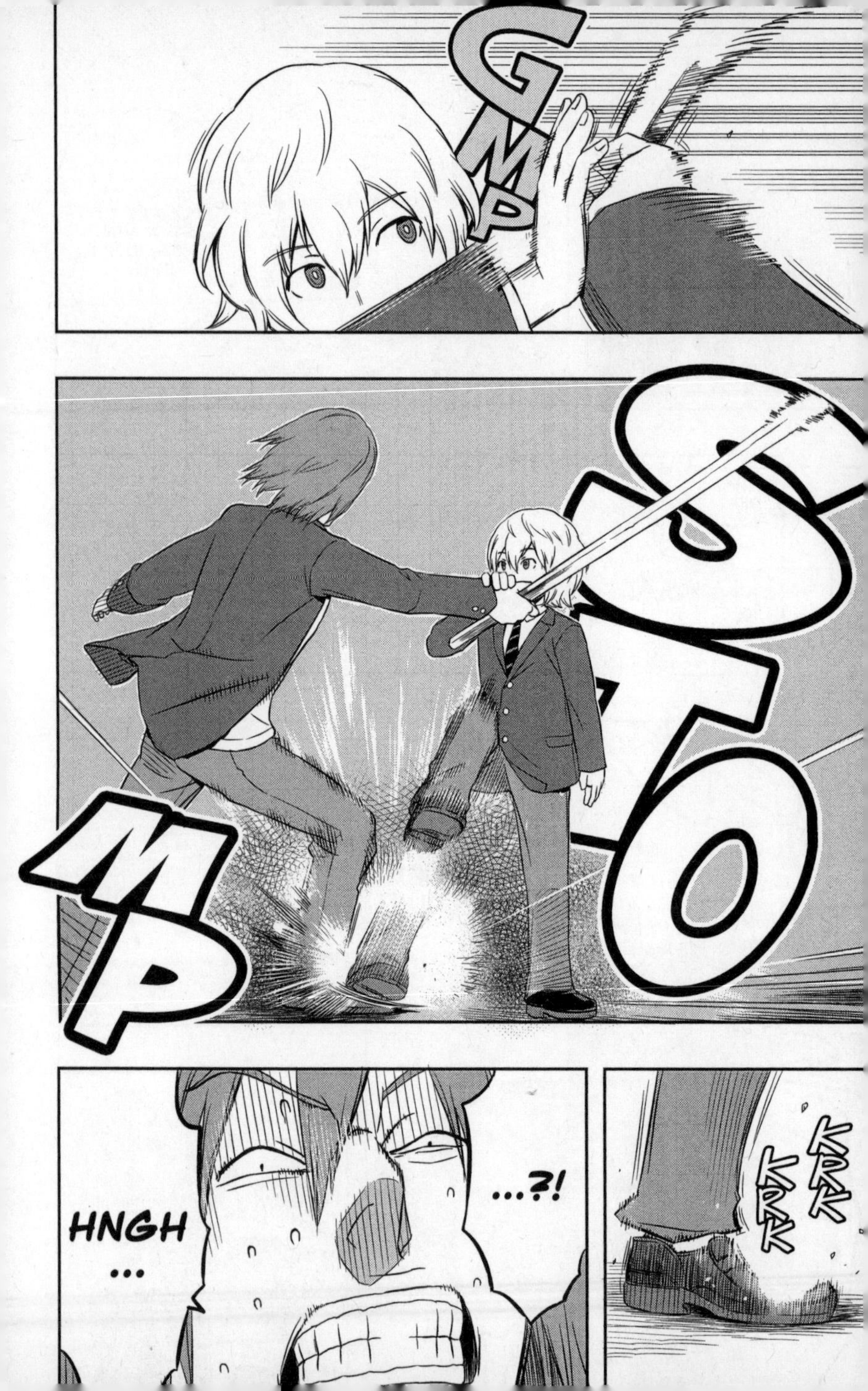
GMP
STOMP
KRAK KRAK
...?!
HNGH ...

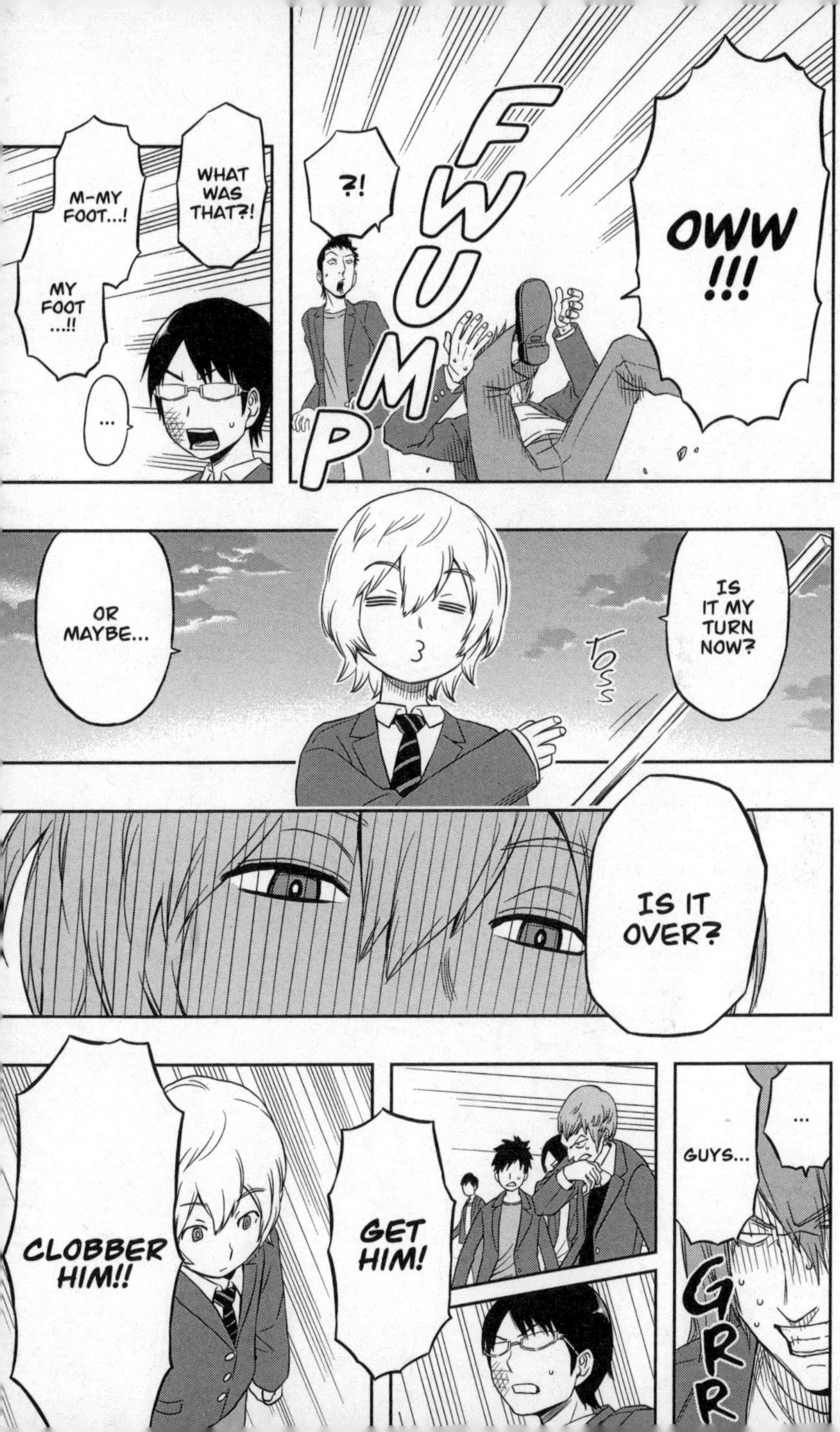
OWW!!!
FWUMP
?!
WHAT WAS THAT?!
M-MY FOOT...!
MY FOOT...!!
...
IS IT MY TURN NOW?
toss
OR MAYBE...
IS IT OVER?
...
GUYS...
GRR
GET HIM!
CLOBBER HIM!!

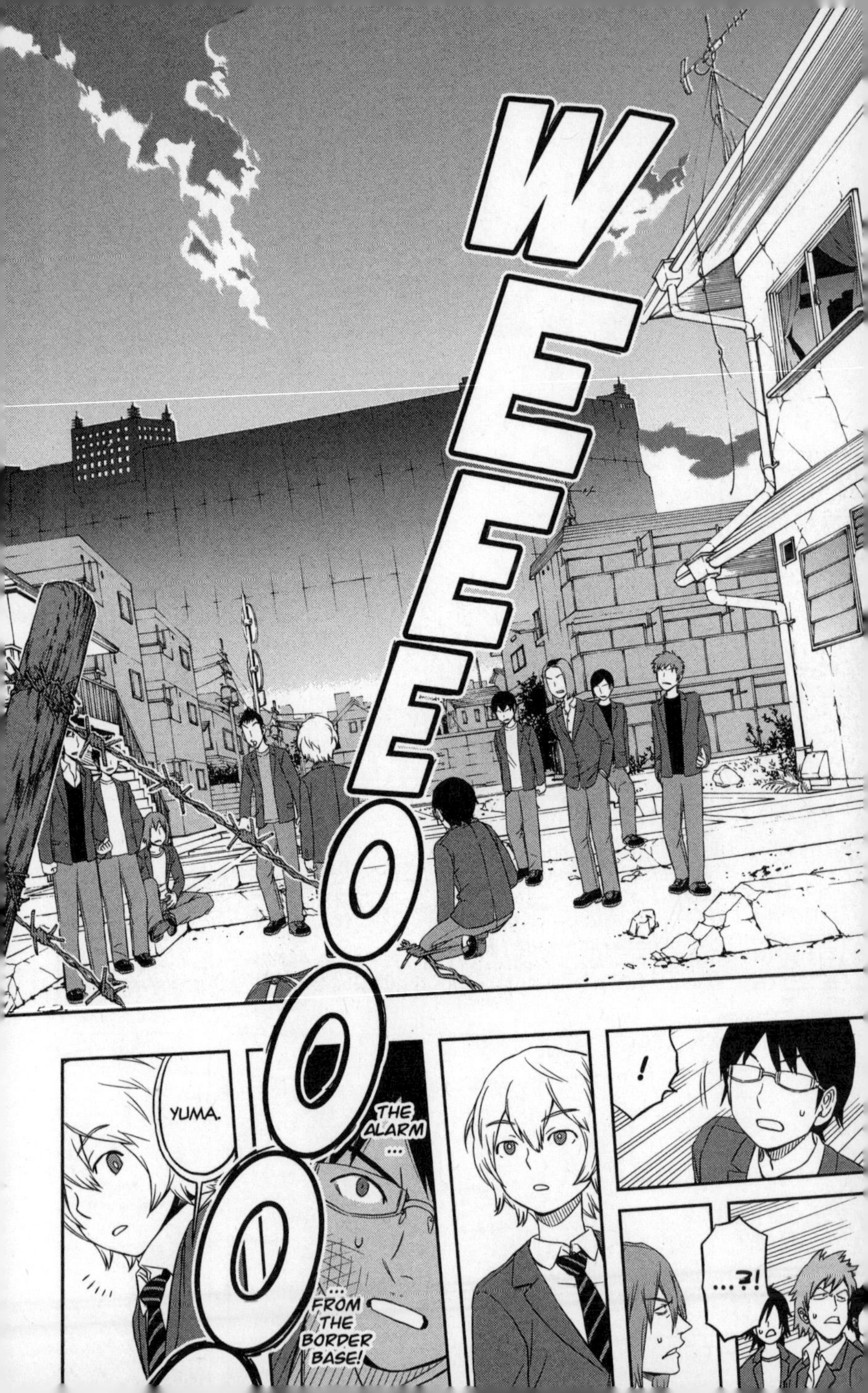
WEEEEEOOOO
!
...?!
THE ALARM ...
... FROM THE BORDER BASE!
YUMA.

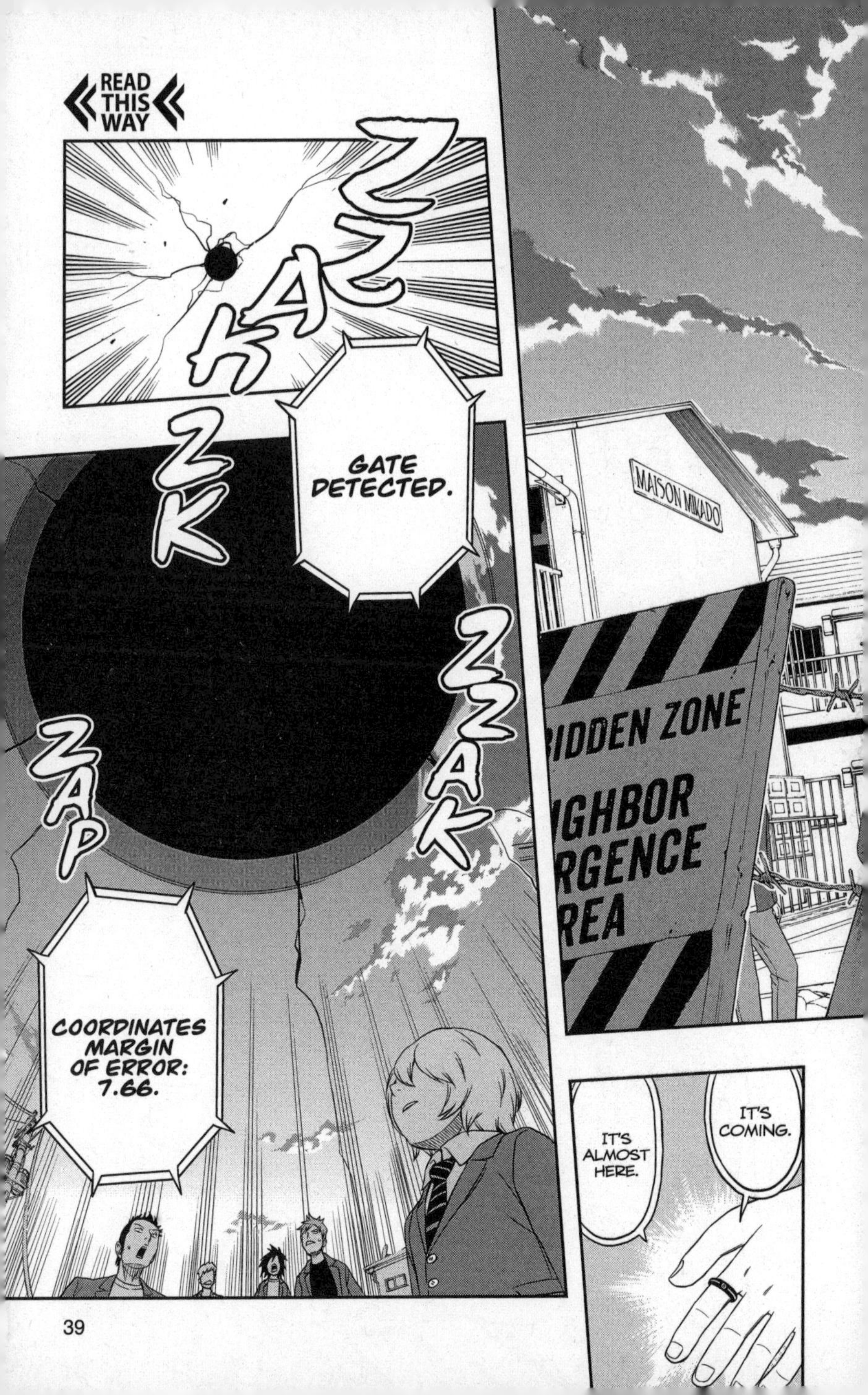
READ THIS WAY
MAISON MIKADO
RIDDEN ZONE
IGHBOR
RGENCE
REA
IT'S COMING.
IT'S ALMOST HERE.
ZZAK
ZK
GATE DETECTED.
ZZAK
ZAP
COORDINATES MARGIN OF ERROR: 7.66.

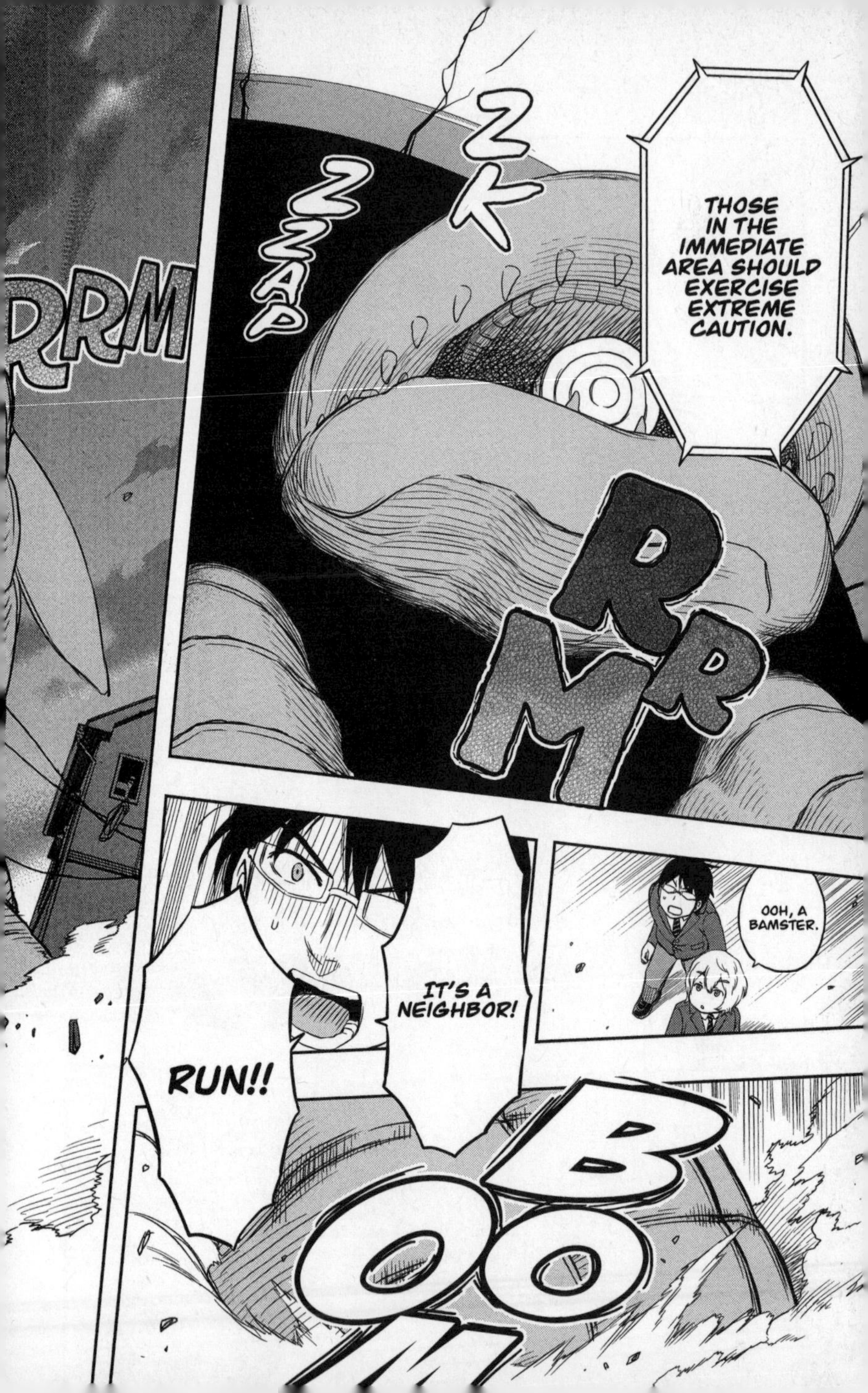
THOSE IN THE IMMEDIATE AREA SHOULD EXERCISE EXTREME CAUTION.
ZK
ZZAP
RRM
OOH, A BAMSTER.
IT'S A NEIGHBOR!
RUN!!
BOOM
RRRM

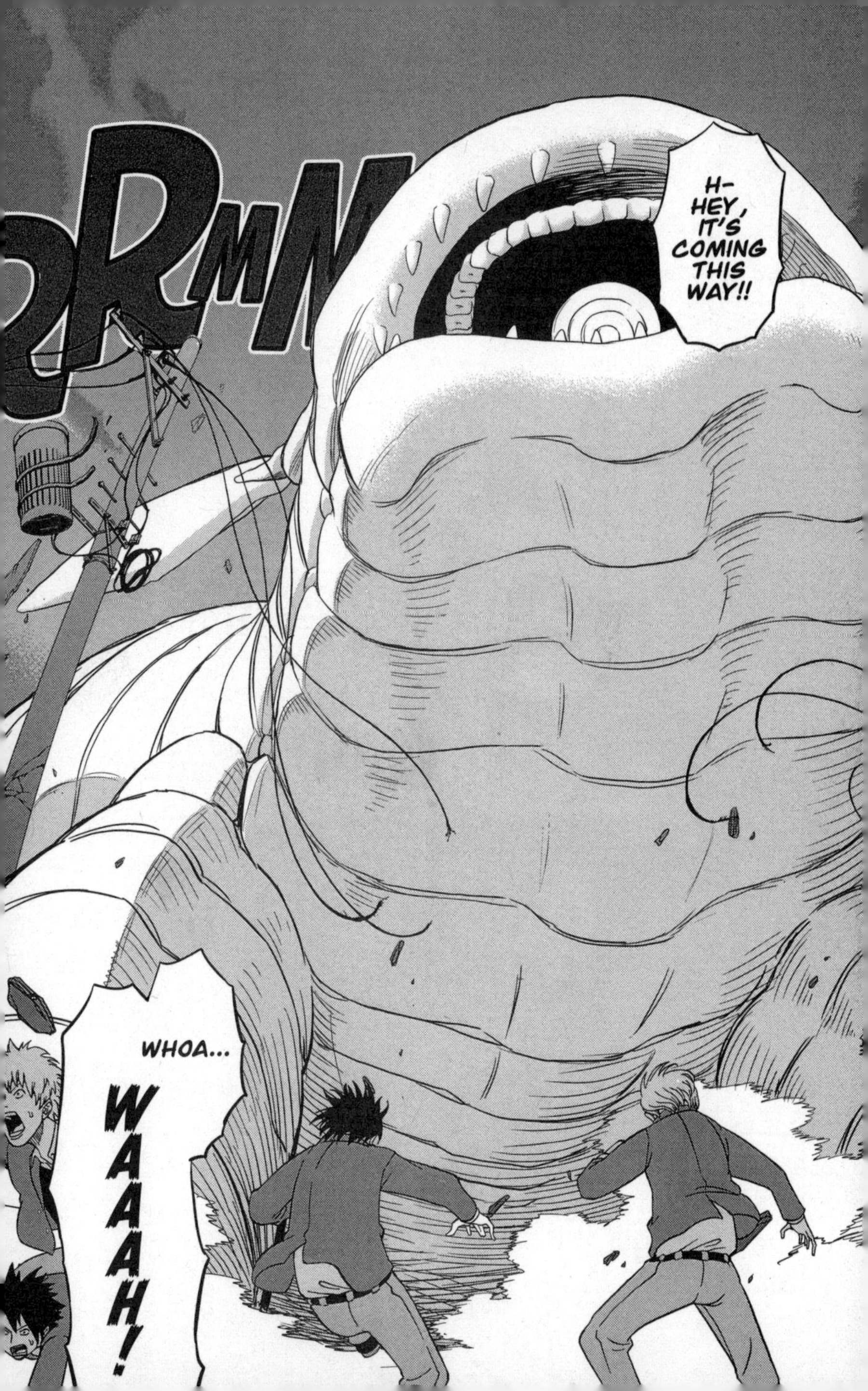
H-HEY, IT'S COMING THIS WAY!!
WHOA...
WAAAAH!

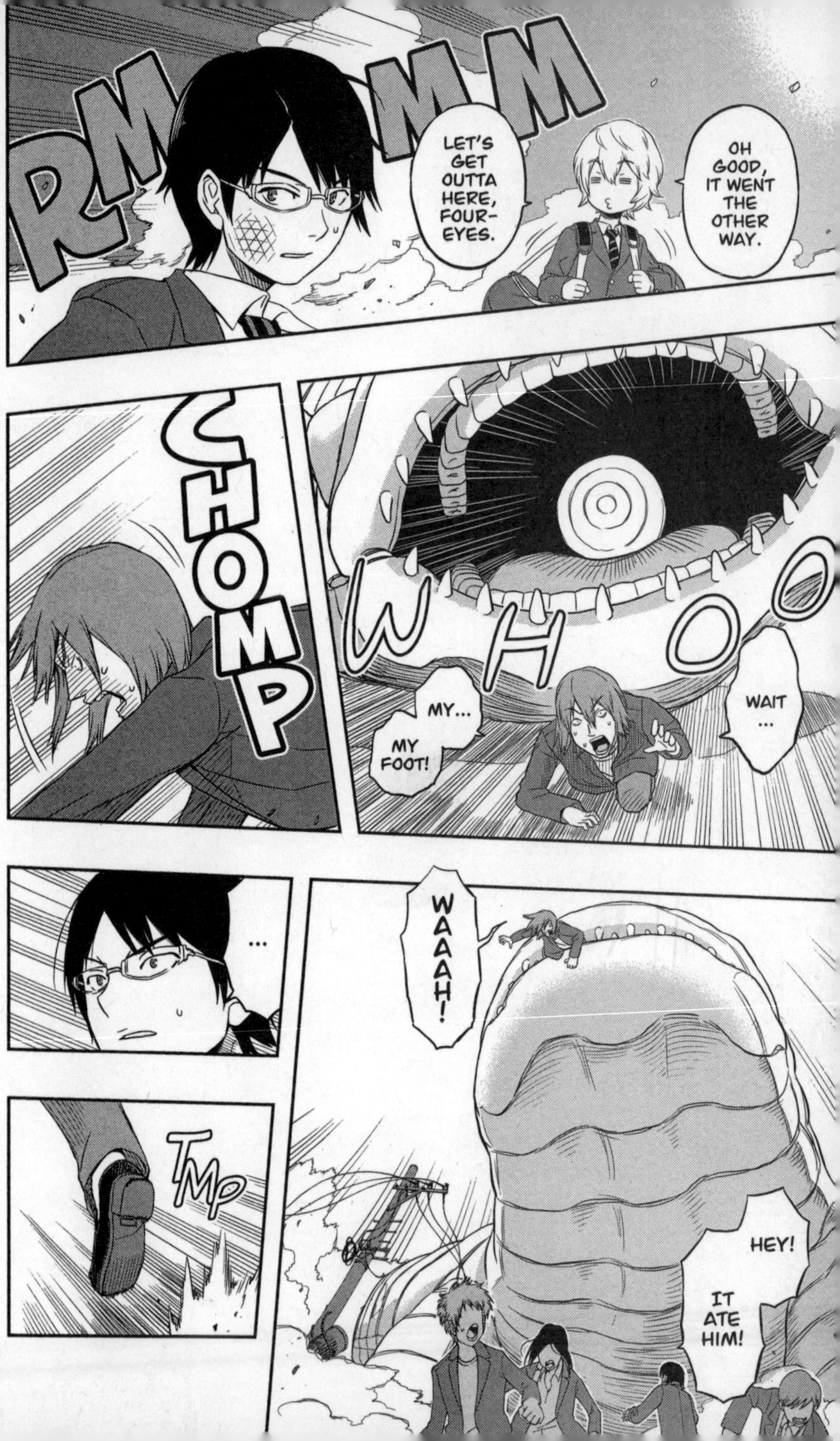
OH GOOD, IT WENT THE OTHER WAY.
LET'S GET OUTTA HERE, FOUR-EYES.
RMMMM
WHOOO
WAIT...
MY...
MY FOOT!
CHOMP
WAAAAH!
HEY!
IT ATE HIM!
...
TMP

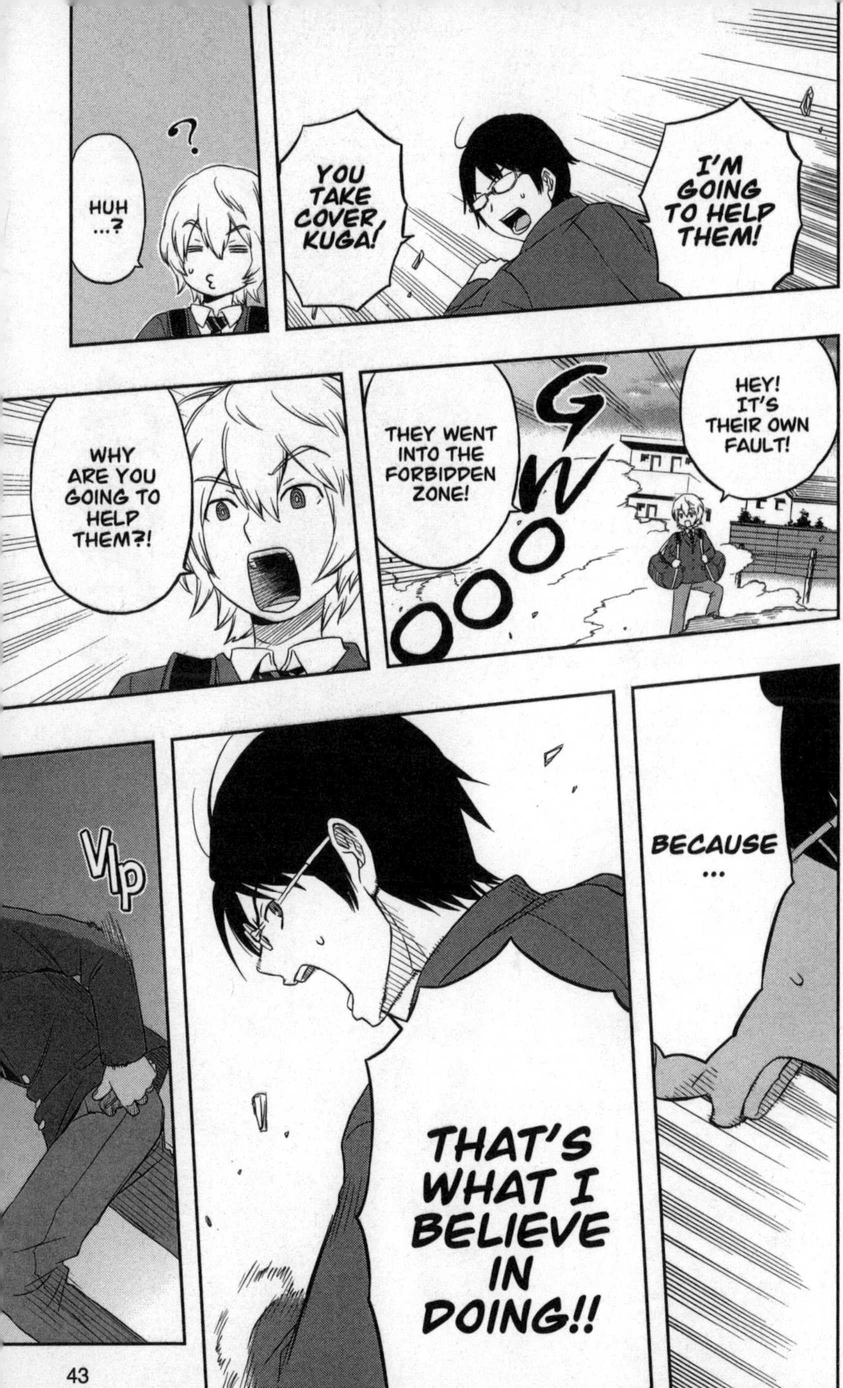
I'M GOING TO HELP THEM!
YOU TAKE COVER, KUGA!
?
HUH ...?
HEY! IT'S THEIR OWN FAULT!
GWOOOO
THEY WENT INTO THE FORBIDDEN ZONE!
WHY ARE YOU GOING TO HELP THEM?!
BECAUSE ...
THAT'S WHAT I BELIEVE IN DOING!!
VIP

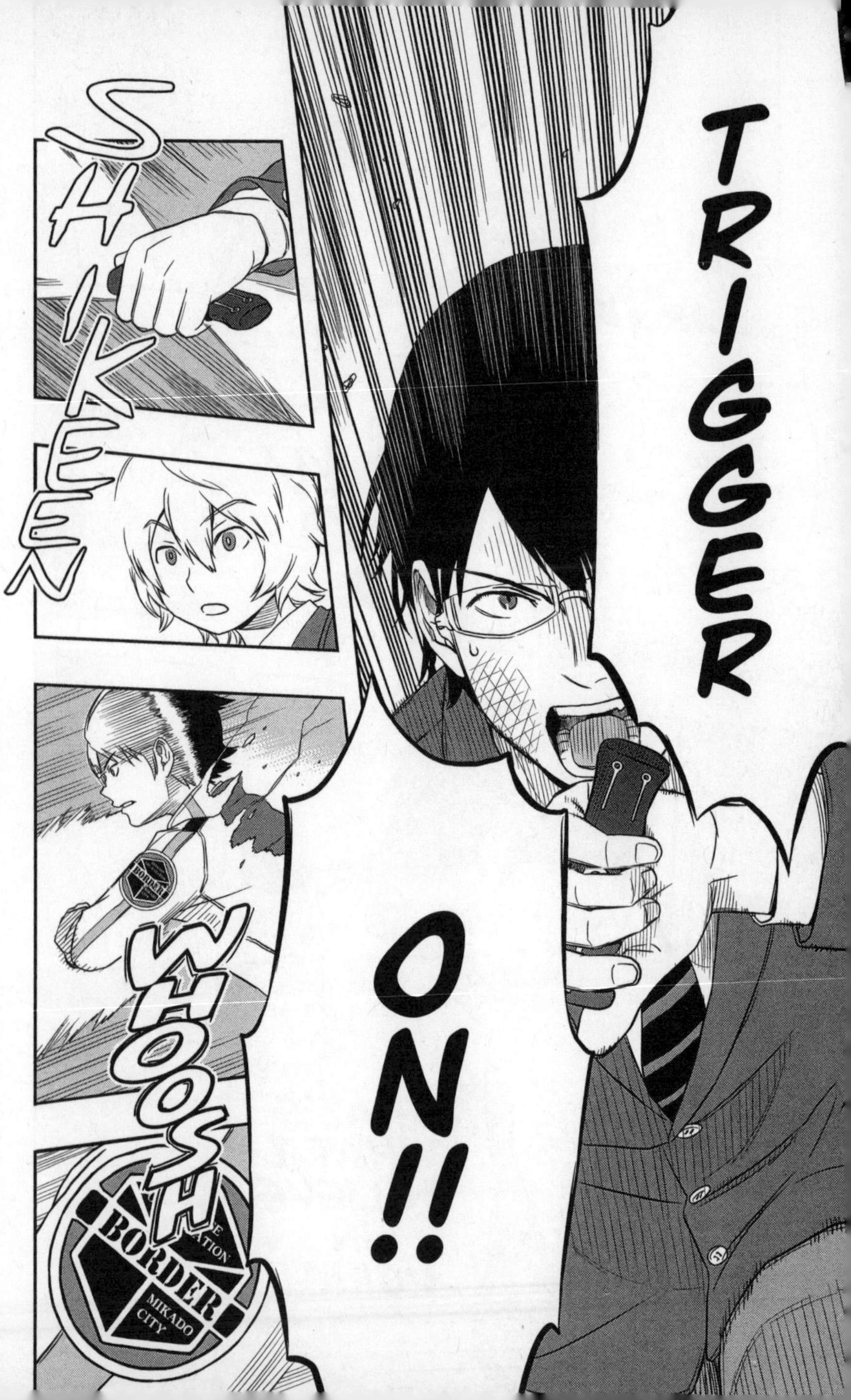
TRIGGER ON!!
SHIKEEN
WHOOSH
BORDER
MIKADO CITY

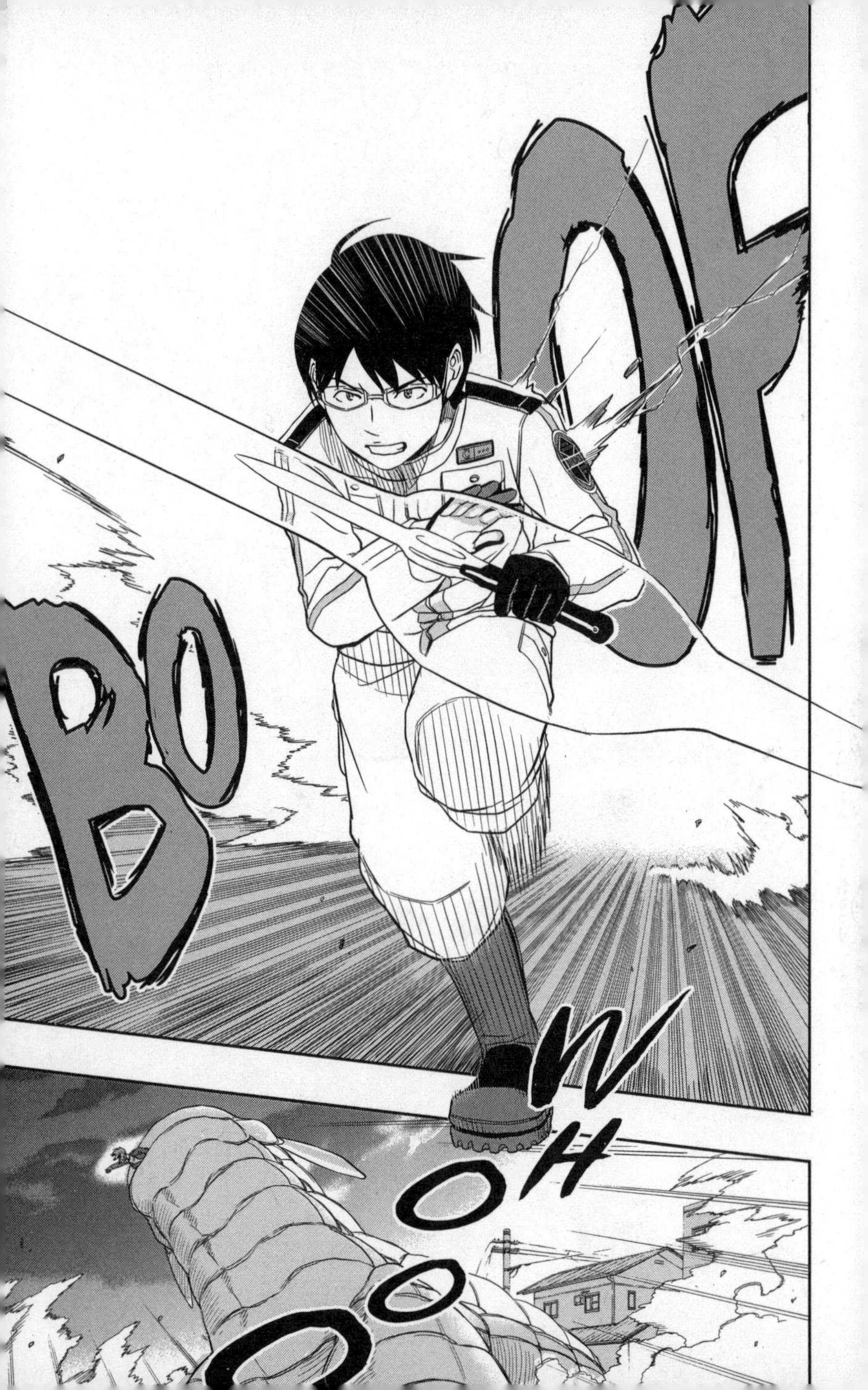
BOOF
WHOOO

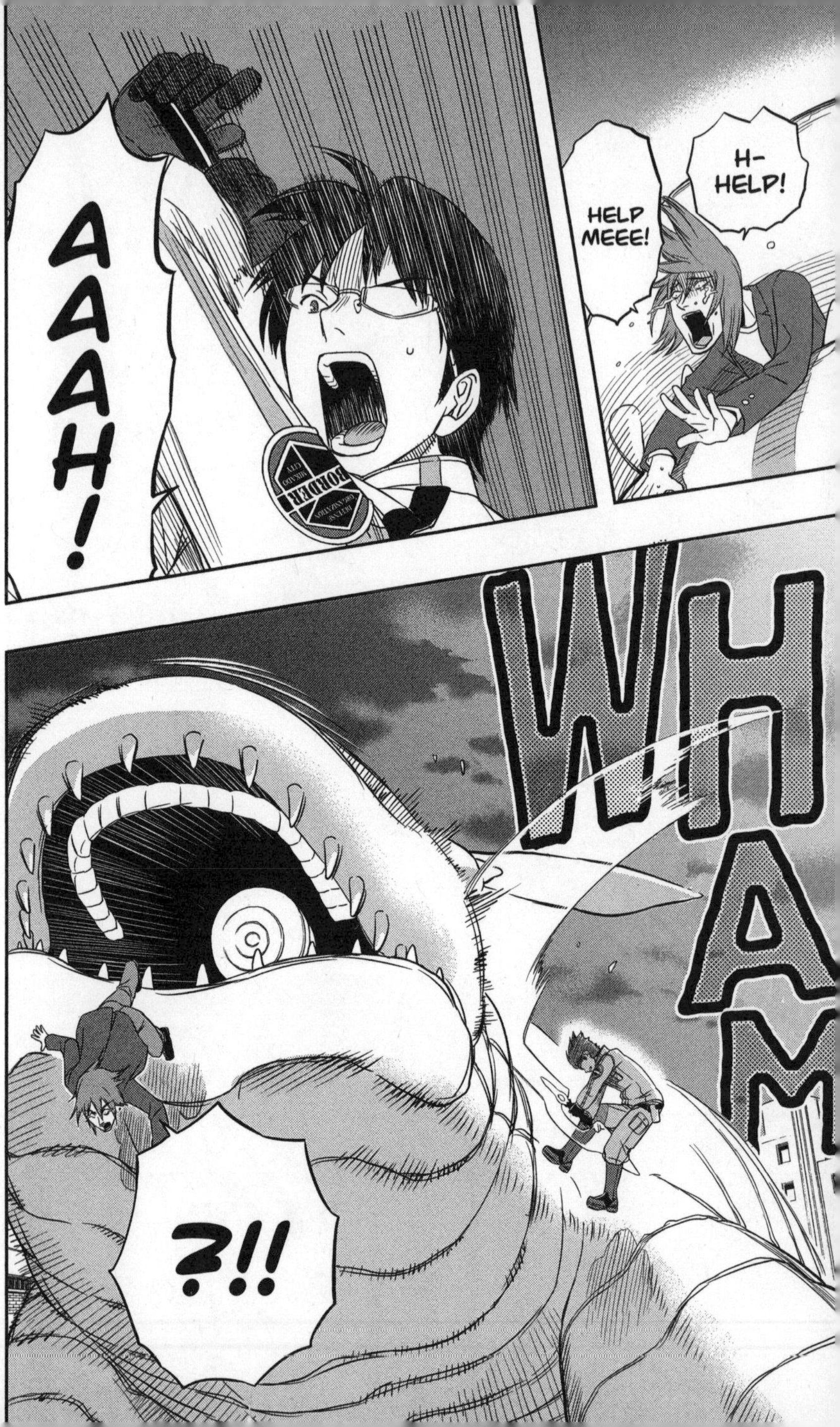
H- HELP!
HELP MEEE!
AAAH!
WHAM
?!!

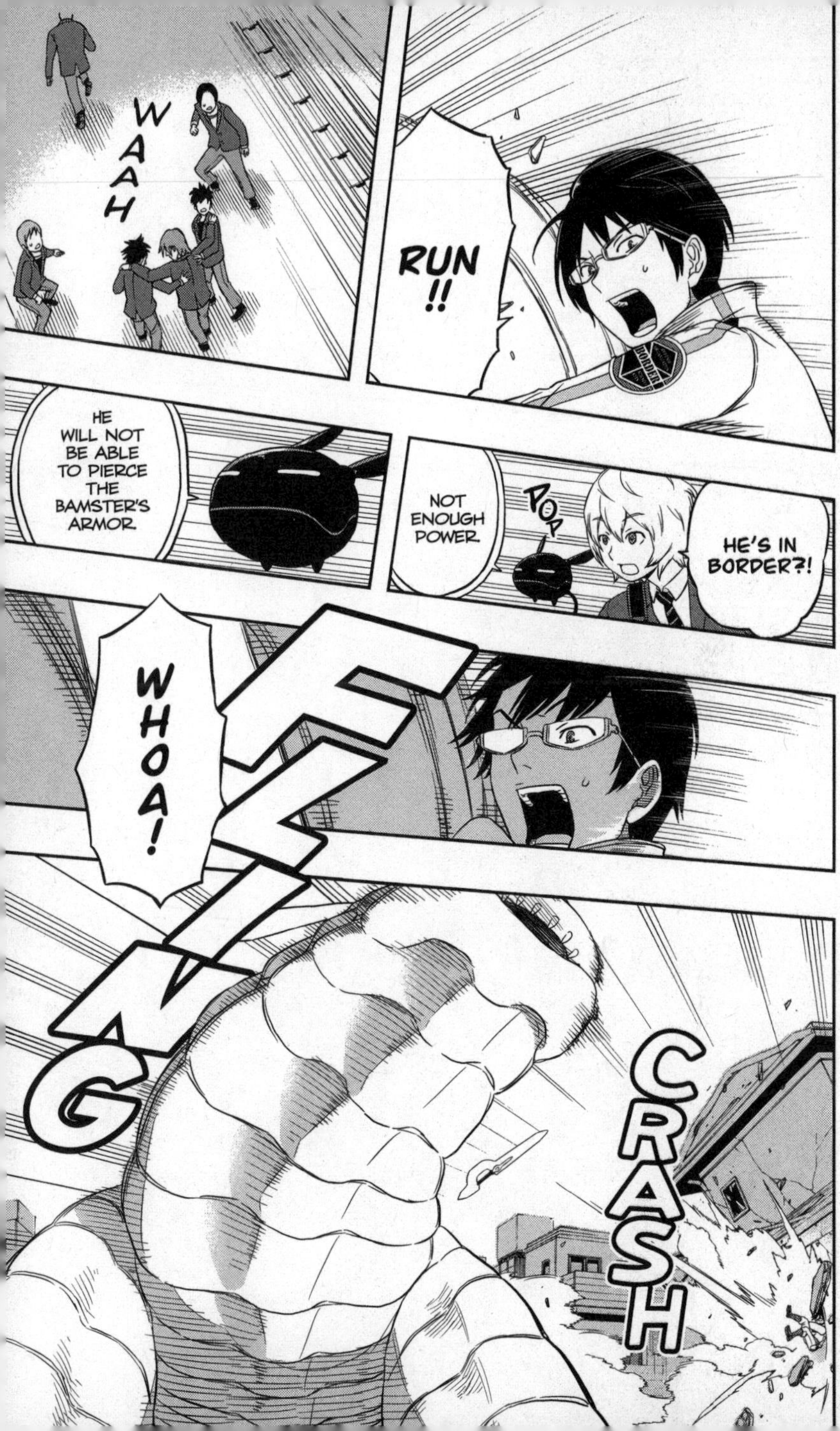
RUN!!
WAAH
HE'S IN BORDER?!
POP
NOT ENOUGH POWER
HE WILL NOT BE ABLE TO PIERCE THE BAMSTER'S ARMOR
WHOA!
FWING
CRASH

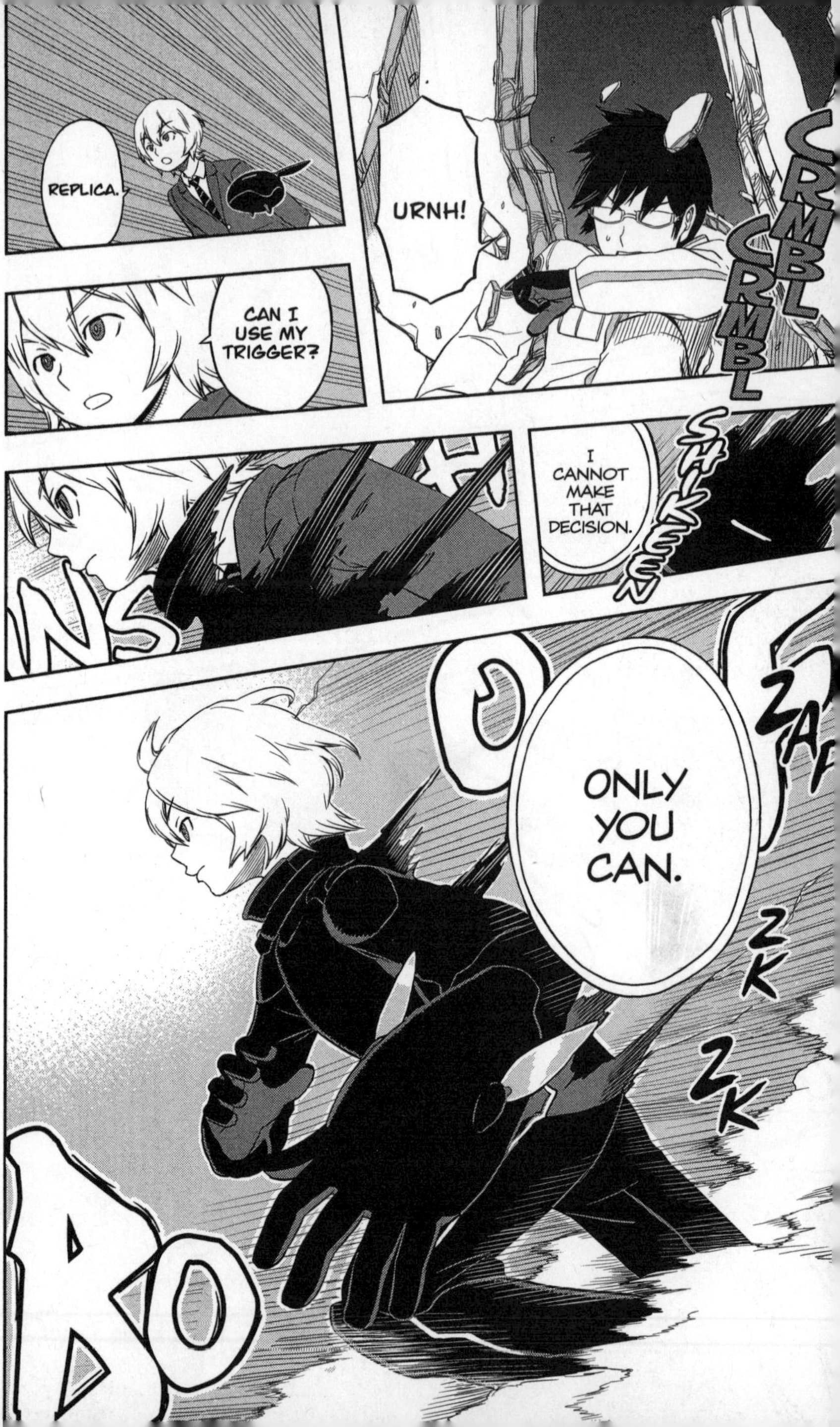
CRMBL
CRMBL
URNH!
REPLICA.
CAN I USE MY TRIGGER?
SHIKEEN
I CANNOT MAKE THAT DECISION.
ONLY YOU CAN.
ZK
ZK

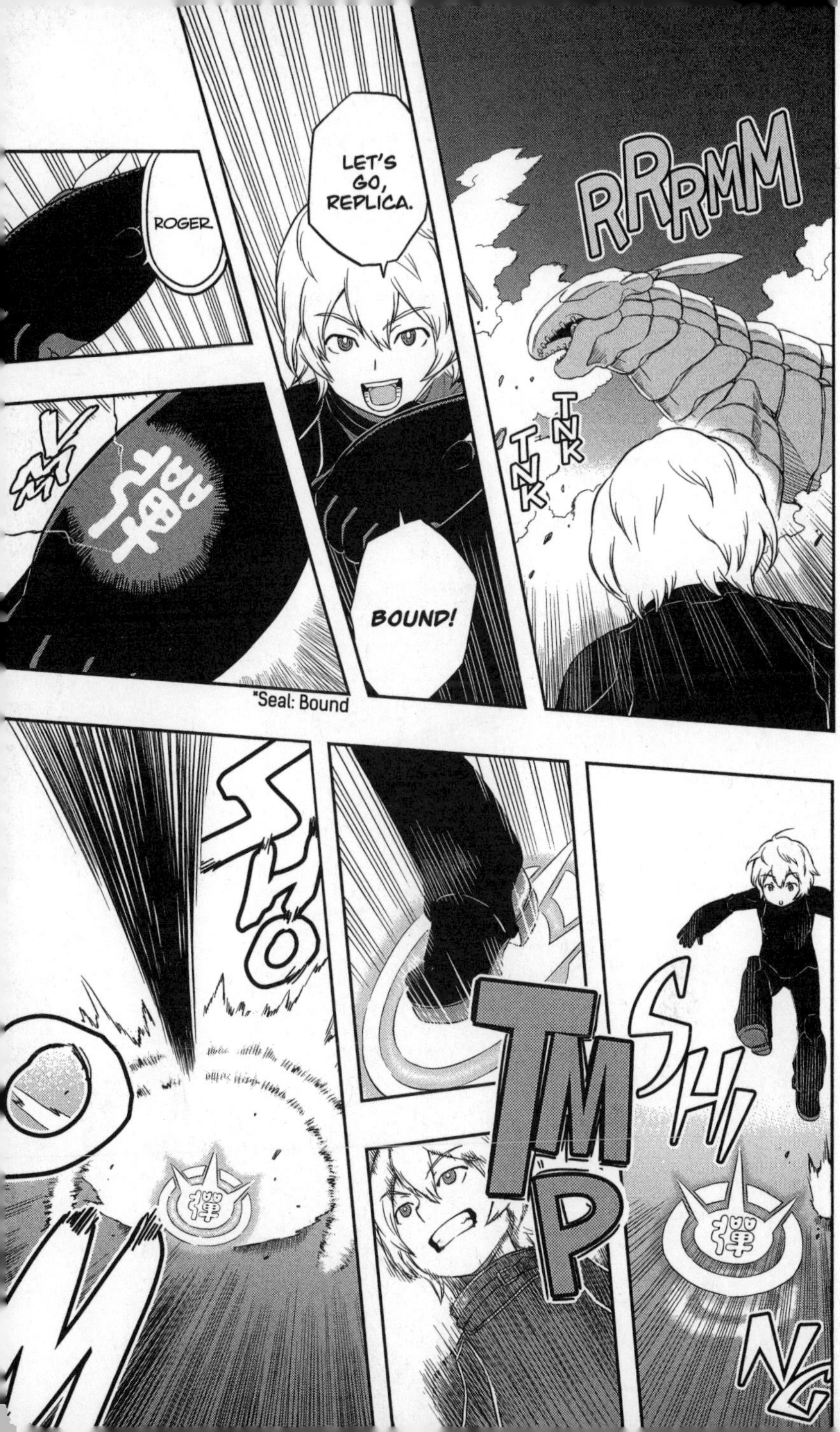
RRRMM
TNK
TNK
LET'S GO, REPLICA.
BOUND!
ROGER.
SHI
NG
TMP
SHO
*Seal: Bound

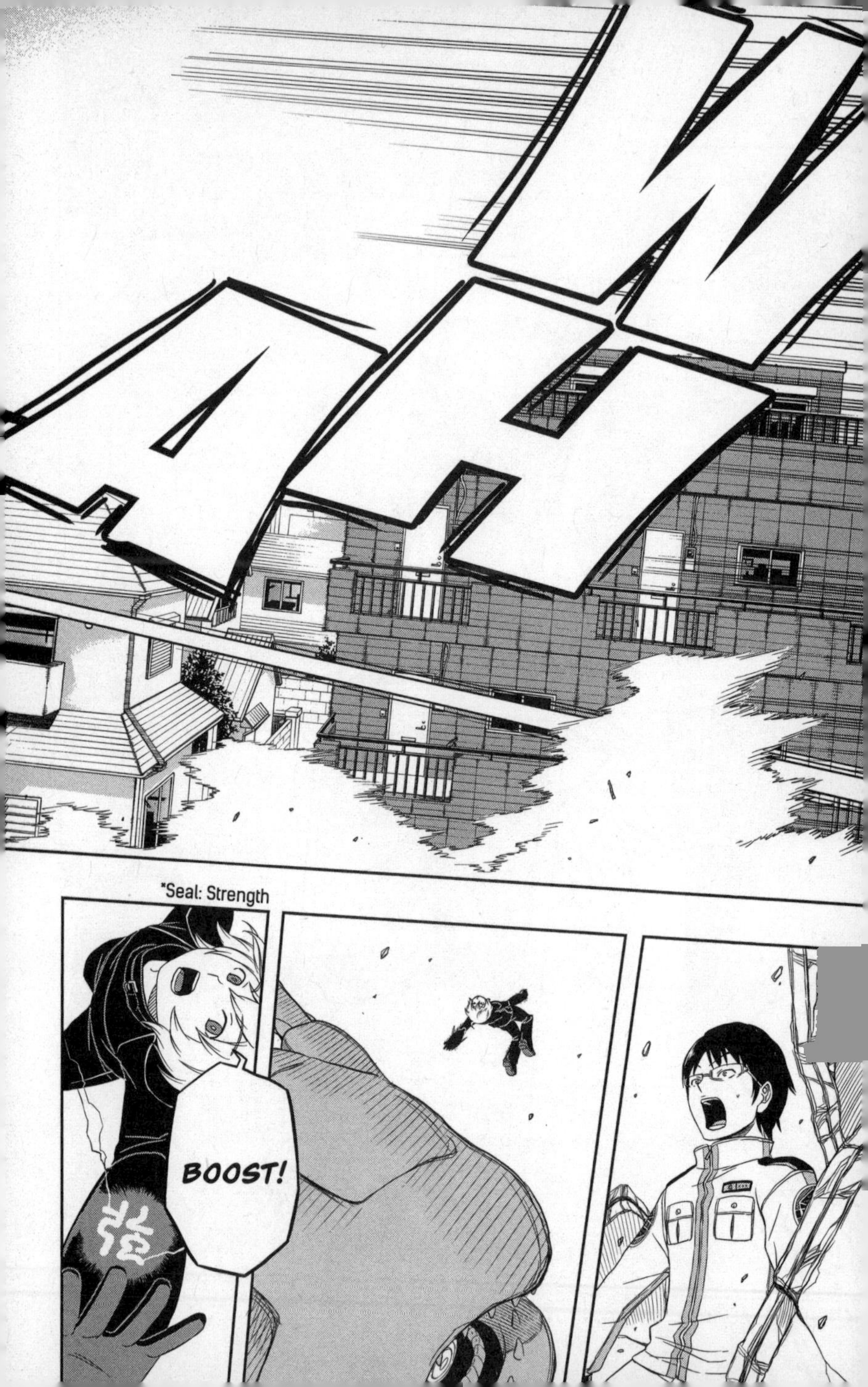
BOOST!
強
*Seal: Strength

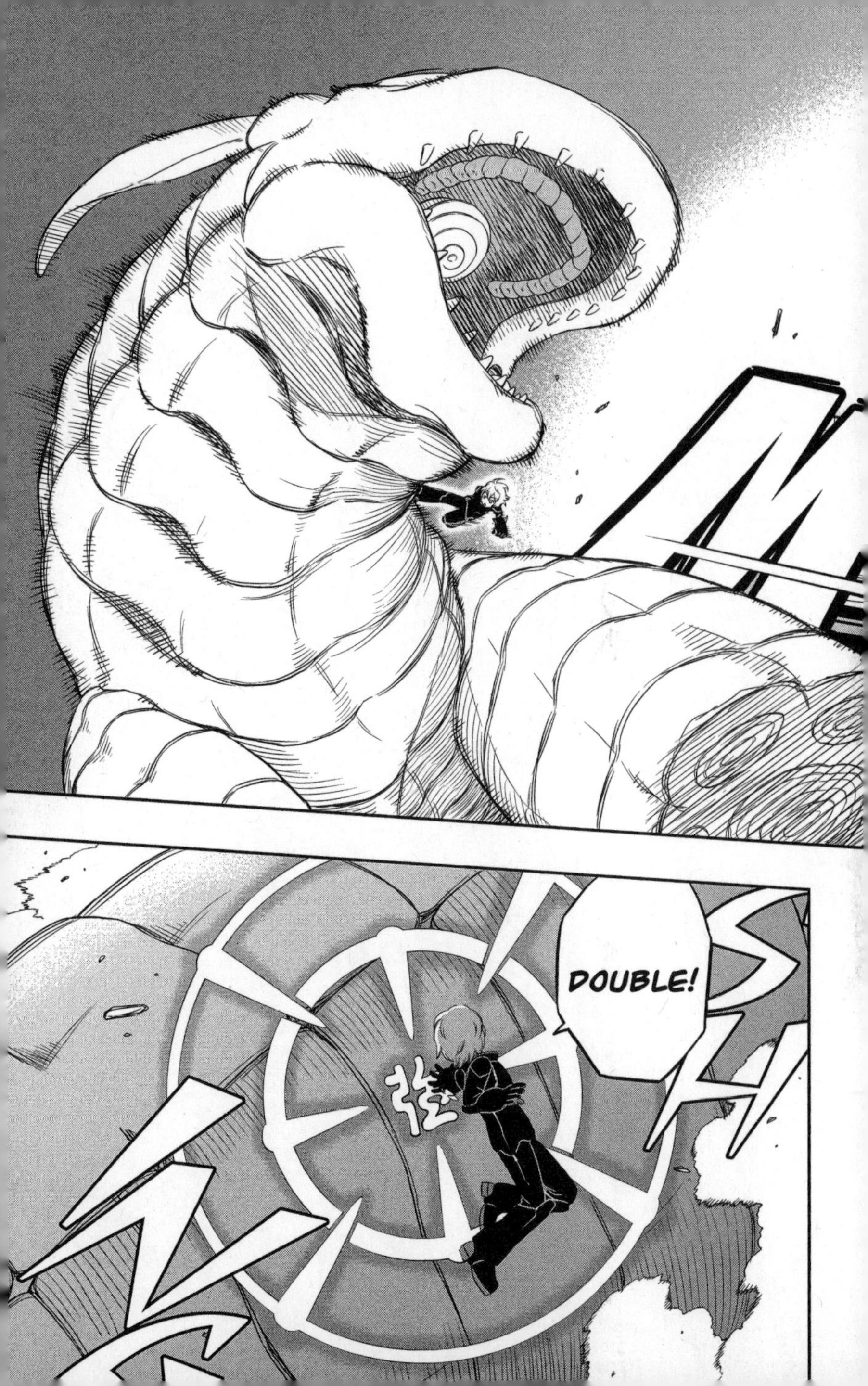
DOUBLE!

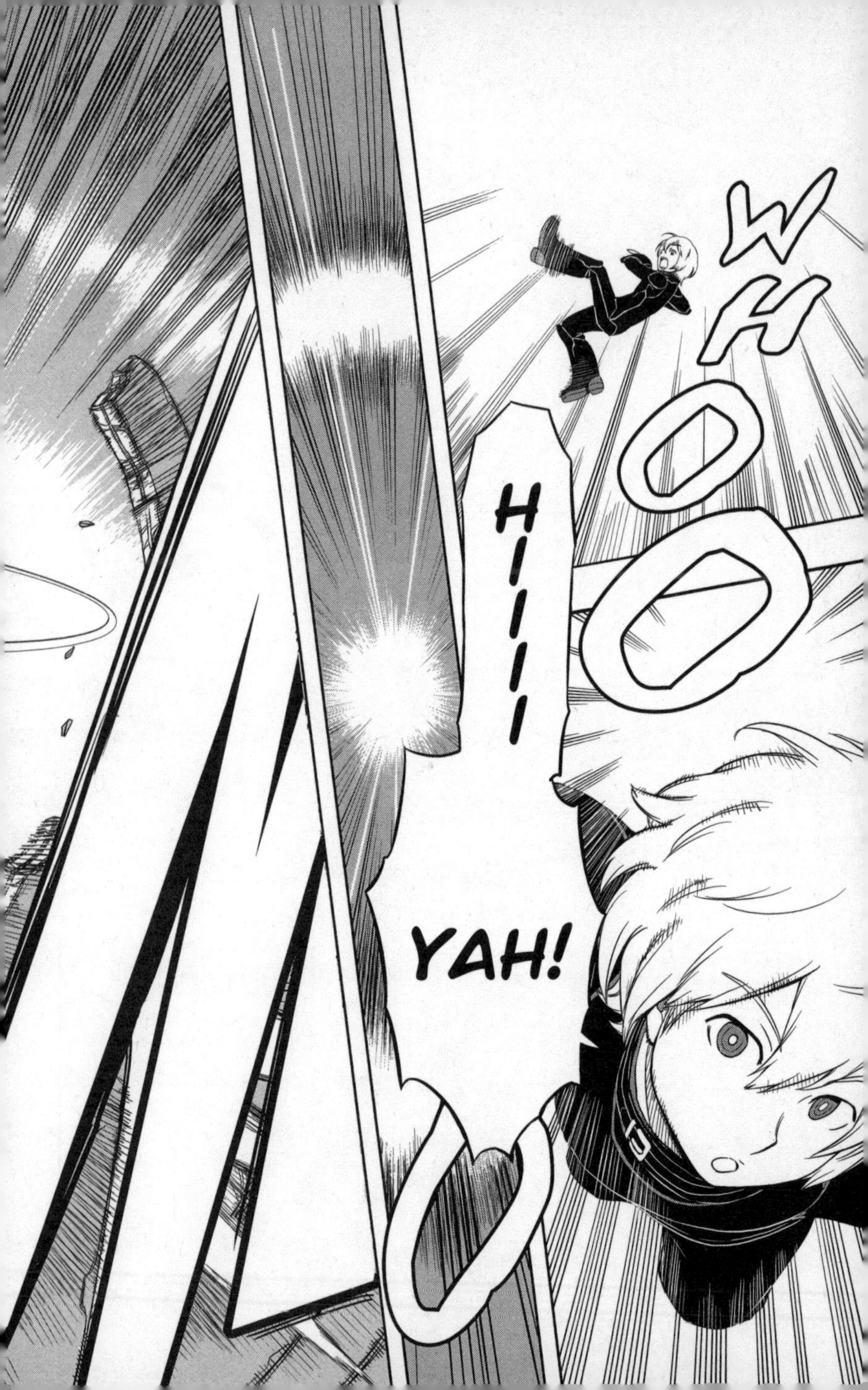
WHOOO
HIIII
YAH!

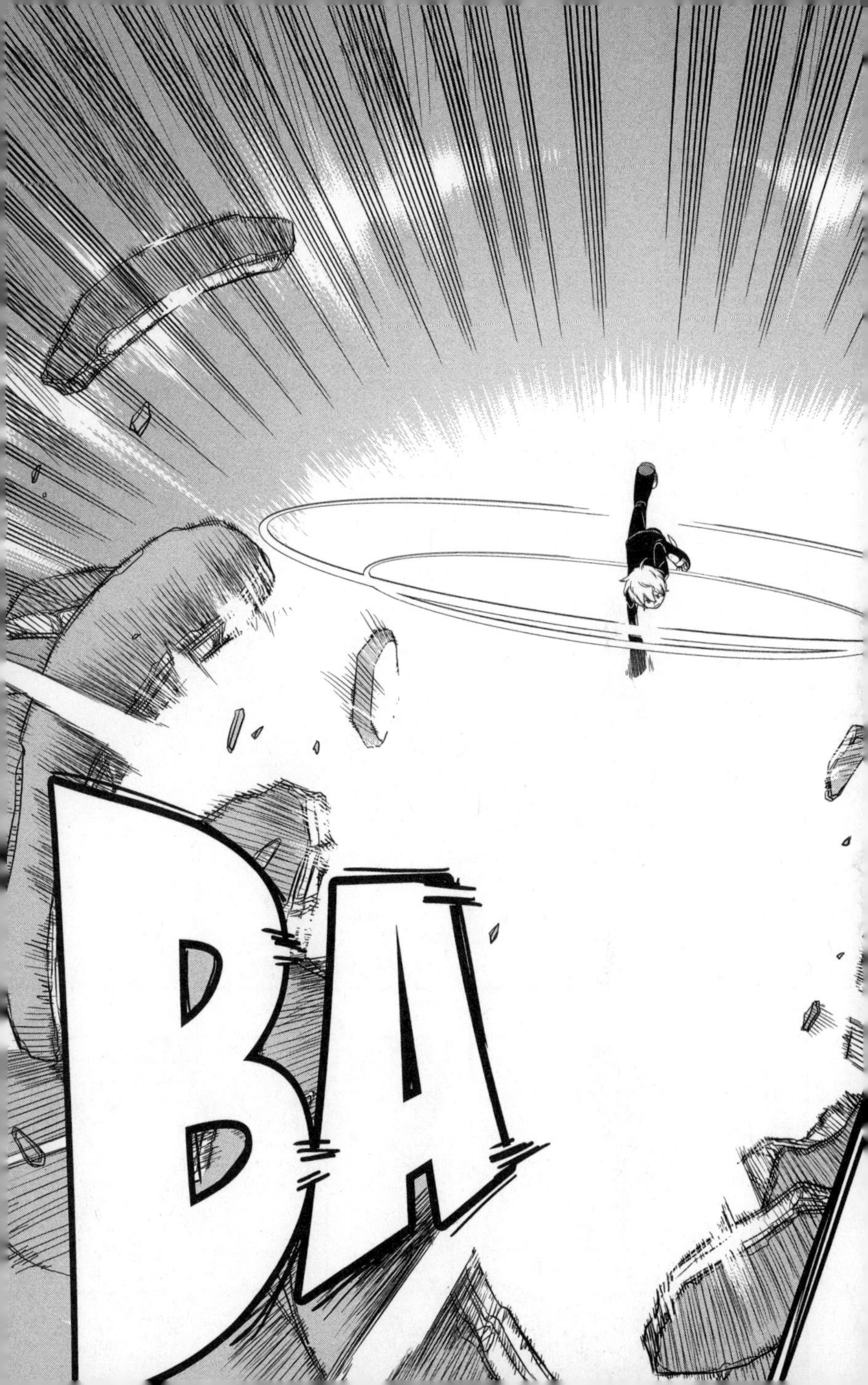
BA

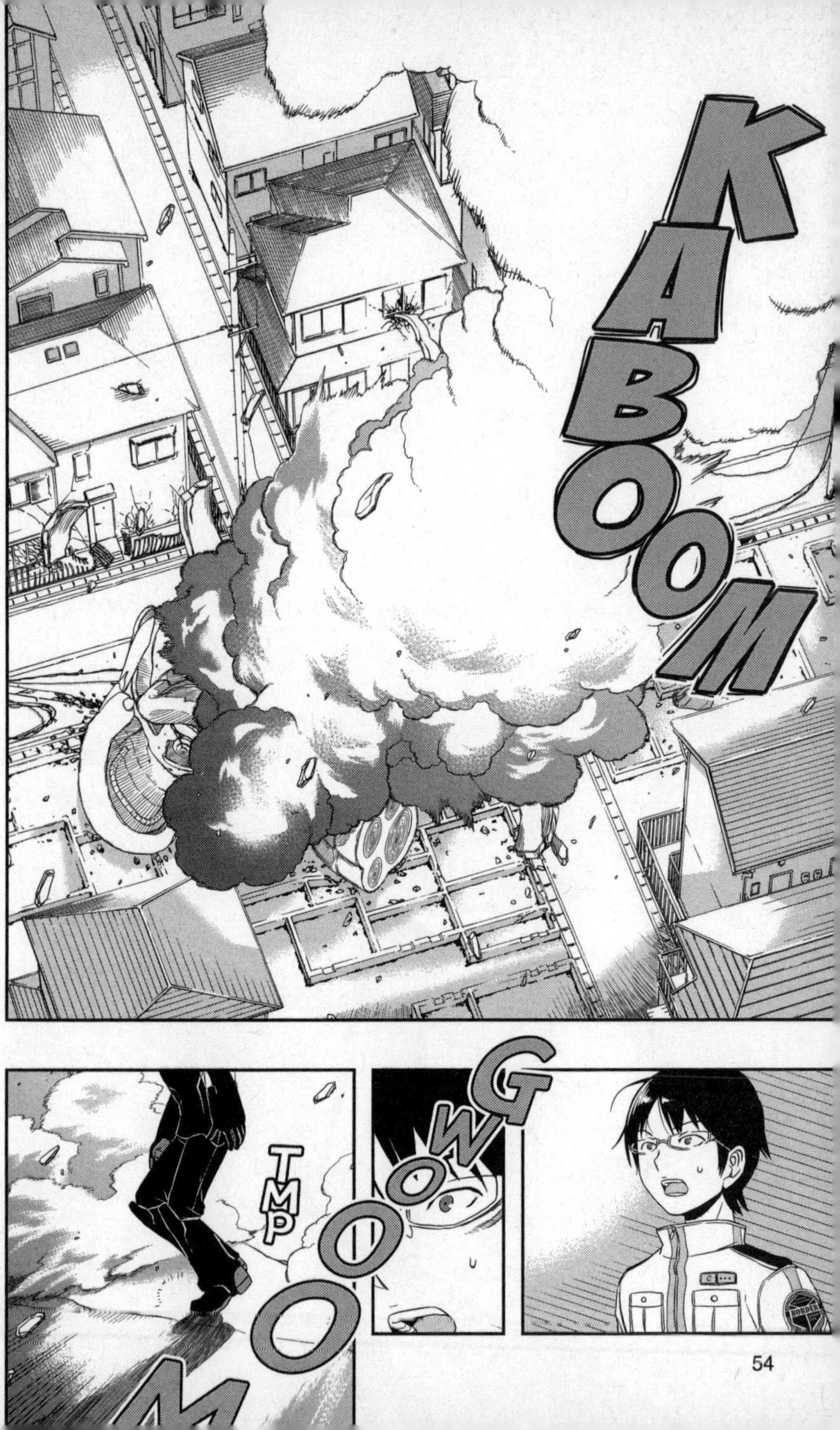
KABOOM
GWOOOOM
TMP

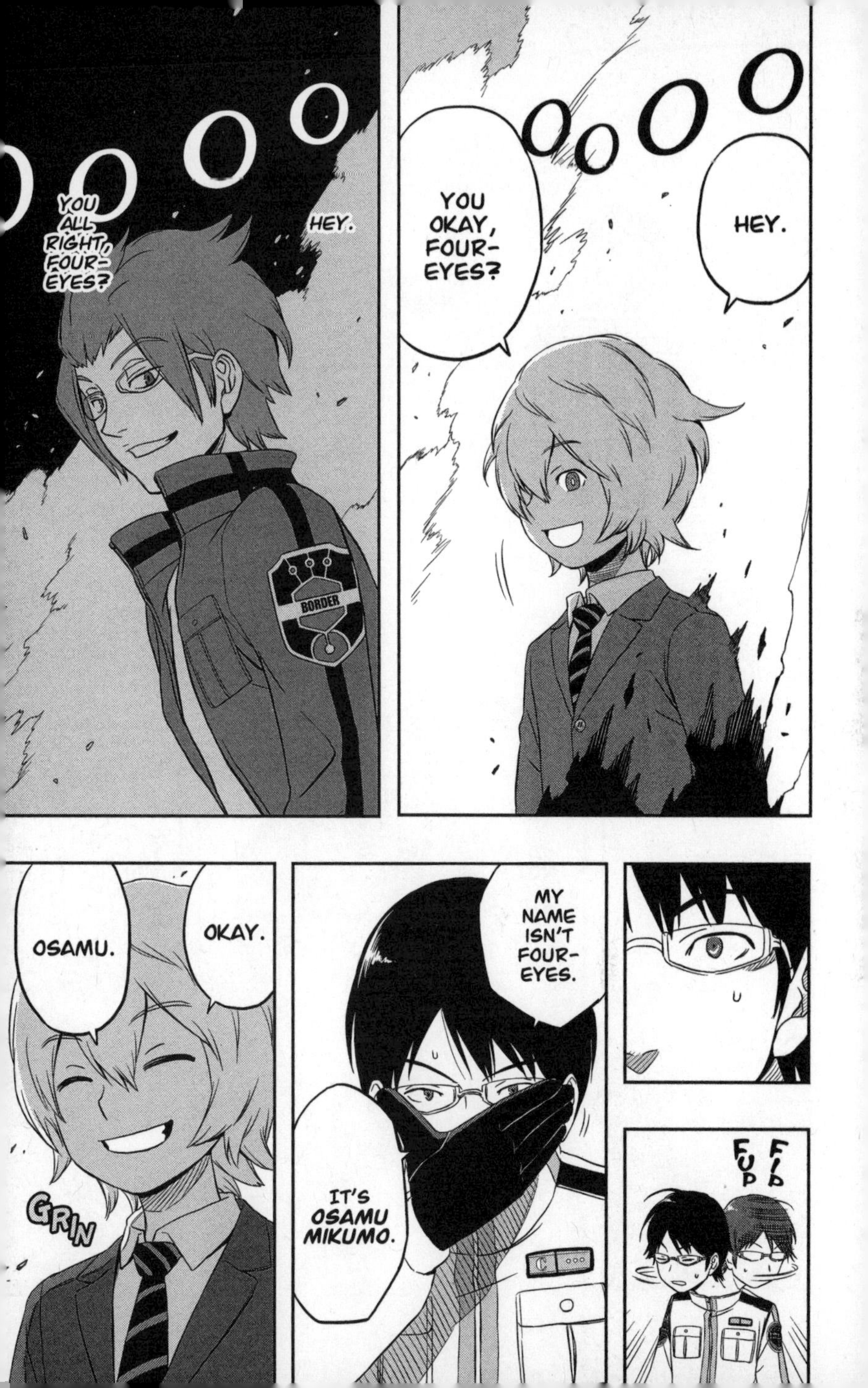
HEY.
YOU OKAY, FOUR-EYES?
HEY.
YOU ALL RIGHT, FOUR-EYES?
FUP
FID
MY NAME ISN'T FOUR-EYES.
IT'S OSAMU MIKUMO.
OKAY.
OSAMU.
GRIN

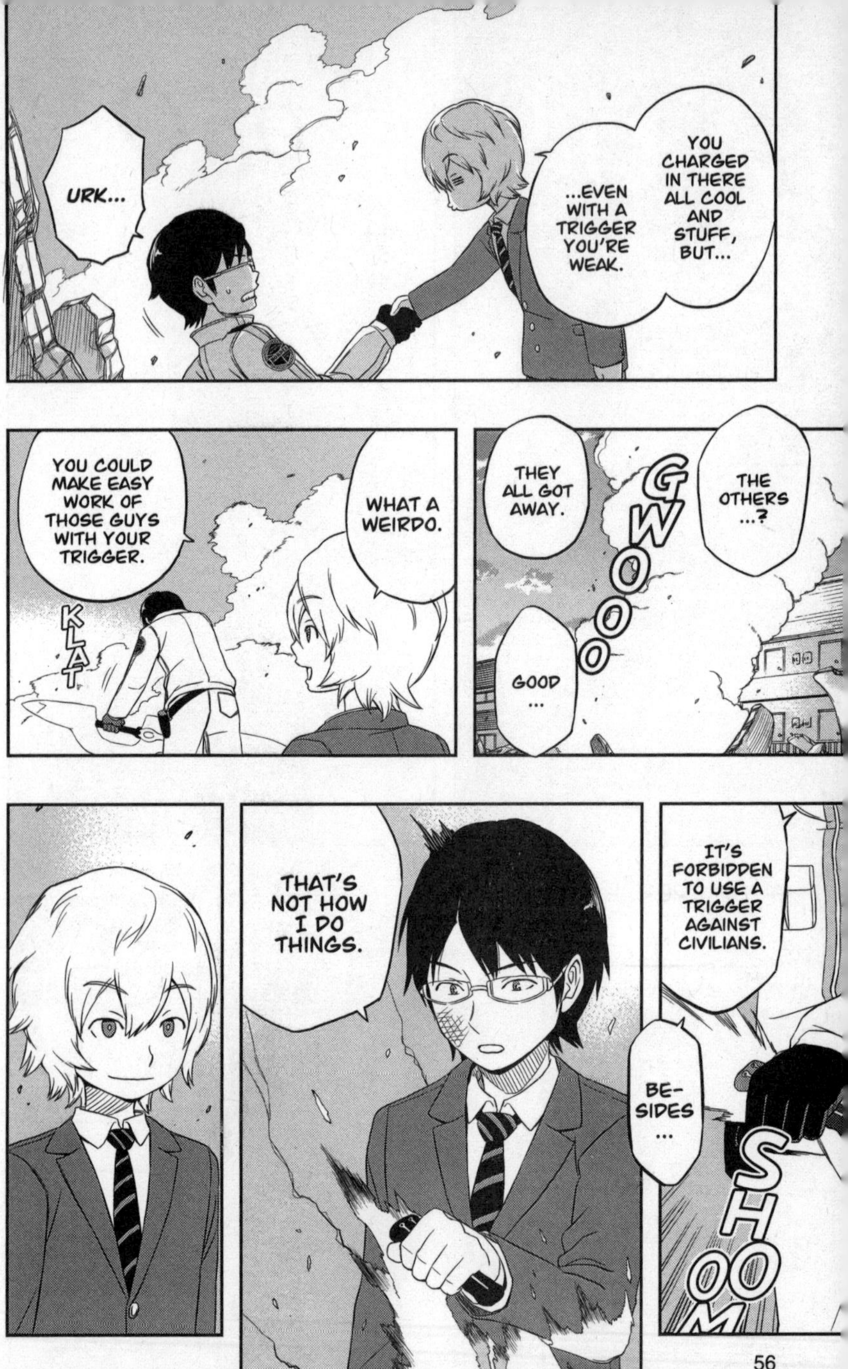
YOU CHARGED IN THERE ALL COOL AND STUFF, BUT...
...EVEN WITH A TRIGGER YOU'RE WEAK.
URK...
THE OTHERS ...?
GWOOOO
THEY ALL GOT AWAY.
GOOD ...
WHAT A WEIRDO.
YOU COULD MAKE EASY WORK OF THOSE GUYS WITH YOUR TRIGGER.
KLAT
IT'S FORBIDDEN TO USE A TRIGGER AGAINST CIVILIANS.
BE-SIDES ...
SHOOOM
THAT'S NOT HOW I DO THINGS.

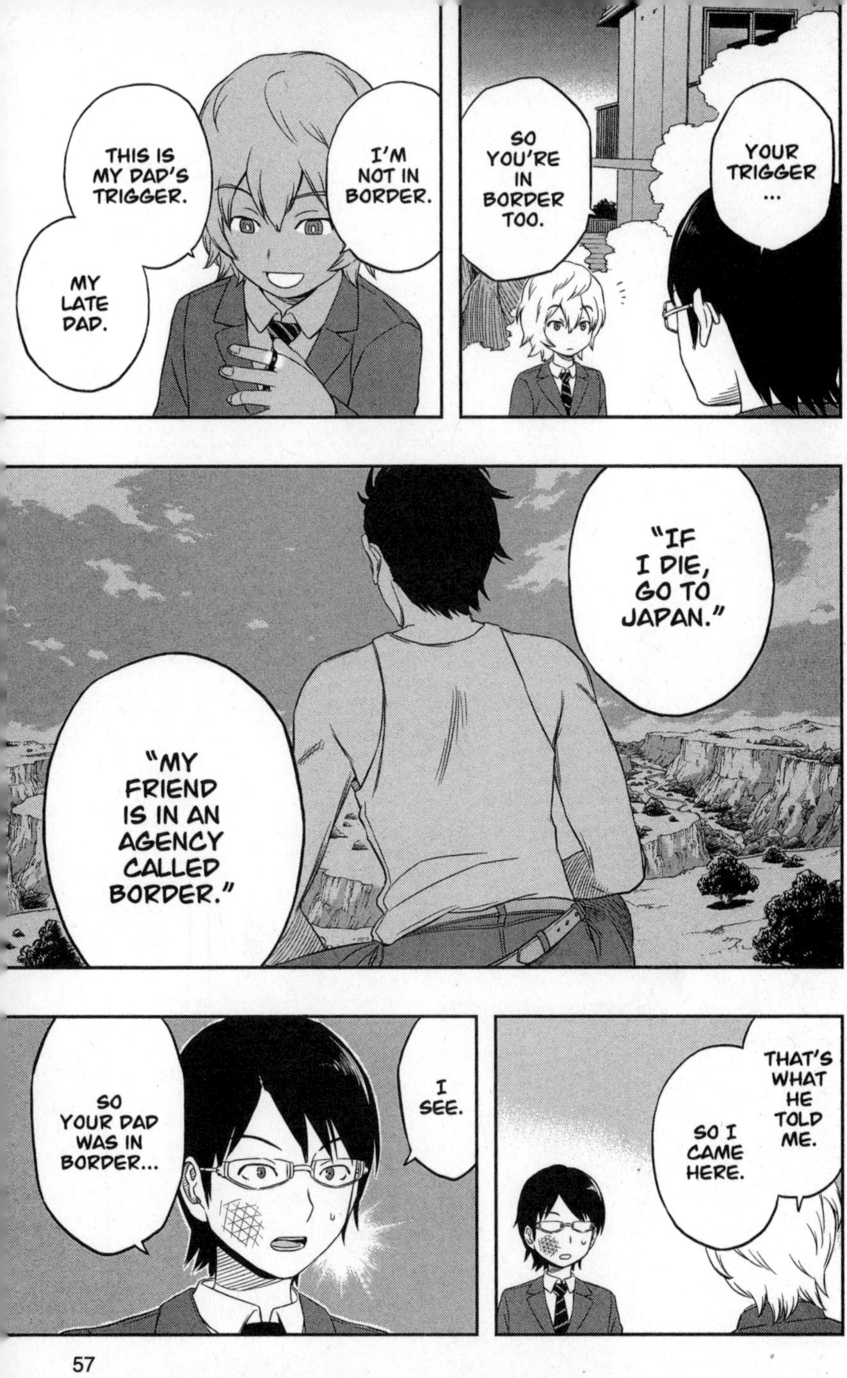
YOUR TRIGGER ...
SO YOU'RE IN BORDER TOO.
I'M NOT IN BORDER.
THIS IS MY DAD'S TRIGGER.
MY LATE DAD.
"IF I DIE, GO TO JAPAN."
"MY FRIEND IS IN AN AGENCY CALLED BORDER."
THAT'S WHAT HE TOLD ME.
SO I CAME HERE.
I SEE.
SO YOUR DAD WAS IN BORDER...

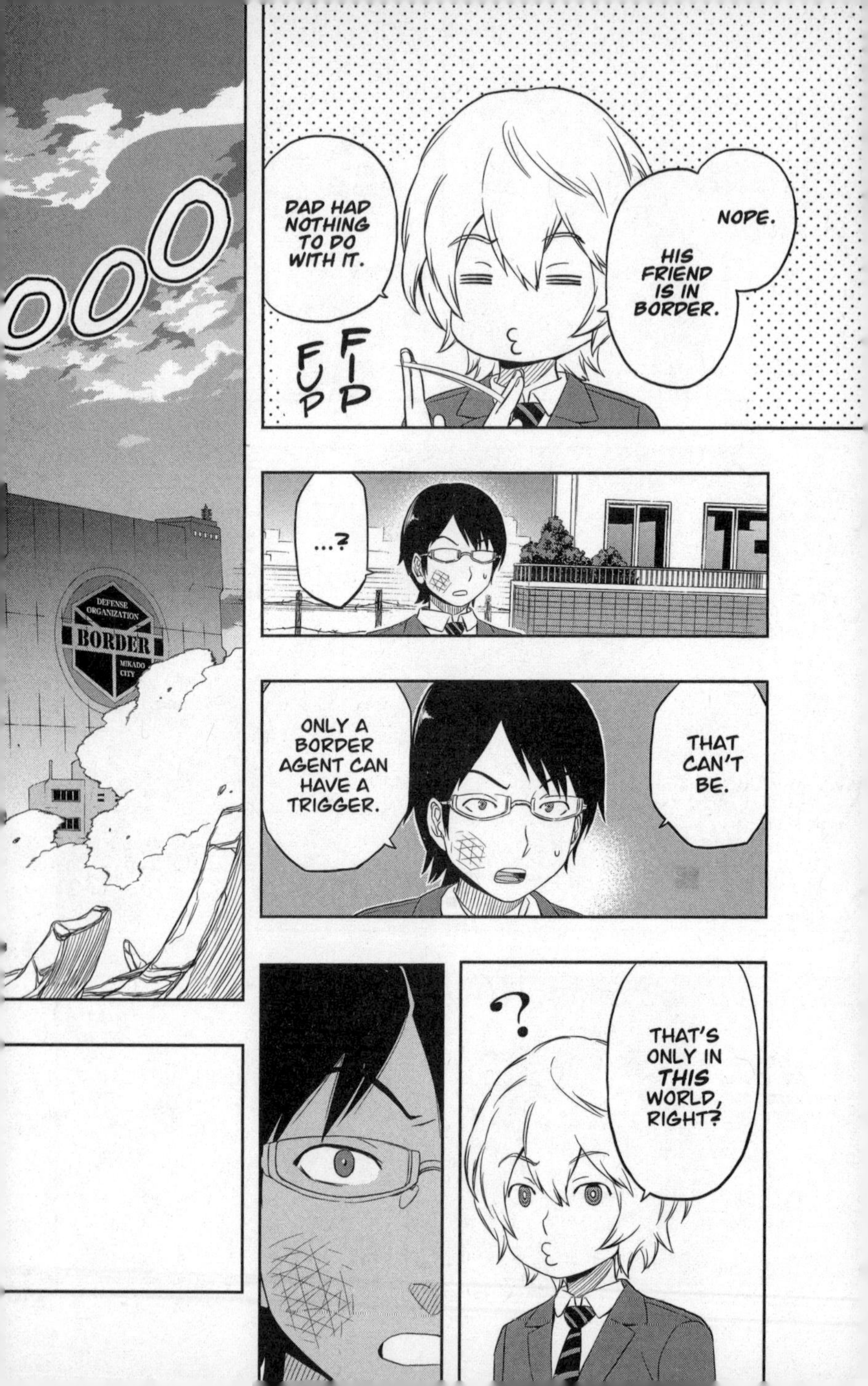
NOPE.
HIS FRIEND IS IN BORDER.
DAD HAD NOTHING TO DO WITH IT.
FIP
FUP
...?
THAT CAN'T BE.
ONLY A BORDER AGENT CAN HAVE A TRIGGER.
OOOO
DEFENSE ORGANIZATION
BORDER
MIKADO CITY
?
THAT'S ONLY IN THIS WORLD, RIGHT?

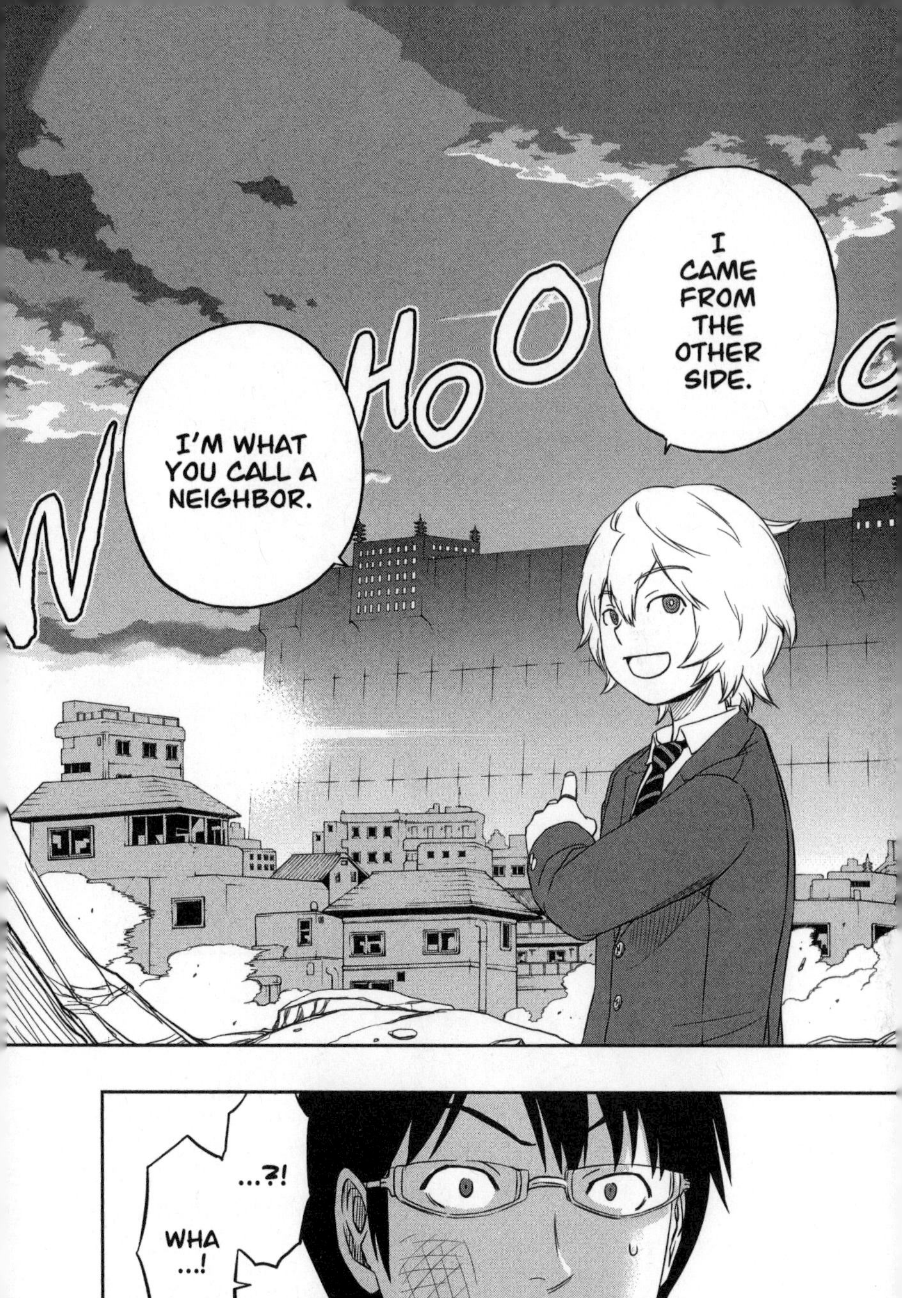
I CAME FROM THE OTHER SIDE.
I'M WHAT YOU CALL A NEIGHBOR.
WHOOO
...?!
WHA ...!

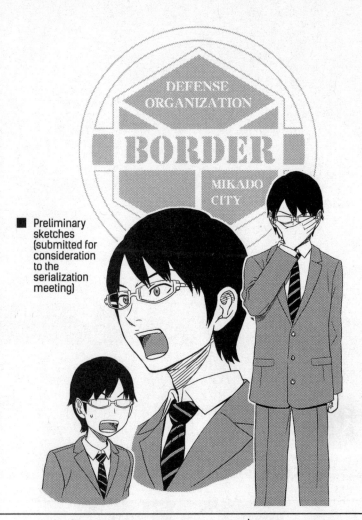

DEFENSE
ORGANIZATION

BORDER

MIKADO
CITY

■ Preliminary
sketches
(submitted for
consideration
to the
serialization
meeting)

Osamu Mikumo

- ■ 15 years old (junior high student)
- ■ Born May 25
- ■ Lepus, Blood type A
- ■ Height: 5'5"
- ■ Likes: Parents' home cooking, bridges

He's very easy to draw for some reason, so a page full of Osamus gets finished quickly. I think he forgives me even when I drawn him weird. Probably.

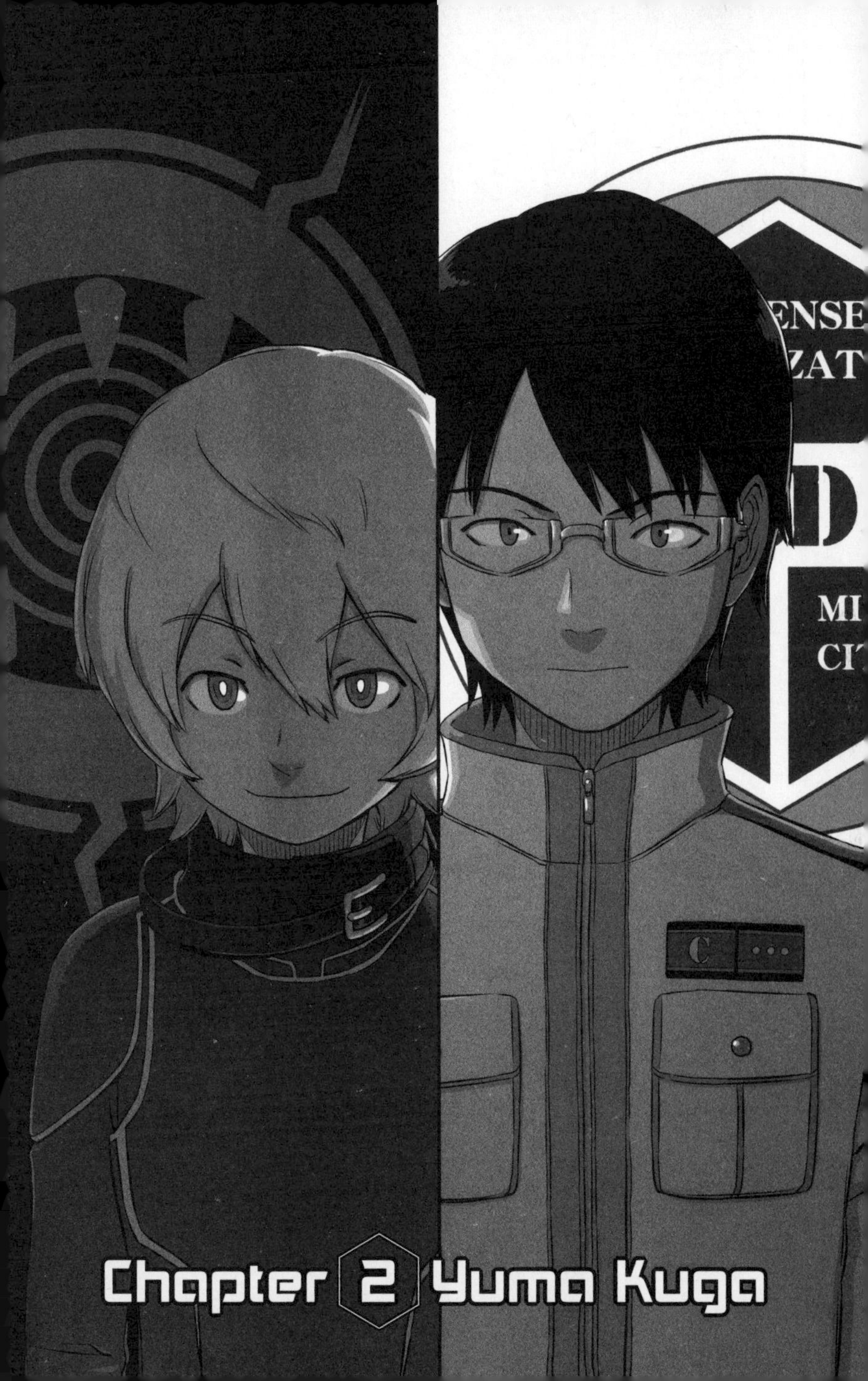

Chapter 2 Yuma Kuga

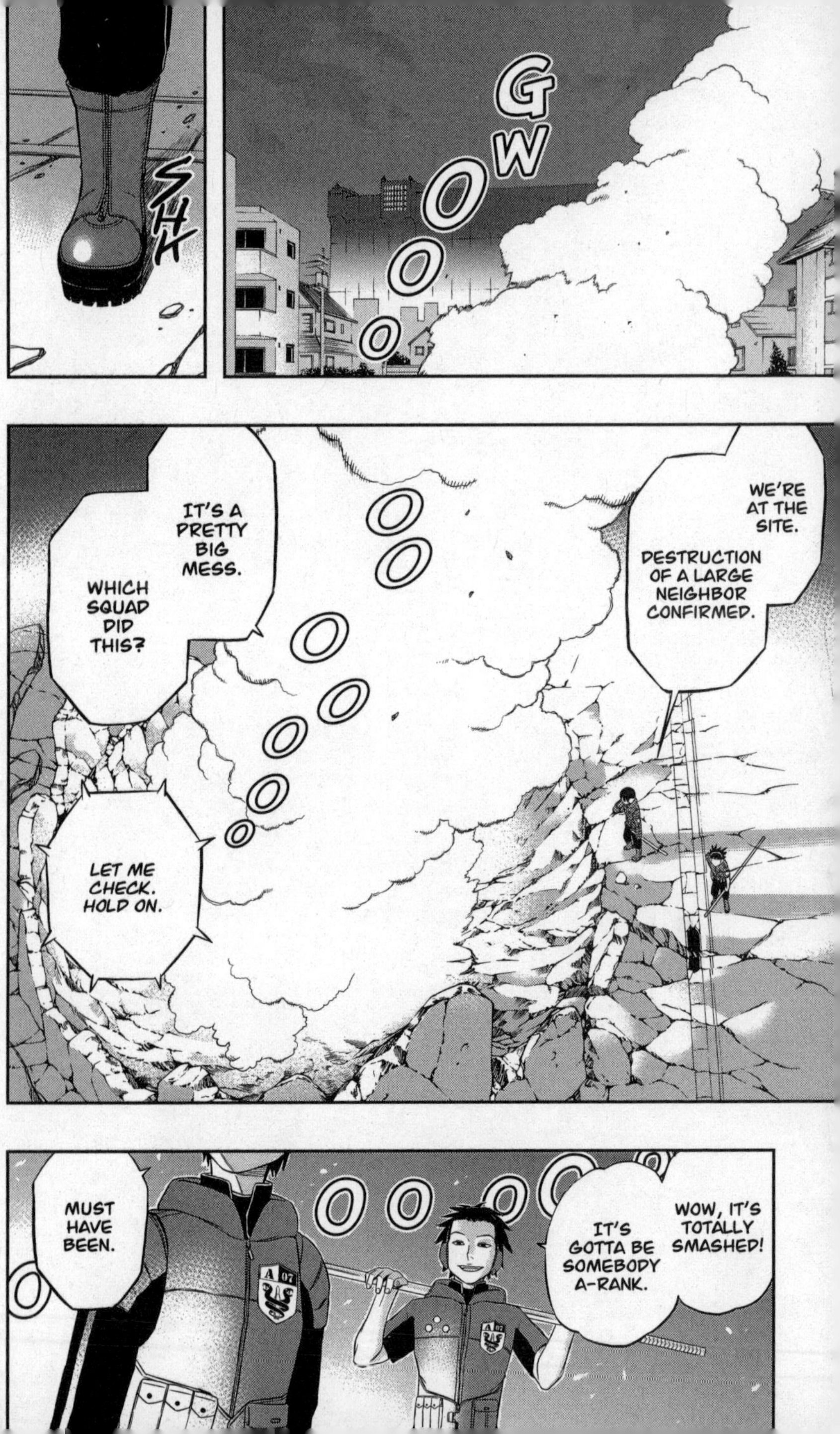
GWOOOO
SHK
WE'RE AT THE SITE.
DESTRUCTION OF A LARGE NEIGHBOR CONFIRMED.
IT'S A PRETTY BIG MESS.
WHICH SQUAD DID THIS?
LET ME CHECK. HOLD ON.
OOOOOOOO
WOW, IT'S TOTALLY SMASHED!
IT'S GOTTA BE SOMEBODY A-RANK.
MUST HAVE BEEN.
OOOOO

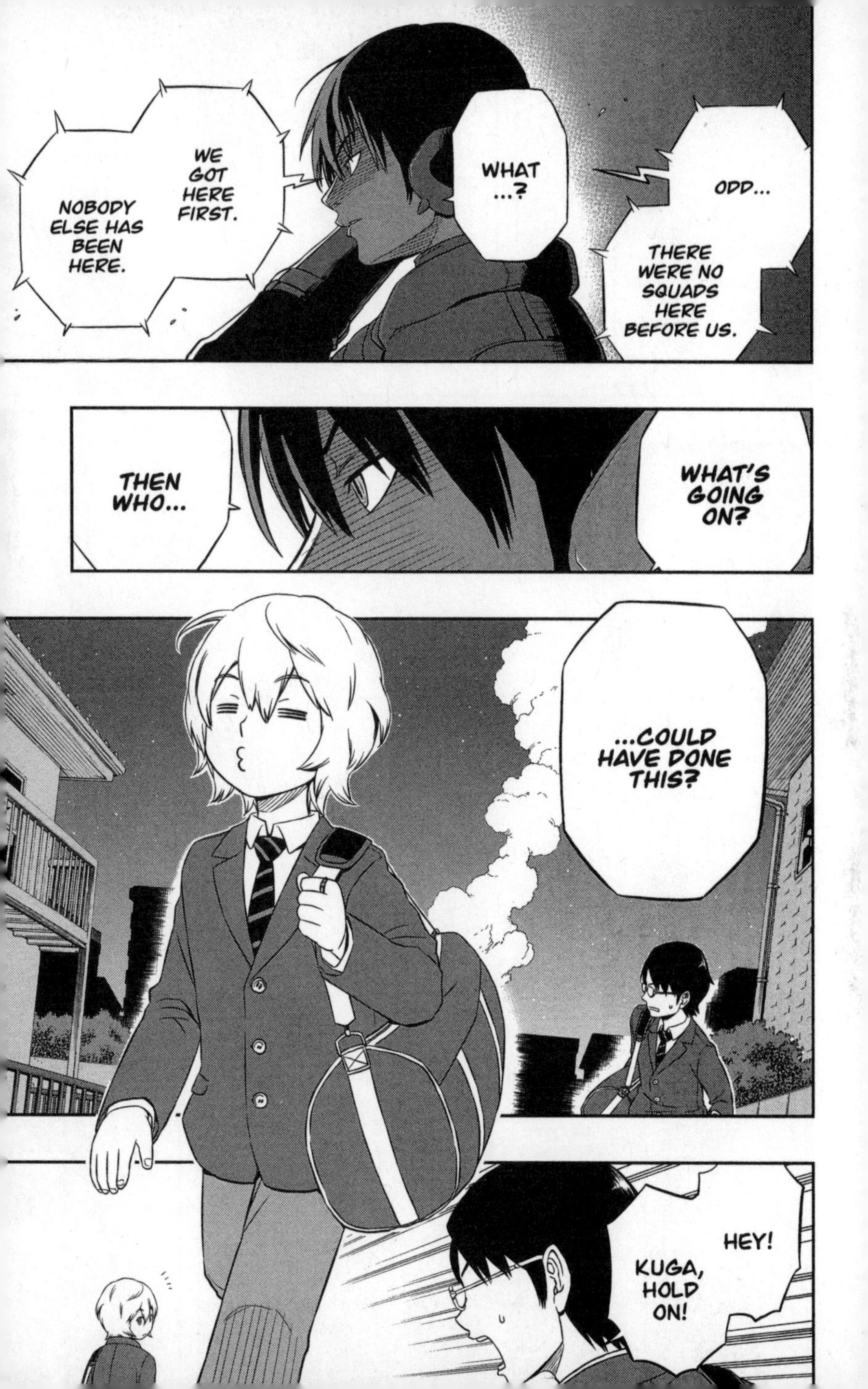
ODD...
THERE WERE NO SQUADS HERE BEFORE US.
WHAT ...?
WE GOT HERE FIRST.
NOBODY ELSE HAS BEEN HERE.
WHAT'S GOING ON?
THEN WHO...
...COULD HAVE DONE THIS?
HEY! KUGA, HOLD ON!

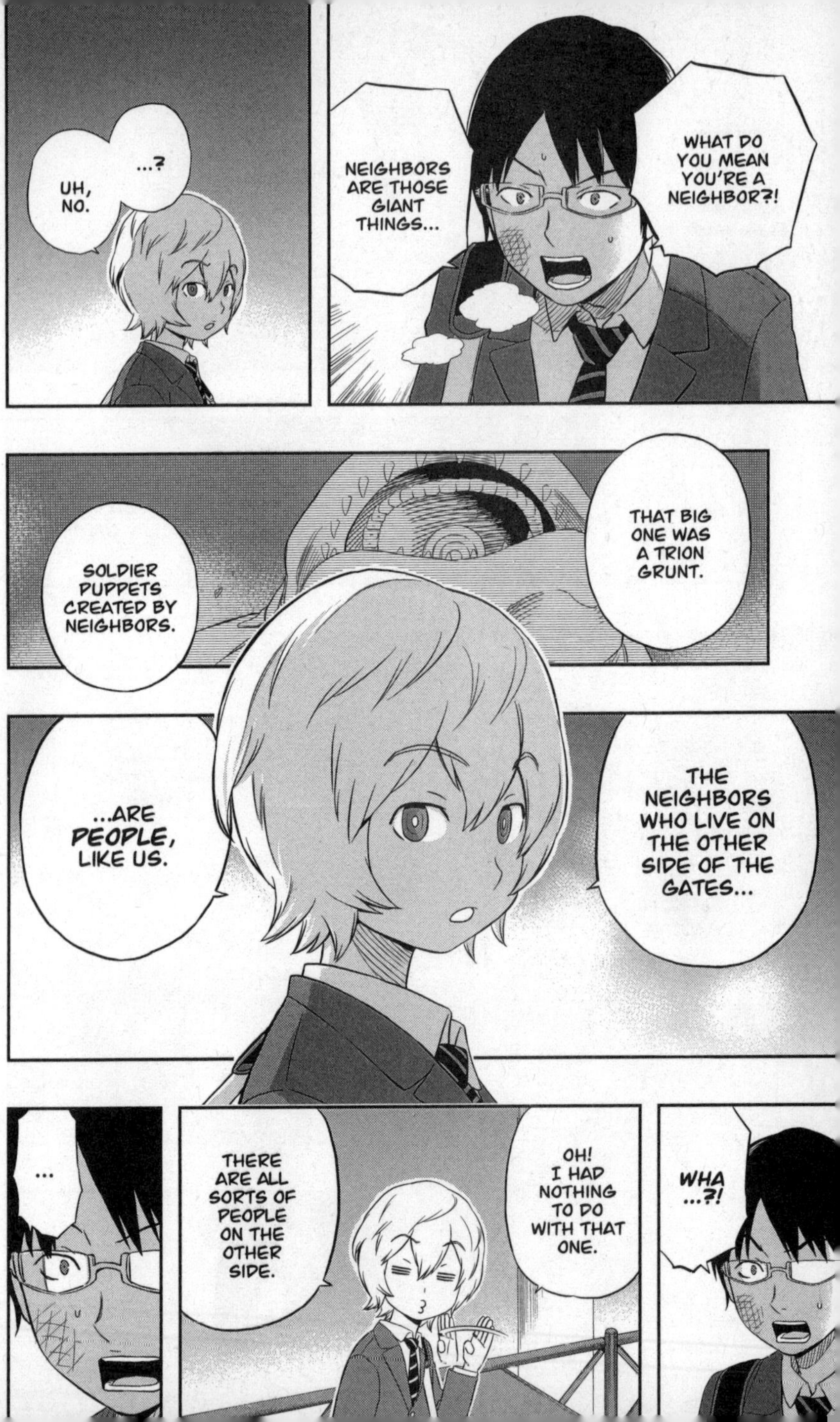
WHAT DO YOU MEAN YOU'RE A NEIGHBOR?!
NEIGHBORS ARE THOSE GIANT THINGS...
...?
UH, NO.
THAT BIG ONE WAS A TRION GRUNT.
SOLDIER PUPPETS CREATED BY NEIGHBORS.
THE NEIGHBORS WHO LIVE ON THE OTHER SIDE OF THE GATES...
...ARE **PEOPLE**, LIKE US.
WHA...?!
OH! I HAD NOTHING TO DO WITH THAT ONE.
THERE ARE ALL SORTS OF PEOPLE ON THE OTHER SIDE.
...

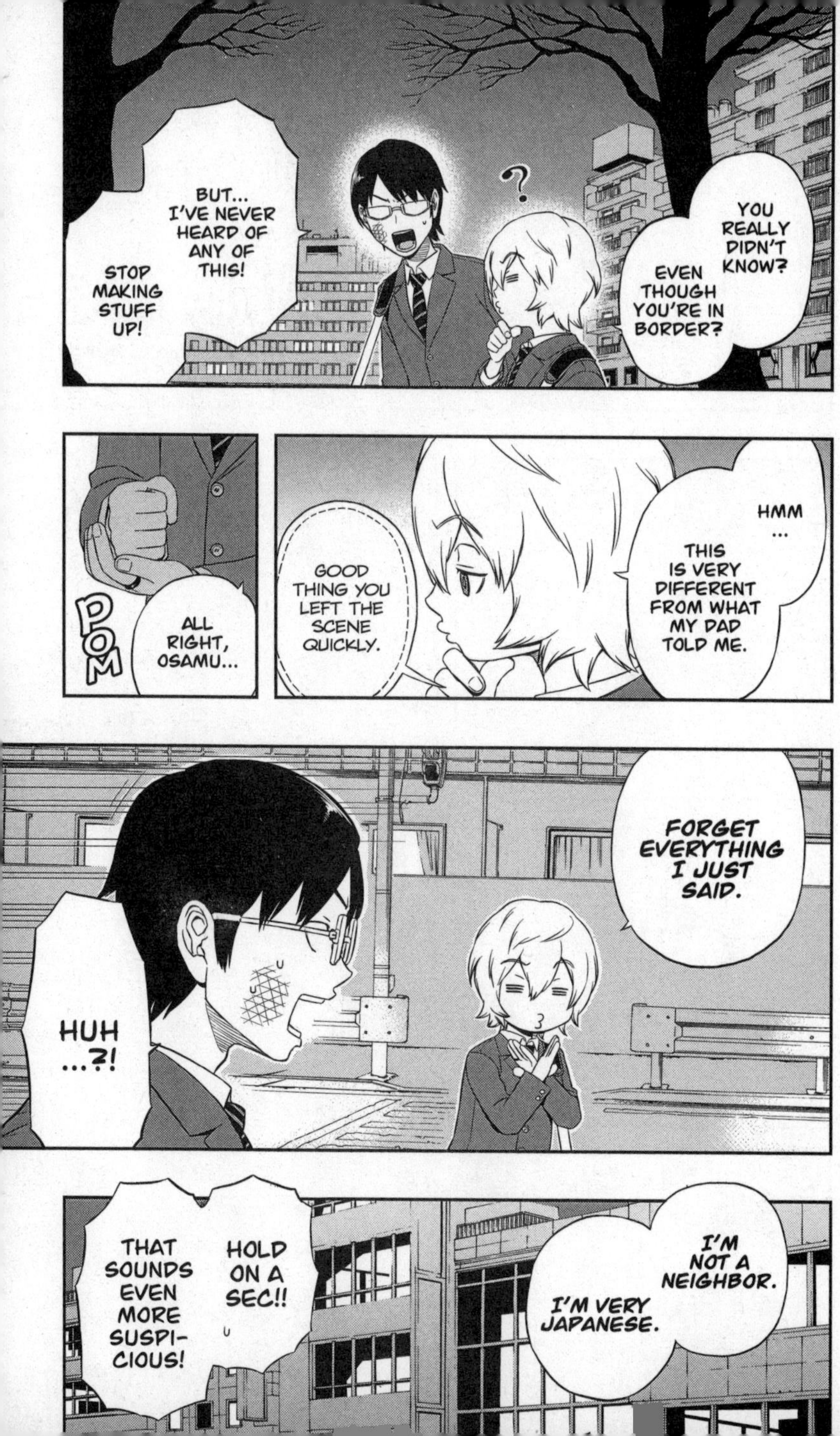
YOU REALLY DIDN'T KNOW?
EVEN THOUGH YOU'RE IN BORDER?
BUT... I'VE NEVER HEARD OF ANY OF THIS!
STOP MAKING STUFF UP!
HMM...
THIS IS VERY DIFFERENT FROM WHAT MY DAD TOLD ME.
GOOD THING YOU LEFT THE SCENE QUICKLY.
POM
ALL RIGHT, OSAMU...
FORGET EVERYTHING I JUST SAID.
HUH...?!
I'M NOT A NEIGHBOR.
I'M VERY JAPANESE.
HOLD ON A SEC!!
THAT SOUNDS EVEN MORE SUSPICIOUS!

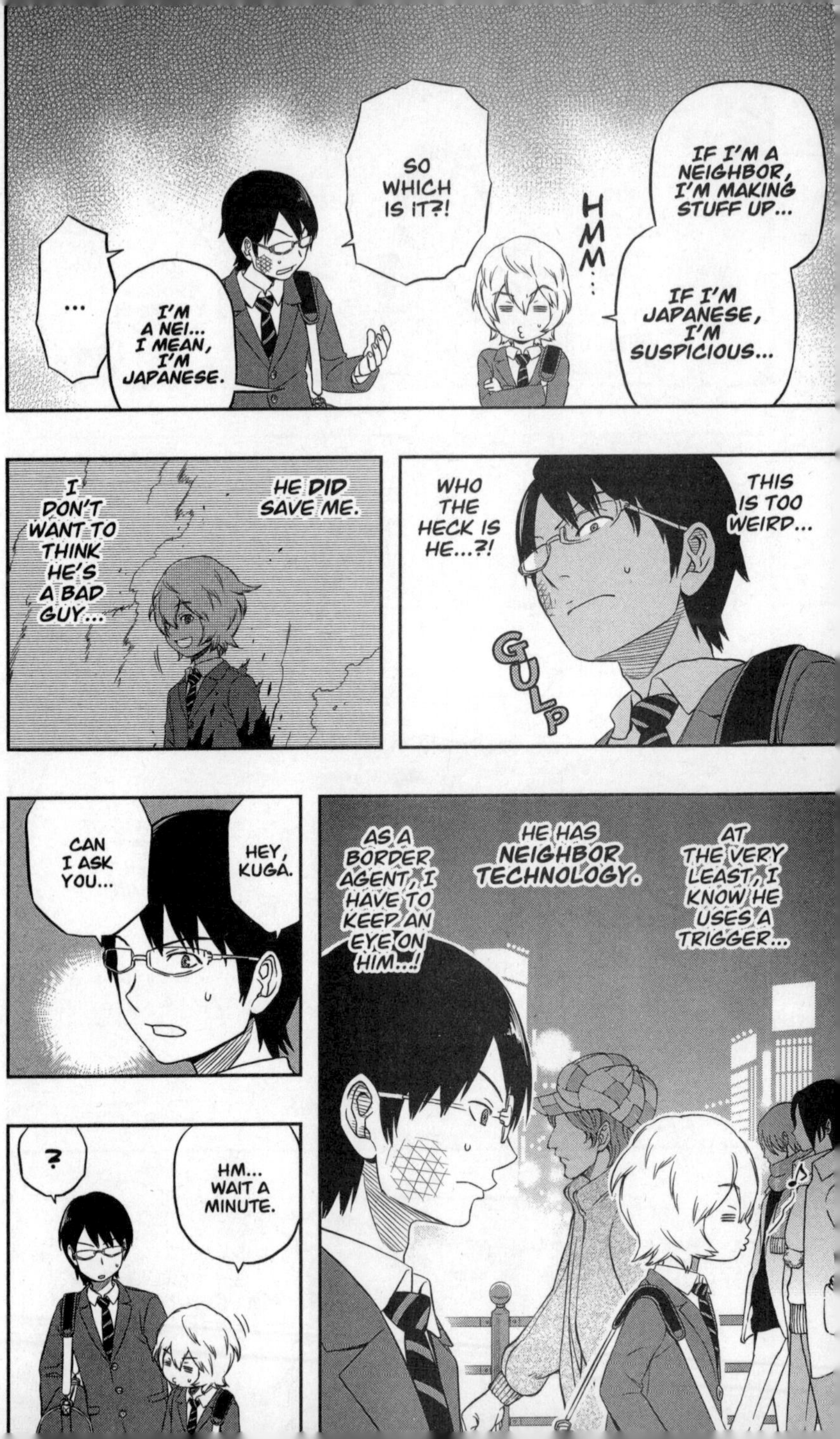
IF I'M A NEIGHBOR, I'M MAKING STUFF UP...
IF I'M JAPANESE, I'M SUSPICIOUS...
HMM...
SO WHICH IS IT?!
I'M A NEI... I MEAN, I'M JAPANESE.
...
THIS IS TOO WEIRD...
WHO THE HECK IS HE...?!
GULP
HE DID SAVE ME.
I DON'T WANT TO THINK HE'S A BAD GUY...
AT THE VERY LEAST, I KNOW HE USES A TRIGGER...
HE HAS NEIGHBOR TECHNOLOGY.
AS A BORDER AGENT, I HAVE TO KEEP AN EYE ON HIM...!
HEY, KUGA.
CAN I ASK YOU...
HM... WAIT A MINUTE.
?

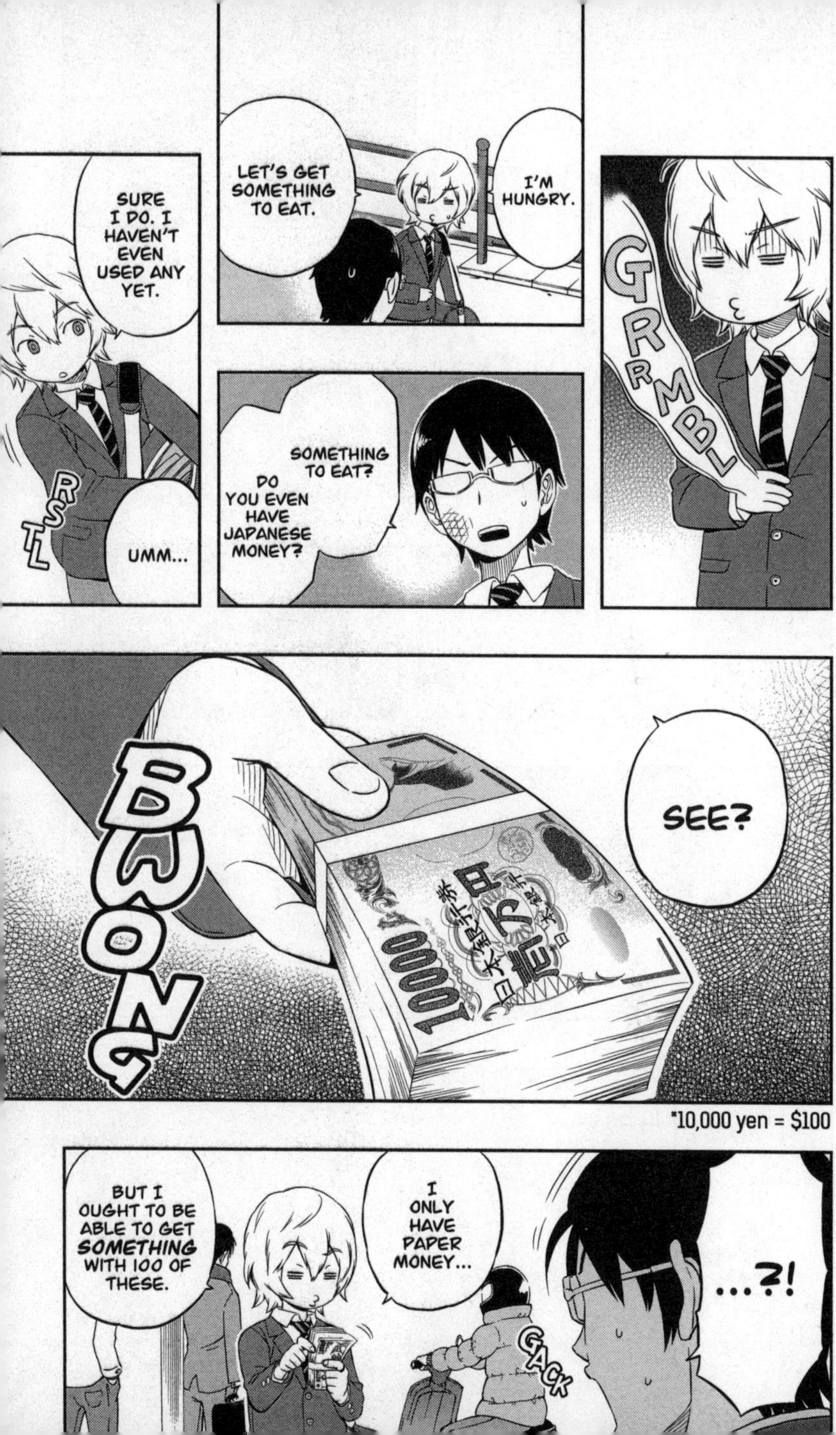
GRRMBL
I'M HUNGRY.
LET'S GET SOMETHING TO EAT.
SOMETHING TO EAT? DO YOU EVEN HAVE JAPANESE MONEY?
SURE I DO. I HAVEN'T EVEN USED ANY YET.
UMM...
RSTL
SEE?
BWONG
10000
...?!
GACK
I ONLY HAVE PAPER MONEY...
BUT I OUGHT TO BE ABLE TO GET **SOMETHING** WITH 100 OF THESE.

*10,000 yen = $100

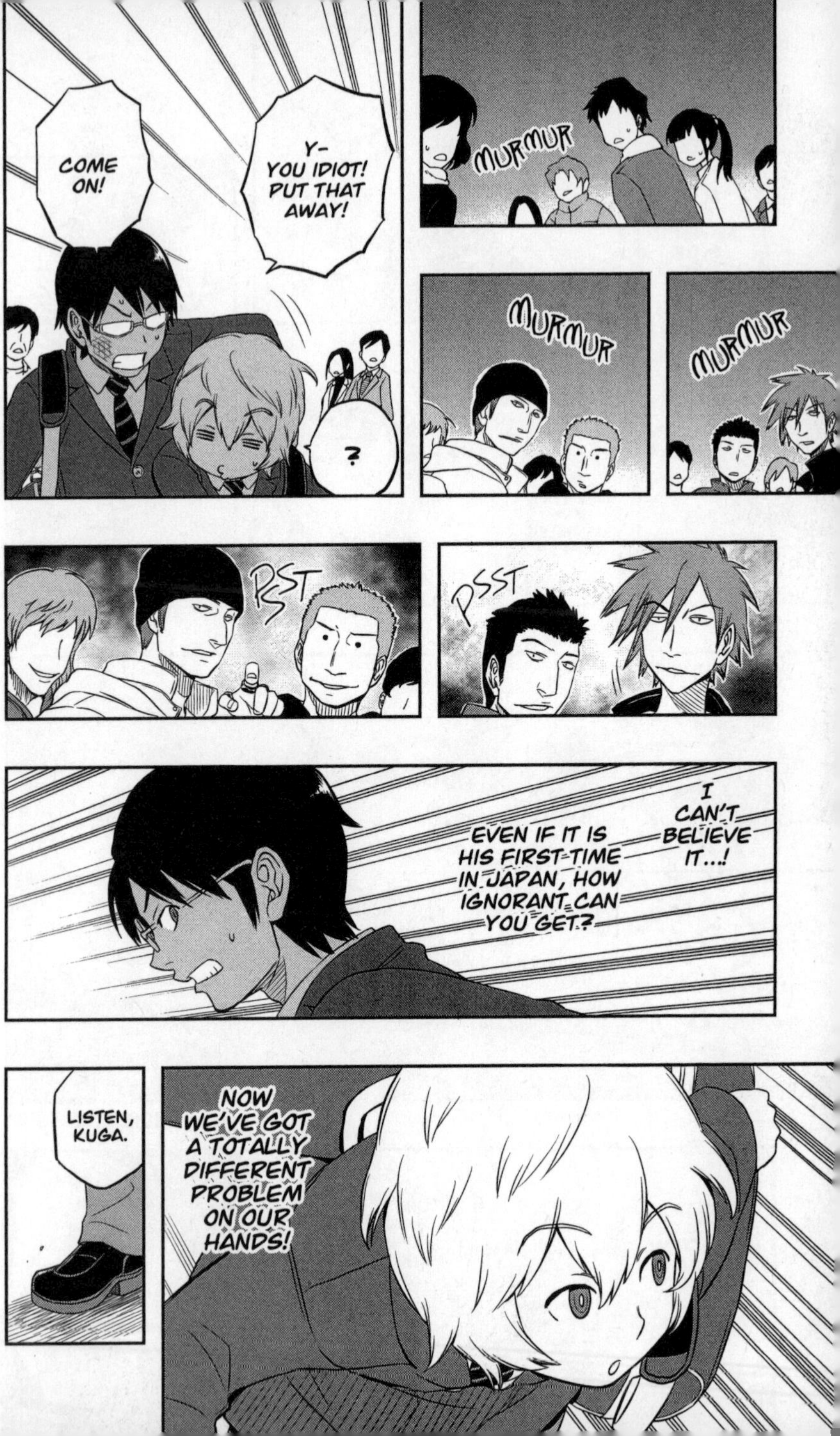
MURMUR
MURMUR
MURMUR
Y- YOU IDIOT! PUT THAT AWAY!
COME ON!
?
PSST
PSST
I CAN'T BELIEVE IT...!
EVEN IF IT IS HIS FIRST TIME IN JAPAN, HOW IGNORANT CAN YOU GET?
NOW WE'VE GOT A TOTALLY DIFFERENT PROBLEM ON OUR HANDS!
LISTEN, KUGA.

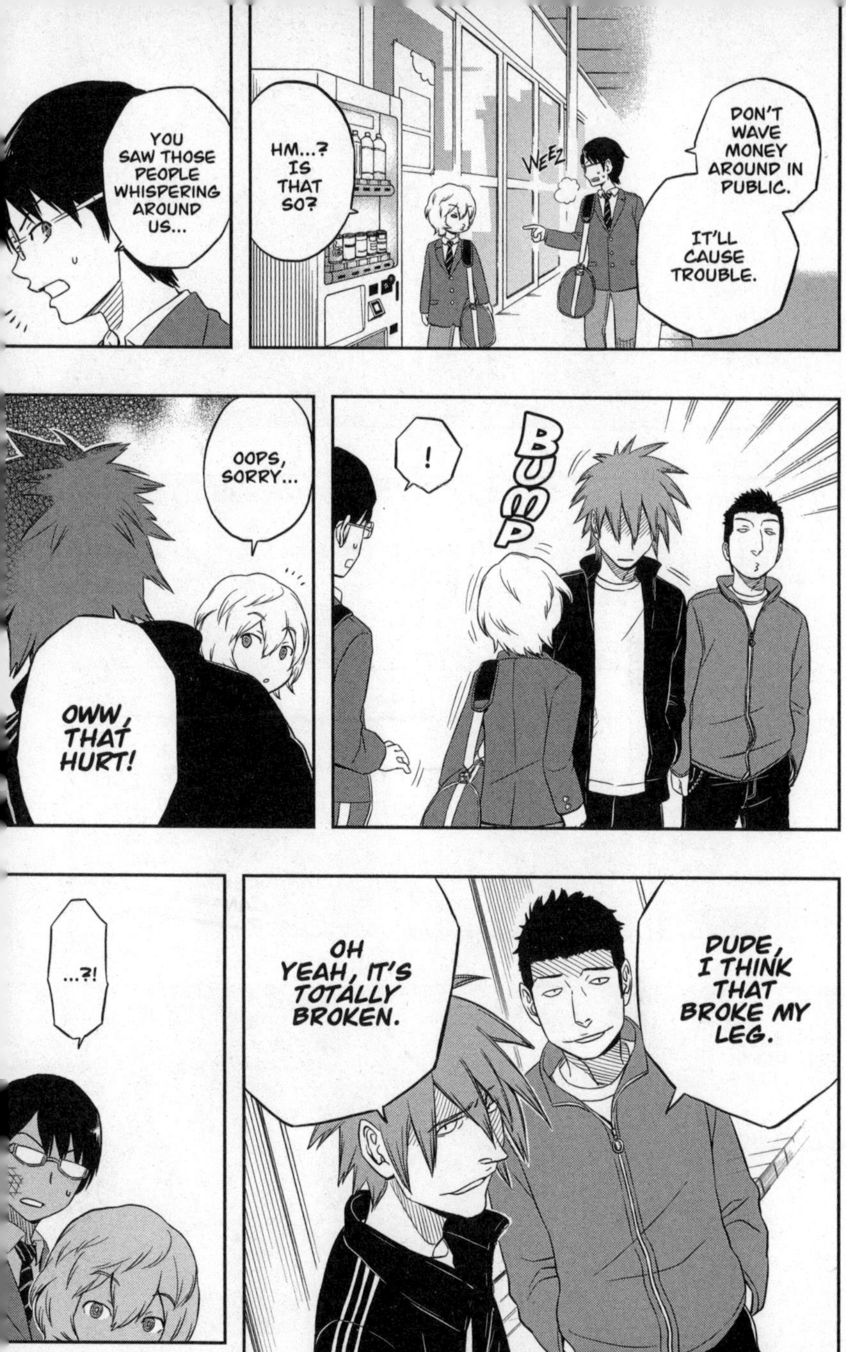
DON'T WAVE MONEY AROUND IN PUBLIC.
IT'LL CAUSE TROUBLE.
WEEZ
HM...? IS THAT SO?
YOU SAW THOSE PEOPLE WHISPERING AROUND US...
BUMP
!
OOPS, SORRY...
OWW, THAT HURT!
DUDE, I THINK THAT BROKE MY LEG.
OH YEAH, IT'S TOTALLY BROKEN.
...?!

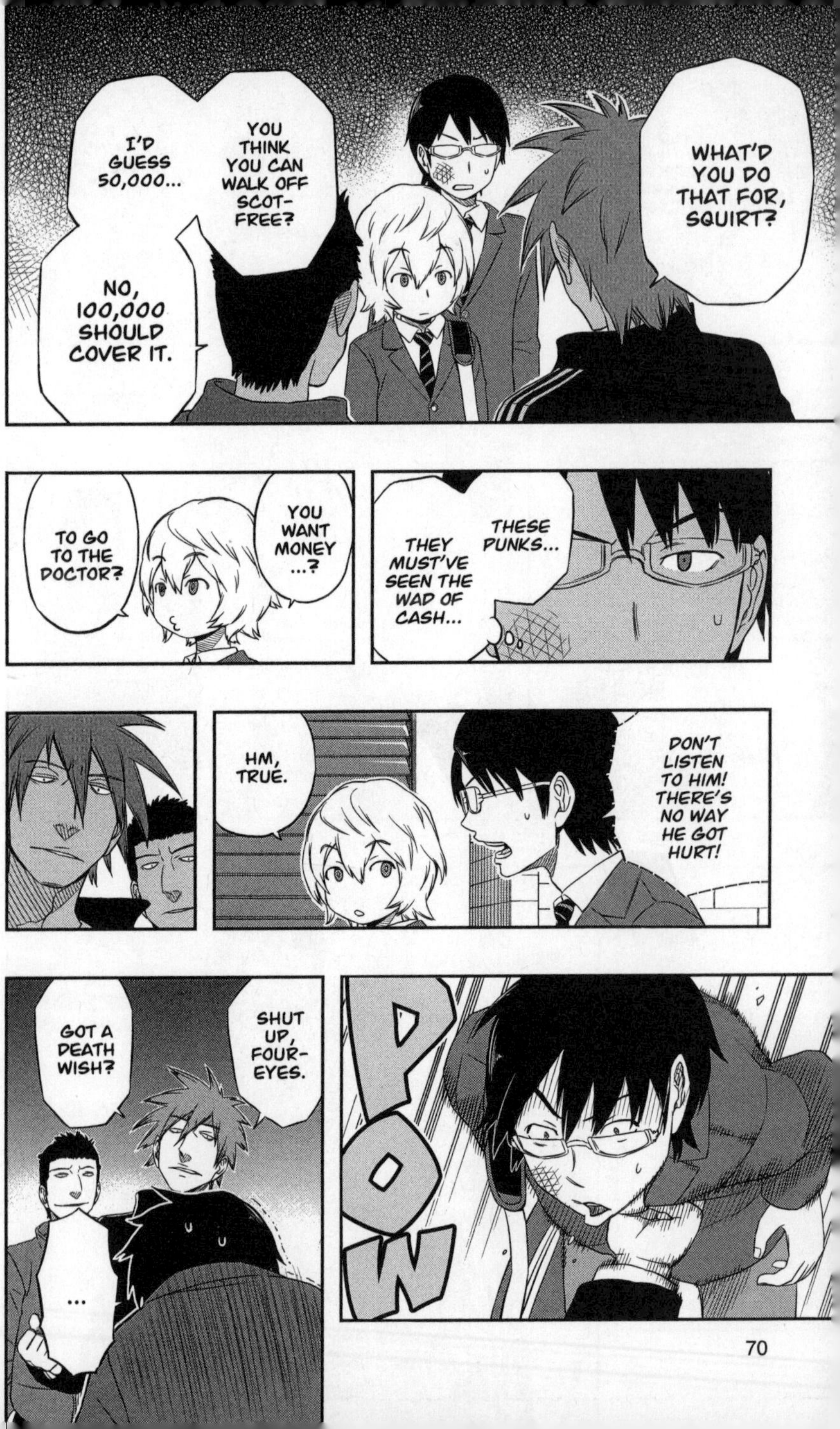
WHAT'D YOU DO THAT FOR, SQUIRT?
YOU THINK YOU CAN WALK OFF SCOT-FREE?
I'D GUESS 50,000...
NO, 100,000 SHOULD COVER IT.
THESE PUNKS...
THEY MUST'VE SEEN THE WAD OF CASH...
YOU WANT MONEY ...?
TO GO TO THE DOCTOR?
DON'T LISTEN TO HIM! THERE'S NO WAY HE GOT HURT!
HM, TRUE.
POW
SHUT UP, FOUR-EYES.
GOT A DEATH WISH?
...

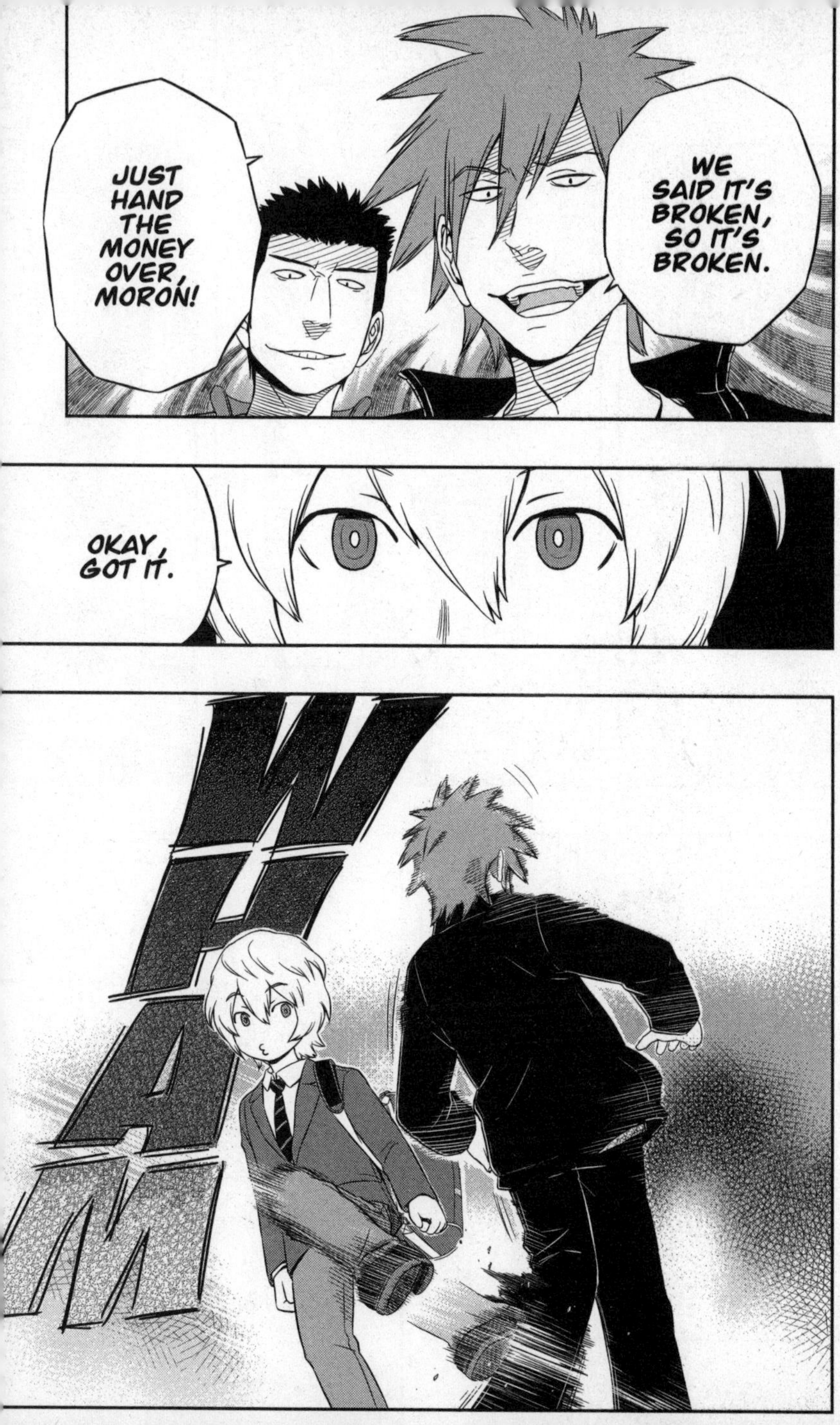
WE SAID IT'S BROKEN, SO IT'S BROKEN.
JUST HAND THE MONEY OVER, MORON!
OKAY, GOT IT.
WHAM

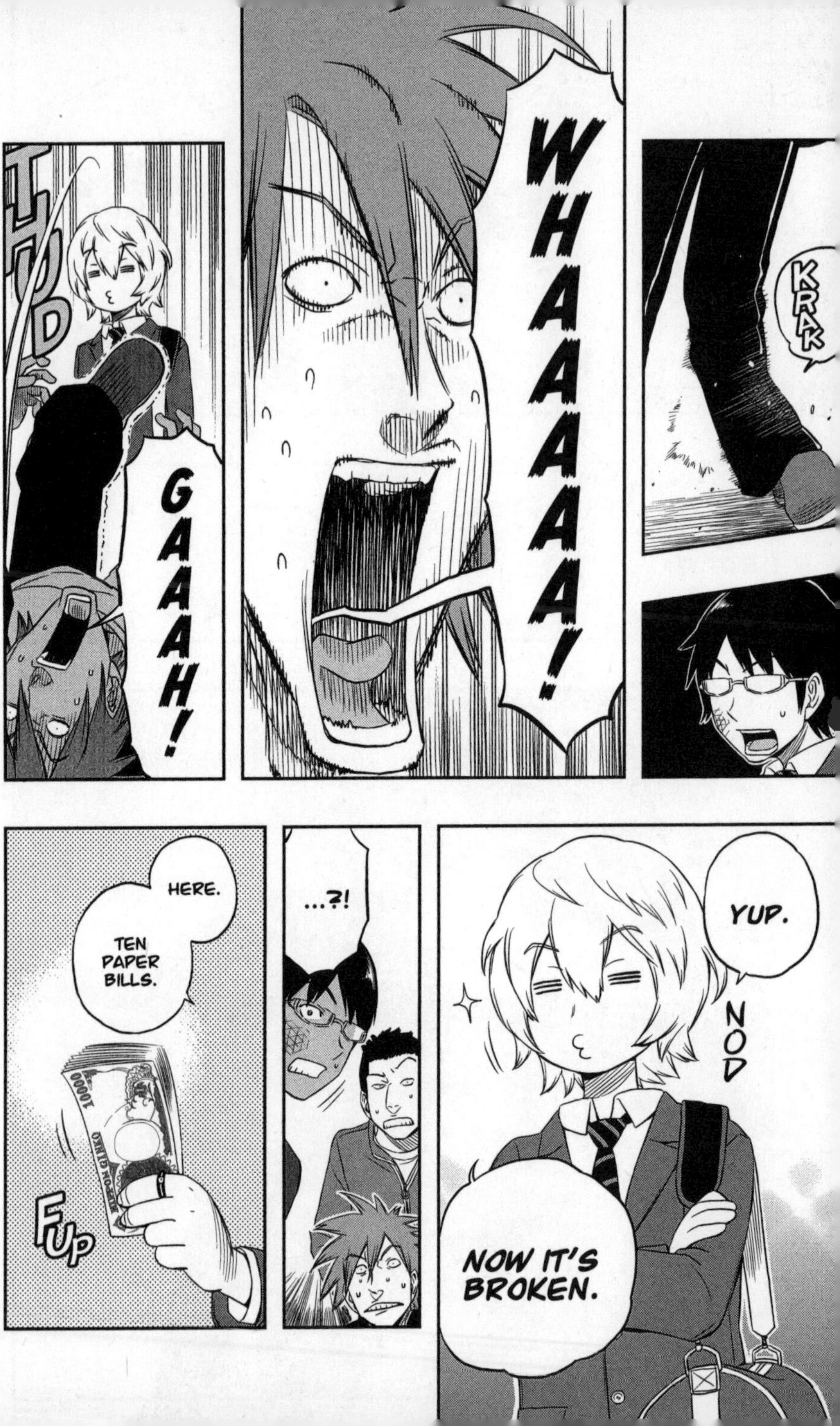
KRAK
WHAAAAAAA!
THUD
GAAAH!
YUP.
NOD
NOW IT'S BROKEN.
...?!
HERE.
TEN PAPER BILLS.
FUP

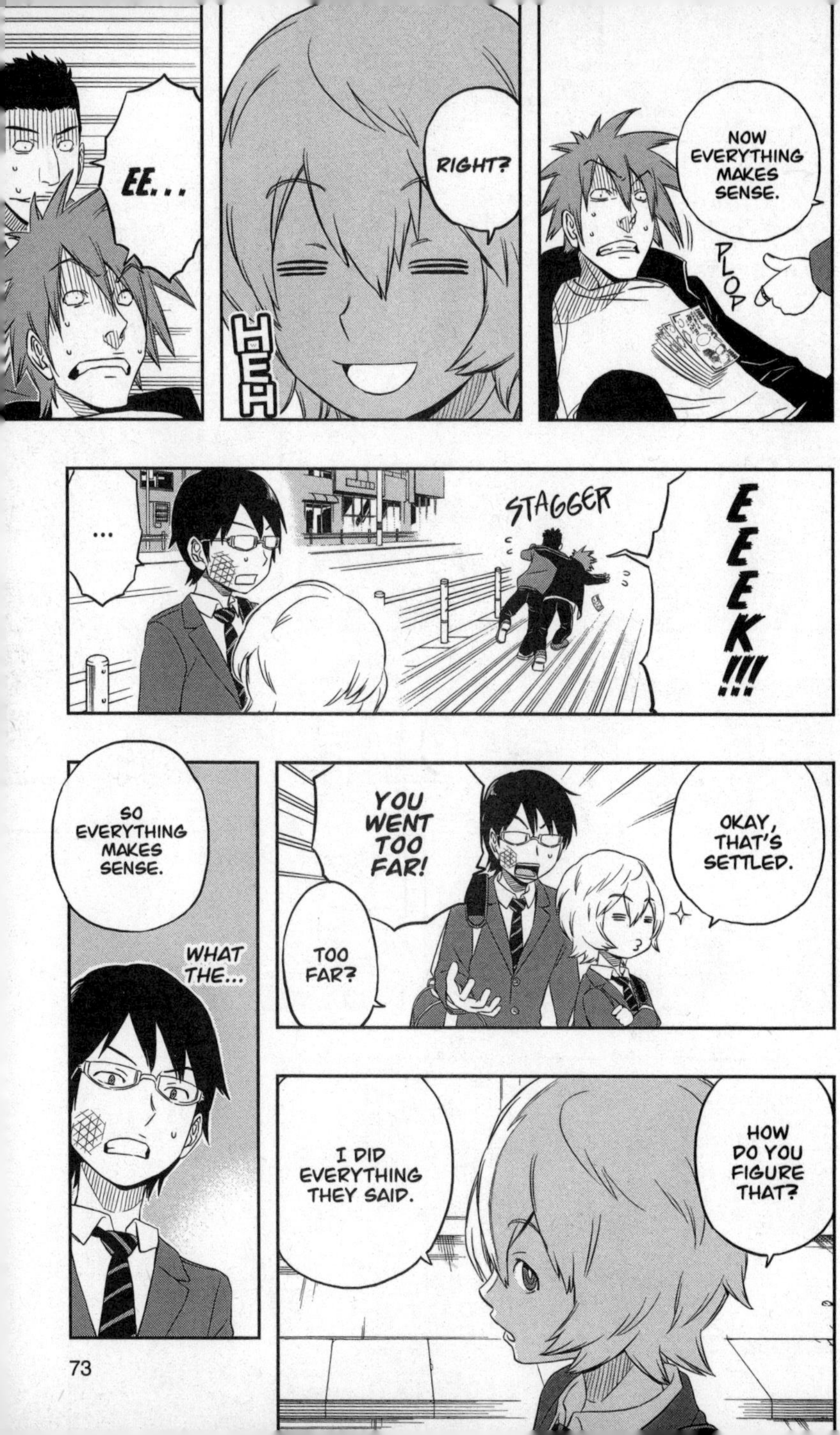
NOW EVERYTHING MAKES SENSE.
PLOP
RIGHT?
HEH
EE...
EEEK!!!
STAGGER
...
OKAY, THAT'S SETTLED.
YOU WENT TOO FAR!
TOO FAR?
HOW DO YOU FIGURE THAT?
I DID EVERYTHING THEY SAID.
SO EVERYTHING MAKES SENSE.
WHAT THE...

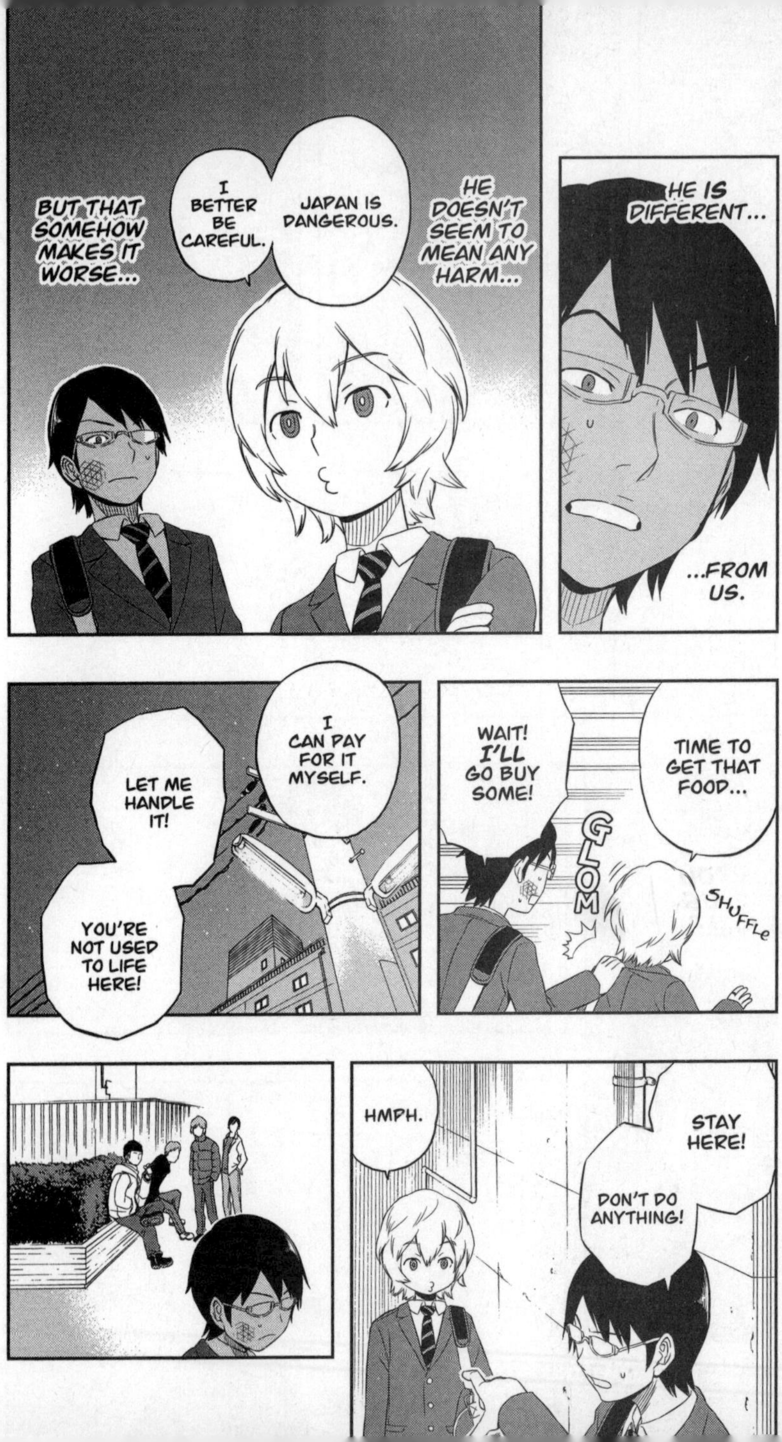
HE IS DIFFERENT...
...FROM US.
HE DOESN'T SEEM TO MEAN ANY HARM...
JAPAN IS DANGEROUS.
I BETTER BE CAREFUL.
BUT THAT SOMEHOW MAKES IT WORSE...
TIME TO GET THAT FOOD...
SHUFFLE
GLOM
WAIT! I'LL GO BUY SOME!
I CAN PAY FOR IT MYSELF.
LET ME HANDLE IT!
YOU'RE NOT USED TO LIFE HERE!
STAY HERE!
DON'T DO ANYTHING!
HMPH.

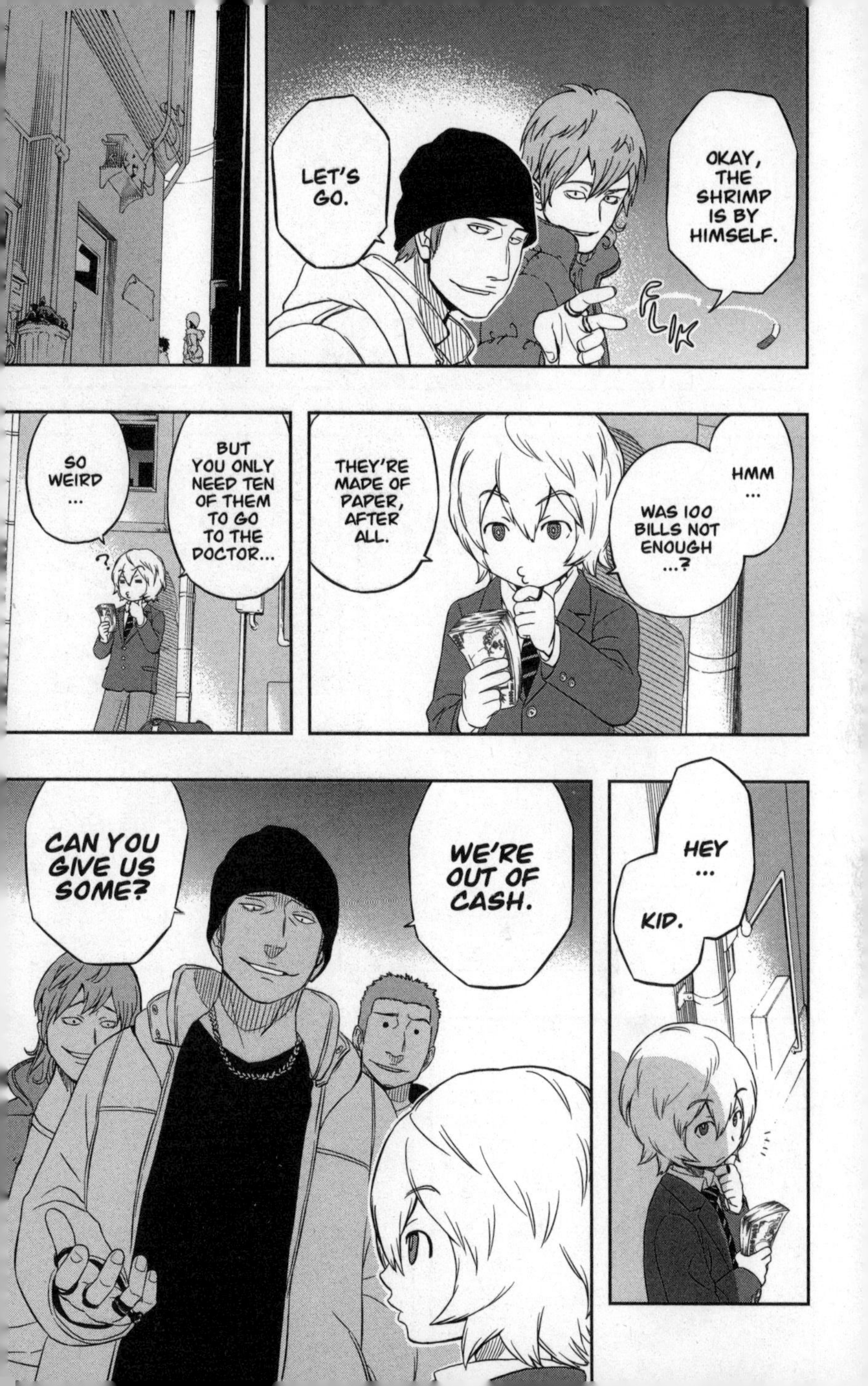
OKAY, THE SHRIMP IS BY HIMSELF.
FLIK
LET'S GO.
HMM...
WAS 100 BILLS NOT ENOUGH...?
THEY'RE MADE OF PAPER, AFTER ALL.
BUT YOU ONLY NEED TEN OF THEM TO GO TO THE DOCTOR...
SO WEIRD...
?
HEY...
KID.
WE'RE OUT OF CASH.
CAN YOU GIVE US SOME?

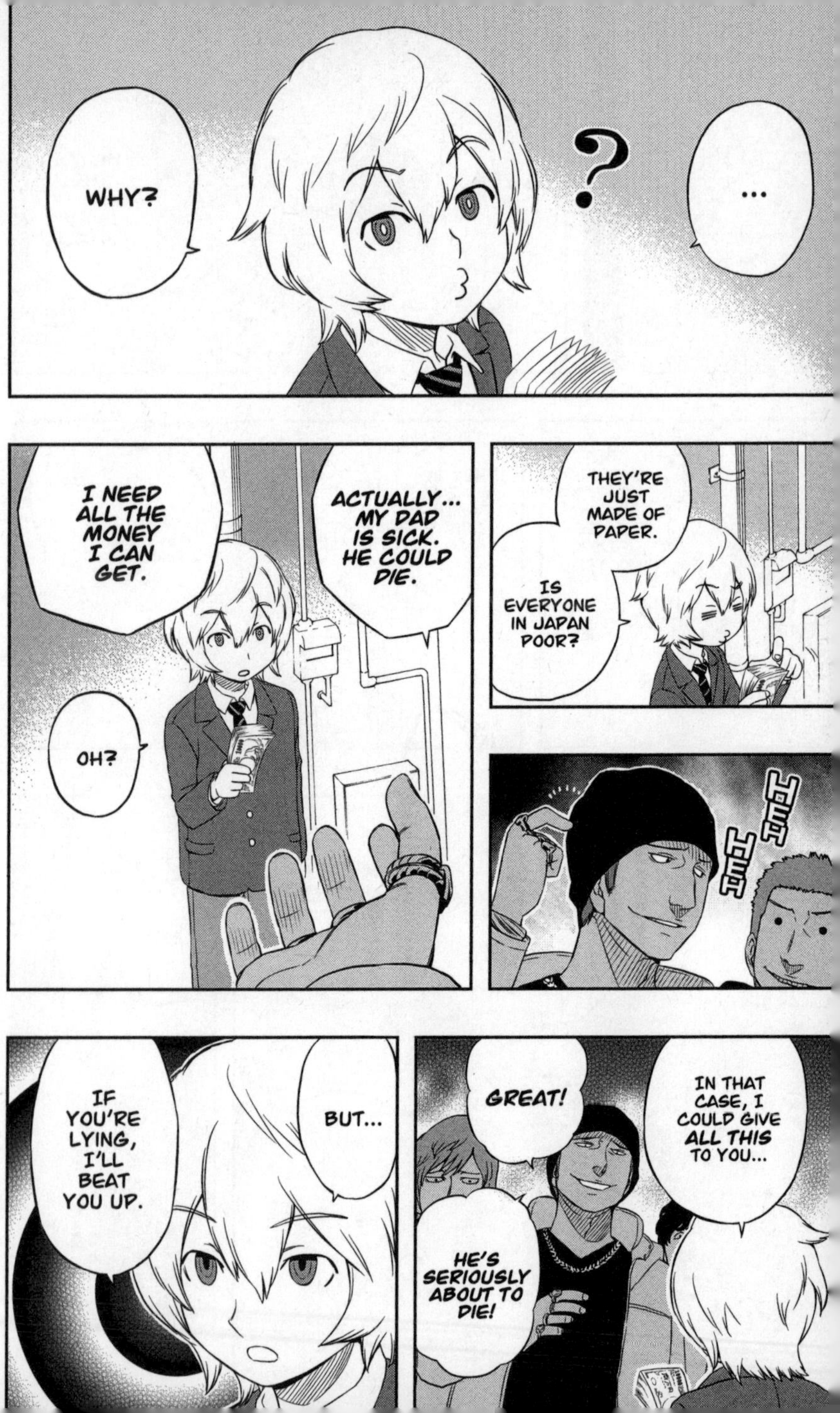
...
?
WHY?
THEY'RE JUST MADE OF PAPER.
IS EVERYONE IN JAPAN POOR?
HEH HEH
ACTUALLY... MY DAD IS SICK. HE COULD DIE.
I NEED ALL THE MONEY I CAN GET.
OH?
IN THAT CASE, I COULD GIVE ALL THIS TO YOU...
GREAT!
HE'S SERIOUSLY ABOUT TO DIE!
BUT...
IF YOU'RE LYING, I'LL BEAT YOU UP.

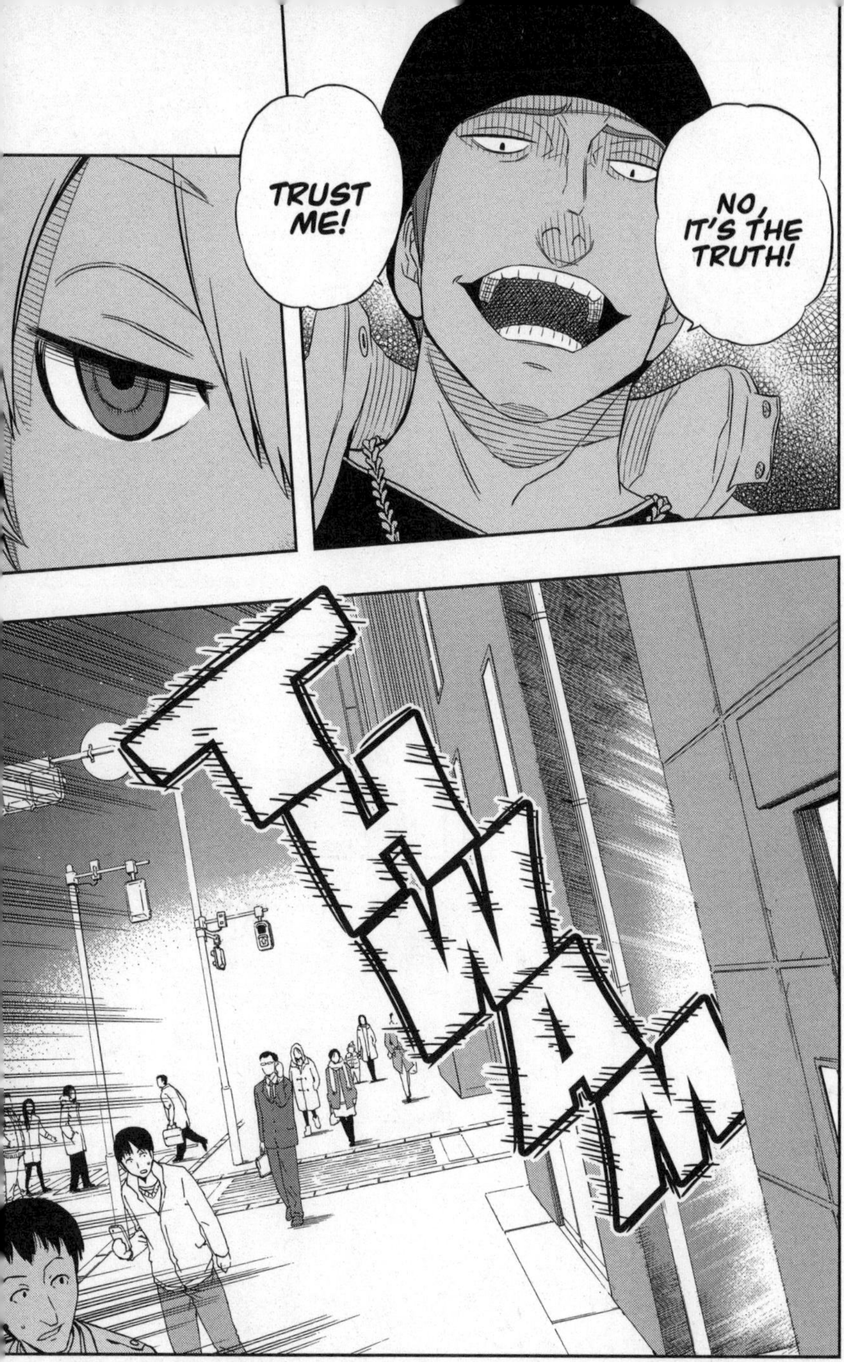
NO, IT'S THE TRUTH!
TRUST ME!
THWAM

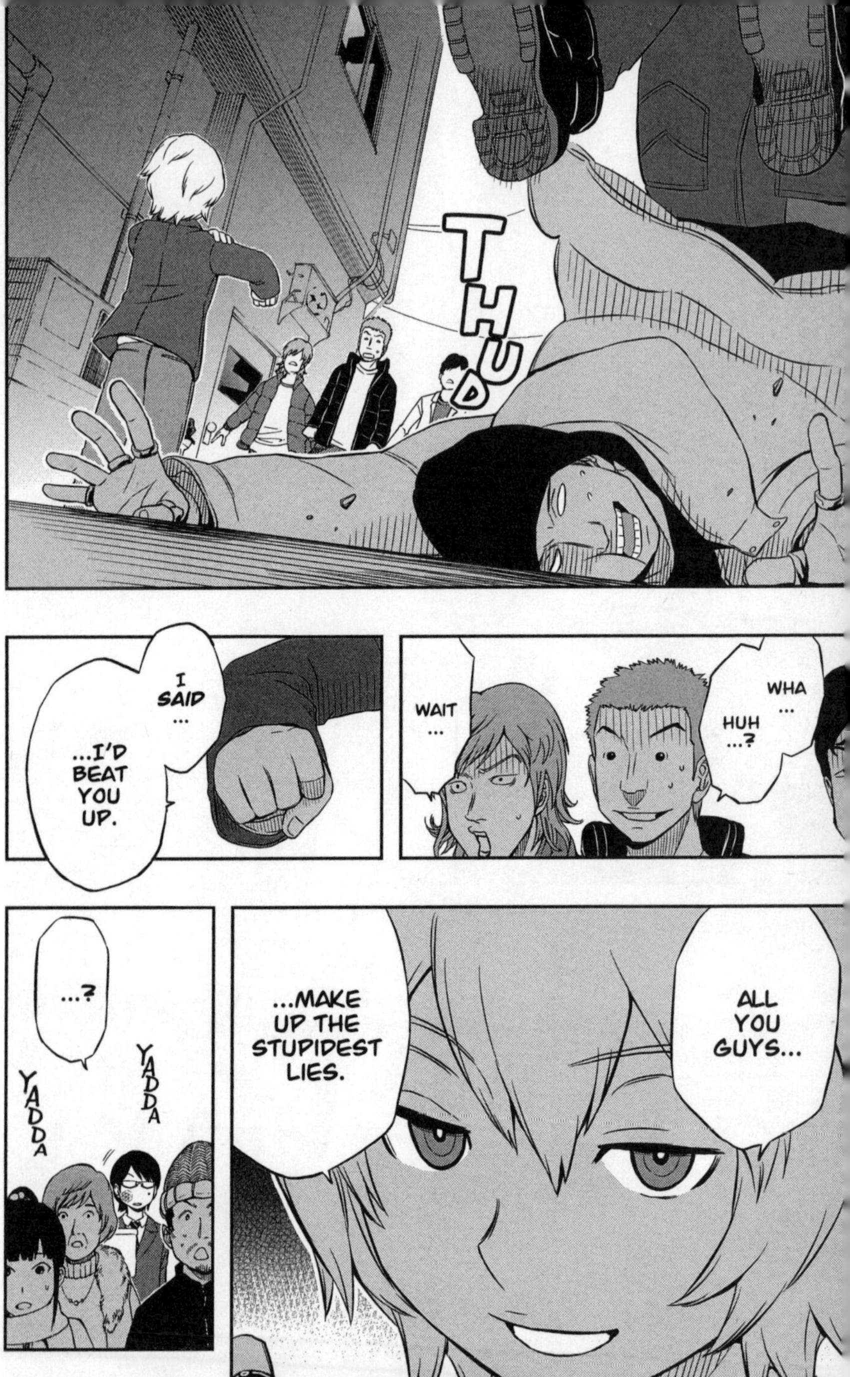
THUD
WHA...
HUH...?
WAIT...
I SAID...
...I'D BEAT YOU UP.
ALL YOU GUYS...
...MAKE UP THE STUPIDEST LIES.
...?
YADDA
YADDA

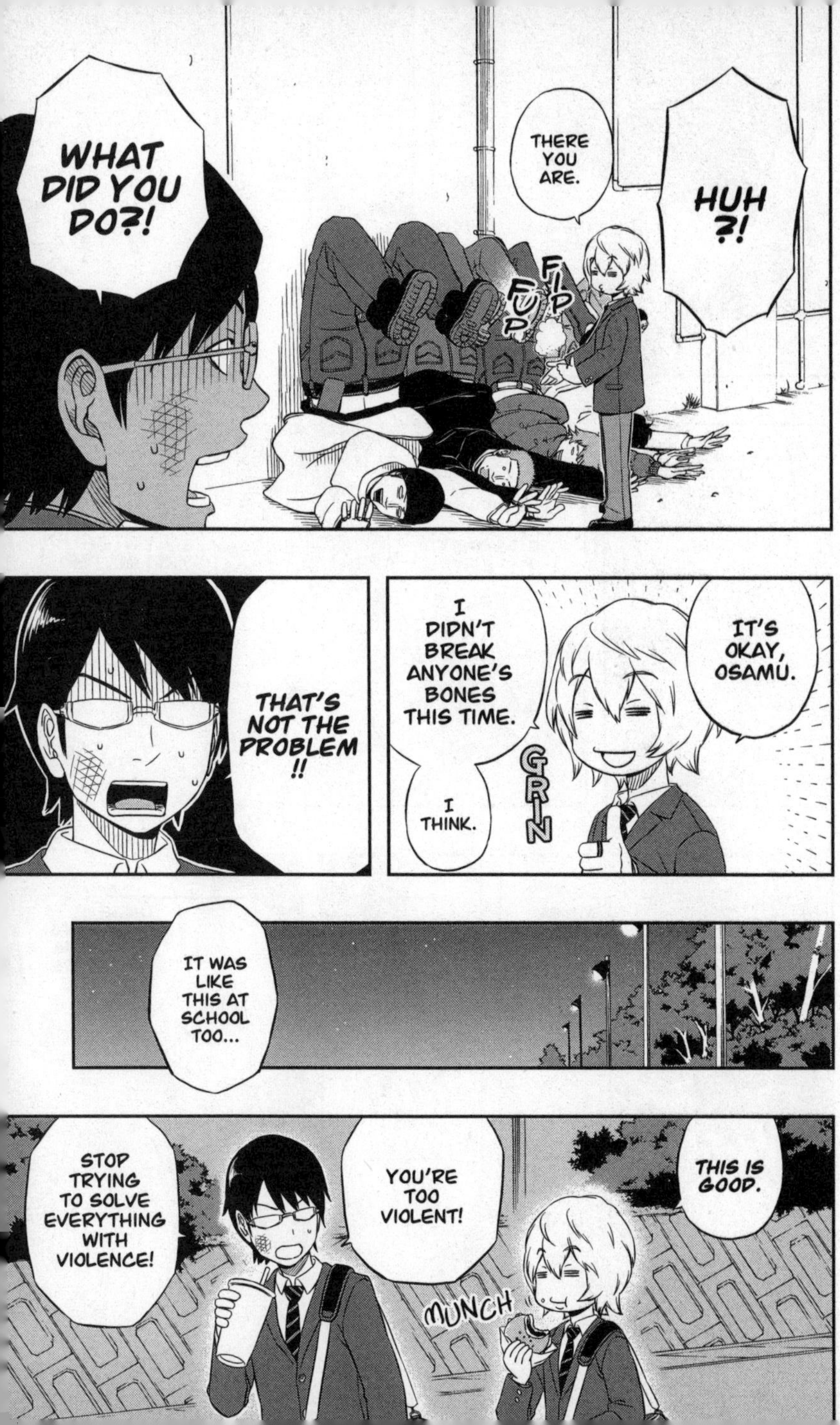
HUH ?!
THERE YOU ARE.
FLIP
FLIP
WHAT DID YOU DO?!
IT'S OKAY, OSAMU.
I DIDN'T BREAK ANYONE'S BONES THIS TIME.
I THINK.
GRIN
THAT'S NOT THE PROBLEM !!
IT WAS LIKE THIS AT SCHOOL TOO...
THIS IS GOOD.
MUNCH
YOU'RE TOO VIOLENT!
STOP TRYING TO SOLVE EVERYTHING WITH VIOLENCE!

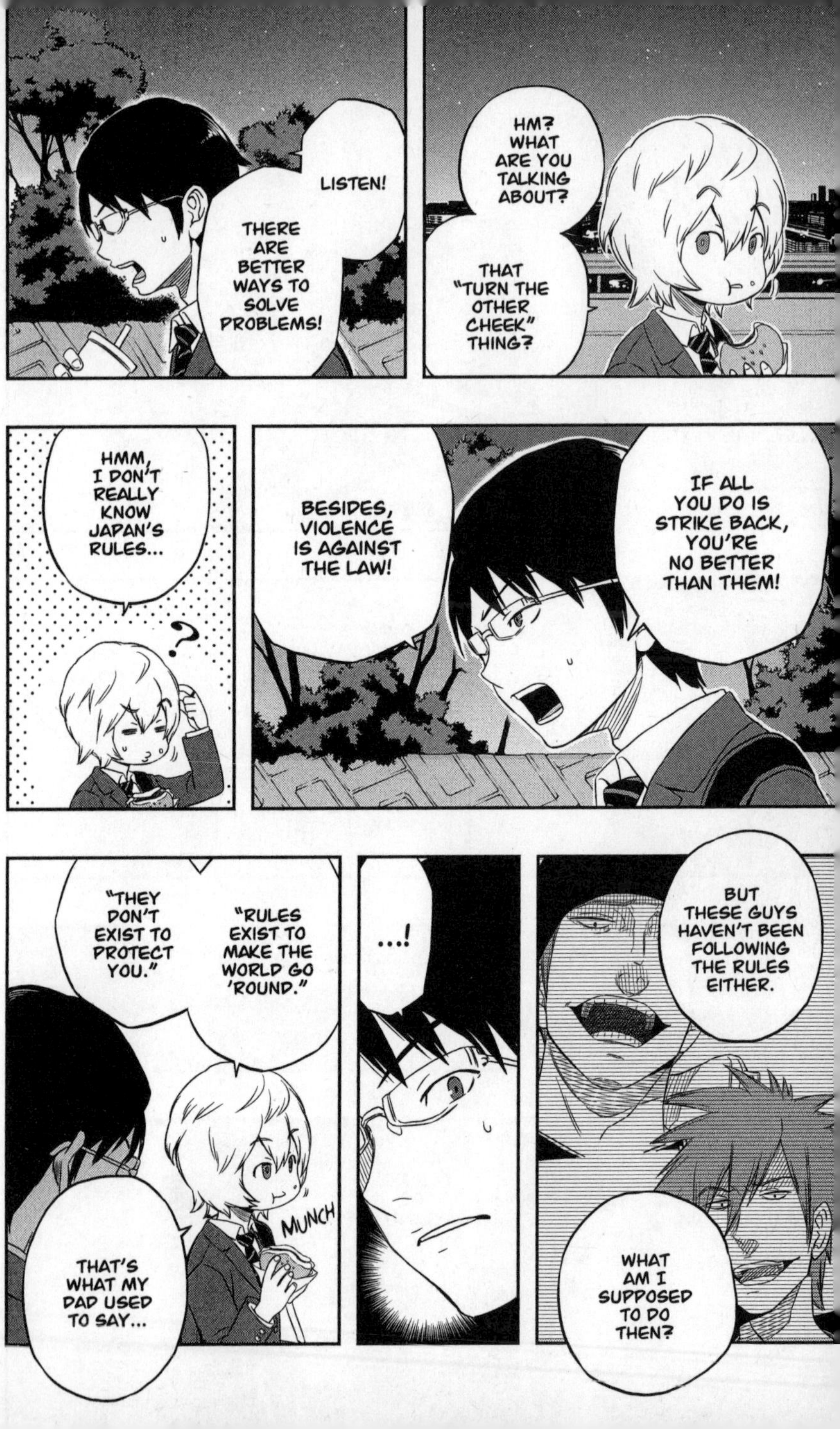
HM? WHAT ARE YOU TALKING ABOUT?
THAT "TURN THE OTHER CHEEK" THING?
LISTEN!
THERE ARE BETTER WAYS TO SOLVE PROBLEMS!
IF ALL YOU DO IS STRIKE BACK, YOU'RE NO BETTER THAN THEM!
BESIDES, VIOLENCE IS AGAINST THE LAW!
HMM, I DON'T REALLY KNOW JAPAN'S RULES...
BUT THESE GUYS HAVEN'T BEEN FOLLOWING THE RULES EITHER.
WHAT AM I SUPPOSED TO DO THEN?
...!
"RULES EXIST TO MAKE THE WORLD GO 'ROUND."
"THEY DON'T EXIST TO PROTECT YOU."
MUNCH
THAT'S WHAT MY DAD USED TO SAY...

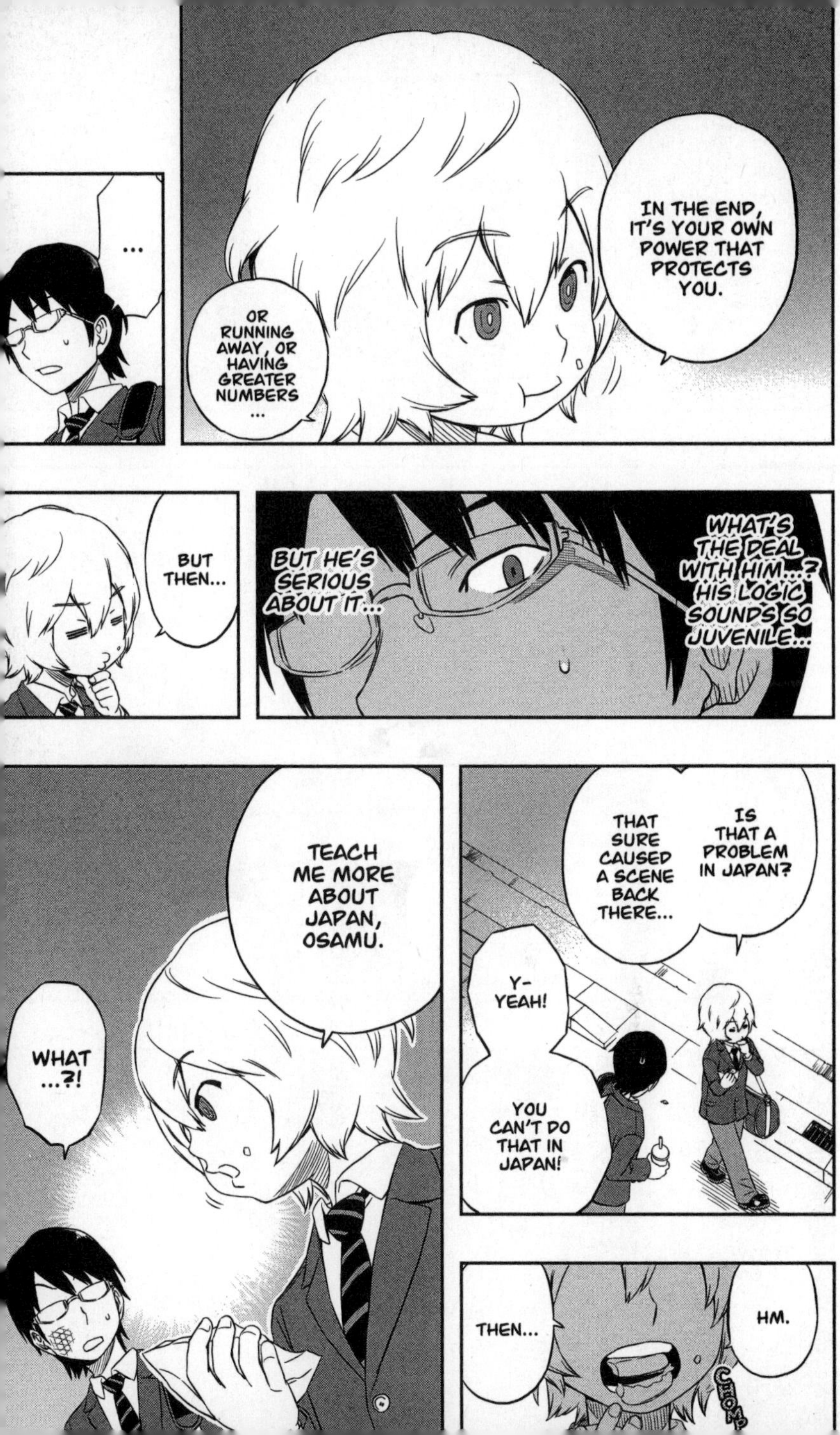
IN THE END, IT'S YOUR OWN POWER THAT PROTECTS YOU.
OR RUNNING AWAY, OR HAVING GREATER NUMBERS...
...
WHAT'S THE DEAL WITH HIM...? HIS LOGIC SOUNDS SO JUVENILE...
BUT HE'S SERIOUS ABOUT IT...
BUT THEN...
IS THAT A PROBLEM IN JAPAN?
THAT SURE CAUSED A SCENE BACK THERE...
Y-YEAH!
YOU CAN'T DO THAT IN JAPAN!
HM.
CHOMP
THEN...
TEACH ME MORE ABOUT JAPAN, OSAMU.
WHAT...?!

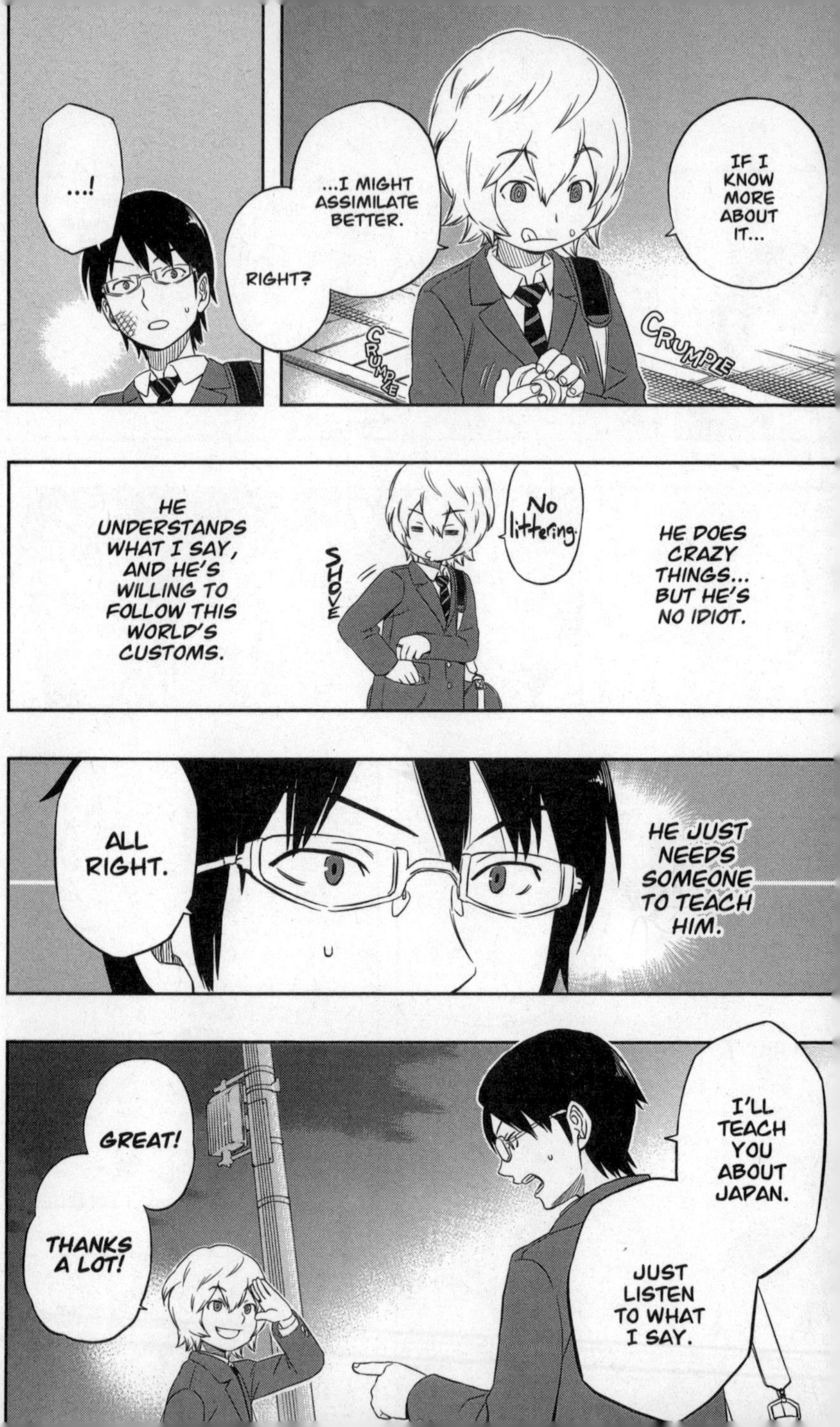
IF I KNOW MORE ABOUT IT...
CRUMPLE
...I MIGHT ASSIMILATE BETTER.
RIGHT?
CRUMPLE
...!
HE DOES CRAZY THINGS... BUT HE'S NO IDIOT.
No littering.
SHOVE
HE UNDERSTANDS WHAT I SAY, AND HE'S WILLING TO FOLLOW THIS WORLD'S CUSTOMS.
HE JUST NEEDS SOMEONE TO TEACH HIM.
ALL RIGHT.
I'LL TEACH YOU ABOUT JAPAN.
JUST LISTEN TO WHAT I SAY.
GREAT!
THANKS A LOT!

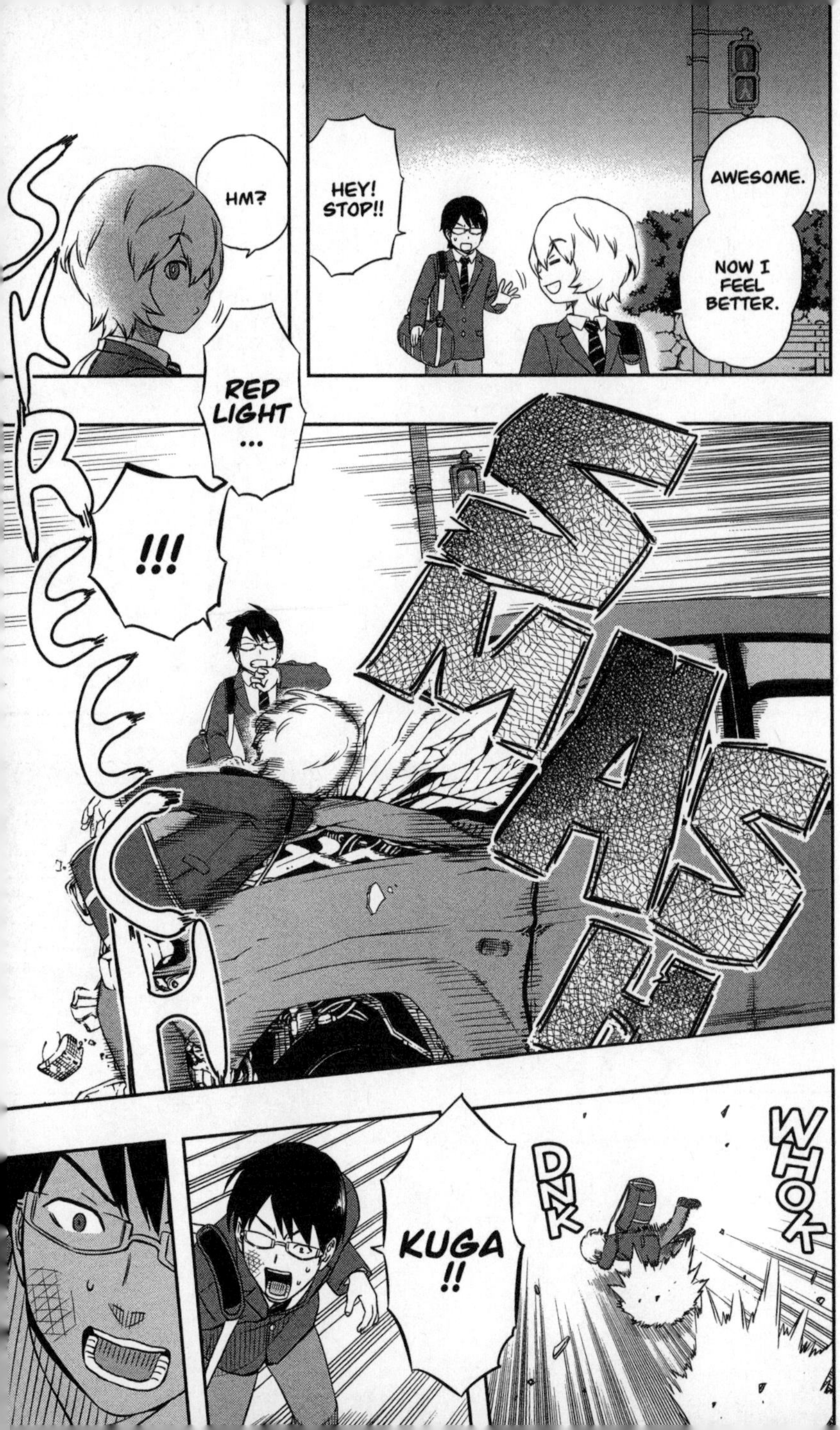
AWESOME.
NOW I FEEL BETTER.
HEY! STOP!!
HM?
RED LIGHT...
SCREECH
!!!
SMASH
WHOK
DNK
KUGA!!

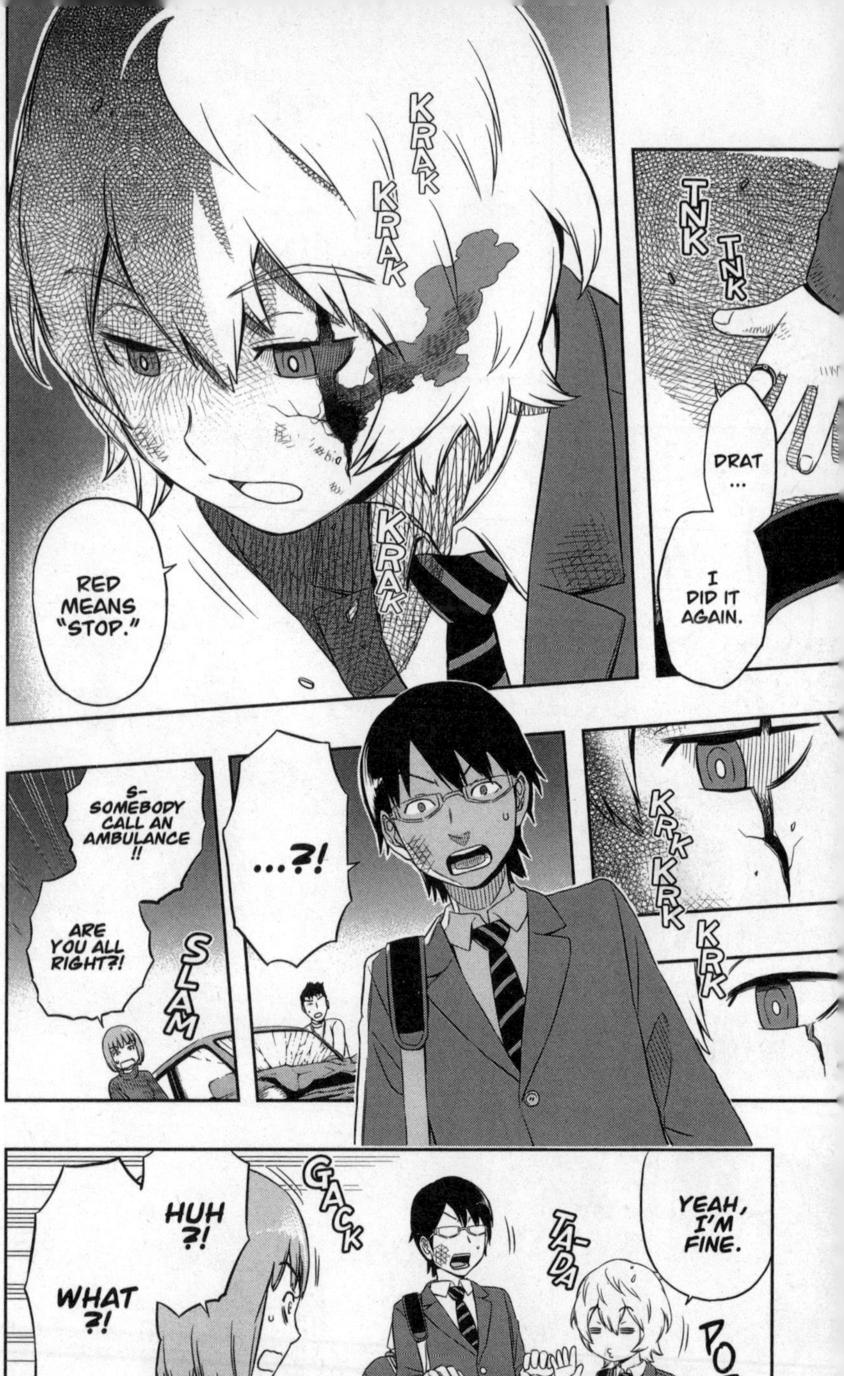
TNK TNK
DRAT ...
I DID IT AGAIN.
KRAK KRAK
RED MEANS "STOP."
KRAK
KRK KRK
KRK KRK
...?!
S- SOMEBODY CALL AN AMBULANCE !!
ARE YOU ALL RIGHT?!
SLAM
YEAH, I'M FINE.
POP
TA-DA
GACK
HUH ?!
WHAT ?!

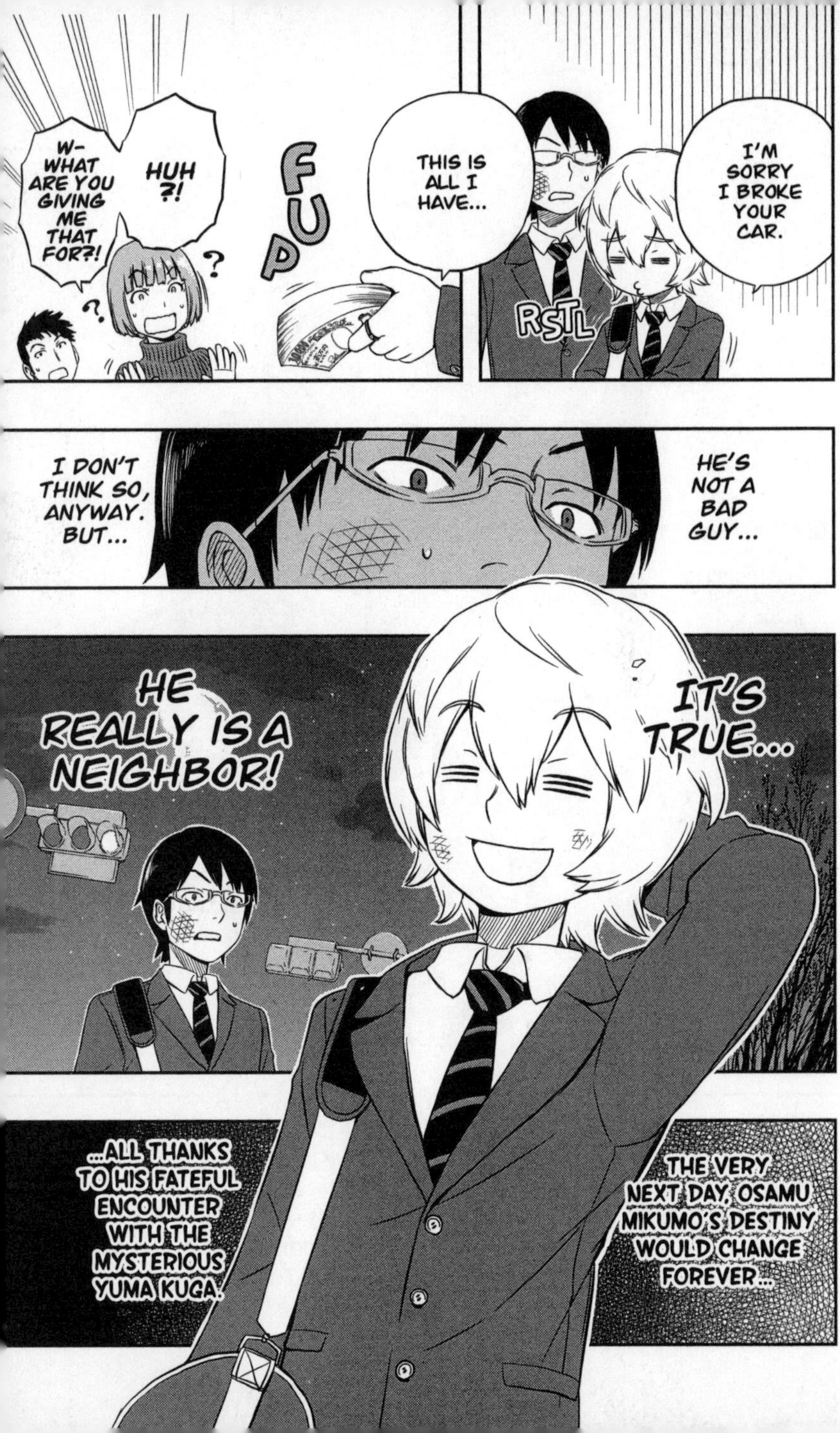

I'M SORRY I BROKE YOUR CAR.
RSTL
THIS IS ALL I HAVE...
FUP
HUH?!
W-WHAT ARE YOU GIVING ME THAT FOR?!
HE'S NOT A BAD GUY...
I DON'T THINK SO, ANYWAY. BUT...
IT'S TRUE...
HE REALLY IS A NEIGHBOR!
THE VERY NEXT DAY, OSAMU MIKUMO'S DESTINY WOULD CHANGE FOREVER...
...ALL THANKS TO HIS FATEFUL ENCOUNTER WITH THE MYSTERIOUS YUMA KUGA.

■ Preliminary sketches (submitted for consideration to the serialization meeting)

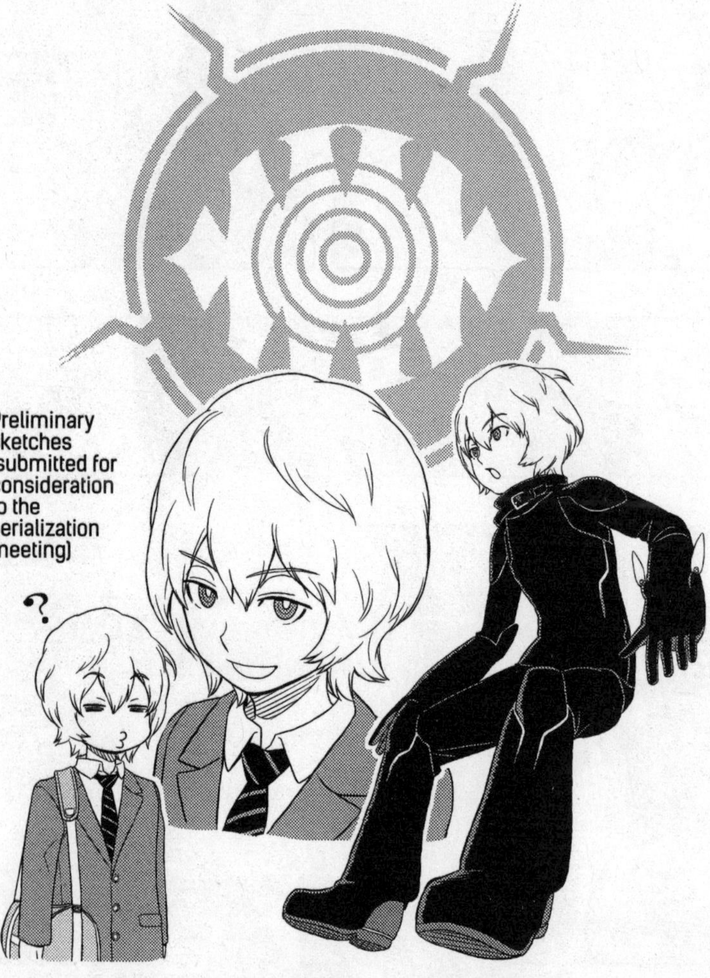
?

Yuma Kuga

- 15 years old (junior high student)
- Born ?
- Zodiac, Blood type unknown
- Height: 4'7"
- Likes: Japanese food

Drawing him used to take a lot of time, but now I'm faster at it. I get the feeling his face looks more and more childish the more I draw him.

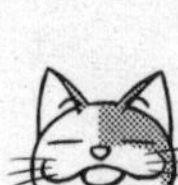

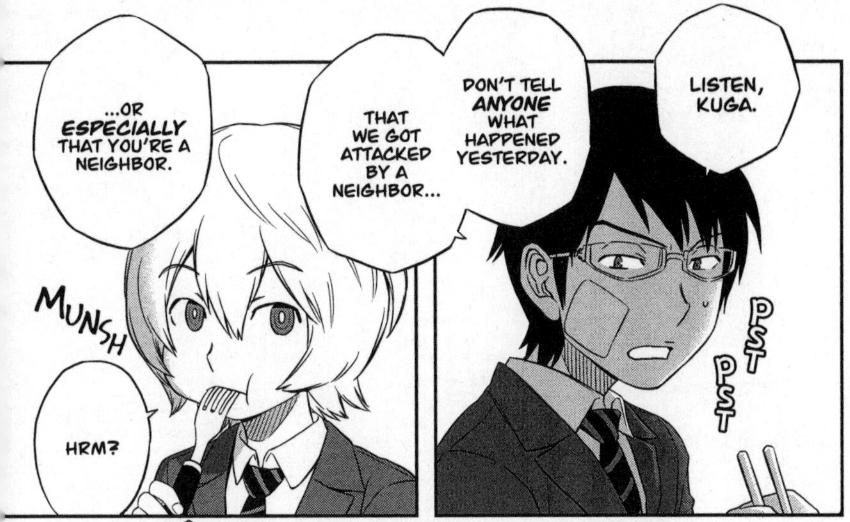
LISTEN, KUGA.
PST PST
DON'T TELL ANYONE WHAT HAPPENED YESTERDAY.
THAT WE GOT ATTACKED BY A NEIGHBOR...
...OR ESPECIALLY THAT YOU'RE A NEIGHBOR.
MUNSH
HRM?

Chapter 3 Yuma Kuga: Part 2

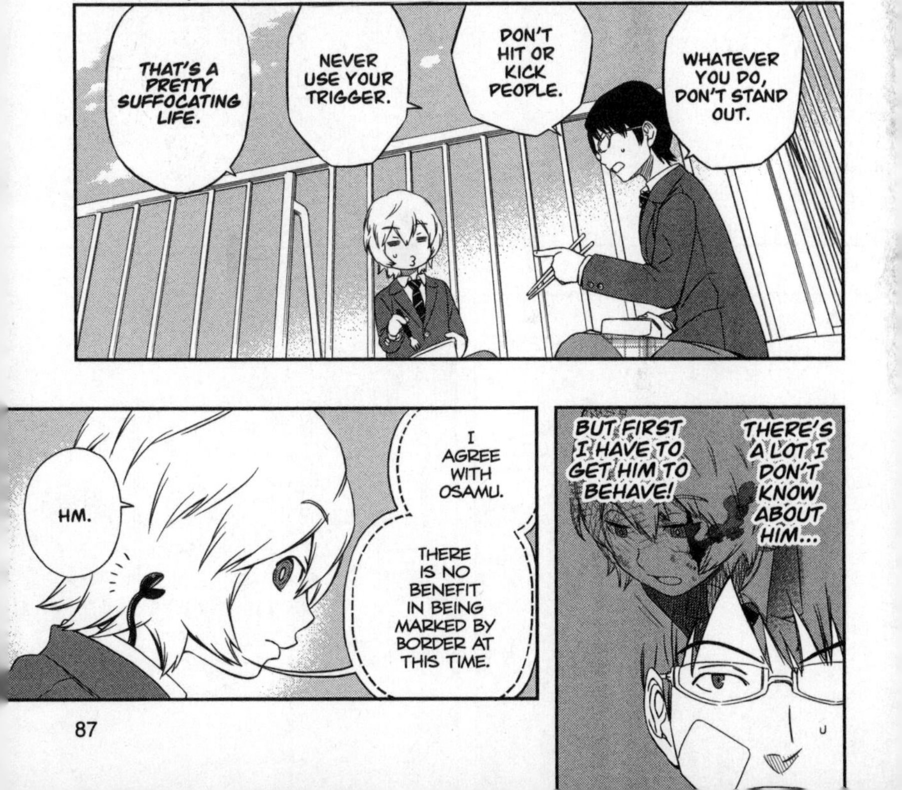
WHATEVER YOU DO, DON'T STAND OUT.
DON'T HIT OR KICK PEOPLE.
NEVER USE YOUR TRIGGER.
THAT'S A PRETTY SUFFOCATING LIFE.
THERE'S A LOT I DON'T KNOW ABOUT HIM...
BUT FIRST I HAVE TO GET HIM TO BEHAVE!
I AGREE WITH OSAMU.
THERE IS NO BENEFIT IN BEING MARKED BY BORDER AT THIS TIME.
HM.

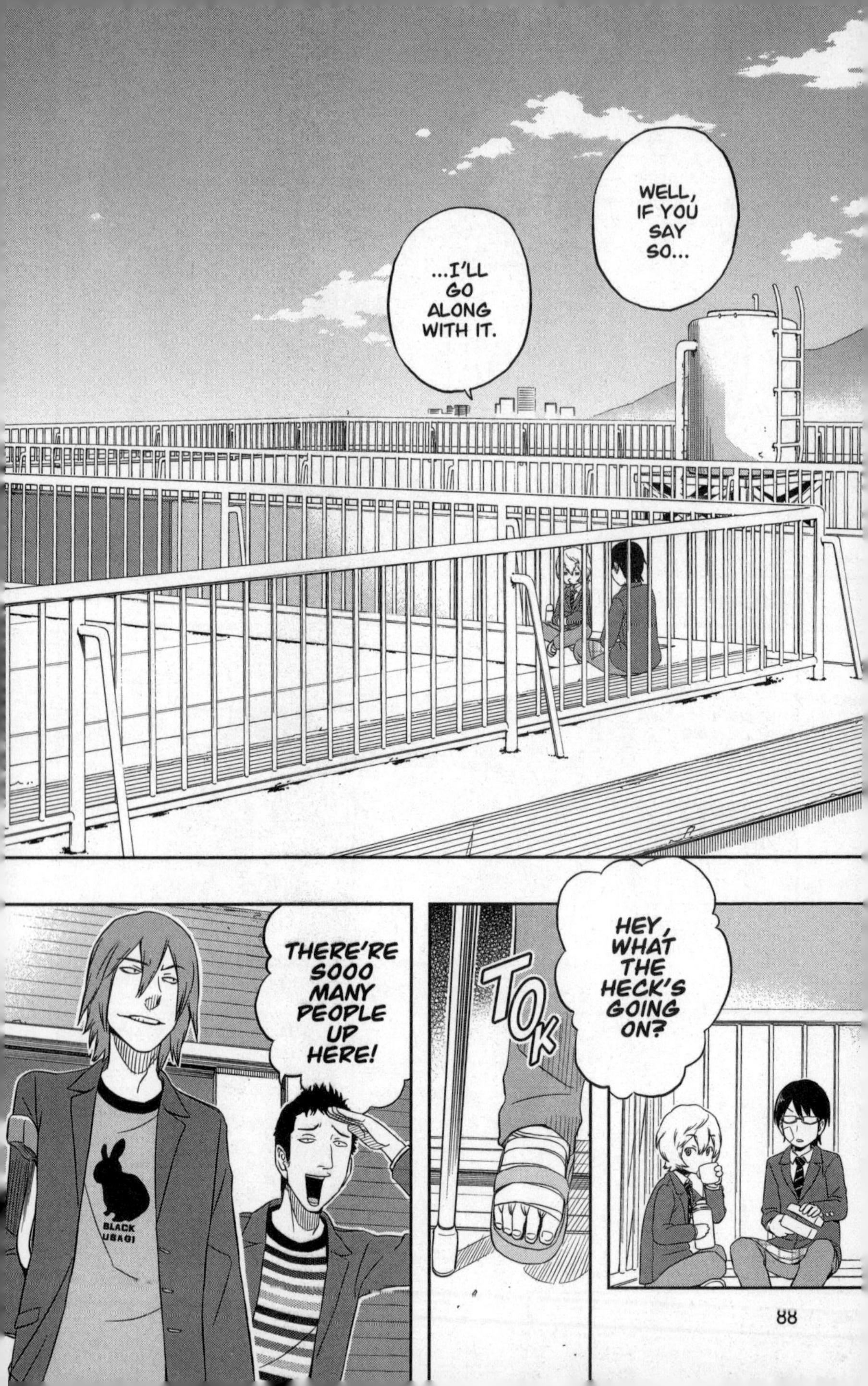
WELL, IF YOU SAY SO...
...I'LL GO ALONG WITH IT.
HEY, WHAT THE HECK'S GOING ON?
TOK
THERE'RE SOOO MANY PEOPLE UP HERE!
BLACK

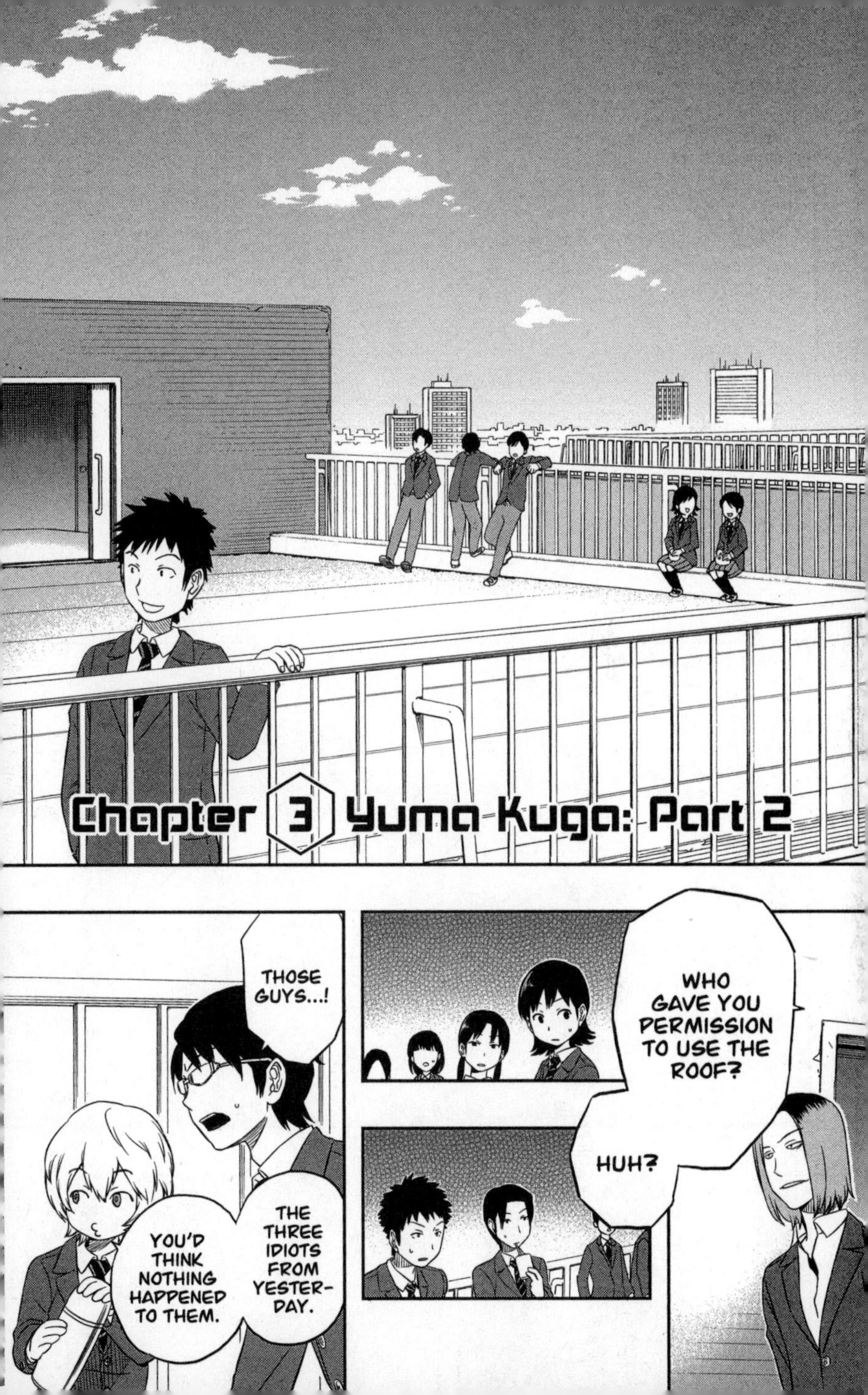
Chapter 3 Yuma Kuga: Part 2
WHO GAVE YOU PERMISSION TO USE THE ROOF?
HUH?
THOSE GUYS...!
THE THREE IDIOTS FROM YESTER-DAY.
YOU'D THINK NOTHING HAPPENED TO THEM.

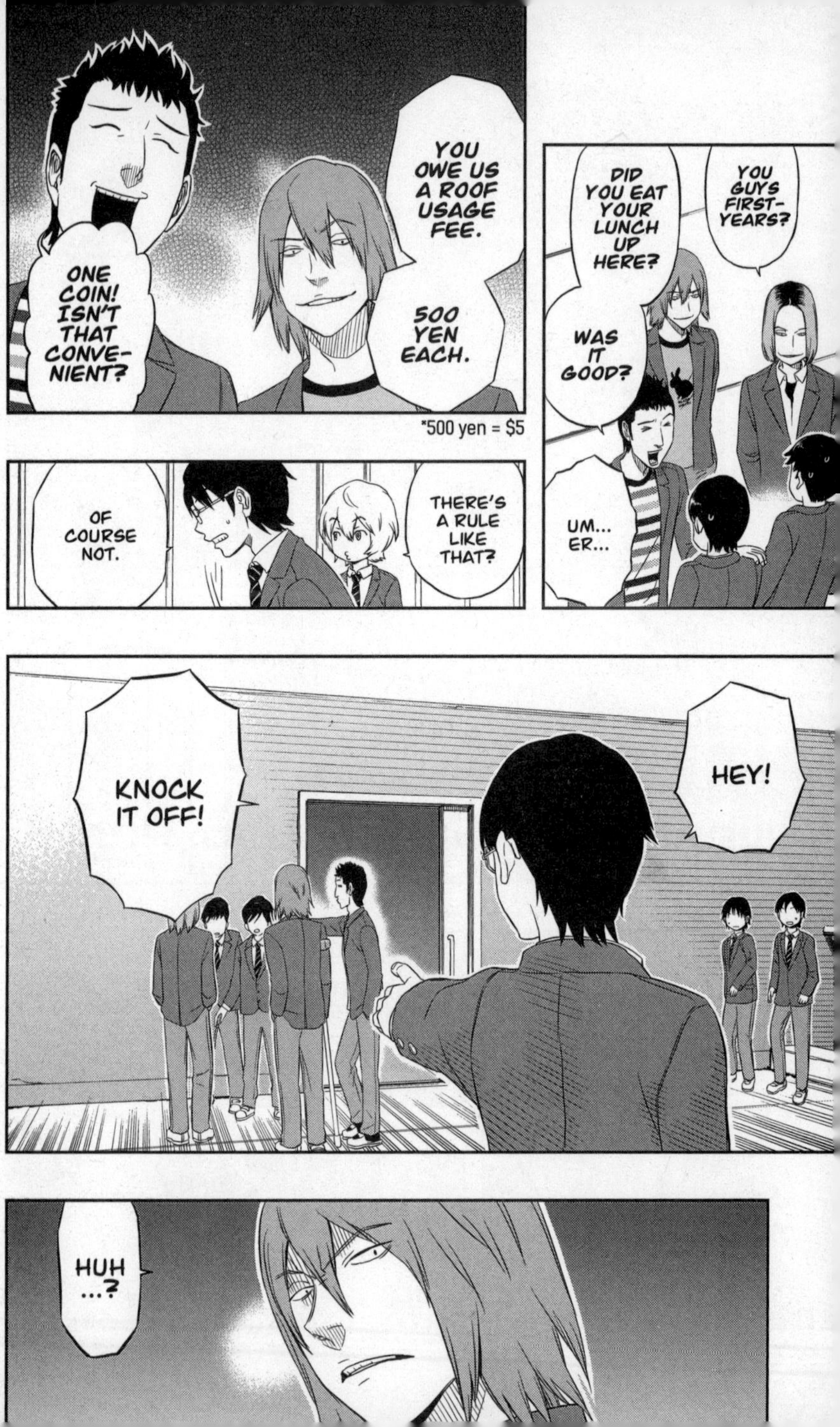
YOU GUYS FIRST-YEARS?
DID YOU EAT YOUR LUNCH UP HERE?
WAS IT GOOD?
UM... ER...
YOU OWE US A ROOF USAGE FEE.
500 YEN EACH.
ONE COIN! ISN'T THAT CONVENIENT?
*500 yen = $5
THERE'S A RULE LIKE THAT?
OF COURSE NOT.
HEY!
KNOCK IT OFF!
HUH ...?

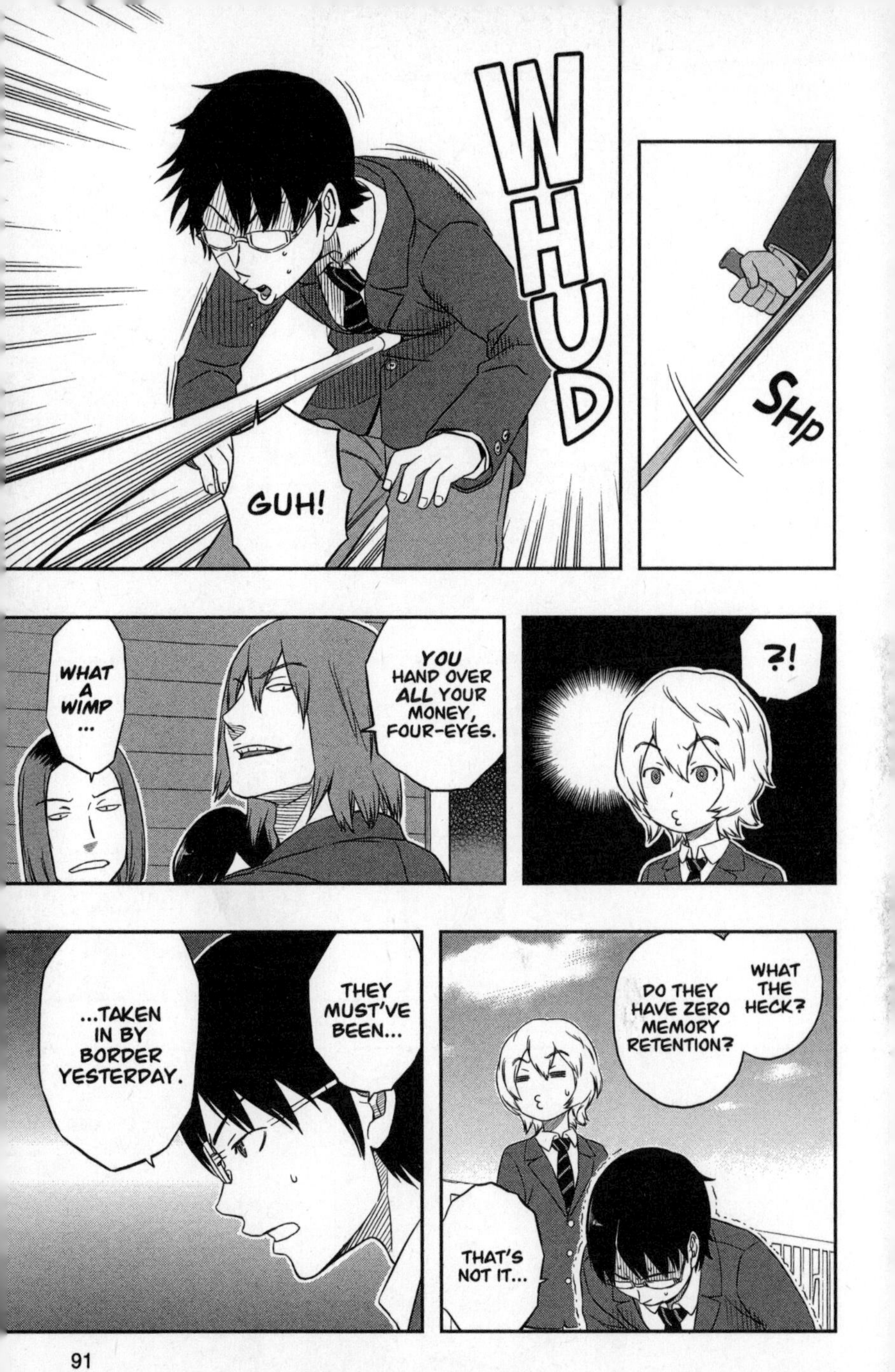

SHp
WHUD
GUH!
?!
YOU HAND OVER ALL YOUR MONEY, FOUR-EYES.
WHAT A WIMP...
WHAT THE HECK?
DO THEY HAVE ZERO MEMORY RETENTION?
THAT'S NOT IT...
THEY MUST'VE BEEN...
...TAKEN IN BY BORDER YESTERDAY.

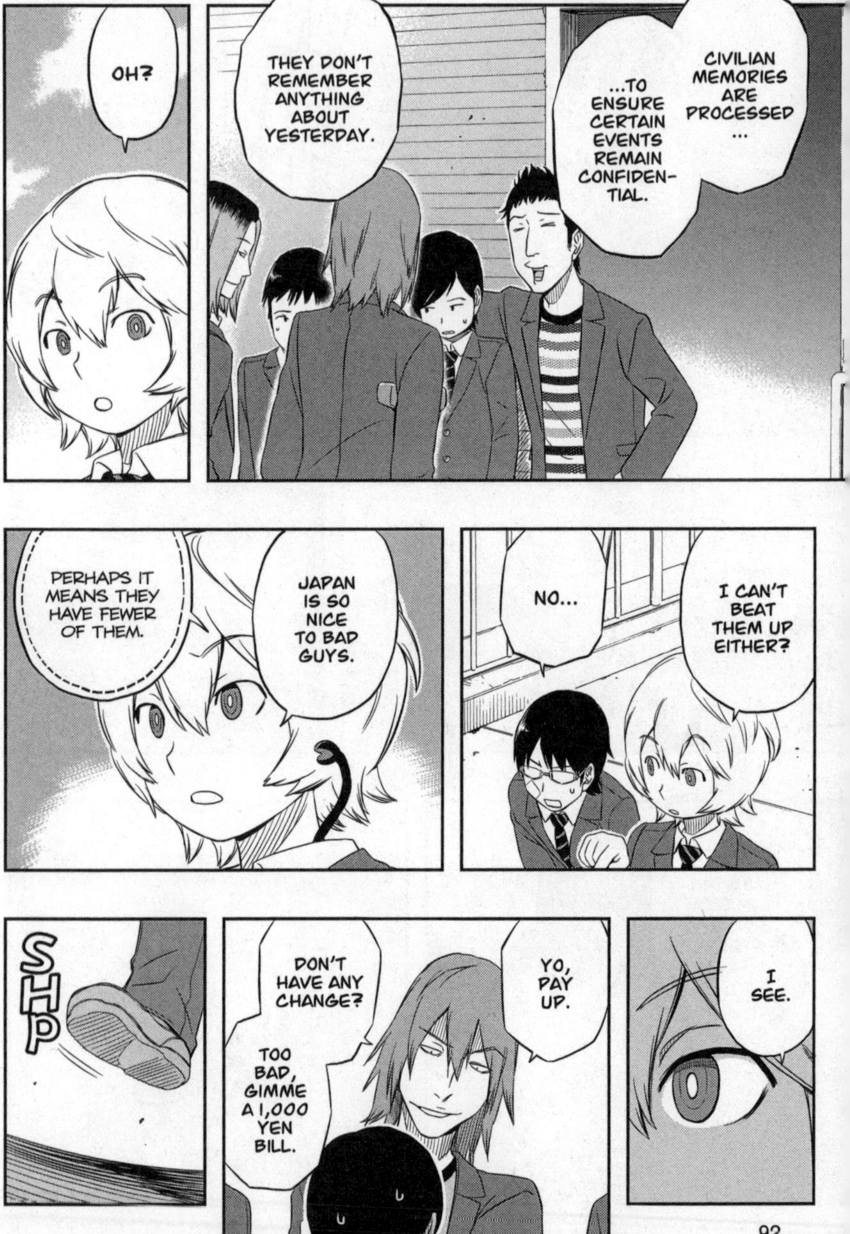
CIVILIAN MEMORIES ARE PROCESSED ...
...TO ENSURE CERTAIN EVENTS REMAIN CONFIDENTIAL.
THEY DON'T REMEMBER ANYTHING ABOUT YESTERDAY.
OH?
I CAN'T BEAT THEM UP EITHER?
NO...
JAPAN IS SO NICE TO BAD GUYS.
PERHAPS IT MEANS THEY HAVE FEWER OF THEM.
I SEE.
YO, PAY UP.
DON'T HAVE ANY CHANGE?
TOO BAD, GIMME A 1,000 YEN BILL.
SHP

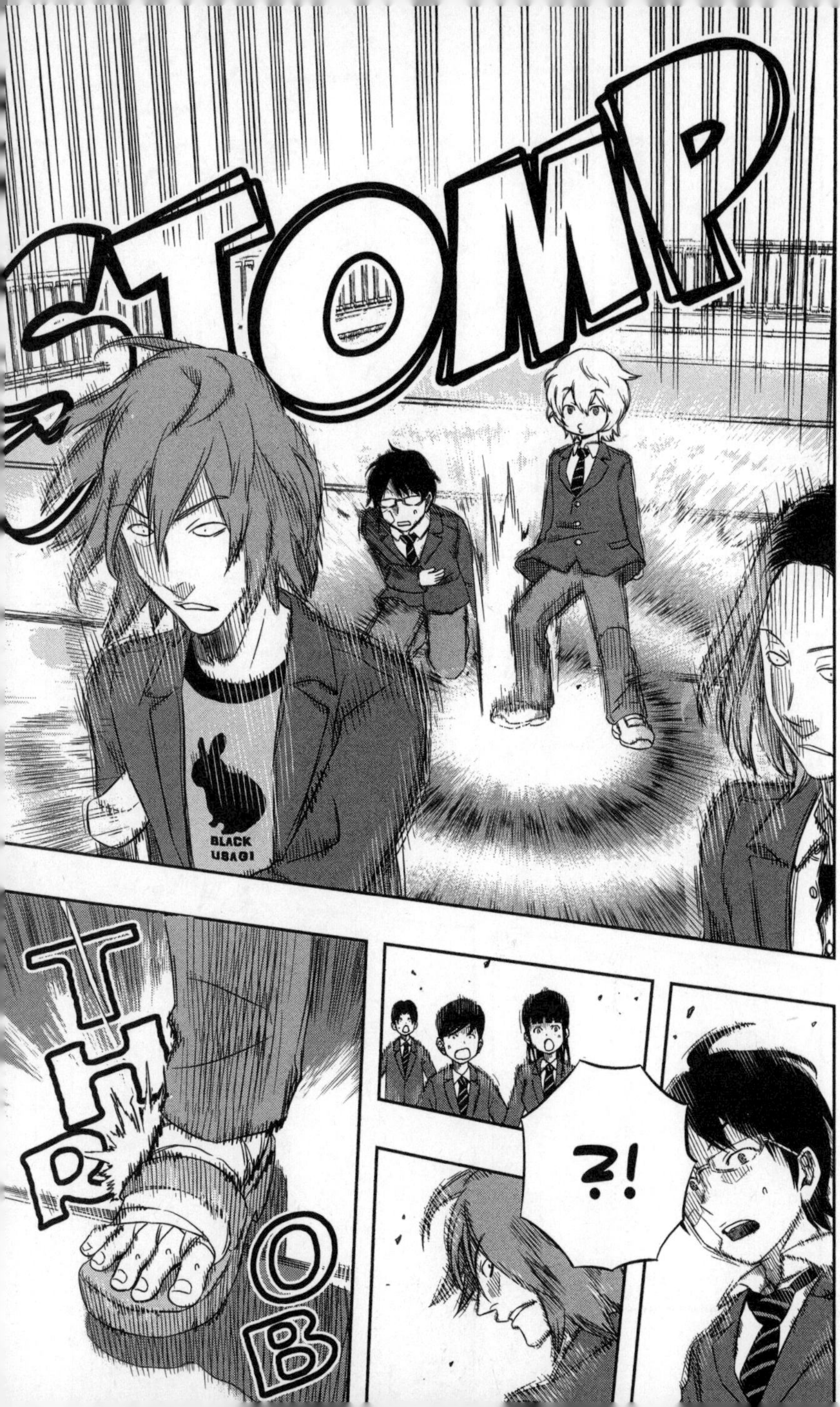
STOMP
BLACK USAGI
THROB
?!

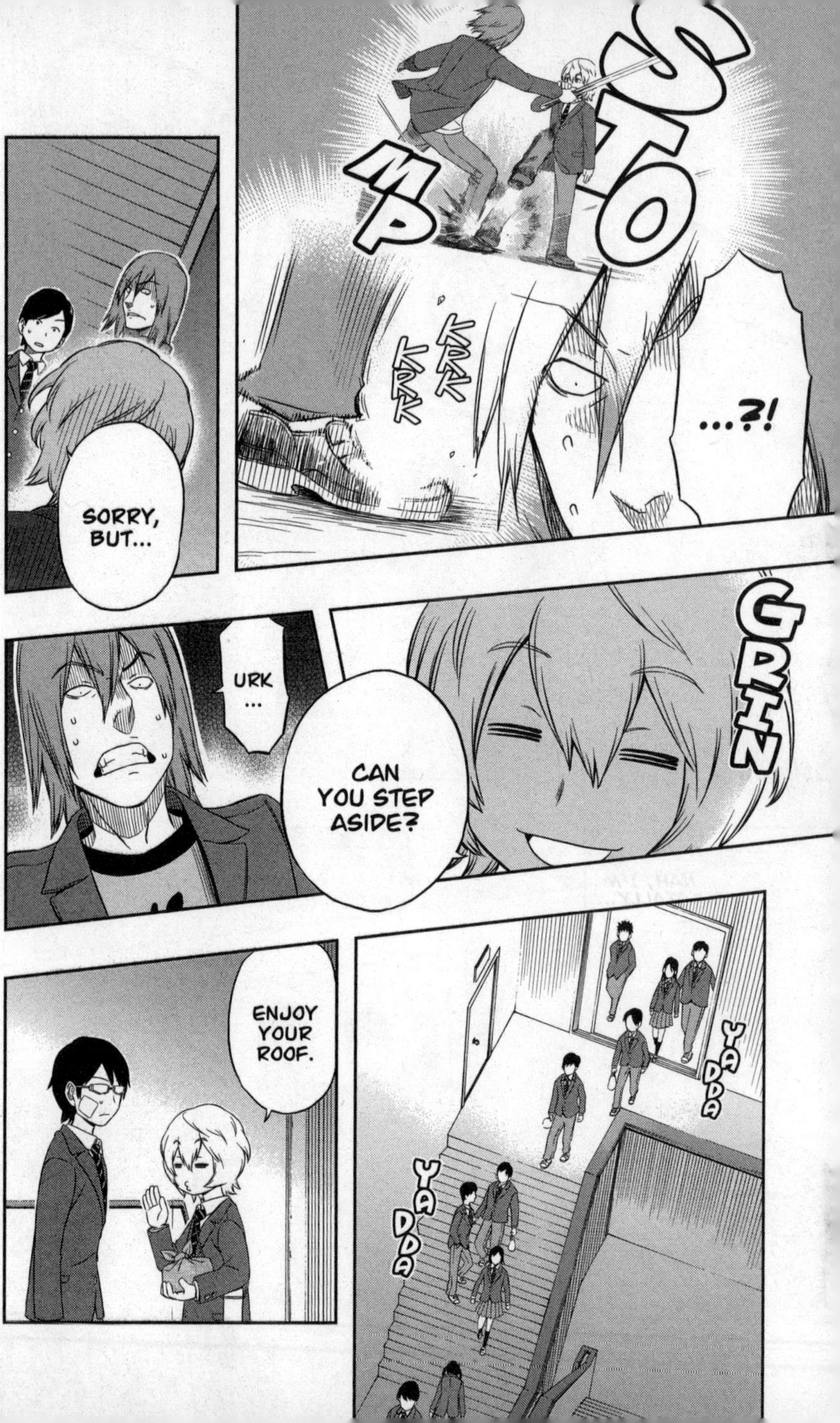
STOMP
KRRK KRRK
...?!
SORRY, BUT...
GRIN
CAN YOU STEP ASIDE?
URK ...
YADDA YADDA
ENJOY YOUR ROOF.

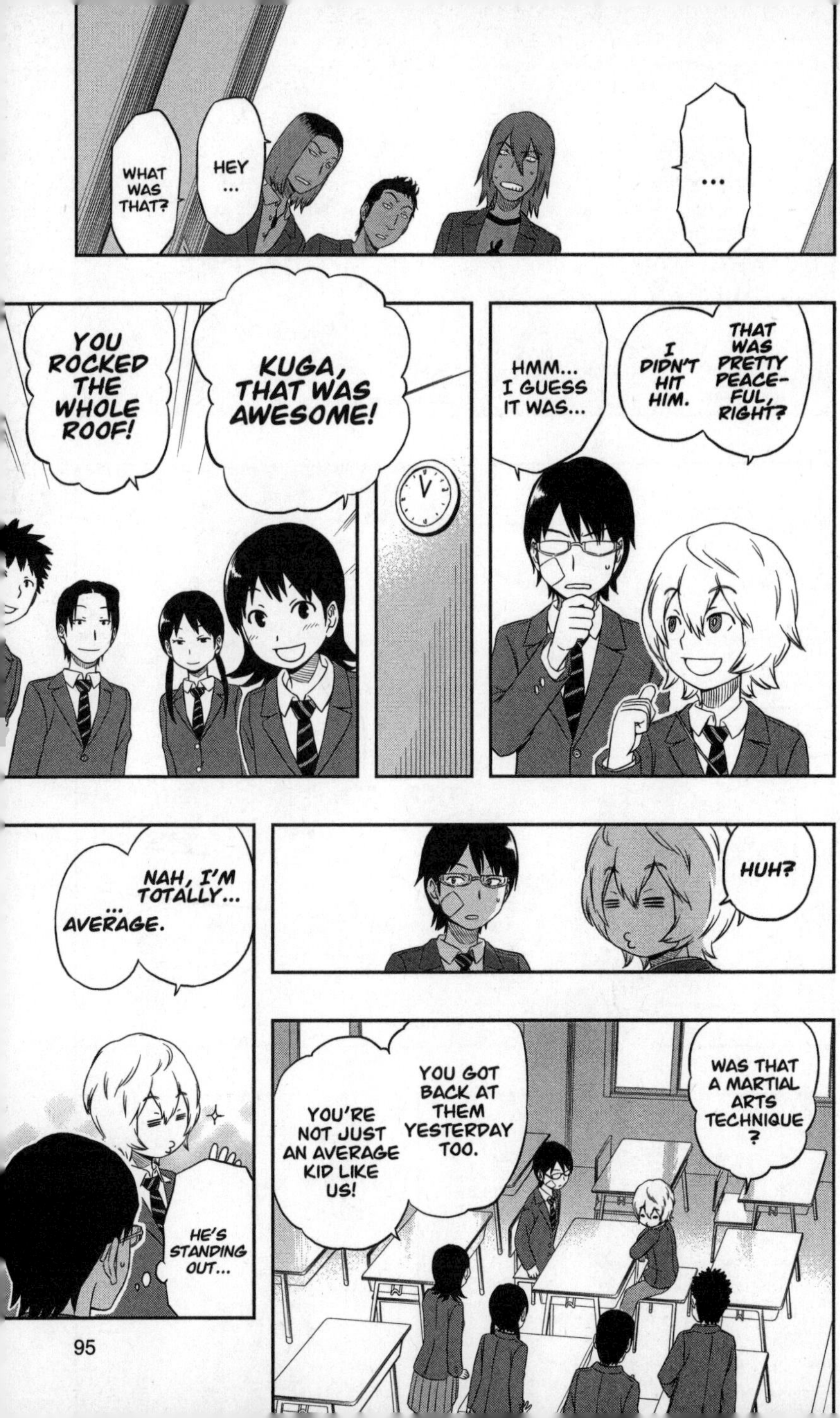
...
HEY ...
WHAT WAS THAT?
THAT WAS PRETTY PEACE-FUL, RIGHT?
I DIDN'T HIT HIM.
HMM... I GUESS IT WAS...
KUGA, THAT WAS AWESOME!
YOU ROCKED THE WHOLE ROOF!
HUH?
WAS THAT A MARTIAL ARTS TECHNIQUE?
YOU GOT BACK AT THEM YESTERDAY TOO.
YOU'RE NOT JUST AN AVERAGE KID LIKE US!
NAH, I'M TOTALLY... ... AVERAGE.
HE'S STANDING OUT...

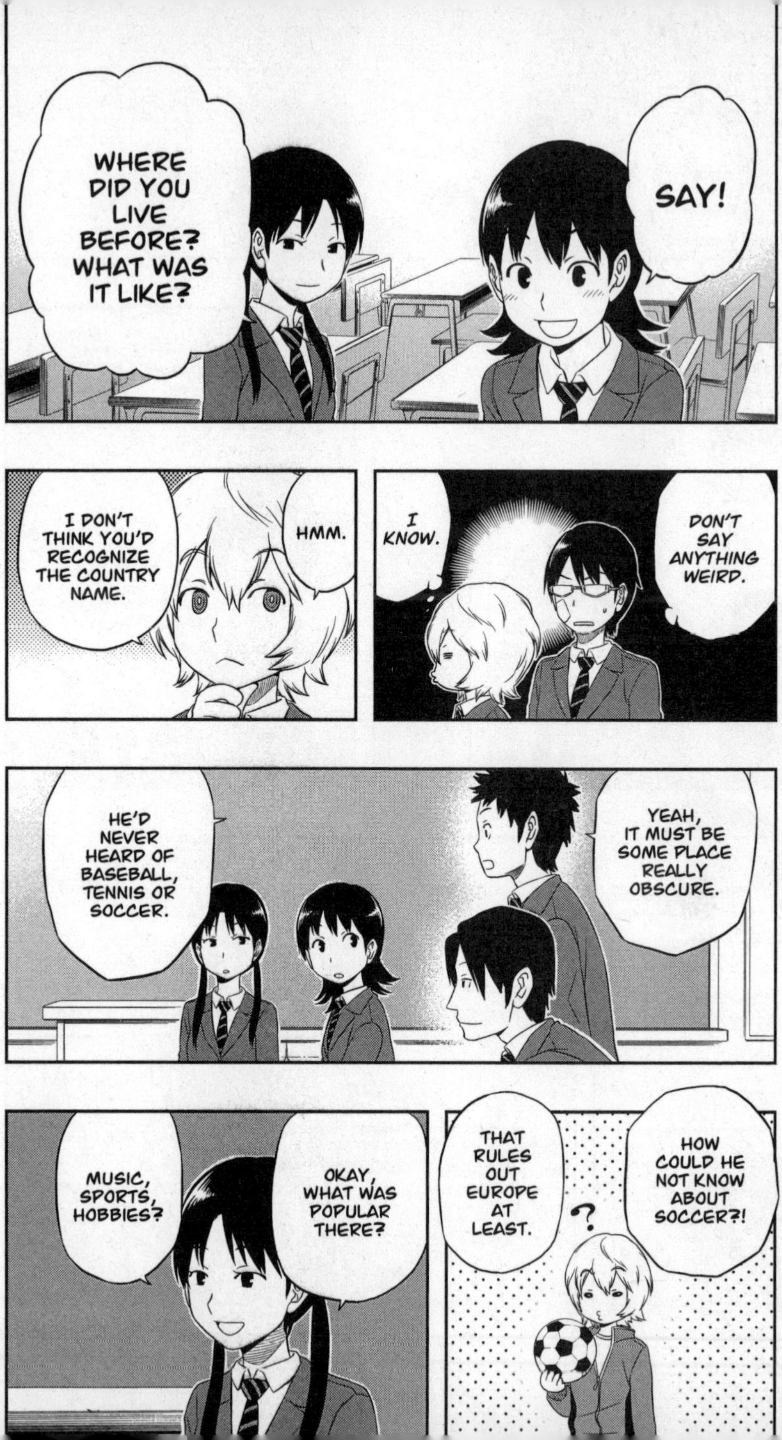
SAY!
WHERE DID YOU LIVE BEFORE? WHAT WAS IT LIKE?
DON'T SAY ANYTHING WEIRD.
I KNOW.
HMM.
I DON'T THINK YOU'D RECOGNIZE THE COUNTRY NAME.
YEAH, IT MUST BE SOME PLACE REALLY OBSCURE.
HE'D NEVER HEARD OF BASEBALL, TENNIS OR SOCCER.
HOW COULD HE NOT KNOW ABOUT SOCCER?!
THAT RULES OUT EUROPE AT LEAST.
?
OKAY, WHAT WAS POPULAR THERE?
MUSIC, SPORTS, HOBBIES?

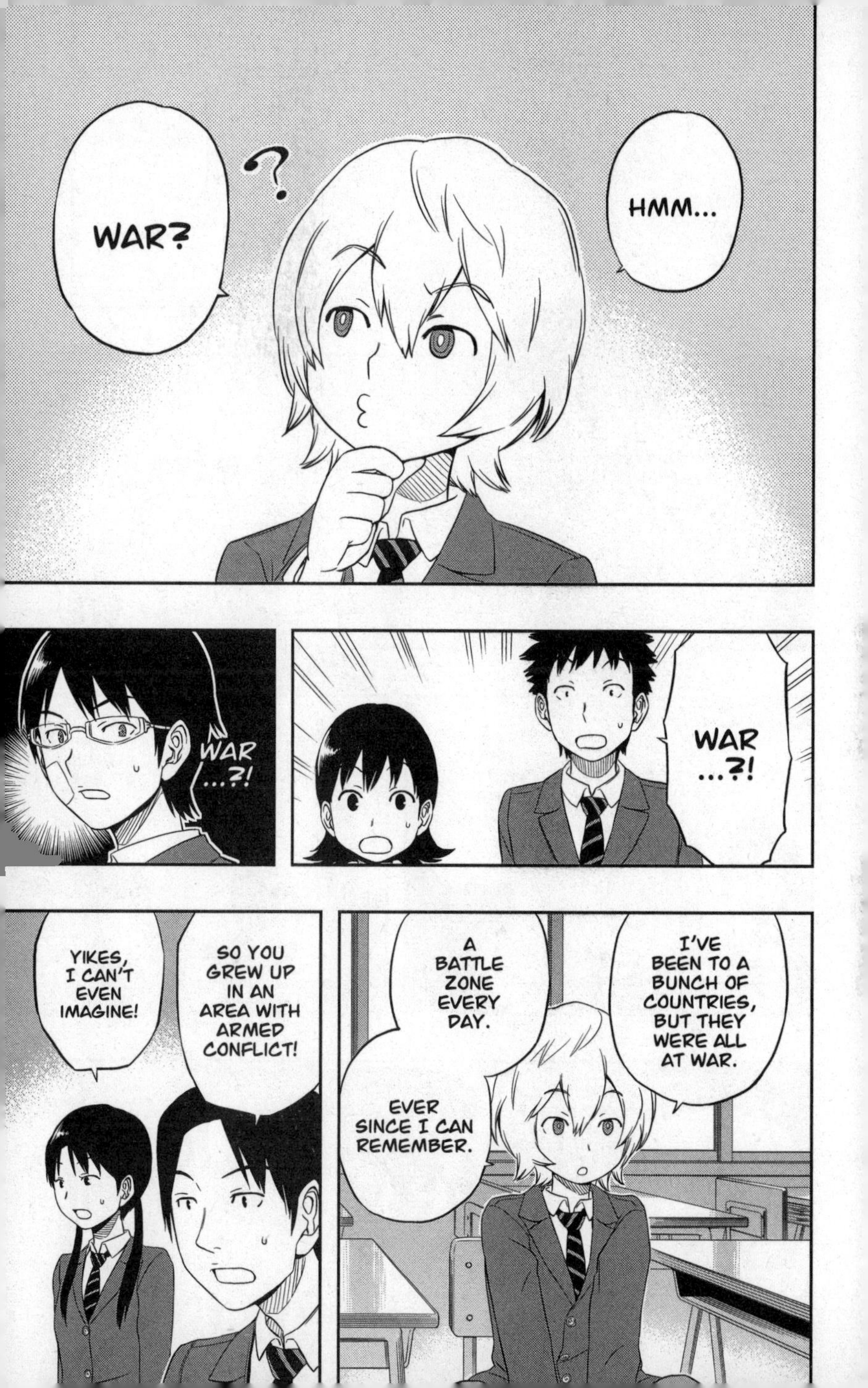
HMM...
WAR?
WAR ...?!
WAR ...?!
I'VE BEEN TO A BUNCH OF COUNTRIES, BUT THEY WERE ALL AT WAR.
A BATTLE ZONE EVERY DAY.
EVER SINCE I CAN REMEMBER.
SO YOU GREW UP IN AN AREA WITH ARMED CONFLICT!
YIKES, I CAN'T EVEN IMAGINE!

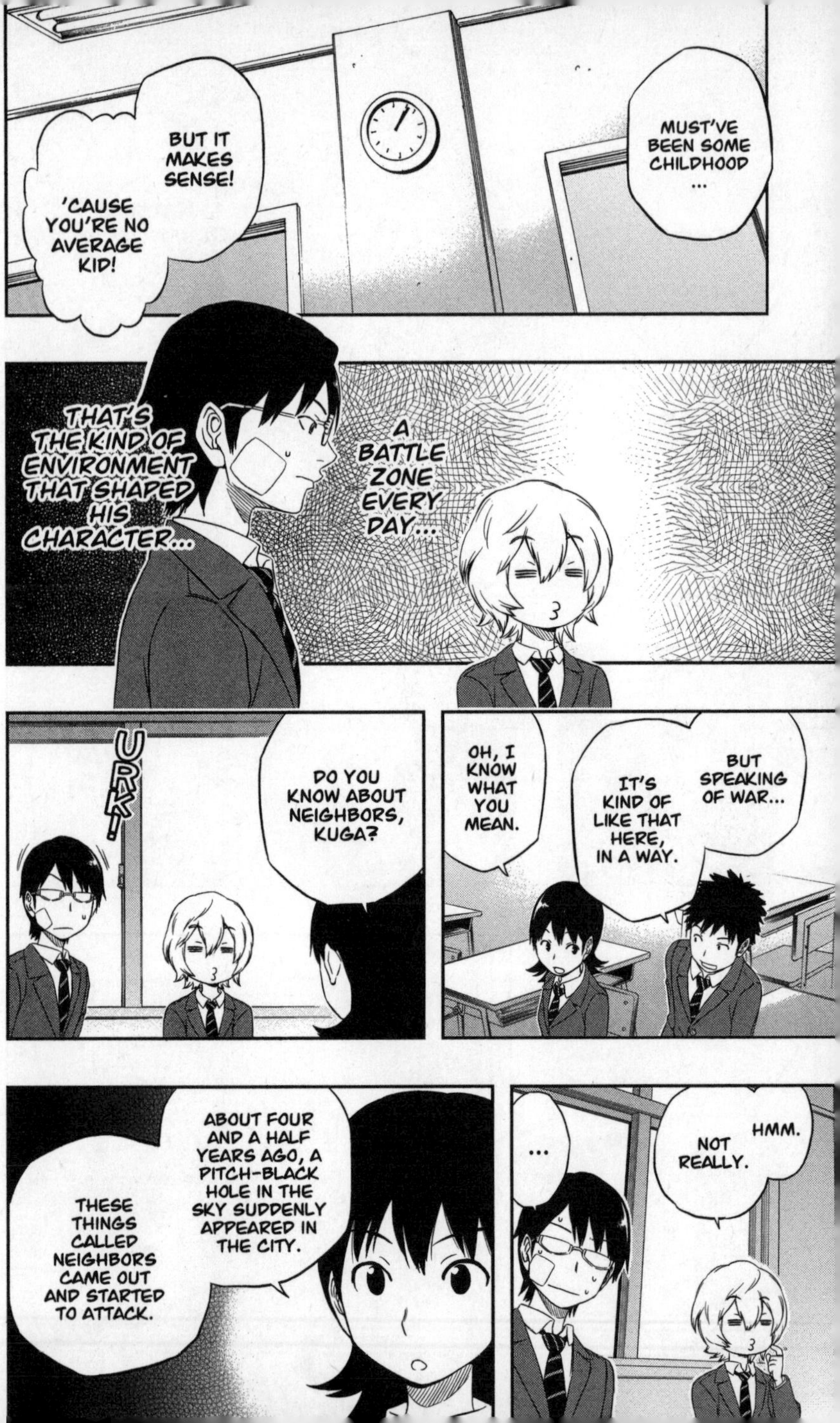
MUST'VE BEEN SOME CHILDHOOD ...
BUT IT MAKES SENSE!
'CAUSE YOU'RE NO AVERAGE KID!
A BATTLE ZONE EVERY DAY...
THAT'S THE KIND OF ENVIRONMENT THAT SHAPED HIS CHARACTER...
BUT SPEAKING OF WAR...
IT'S KIND OF LIKE THAT HERE, IN A WAY.
OH, I KNOW WHAT YOU MEAN.
DO YOU KNOW ABOUT NEIGHBORS, KUGA?
URK!
HMM.
NOT REALLY.
...
ABOUT FOUR AND A HALF YEARS AGO, A PITCH-BLACK HOLE IN THE SKY SUDDENLY APPEARED IN THE CITY.
THESE THINGS CALLED NEIGHBORS CAME OUT AND STARTED TO ATTACK.

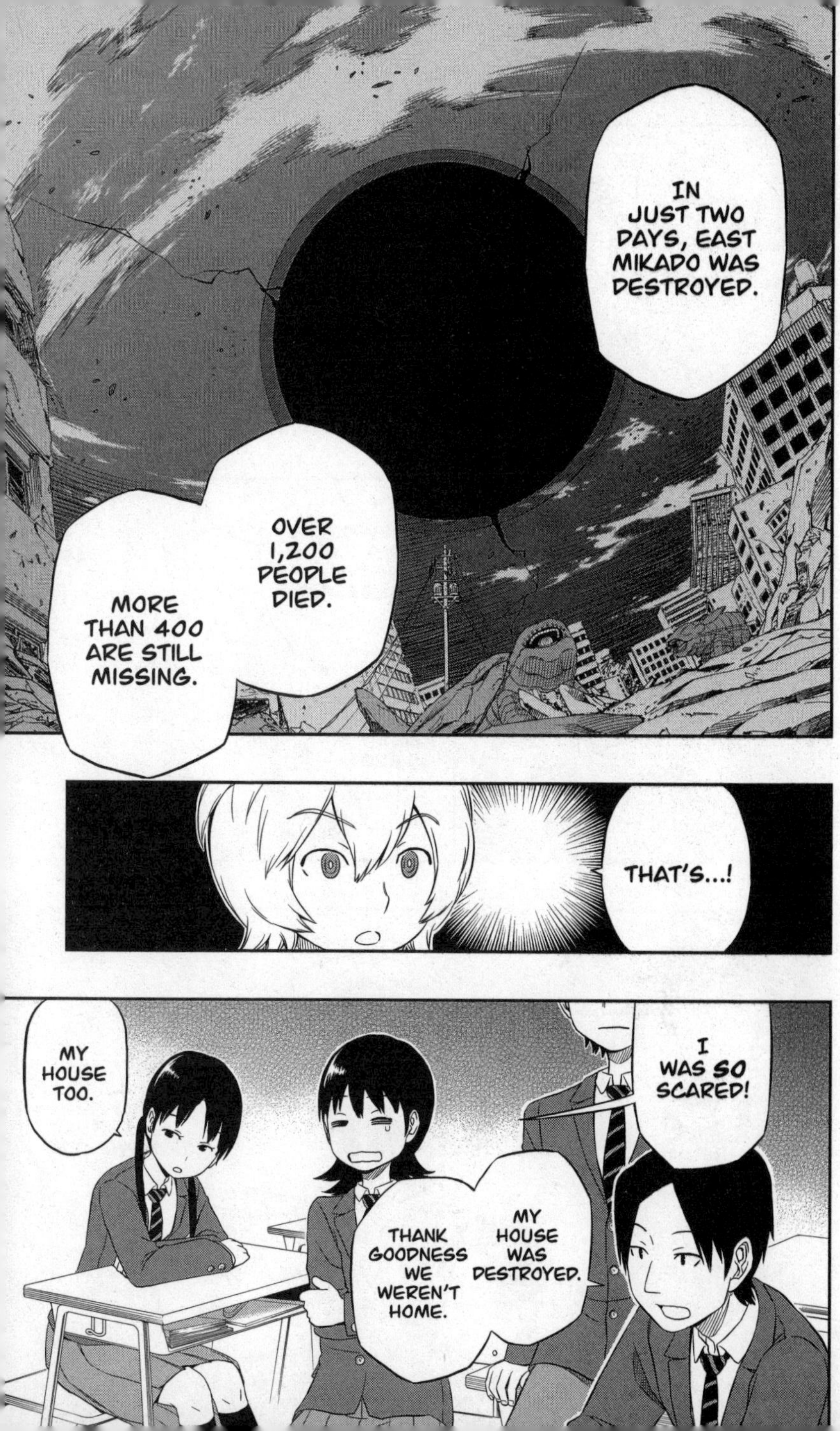
IN JUST TWO DAYS, EAST MIKADO WAS DESTROYED.
OVER 1,200 PEOPLE DIED.
MORE THAN 400 ARE STILL MISSING.
THAT'S...!
I WAS SO SCARED!
MY HOUSE WAS DESTROYED.
THANK GOODNESS WE WEREN'T HOME.
MY HOUSE TOO.

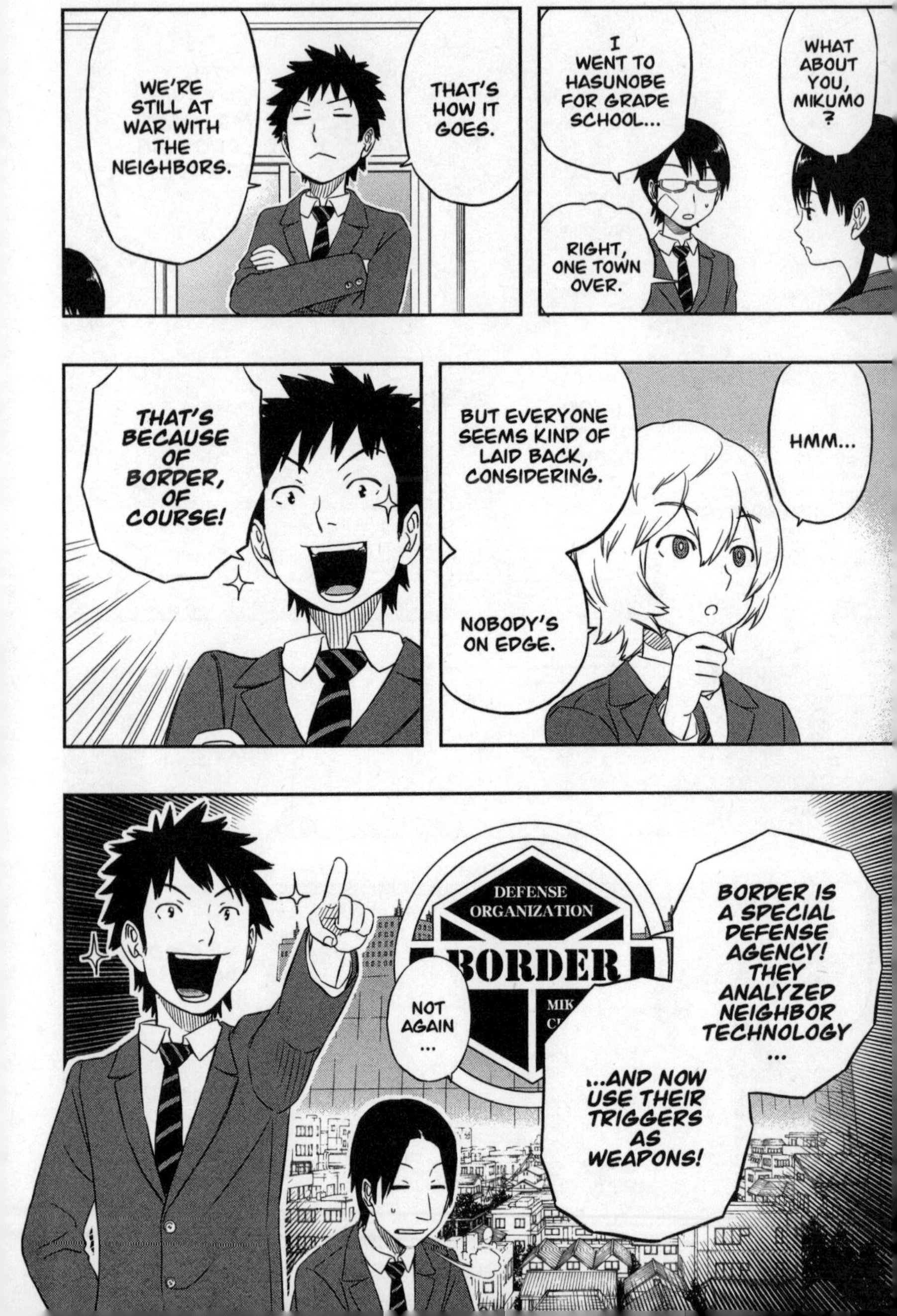
WHAT ABOUT YOU, MIKUMO?
I WENT TO HASUNOBE FOR GRADE SCHOOL...
RIGHT, ONE TOWN OVER.
THAT'S HOW IT GOES.
WE'RE STILL AT WAR WITH THE NEIGHBORS.
HMM...
BUT EVERYONE SEEMS KIND OF LAID BACK, CONSIDERING.
NOBODY'S ON EDGE.
THAT'S BECAUSE OF BORDER, OF COURSE!
BORDER IS A SPECIAL DEFENSE AGENCY! THEY ANALYZED NEIGHBOR TECHNOLOGY...
...AND NOW USE THEIR TRIGGERS AS WEAPONS!
DEFENSE ORGANIZATION
BORDER
NOT AGAIN...

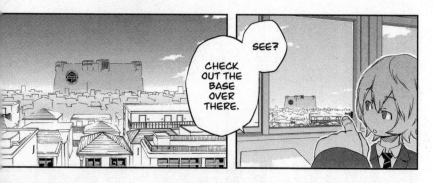

SEE?
CHECK OUT THE BASE OVER THERE.
BEFORE THEY BUILT THAT BASE...
... NEIGHBORS POPPED UP ALL OVER TOWN.
BUT THE GUIDANCE BEACON THERE...
...LIMITS WHERE THEY APPEAR TO THE AREA AROUND THE BASE.
SO THE CITY'S SAFE, AND WE CAN RELAX.
MAN, I WANNA JOIN BORDER TOO!
I WONDER HOW I CAN APPLY?
SIGH
YOU'D BE IN OVER YOUR HEAD.
HM?
IF YOU WANT TO JOIN, YOU COULD ASK...
!!
URK

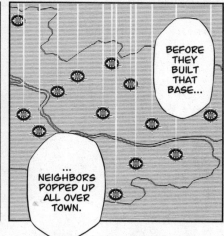

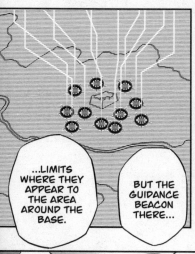

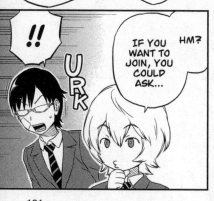

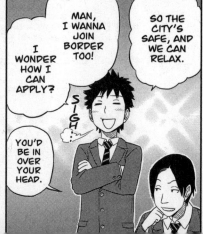

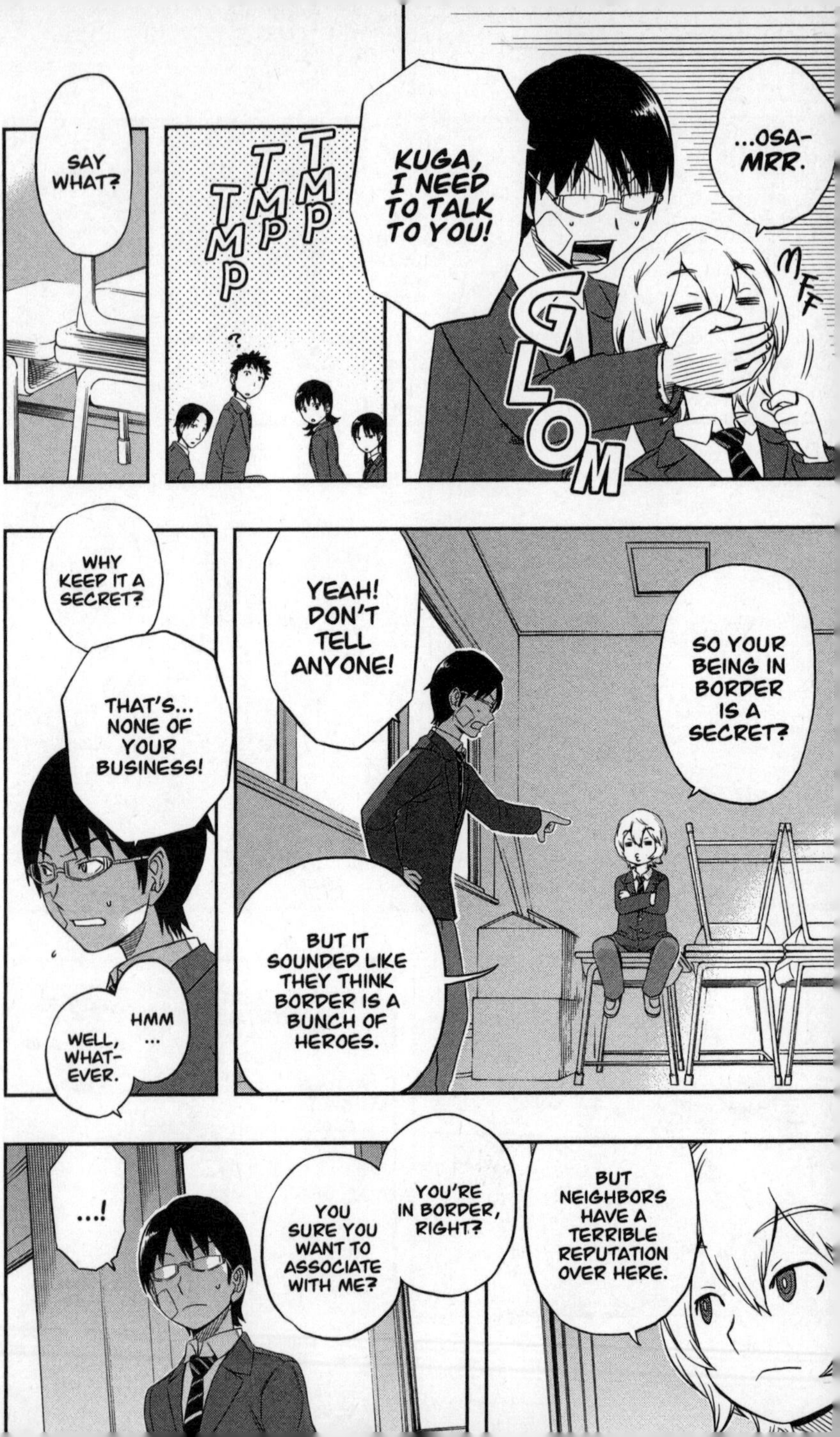
...OSA-MRR.
MFF
KUGA, I NEED TO TALK TO YOU!
GLOM
TMP TMP TMP
?
SAY WHAT?
SO YOUR BEING IN BORDER IS A SECRET?
YEAH! DON'T TELL ANYONE!
BUT IT SOUNDED LIKE THEY THINK BORDER IS A BUNCH OF HEROES.
WHY KEEP IT A SECRET?
THAT'S... NONE OF YOUR BUSINESS!
HMM...
WELL, WHATEVER.
BUT NEIGHBORS HAVE A TERRIBLE REPUTATION OVER HERE.
YOU'RE IN BORDER, RIGHT?
YOU SURE YOU WANT TO ASSOCIATE WITH ME?
...!

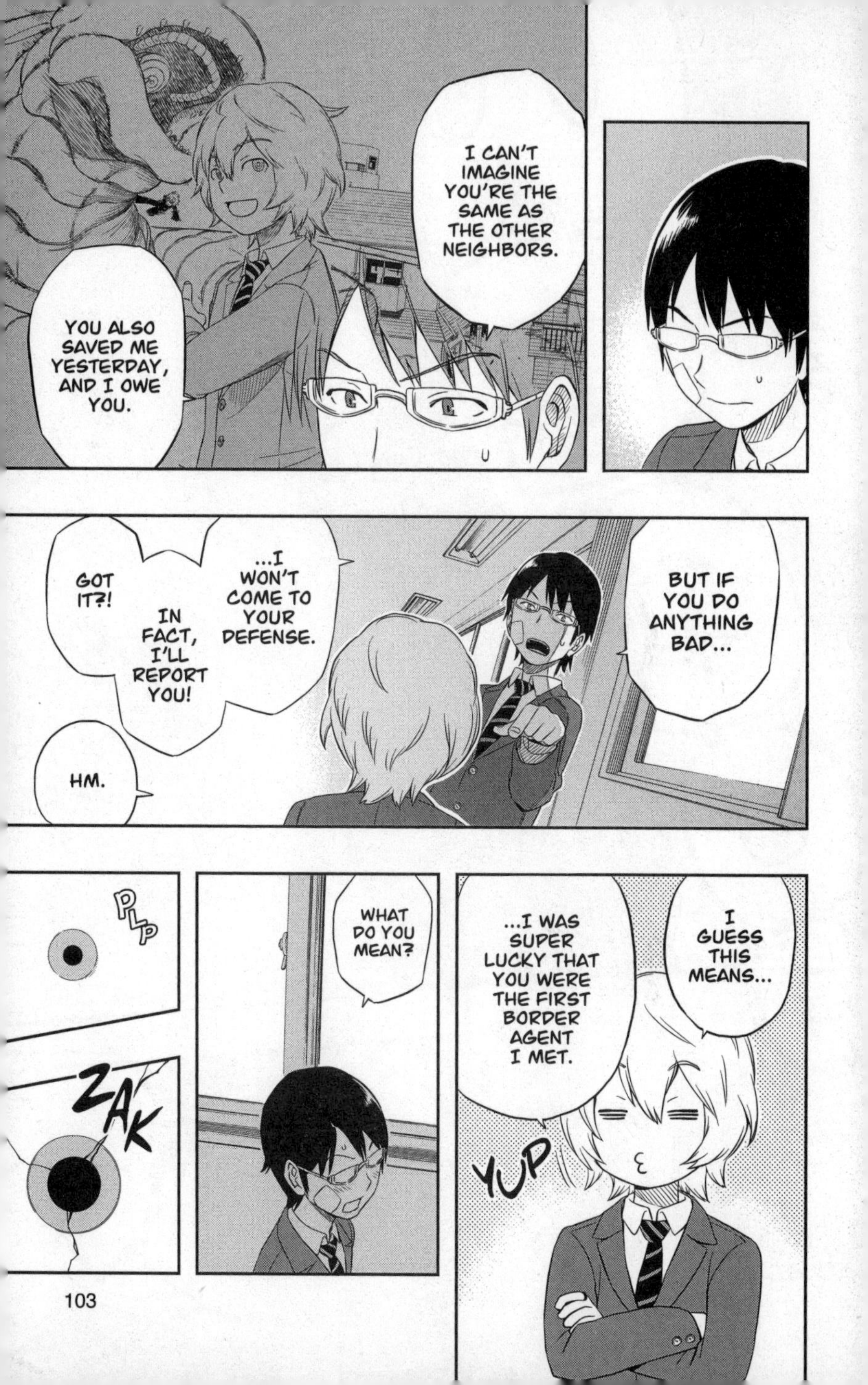
I CAN'T IMAGINE YOU'RE THE SAME AS THE OTHER NEIGHBORS.
YOU ALSO SAVED ME YESTERDAY, AND I OWE YOU.
BUT IF YOU DO ANYTHING BAD...
...I WON'T COME TO YOUR DEFENSE.
IN FACT, I'LL REPORT YOU!
GOT IT?!
HM.
I GUESS THIS MEANS...
...I WAS SUPER LUCKY THAT YOU WERE THE FIRST BORDER AGENT I MET.
YUP
WHAT DO YOU MEAN?
PLP
ZAK

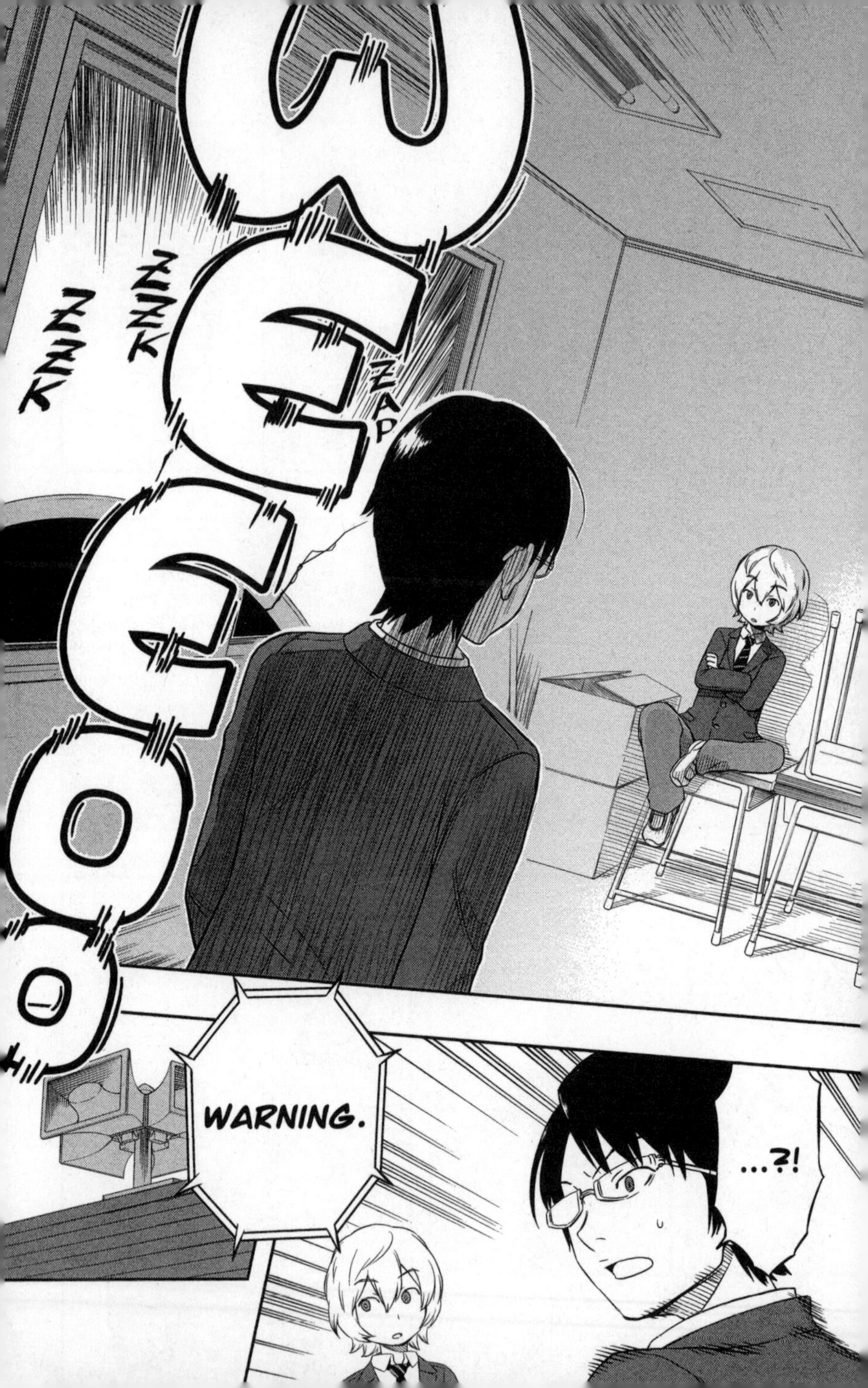
ZAP
...?!
WARNING.

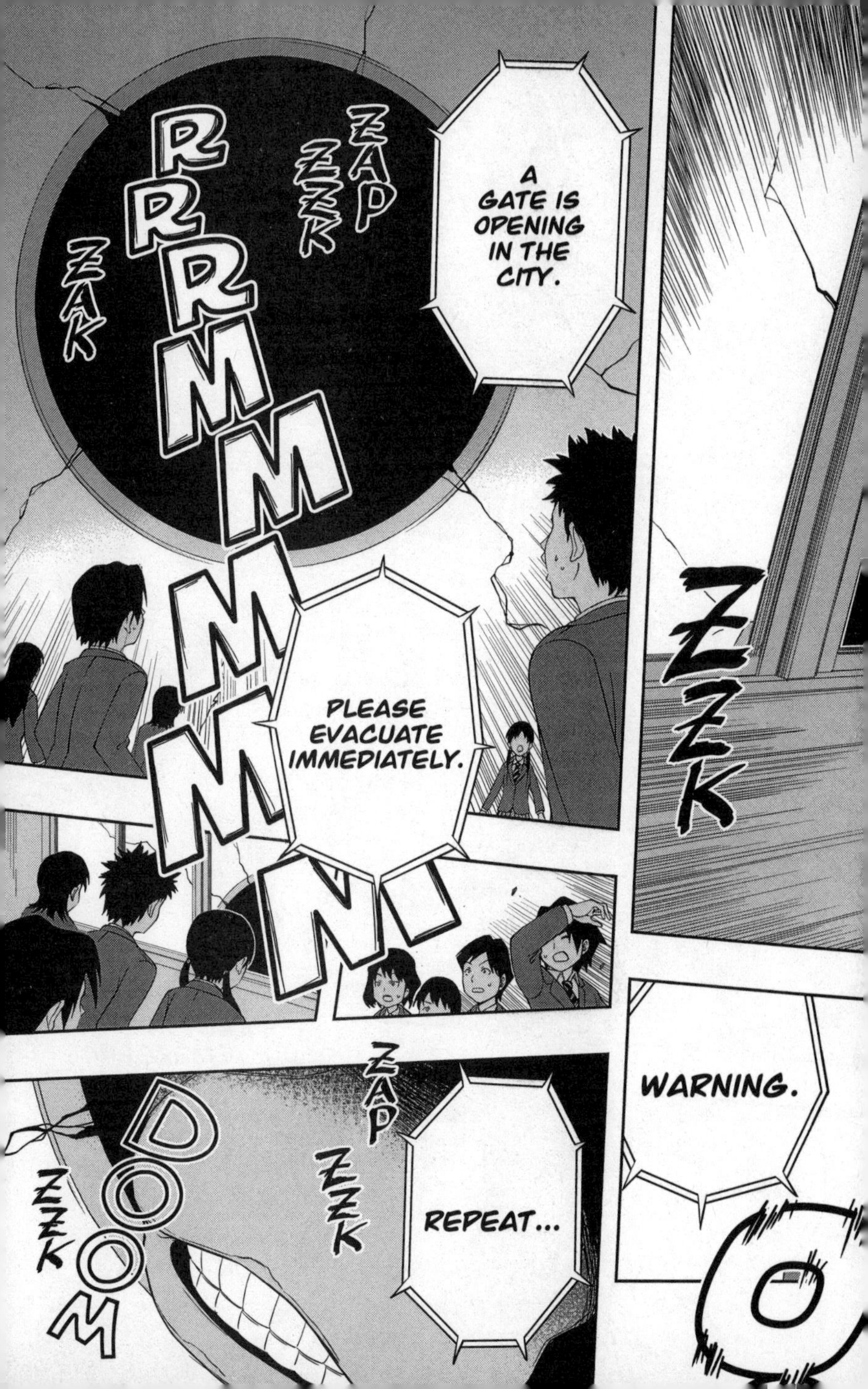
ZZZK
A GATE IS OPENING IN THE CITY.
ZAP
ZZZK
RRRMMMMMN
ZAK
PLEASE EVACUATE IMMEDIATELY.
WARNING.
ZAP
REPEAT...
ZZZK
DOOM
ZZZK

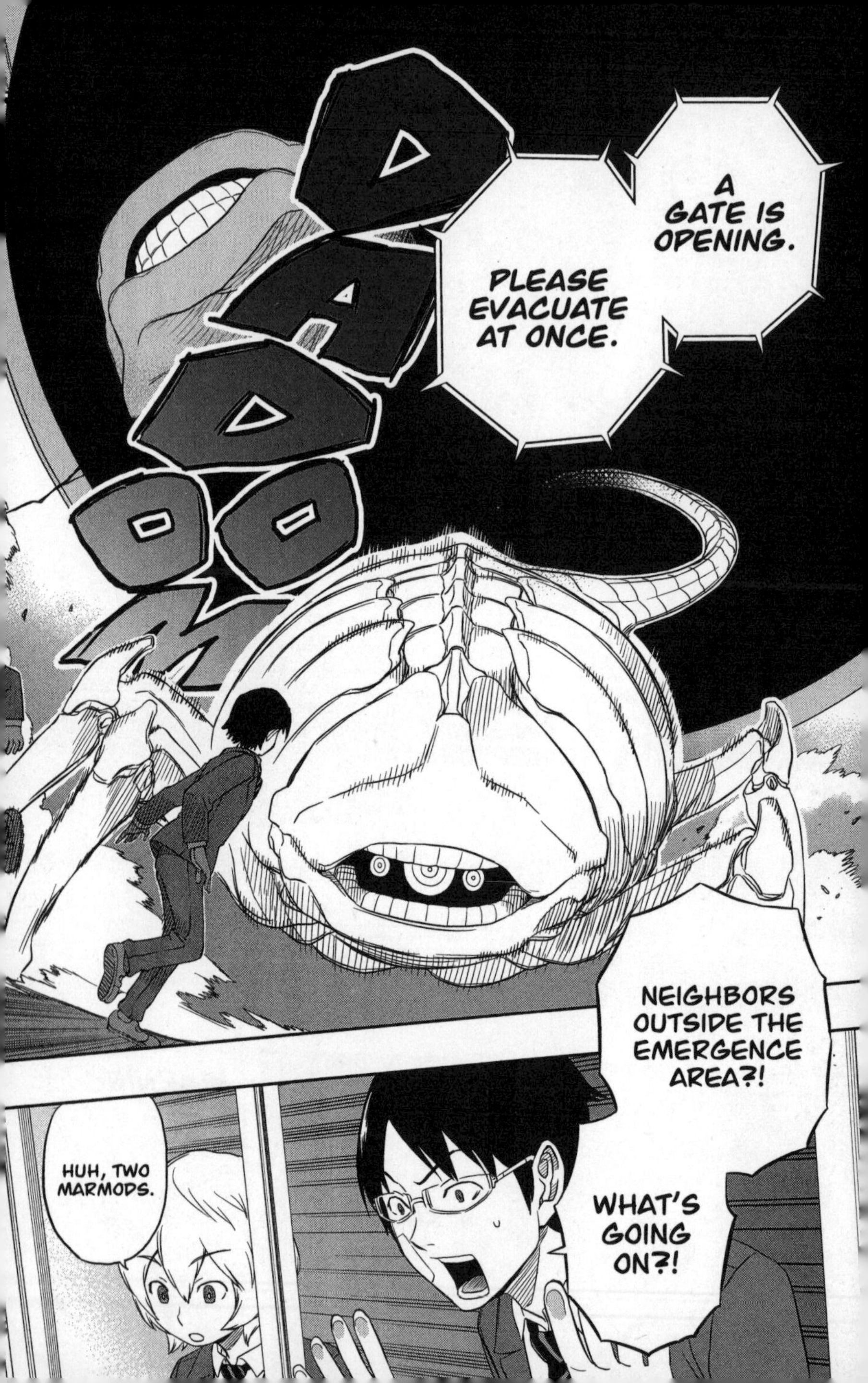
A GATE IS OPENING.
PLEASE EVACUATE AT ONCE.
NEIGHBORS OUTSIDE THE EMERGENCE AREA?!
WHAT'S GOING ON?!
HUH, TWO MARMODS.

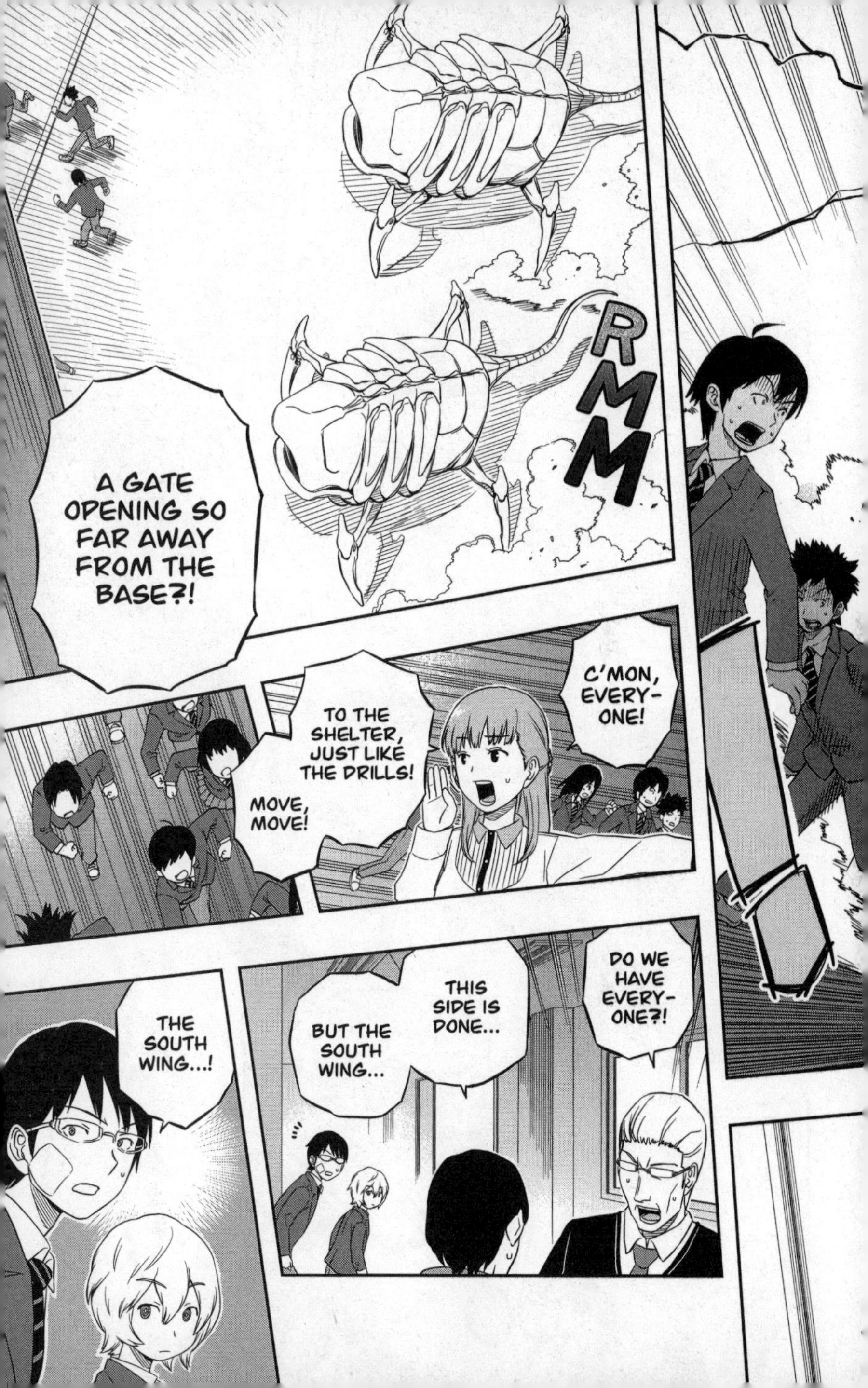
RMM
A GATE OPENING SO FAR AWAY FROM THE BASE?!
C'MON, EVERY-ONE!
TO THE SHELTER, JUST LIKE THE DRILLS!
MOVE, MOVE!
DO WE HAVE EVERY-ONE?!
THIS SIDE IS DONE...
BUT THE SOUTH WING...
THE SOUTH WING...!

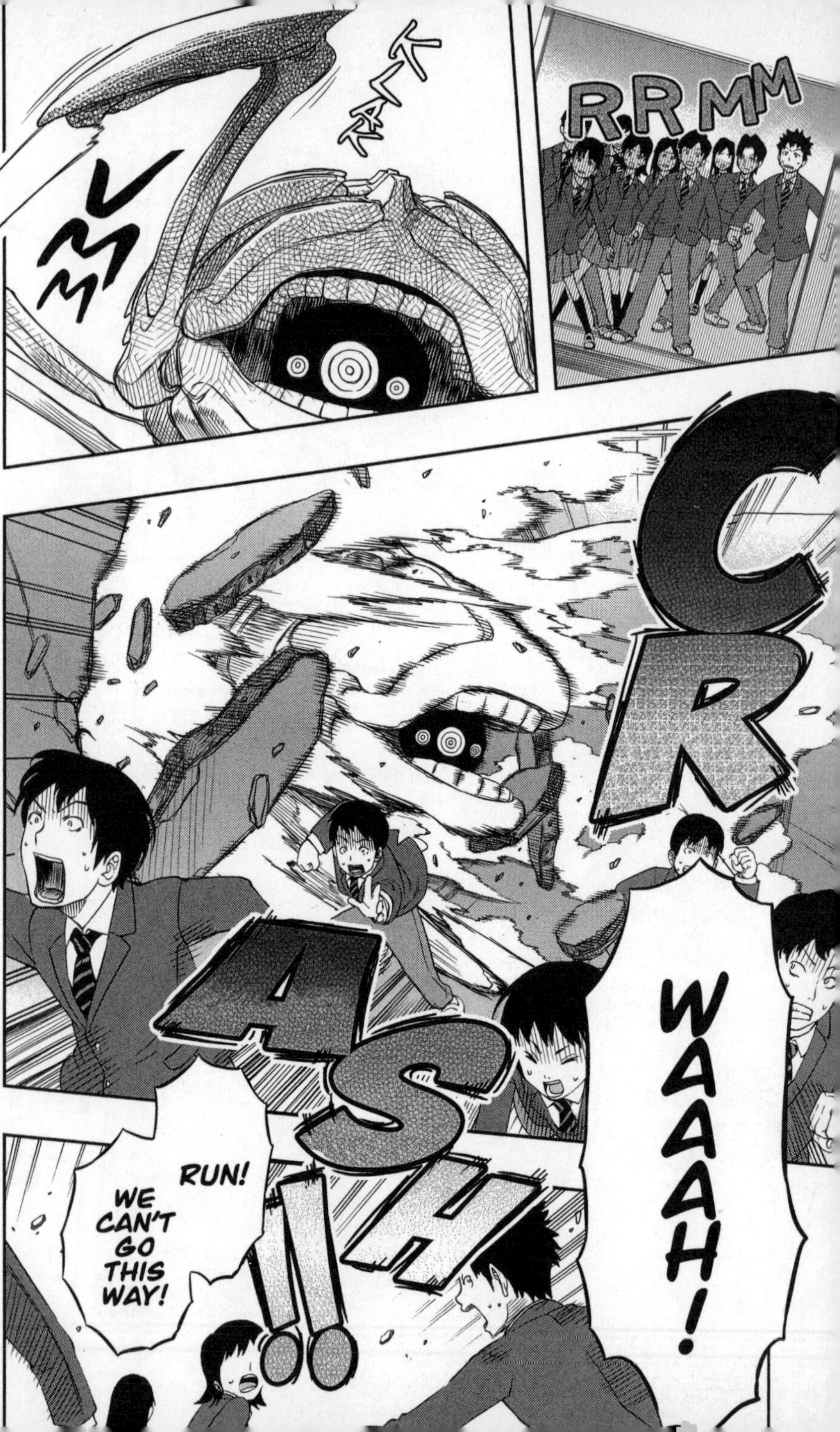
RRMM
KLAK
VMM
CRASH!!
WAAAH!
RUN!
WE CAN'T GO THIS WAY!

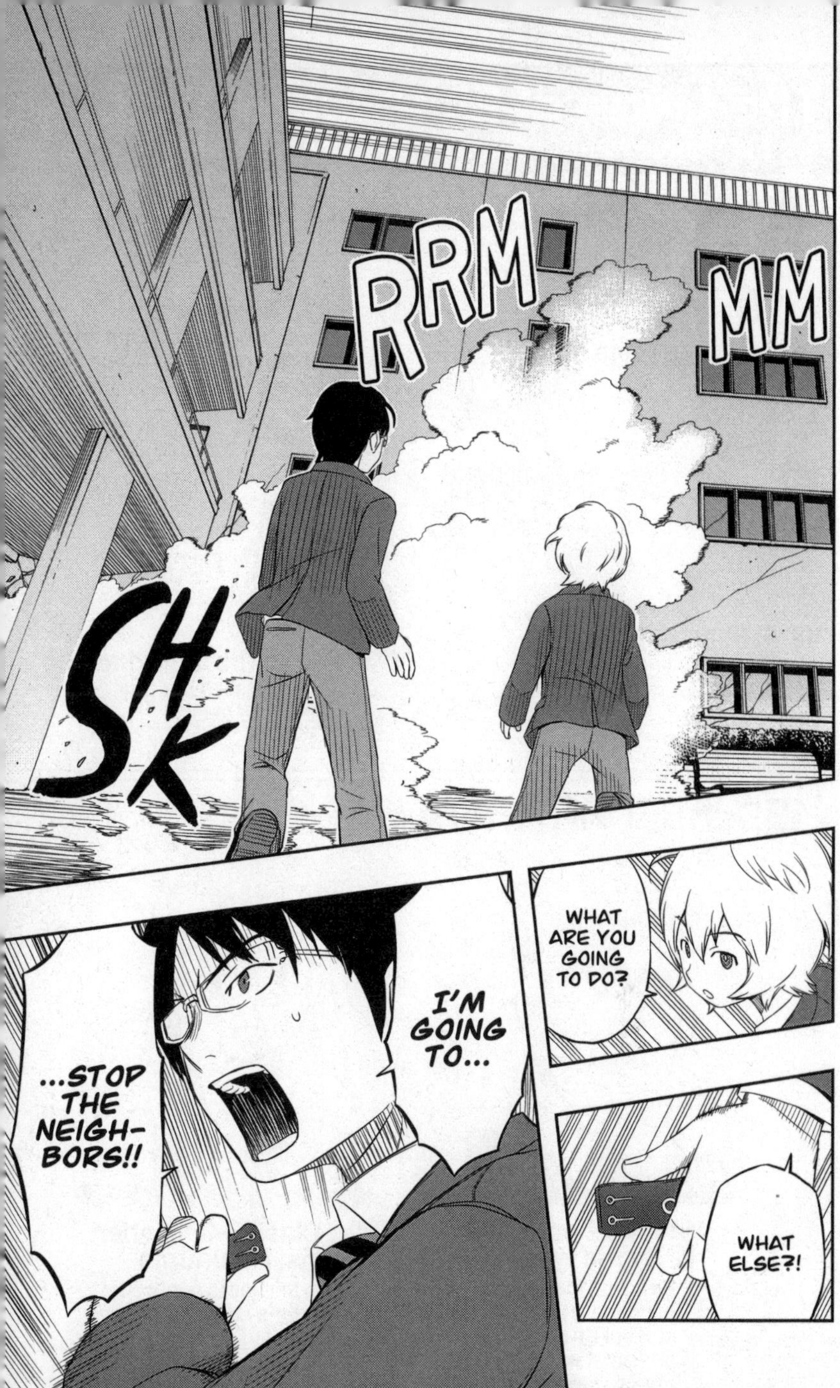
RRM
MM
SHK
WHAT ARE YOU GOING TO DO?
WHAT ELSE?!
I'M GOING TO...
...STOP THE NEIGHBORS!!

The Lives of Bit Players: Part 1
For people who, for some reason, salivate over trivia.

■ The Three Idiots (Chapter 1~)

I'd like to draw them at least one more time.

No. 1: Ringleader
The worst of them. I hope he improves his danger detection skills and survives.

No. 3: Roots Showing
Just being a delinquent on the side. He gets good grades and comes from a rich family.

No. 2: The Annoying One
I don't dislike this guy. He's easy to draw.

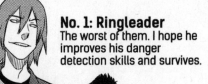

■ School Teachers (Chapter 1~)

Senior Teacher: Mr. Moribayashi
He's a good teacher, concerned about his students' futures and strict with troublemakers. 

Class 3-3 Teacher: Ms. Mizunuma 
She looks pretty cute for a character I spent so little time designing. She's probably popular with the students.

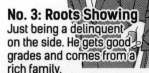

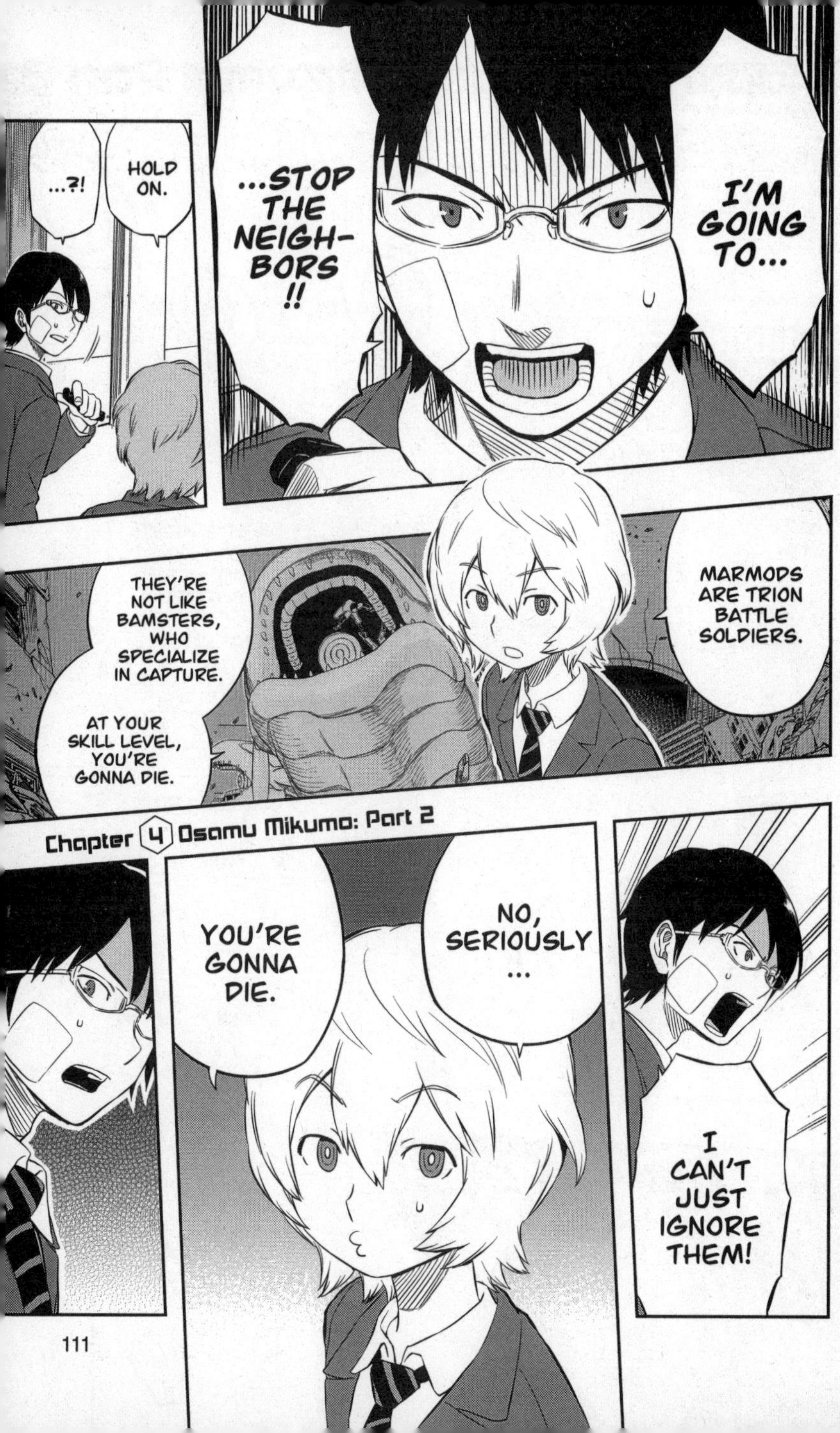
I'M GOING TO...
...STOP THE NEIGH-BORS!!
HOLD ON.
...?!
MARMODS ARE TRION BATTLE SOLDIERS.
THEY'RE NOT LIKE BAMSTERS, WHO SPECIALIZE IN CAPTURE.
AT YOUR SKILL LEVEL, YOU'RE GONNA DIE.
Chapter 4 Osamu Mikumo: Part 2
I CAN'T JUST IGNORE THEM!
NO, SERIOUSLY...
YOU'RE GONNA DIE.

Chapter 4 Osamu Mikumo: Part 2

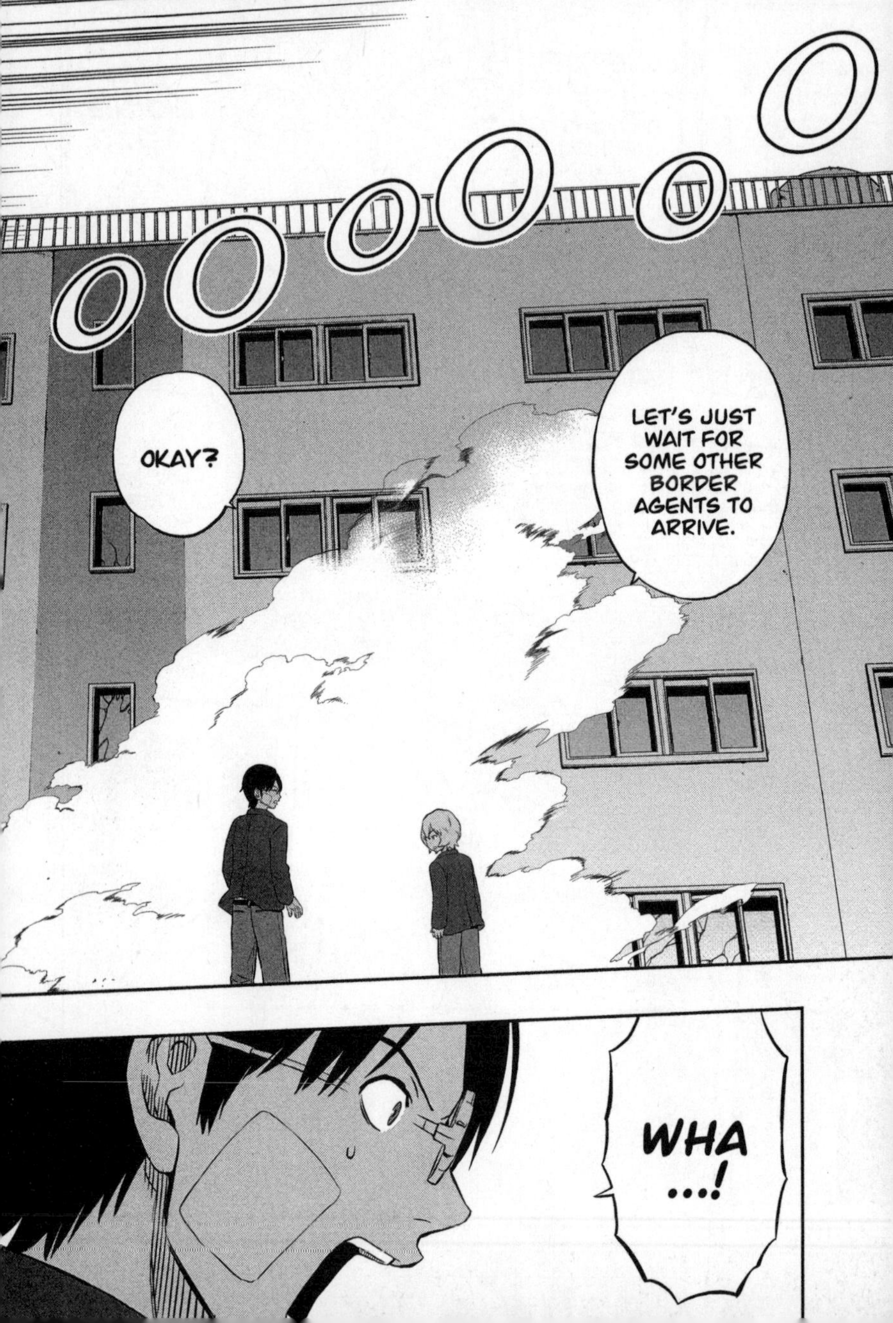
LET'S JUST WAIT FOR SOME OTHER BORDER AGENTS TO ARRIVE.
OKAY?
WHA ...!

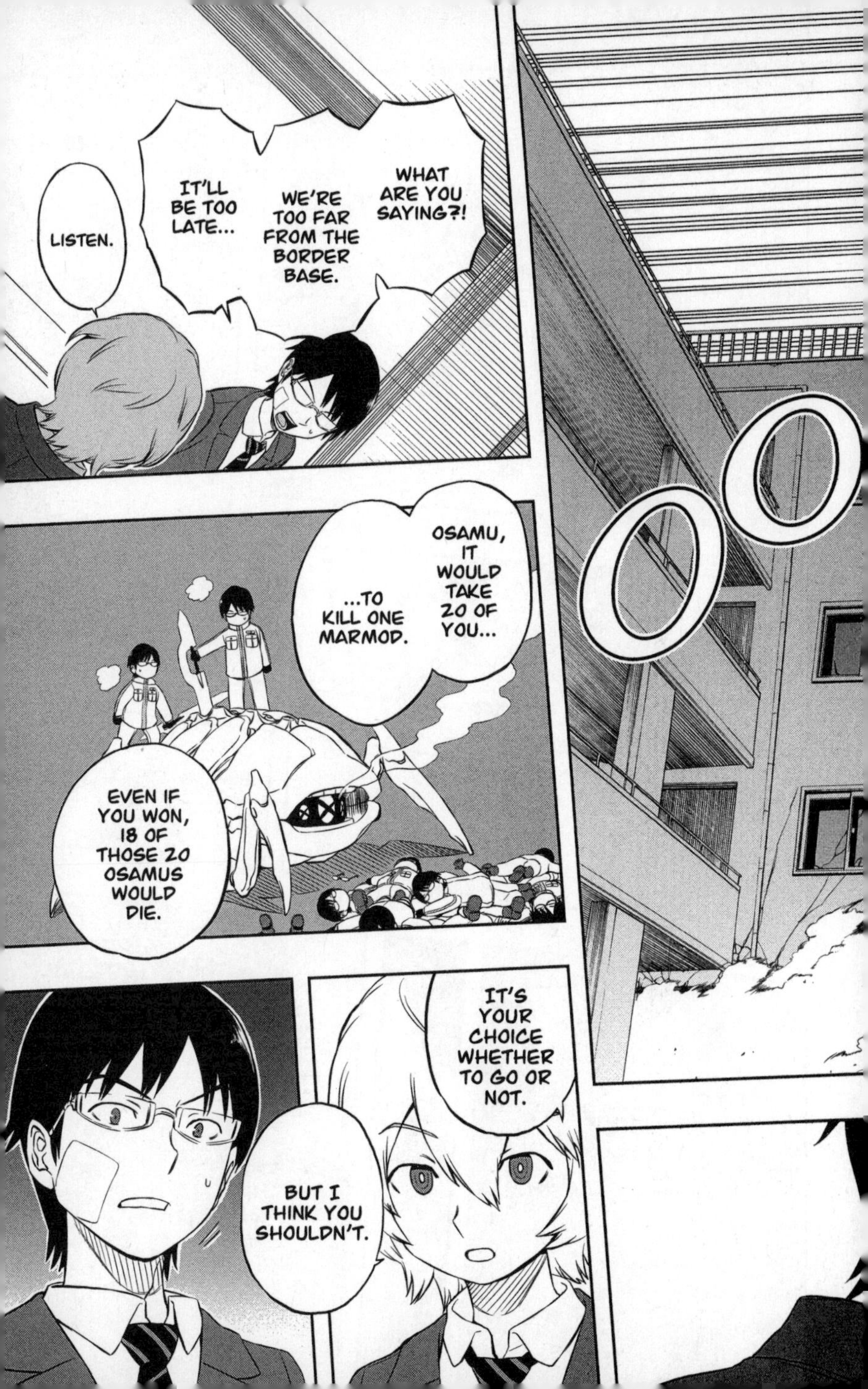
WHAT ARE YOU SAYING?!
WE'RE TOO FAR FROM THE BORDER BASE.
IT'LL BE TOO LATE...
LISTEN.
OSAMU, IT WOULD TAKE 20 OF YOU...
...TO KILL ONE MARMOD.
EVEN IF YOU WON, 18 OF THOSE 20 OSAMUS WOULD DIE.
IT'S YOUR CHOICE WHETHER TO GO OR NOT.
BUT I THINK YOU SHOULDN'T.

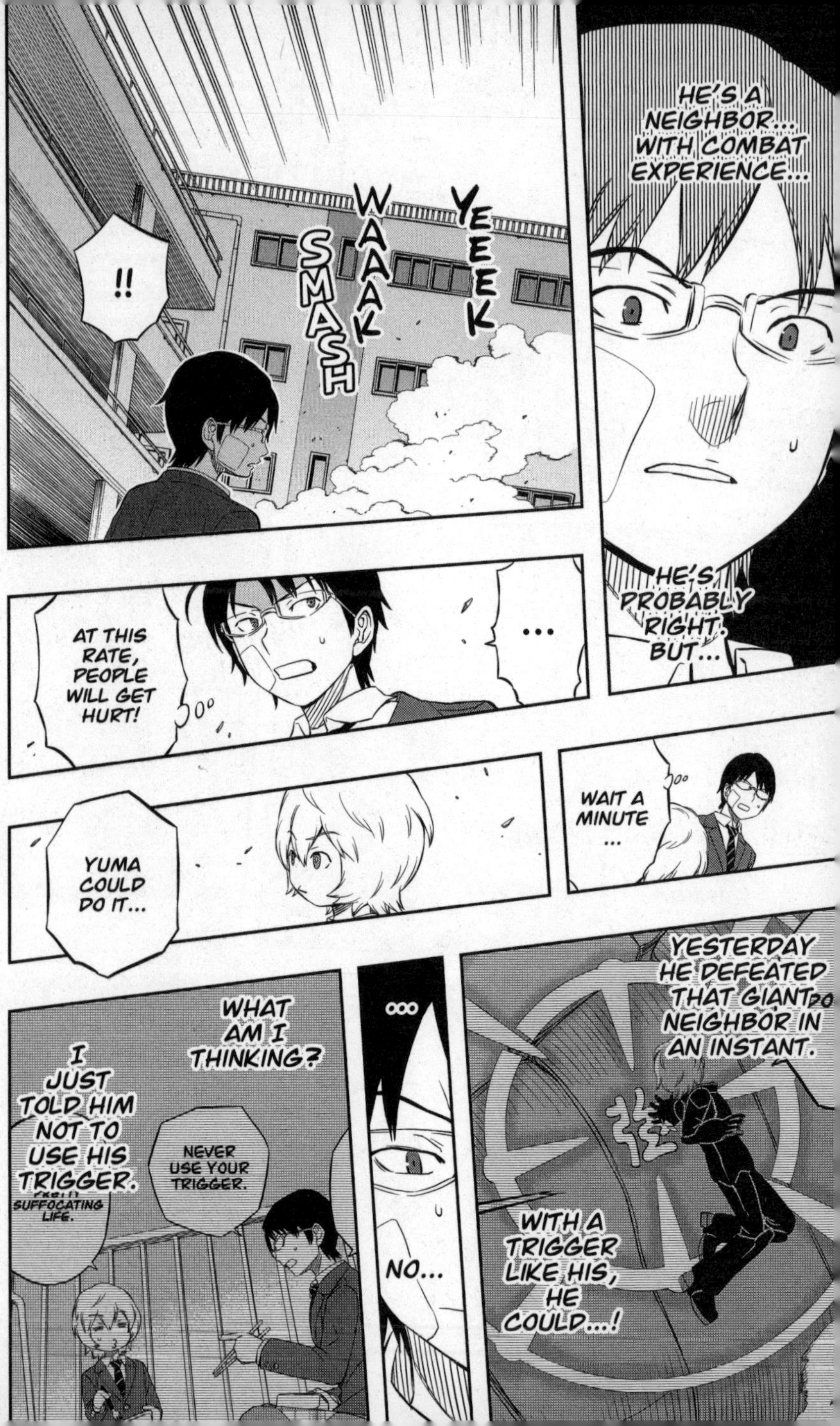
HE'S A NEIGHBOR... WITH COMBAT EXPERIENCE...
HE'S PROBABLY RIGHT. BUT...
YEEEK
WAAAK
SMASH
!!
...
AT THIS RATE, PEOPLE WILL GET HURT!
WAIT A MINUTE ...
YUMA COULD DO IT...
YESTERDAY HE DEFEATED THAT GIANT NEIGHBOR IN AN INSTANT.
WITH A TRIGGER LIKE HIS, HE COULD...!
...
NO...
WHAT AM I THINKING?
I JUST TOLD HIM NOT TO USE HIS TRIGGER.
NEVER USE YOUR TRIGGER.
SUFFOCATING LIFE.

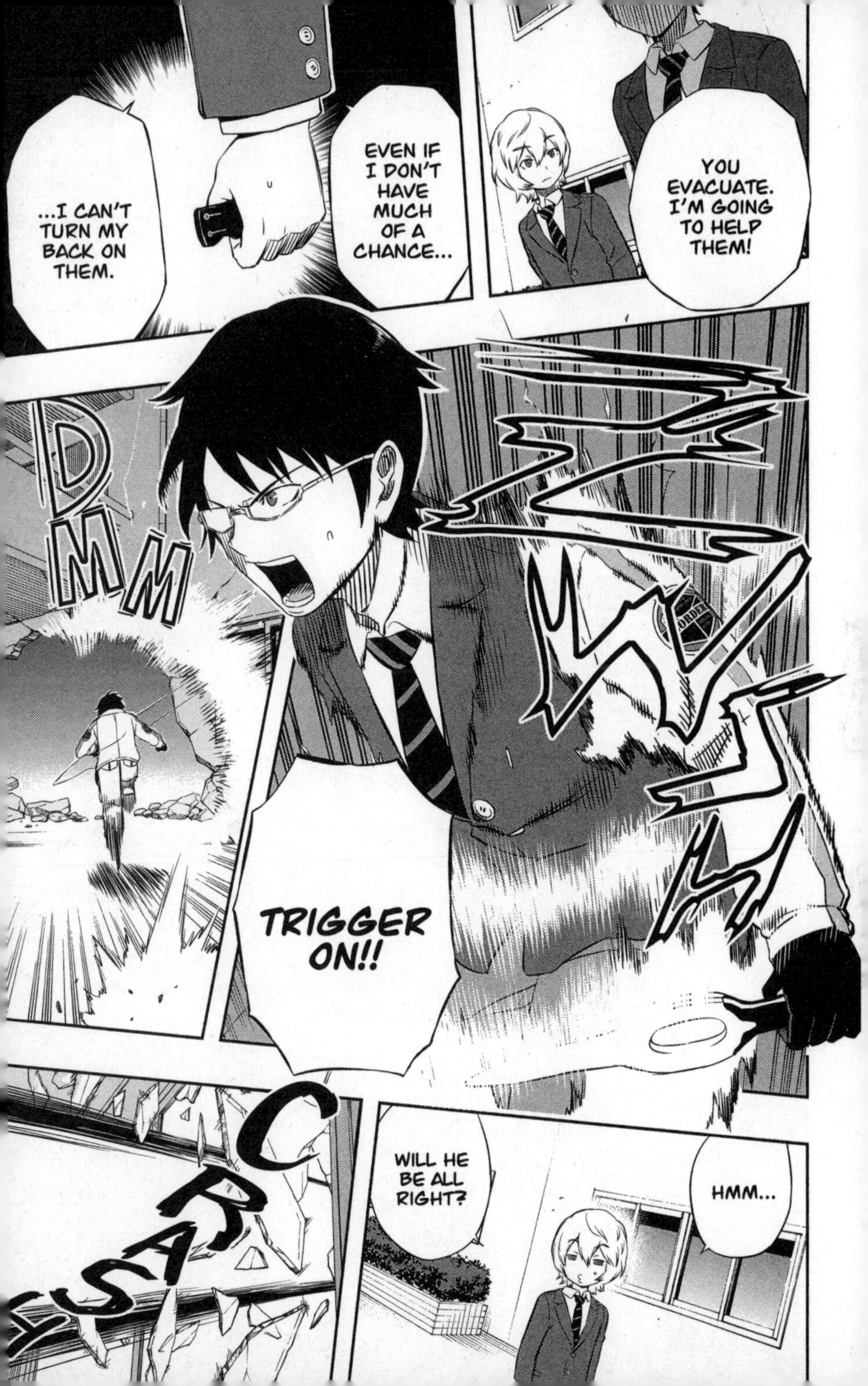
YOU EVACUATE. I'M GOING TO HELP THEM!
EVEN IF I DON'T HAVE MUCH OF A CHANCE...
...I CAN'T TURN MY BACK ON THEM.
TRIGGER ON!!
DMM
WILL HE BE ALL RIGHT?
HMM...
CRASS

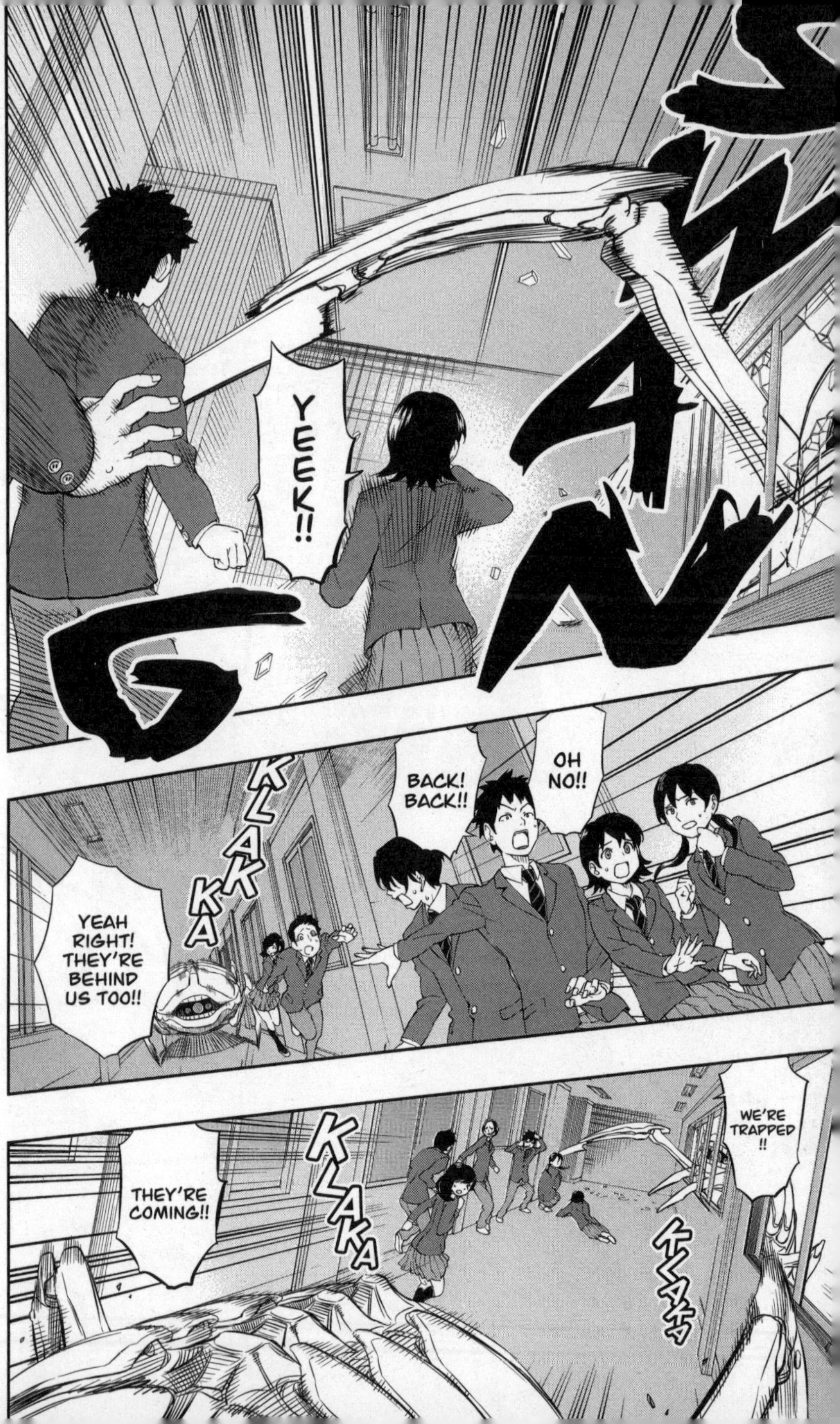
GAN
YEEK!!
OH NO!!
BACK! BACK!!
KLAKAKA
YEAH RIGHT! THEY'RE BEHIND US TOO!!
WE'RE TRAPPED !!
KLAKA
KLAKA
THEY'RE COMING!!

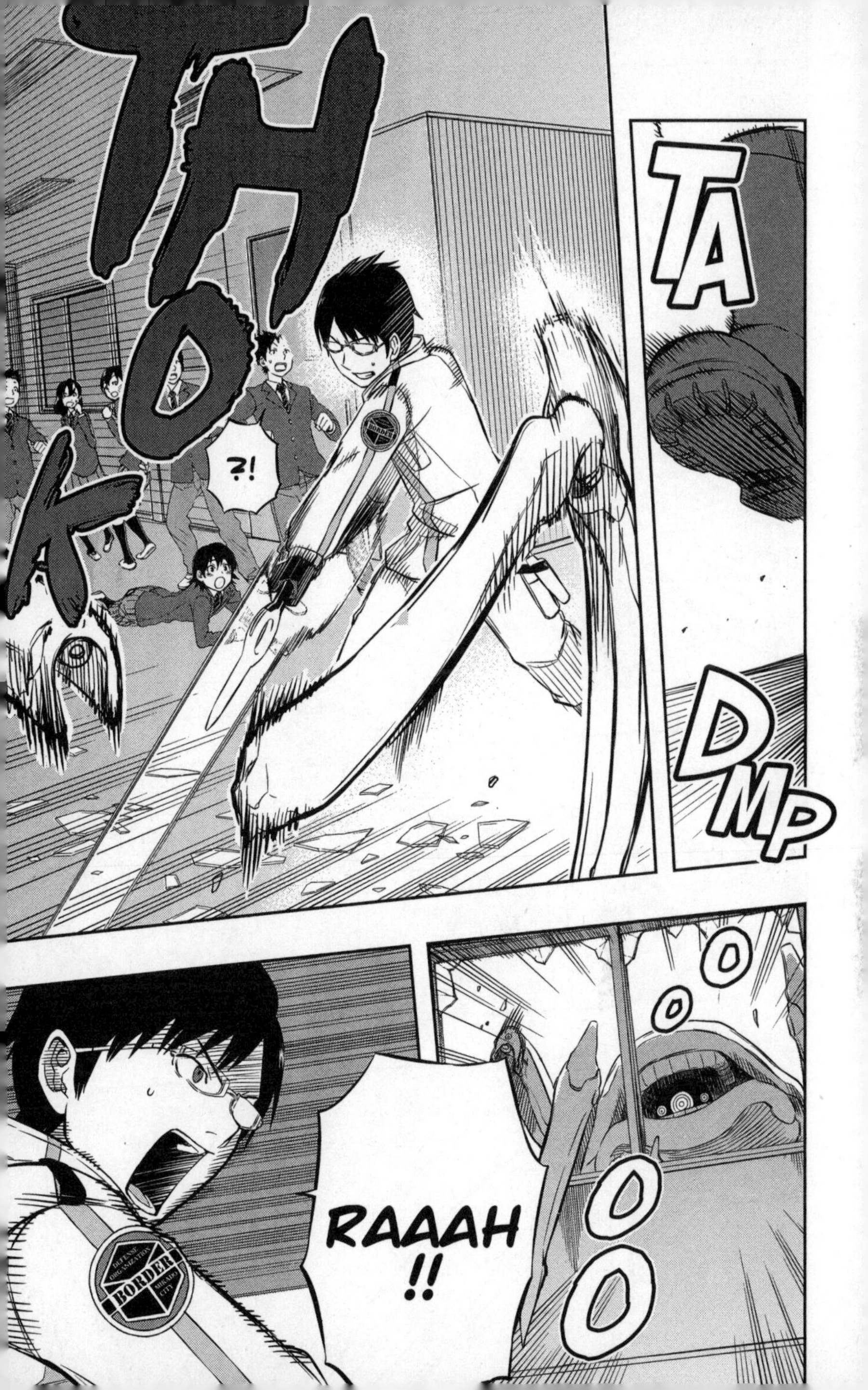
TA
DMP
THOK
?!
OOOOO
RAAAH!!

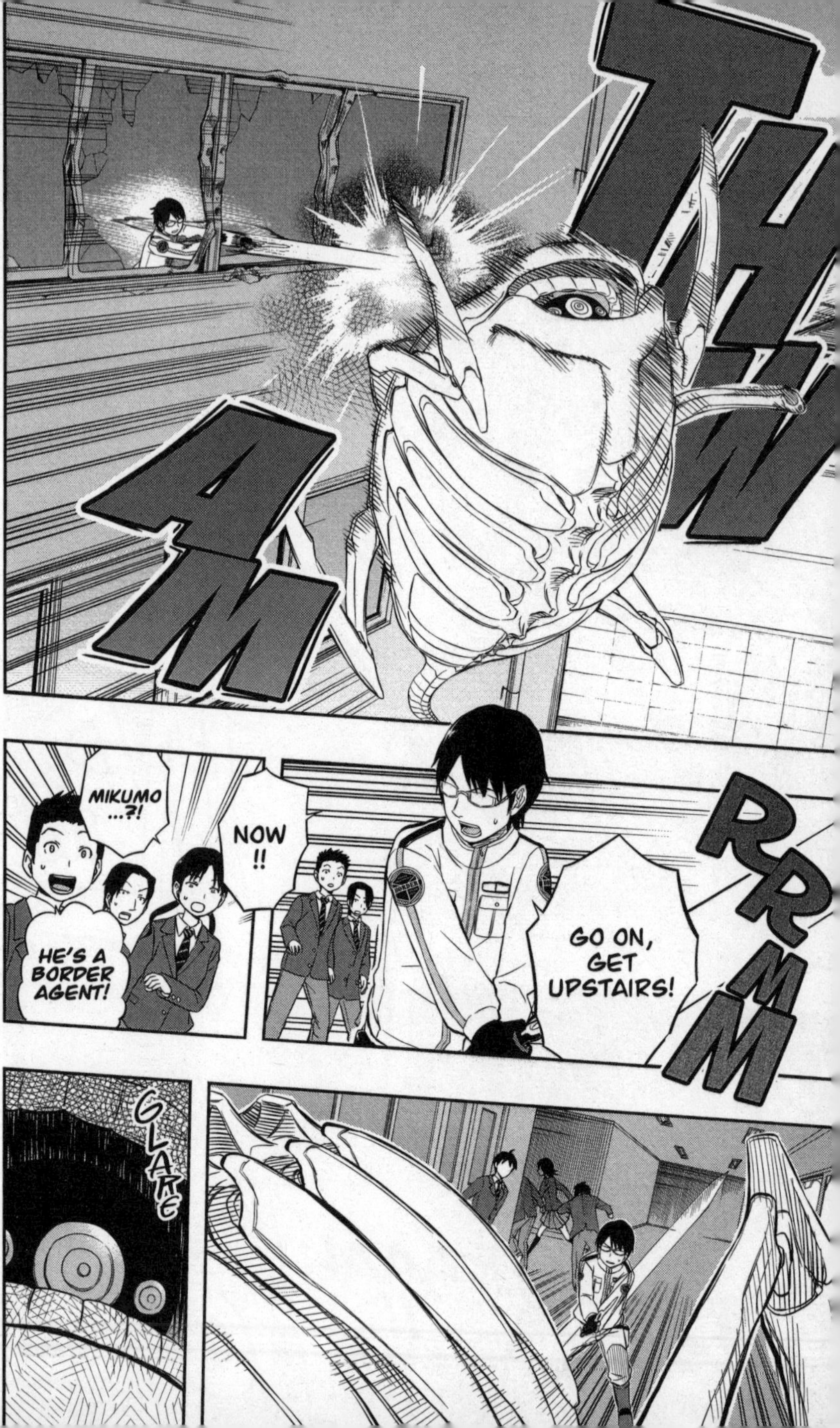
THWAM
RRMMM
GO ON, GET UPSTAIRS!
NOW !!
MIKUMO ...?!
HE'S A BORDER AGENT!
GLARE

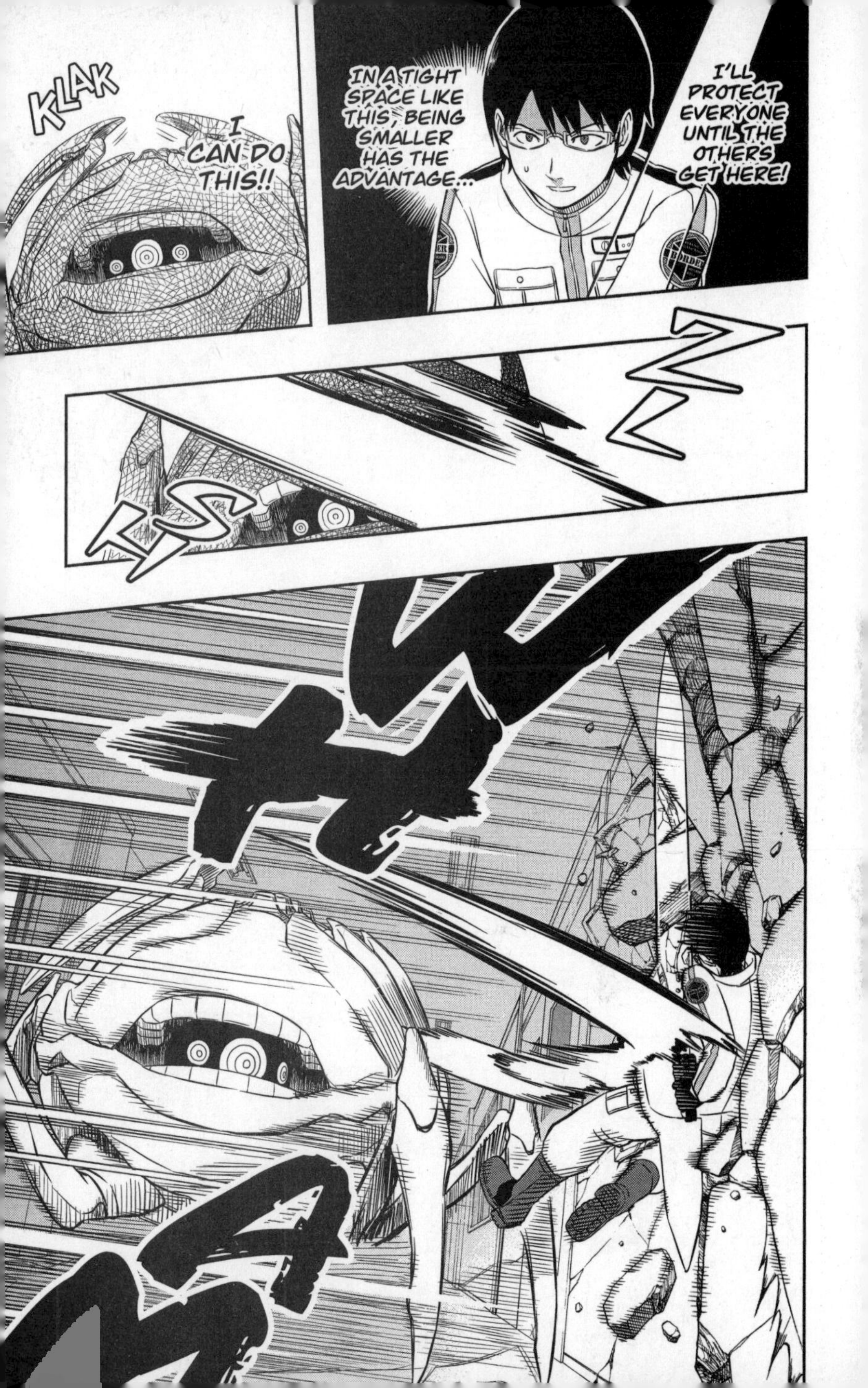
I'LL PROTECT EVERYONE UNTIL THE OTHERS GET HERE!
IN A TIGHT SPACE LIKE THIS, BEING SMALLER HAS THE ADVANTAGE...
KLAK
I CAN DO THIS!!

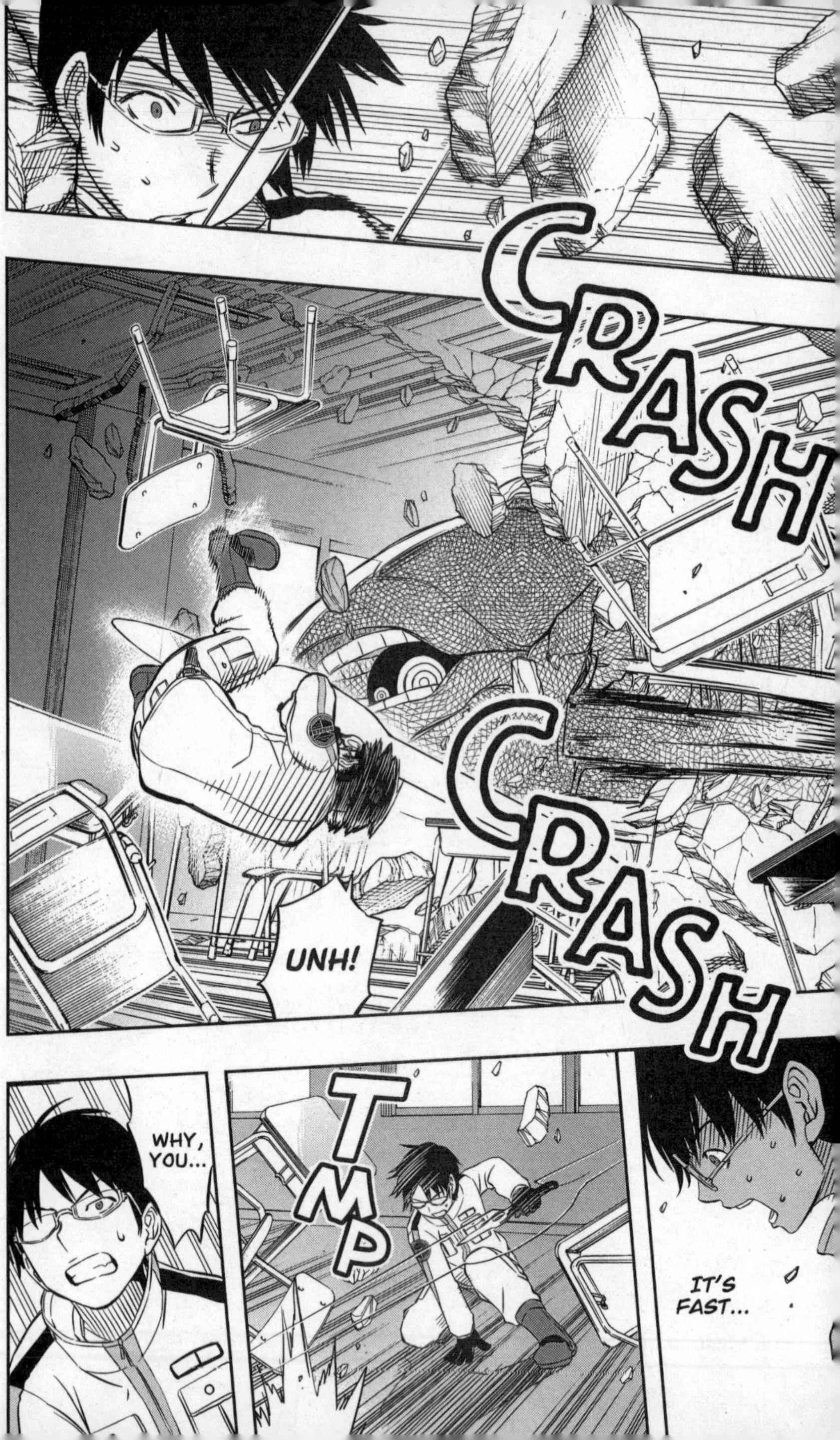
CRASH
CRASH
UNH!
IT'S FAST...
TMP
WHY, YOU...

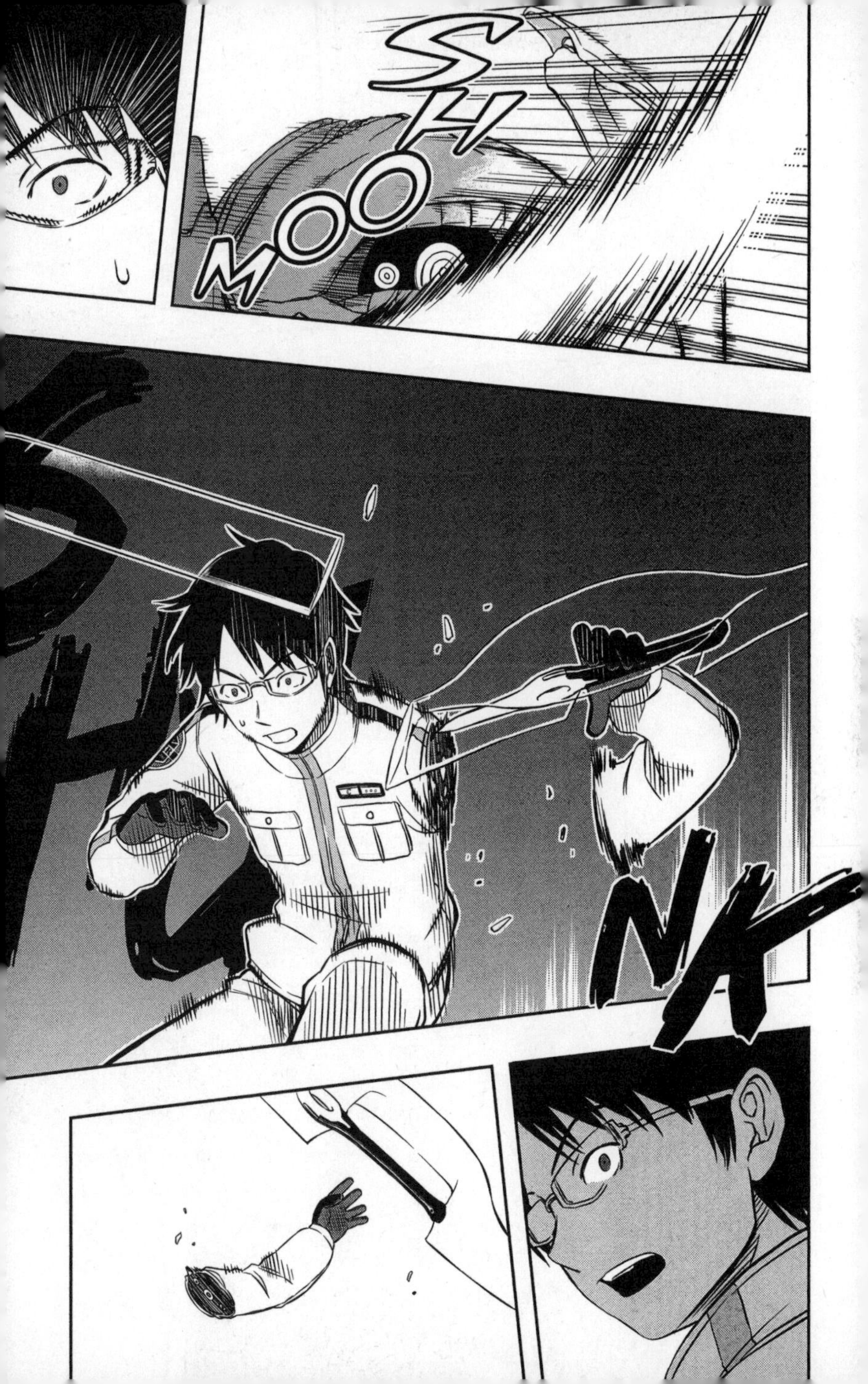
SHOOM
SHNK

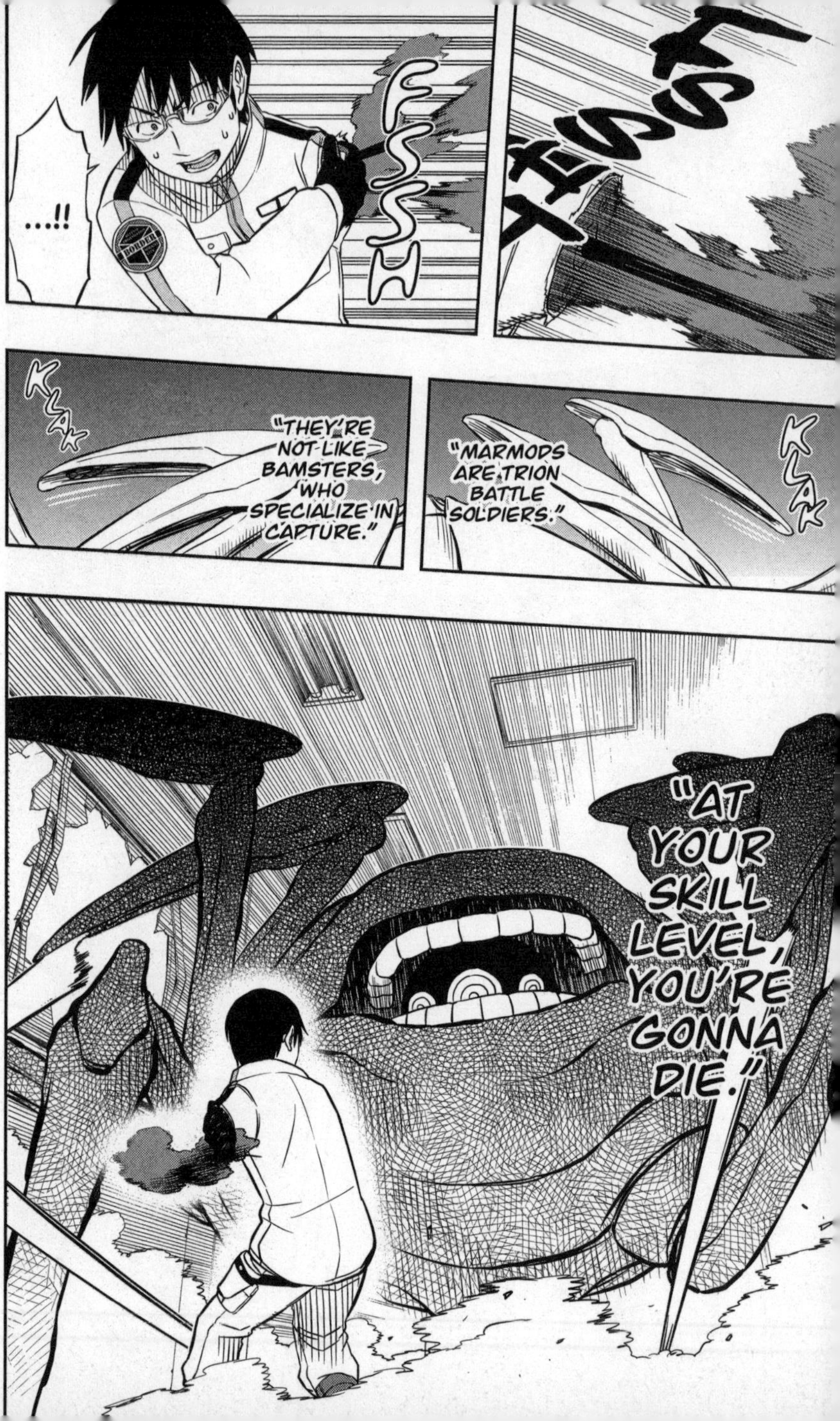
FSST
FSSH
...!!
KLAK
"MARMODS ARE TRION BATTLE SOLDIERS."
"THEY'RE NOT LIKE BAMSTERS, WHO SPECIALIZE IN CAPTURE."
KLAK
"AT YOUR SKILL LEVEL, YOU'RE GONNA DIE."

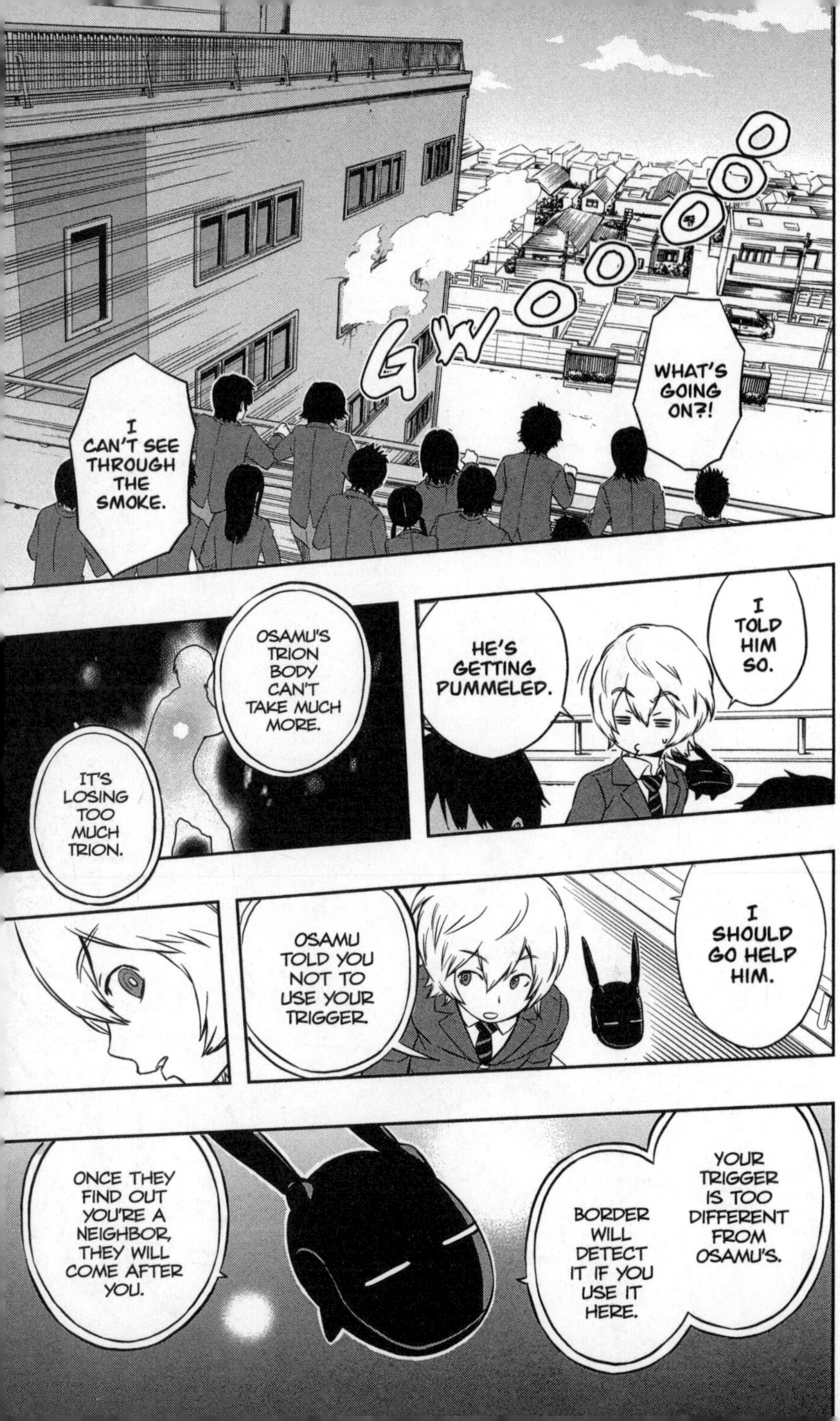
GWOOOOO
WHAT'S GOING ON?!
I CAN'T SEE THROUGH THE SMOKE.
I TOLD HIM SO.
HE'S GETTING PUMMELED.
OSAMU'S TRION BODY CAN'T TAKE MUCH MORE.
IT'S LOSING TOO MUCH TRION.
I SHOULD GO HELP HIM.
OSAMU TOLD YOU NOT TO USE YOUR TRIGGER.
YOUR TRIGGER IS TOO DIFFERENT FROM OSAMU'S.
BORDER WILL DETECT IT IF YOU USE IT HERE.
ONCE THEY FIND OUT YOU'RE A NEIGHBOR, THEY WILL COME AFTER YOU.

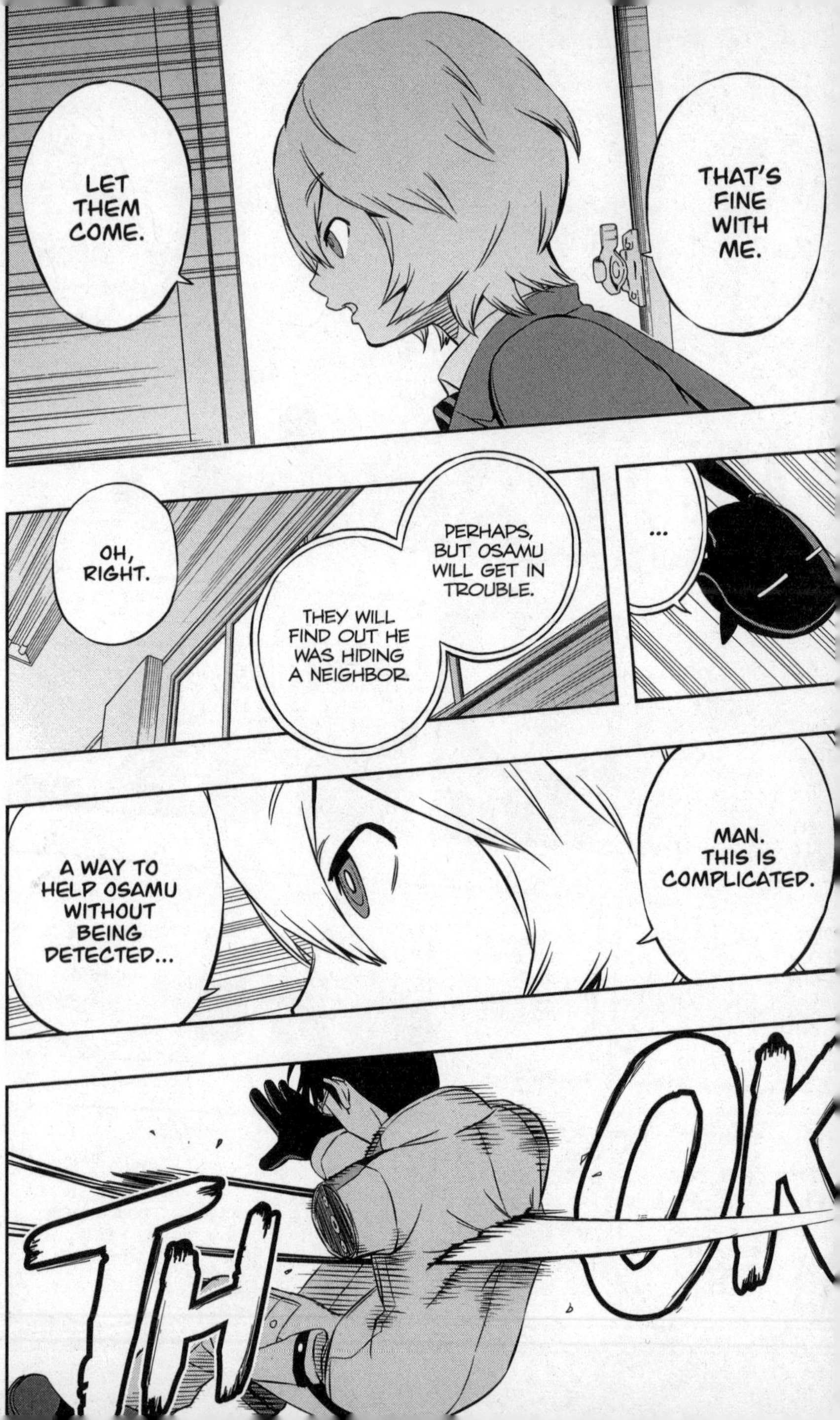
THAT'S FINE WITH ME.
LET THEM COME.
...
PERHAPS, BUT OSAMU WILL GET IN TROUBLE.
THEY WILL FIND OUT HE WAS HIDING A NEIGHBOR.
OH, RIGHT.
MAN. THIS IS COMPLICATED.
A WAY TO HELP OSAMU WITHOUT BEING DETECTED...
THOK

READ THIS WAY

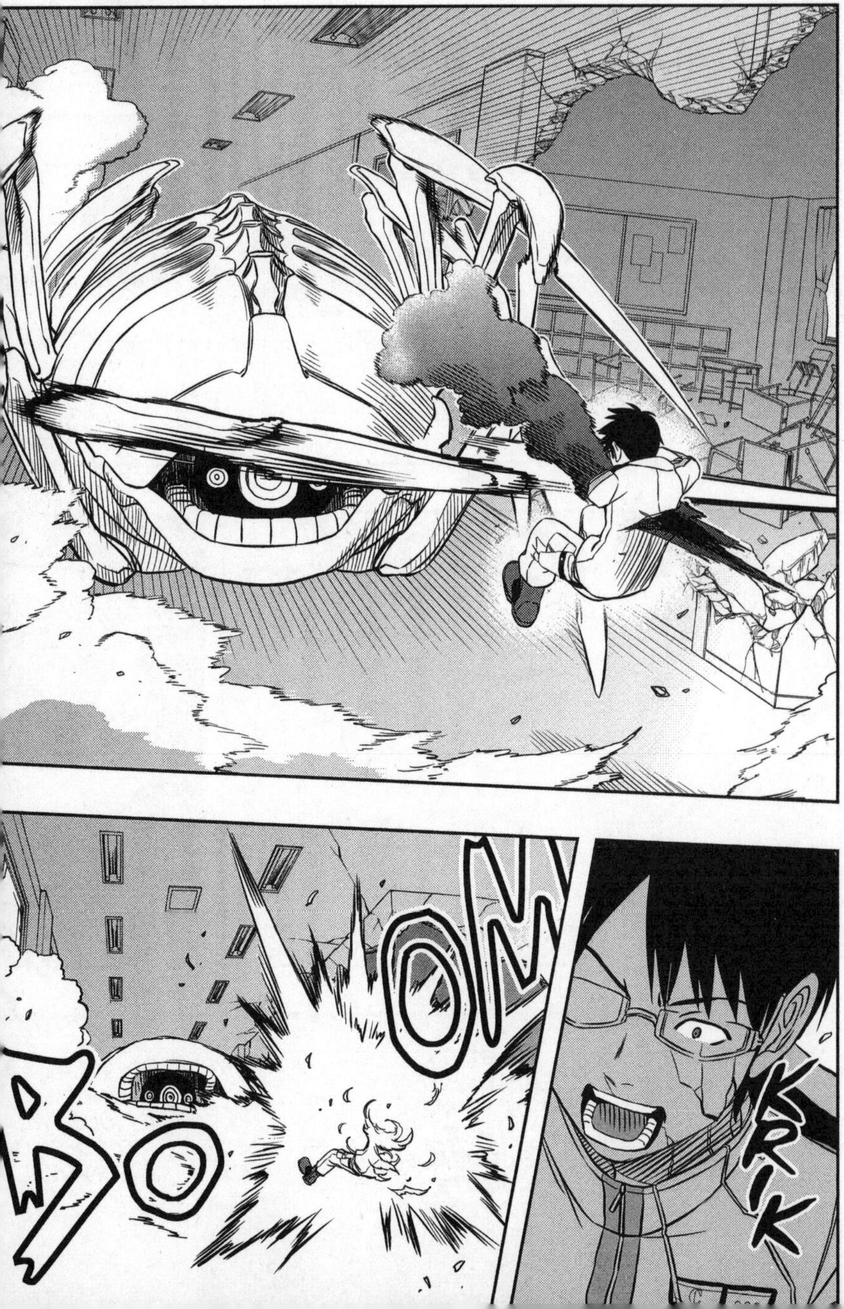
KRIK
BOOM

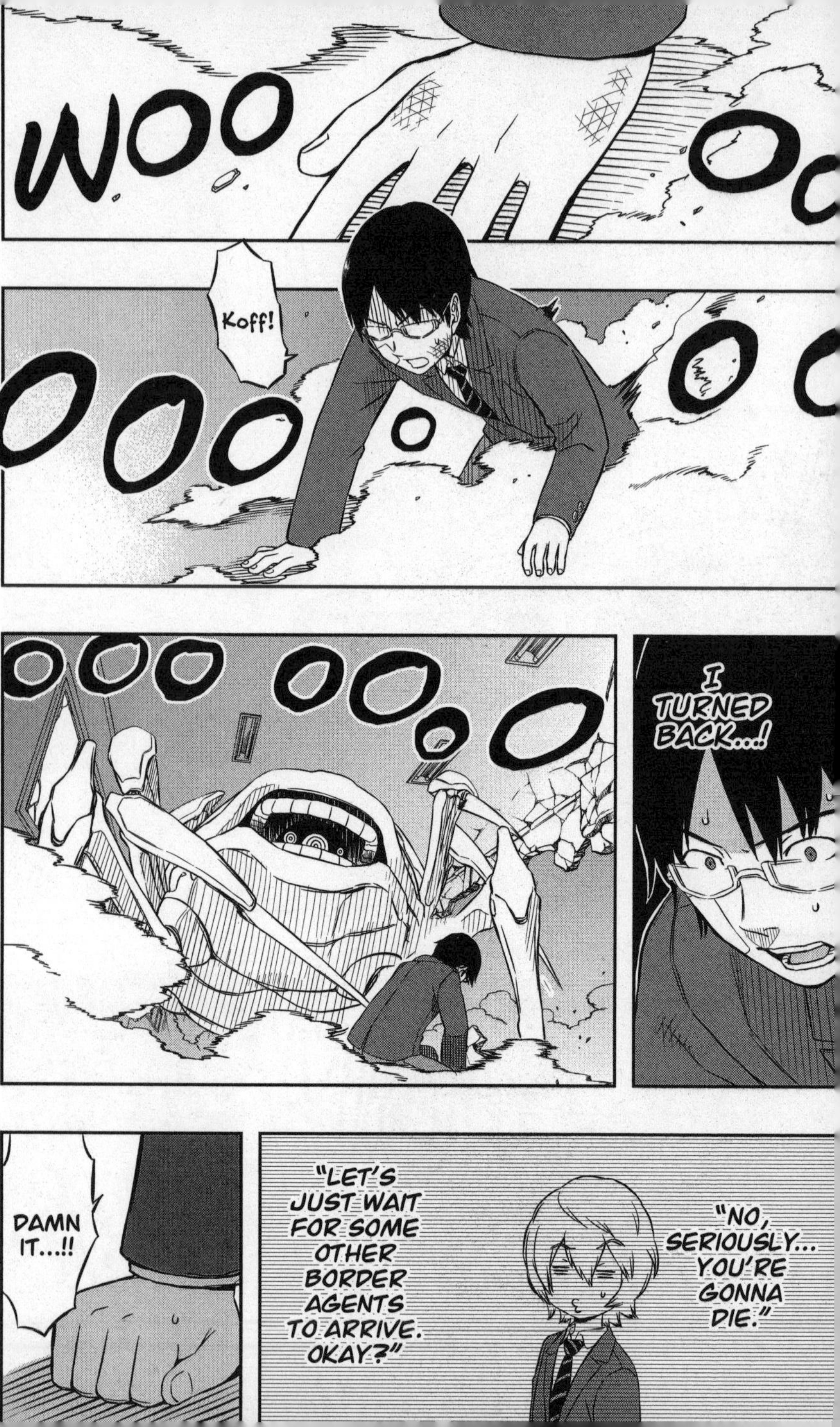

WOOOO
Koff!
OOOOOOO
I TURNED BACK...!
OOOOOOO
"NO, SERIOUSLY... YOU'RE GONNA DIE."
"LET'S JUST WAIT FOR SOME OTHER BORDER AGENTS TO ARRIVE. OKAY?"
DAMN IT...!!

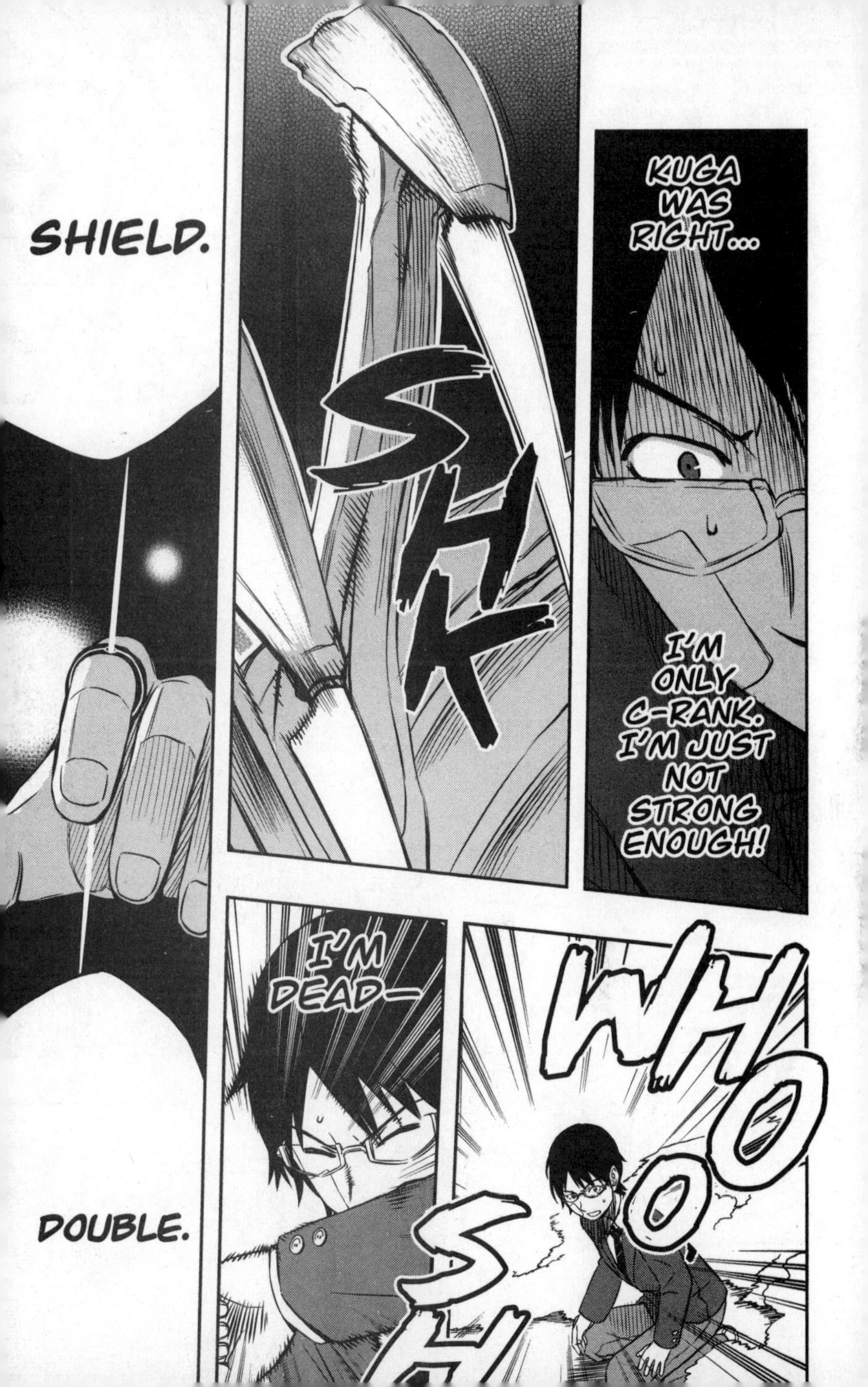
KUGA WAS RIGHT...
I'M ONLY C-RANK. I'M JUST NOT STRONG ENOUGH!
SHK
WHOOSH
I'M DEAD—
SHIELD.
DOUBLE.

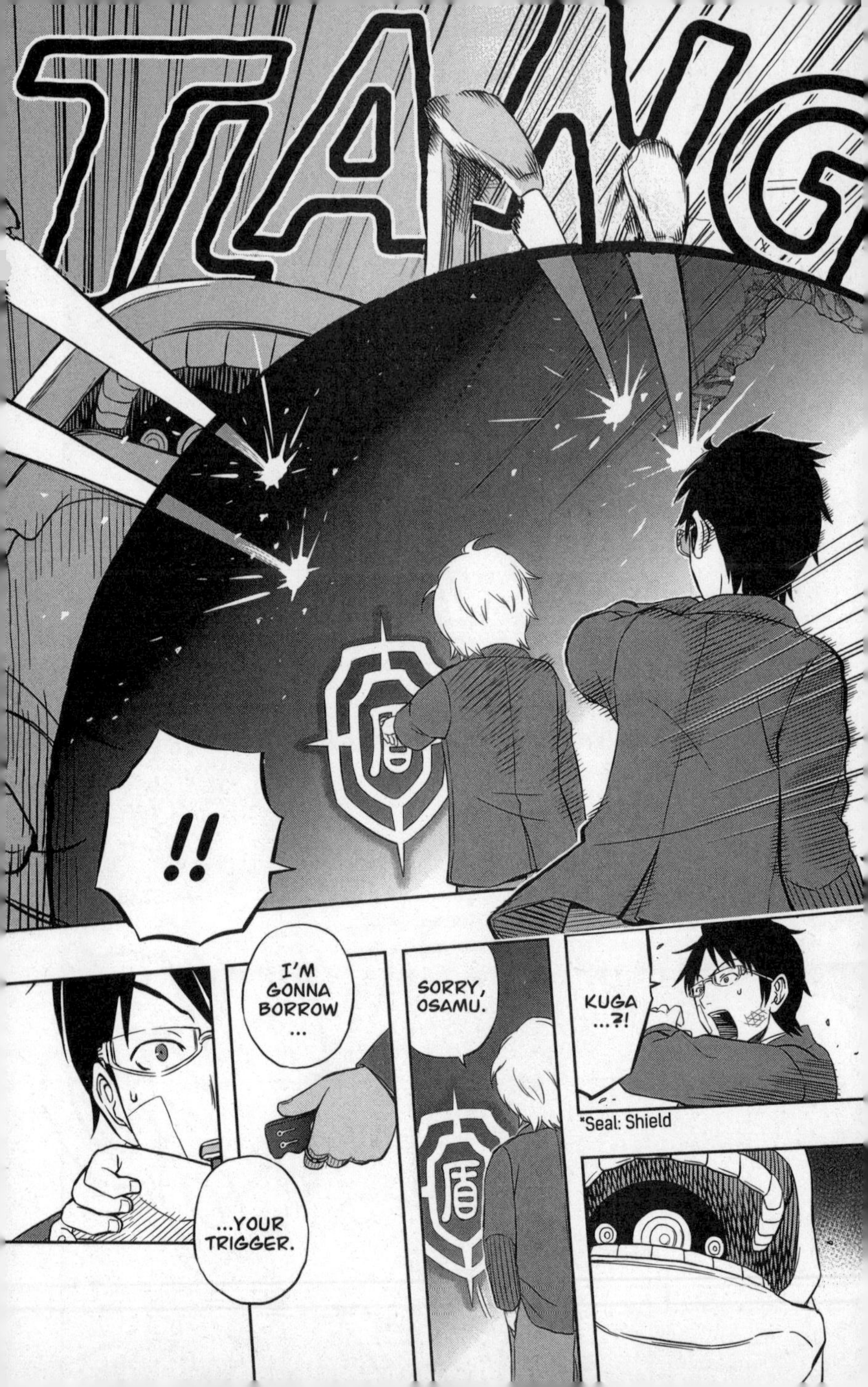
TANG
!!
KUGA ...?!
*Seal: Shield
SORRY, OSAMU.
I'M GONNA BORROW ...
...YOUR TRIGGER.

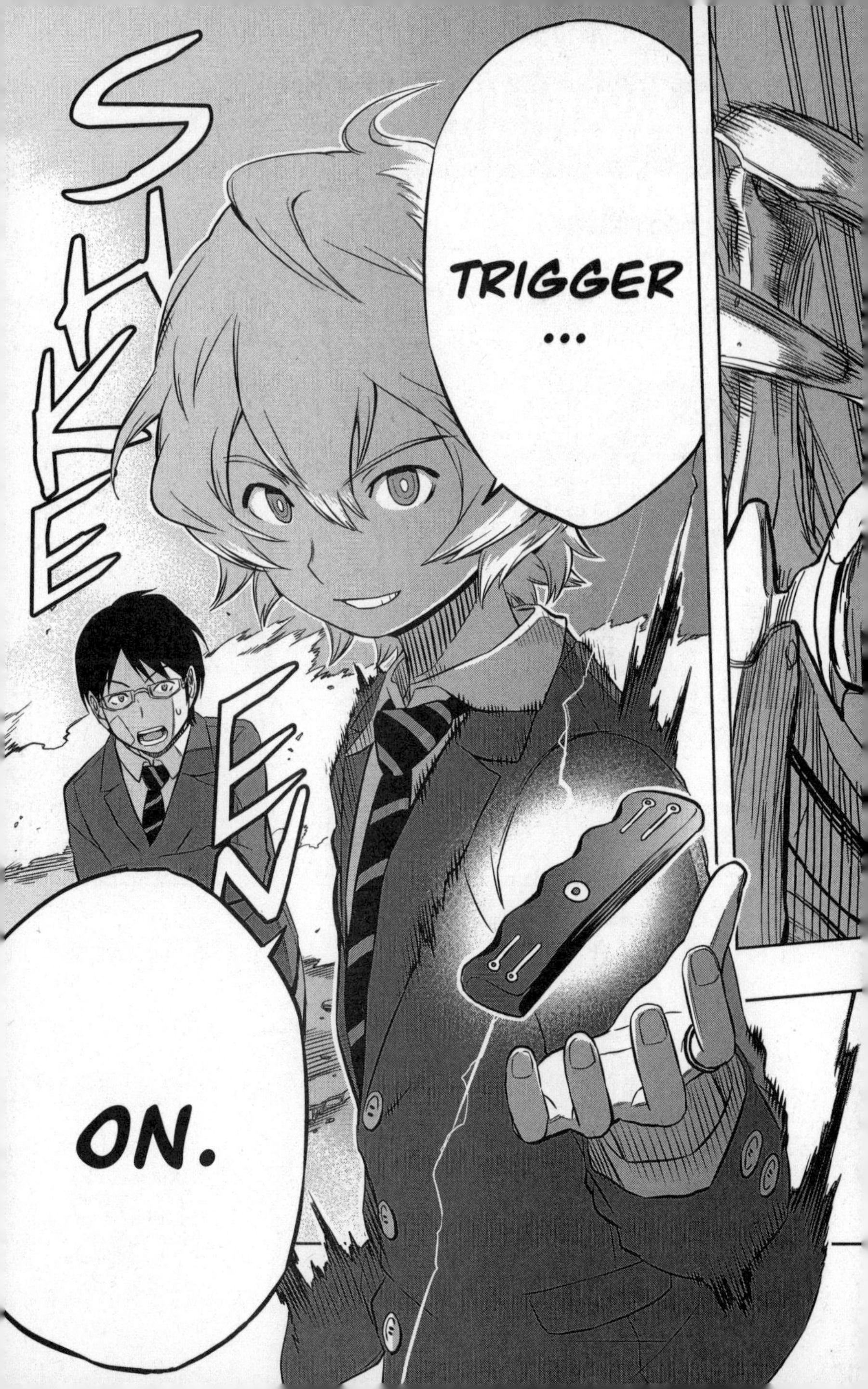
TRIGGER ...
ON.

The Lives of Bit Players: Part 2

For bit player enthusiasts. Supposedly one out of every 200 people is a "BPE."

Classmates

(Chapter 3~)

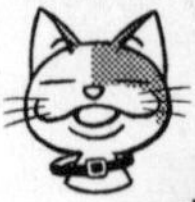

I get the feeling Osamu doesn't have many friends...

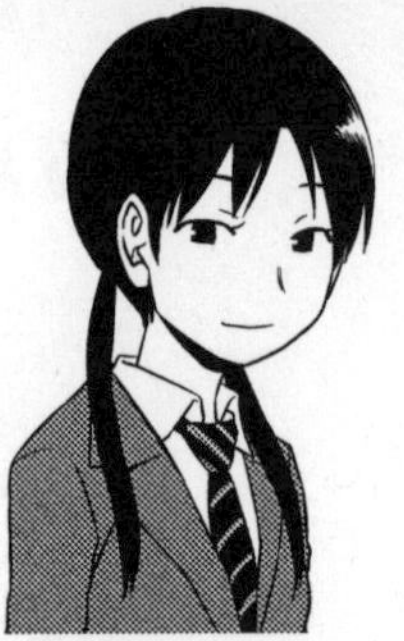

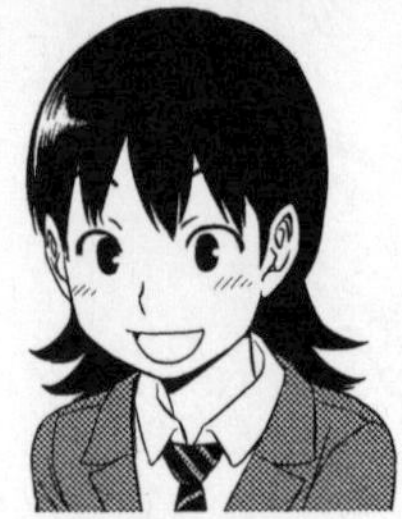

Futatsugi
Outgoing, likes celebrities. Despite appearances, she's into the arts.

Ichinose
Probably popular with the boys. Despite appearances, she's into sports.

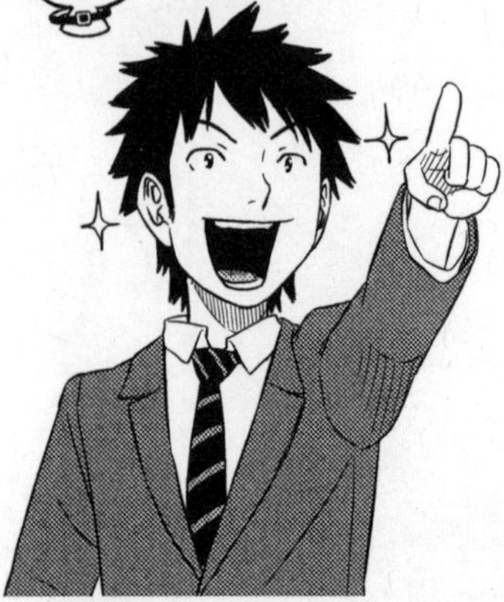

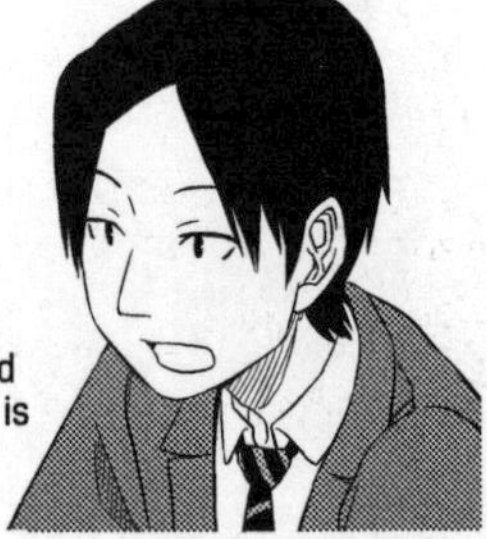

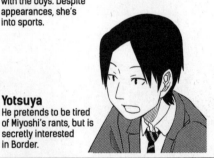

Miyoshi
A useful character who explains Border. Good luck enlisting!

Yotsuya
He pretends to be tired of Miyoshi's rants, but is secretly interested in Border.

Arashiyama's Siblings

(Chapter 6)

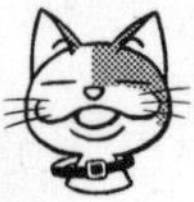

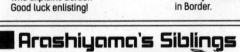

They're twins.

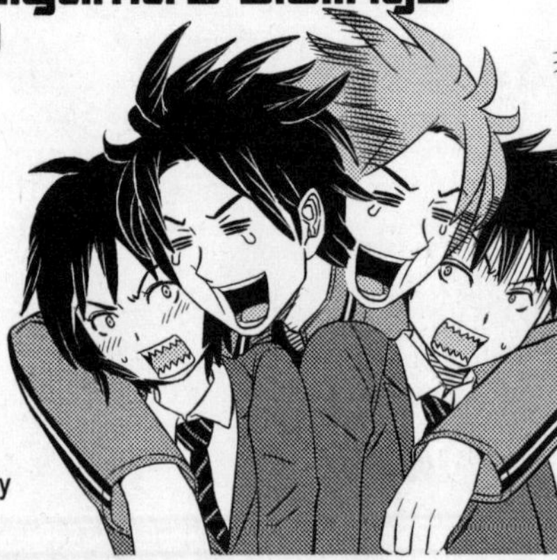

Saho
Captain of the volleyball team. In 8th grade. I hope she secretly admires her brother.

Fuku
Vice captain of the track team. In 8th grade. I hope his goal is to surpass his brother.

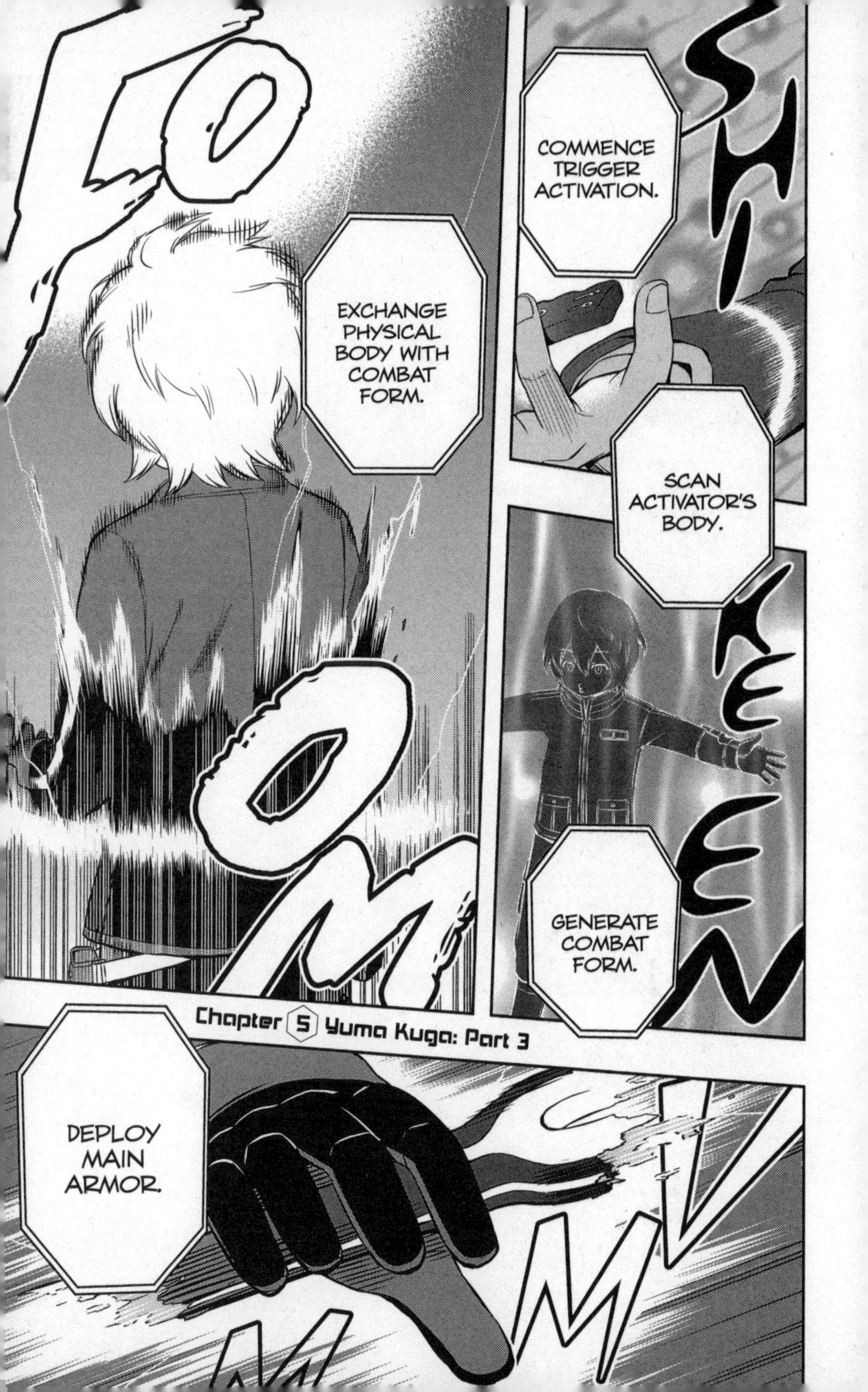

COMMENCE TRIGGER ACTIVATION.
SHII
SCAN ACTIVATOR'S BODY.
KEEN
GENERATE COMBAT FORM.
LOOM
EXCHANGE PHYSICAL BODY WITH COMBAT FORM.
Chapter 5 Yuma Kuga: Part 3
VMMM
DEPLOY MAIN ARMOR.

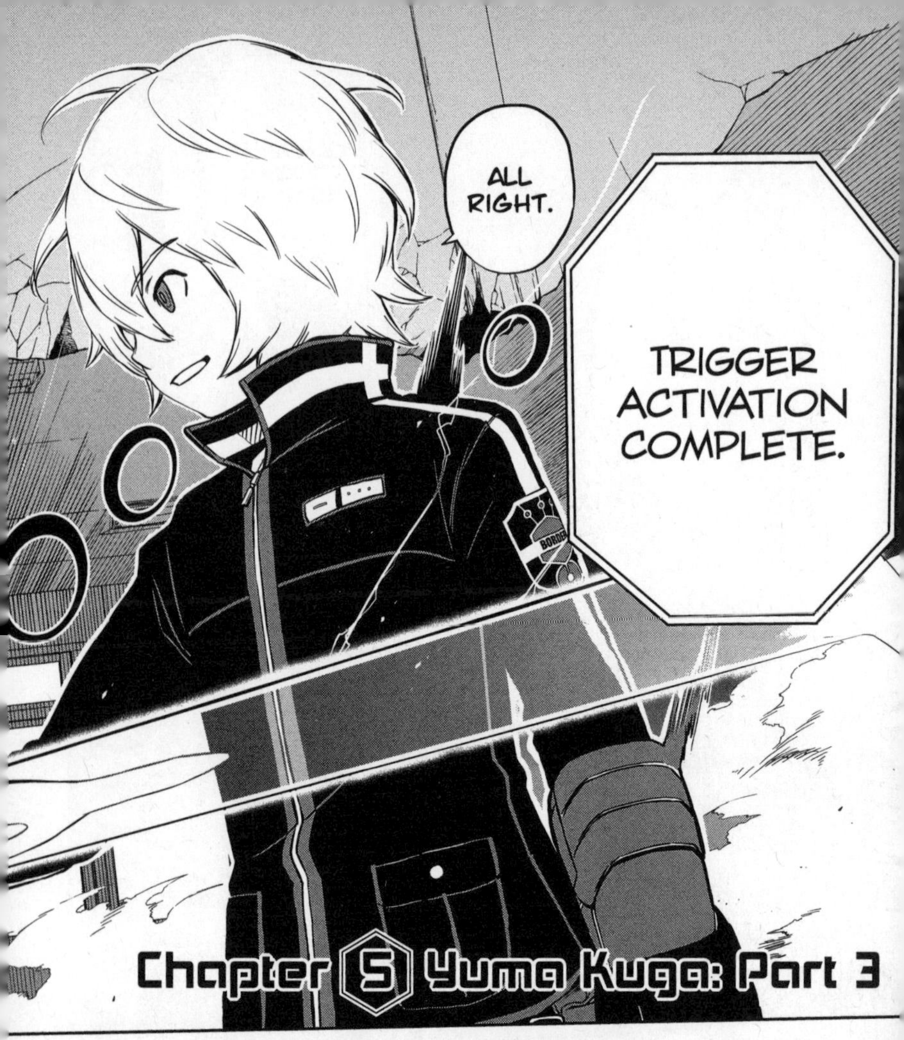
TRIGGER ACTIVATION COMPLETE.
ALL RIGHT.
Chapter 5 Yuma Kuga: Part 3
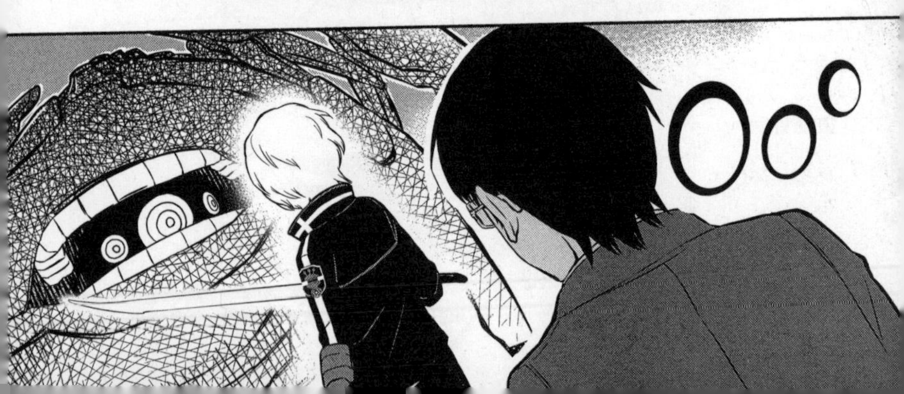

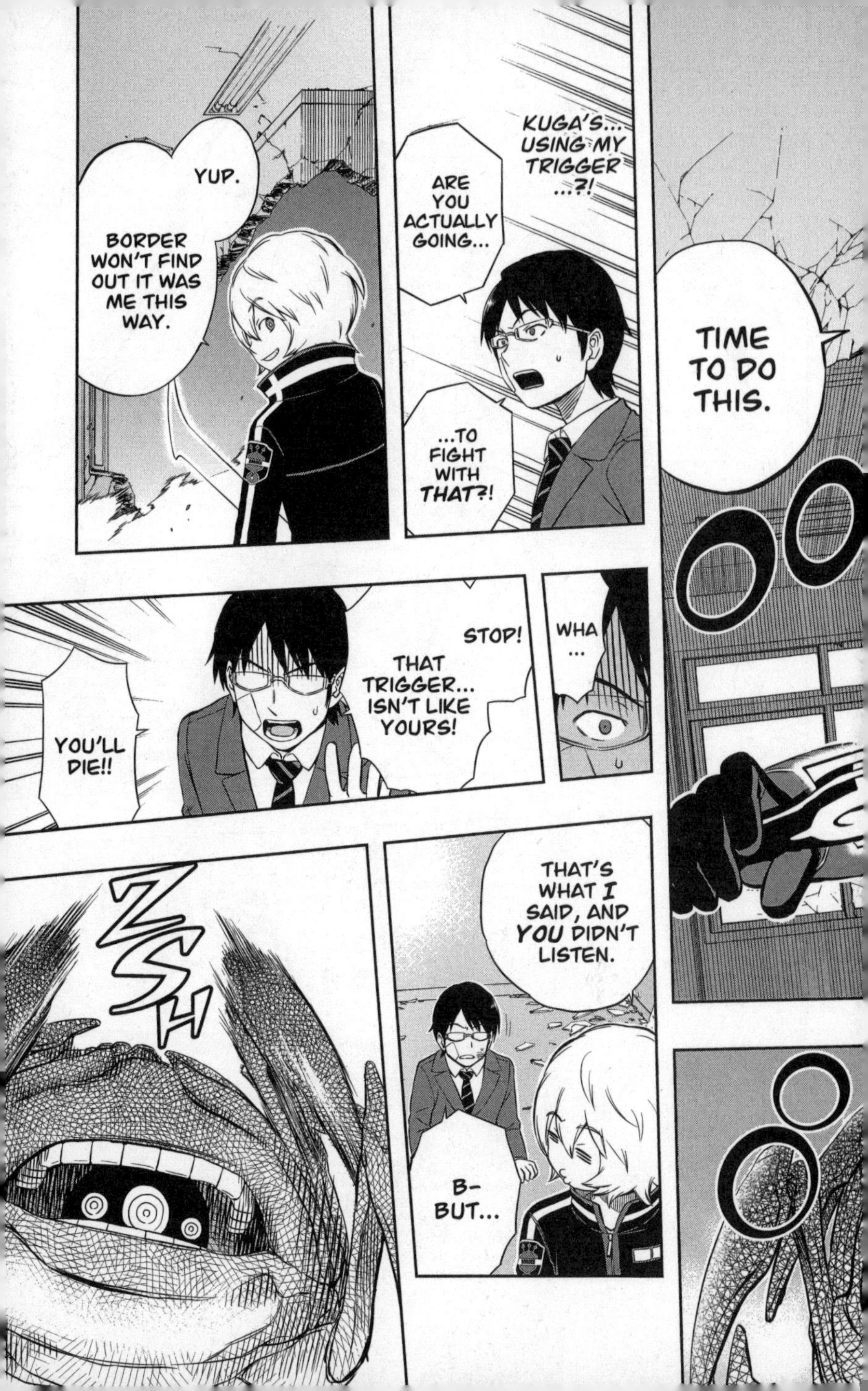
TIME TO DO THIS.
KUGA'S... USING MY TRIGGER ...?!
ARE YOU ACTUALLY GOING...
...TO FIGHT WITH THAT?!
YUP.
BORDER WON'T FIND OUT IT WAS ME THIS WAY.
WHA ...
STOP!
THAT TRIGGER... ISN'T LIKE YOURS!
YOU'LL DIE!!
THAT'S WHAT I SAID, AND YOU DIDN'T LISTEN.
B- BUT...
ZSH

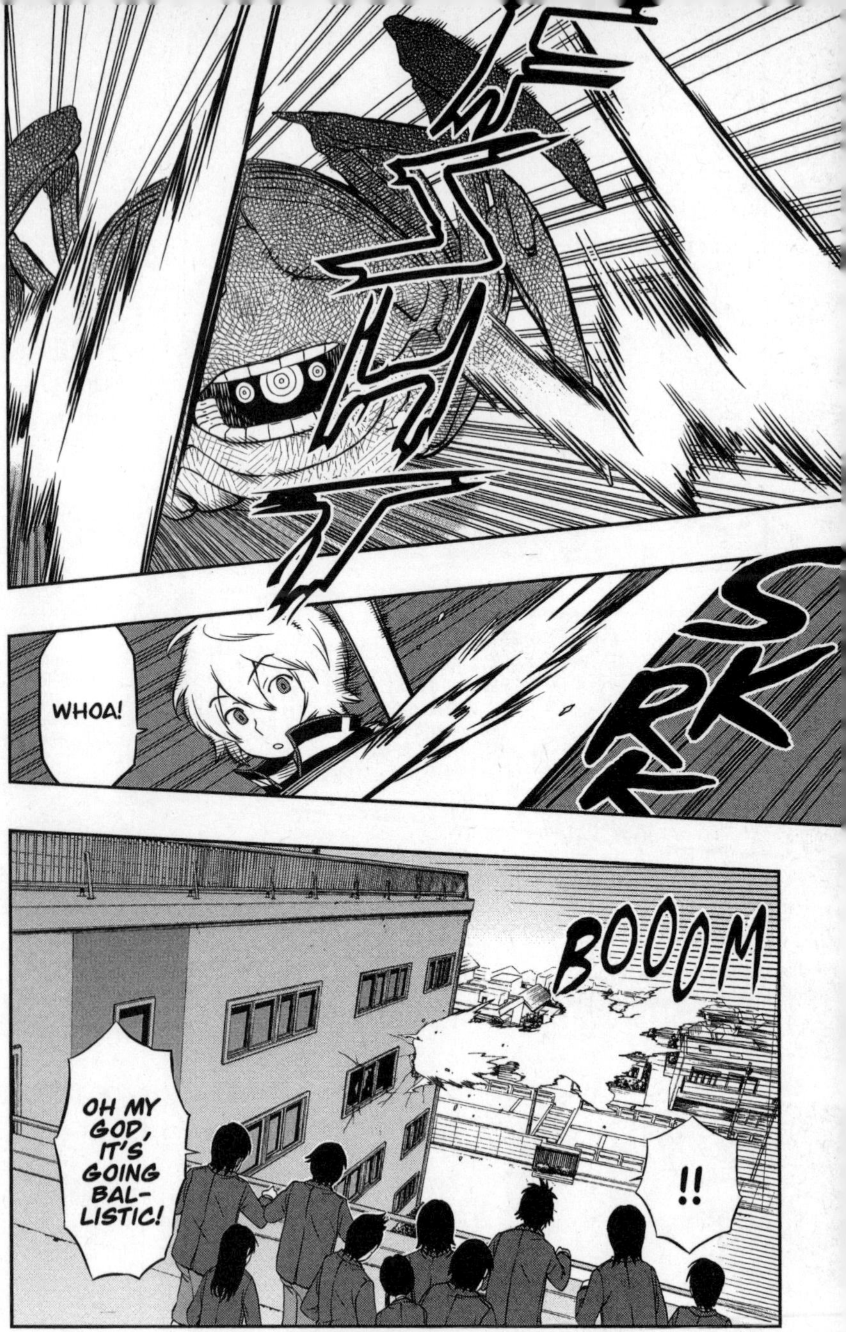
SRK
WHOA!
BOOOM
!!
OH MY GOD, IT'S GOING BAL-LISTIC!

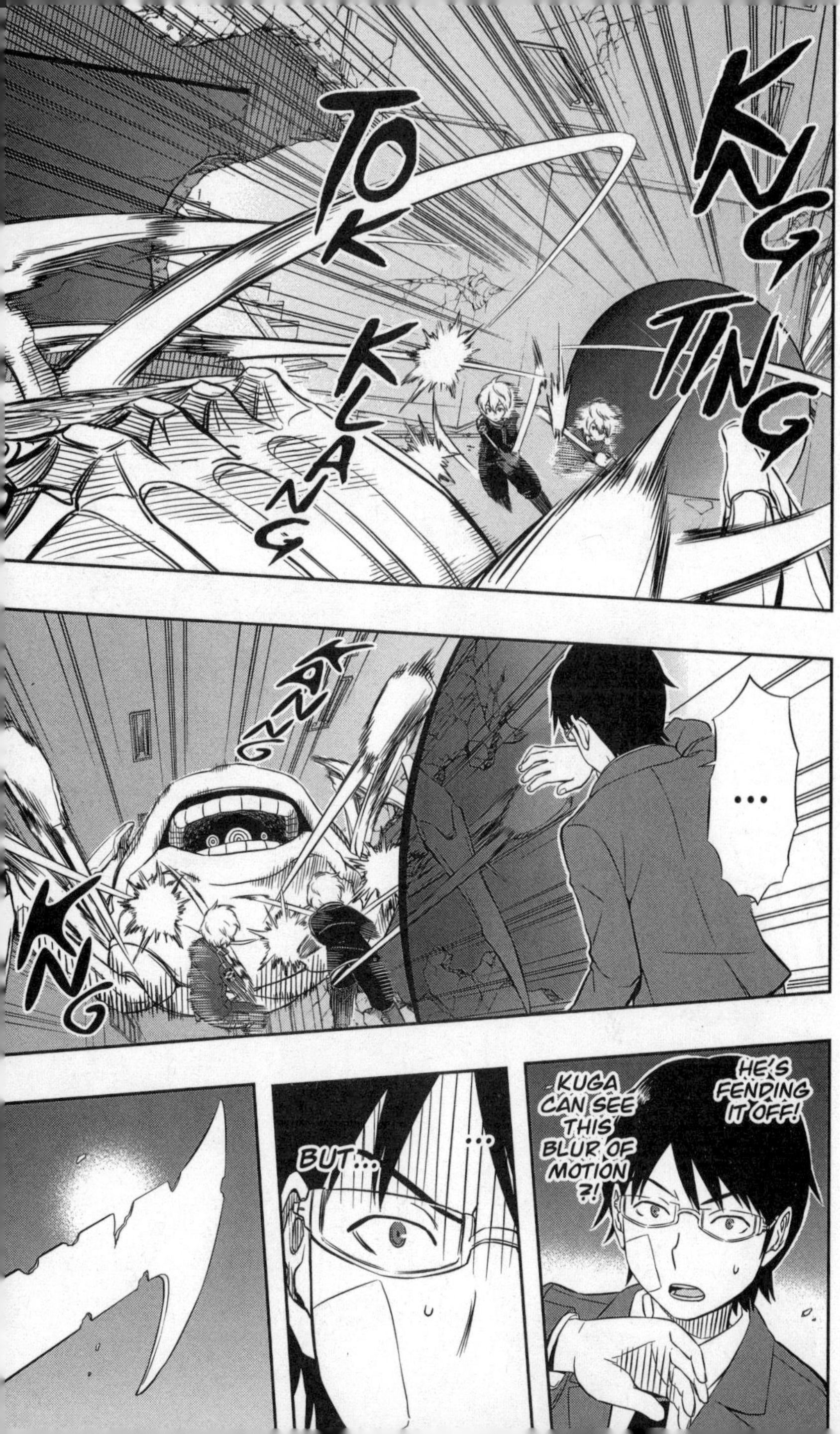
KNG
TING
TOK
KLANG
...
KANNG
KNG
HE'S FENDING IT OFF!
KUGA CAN SEE THIS BLUR OF MOTION ?!
...
BUT...

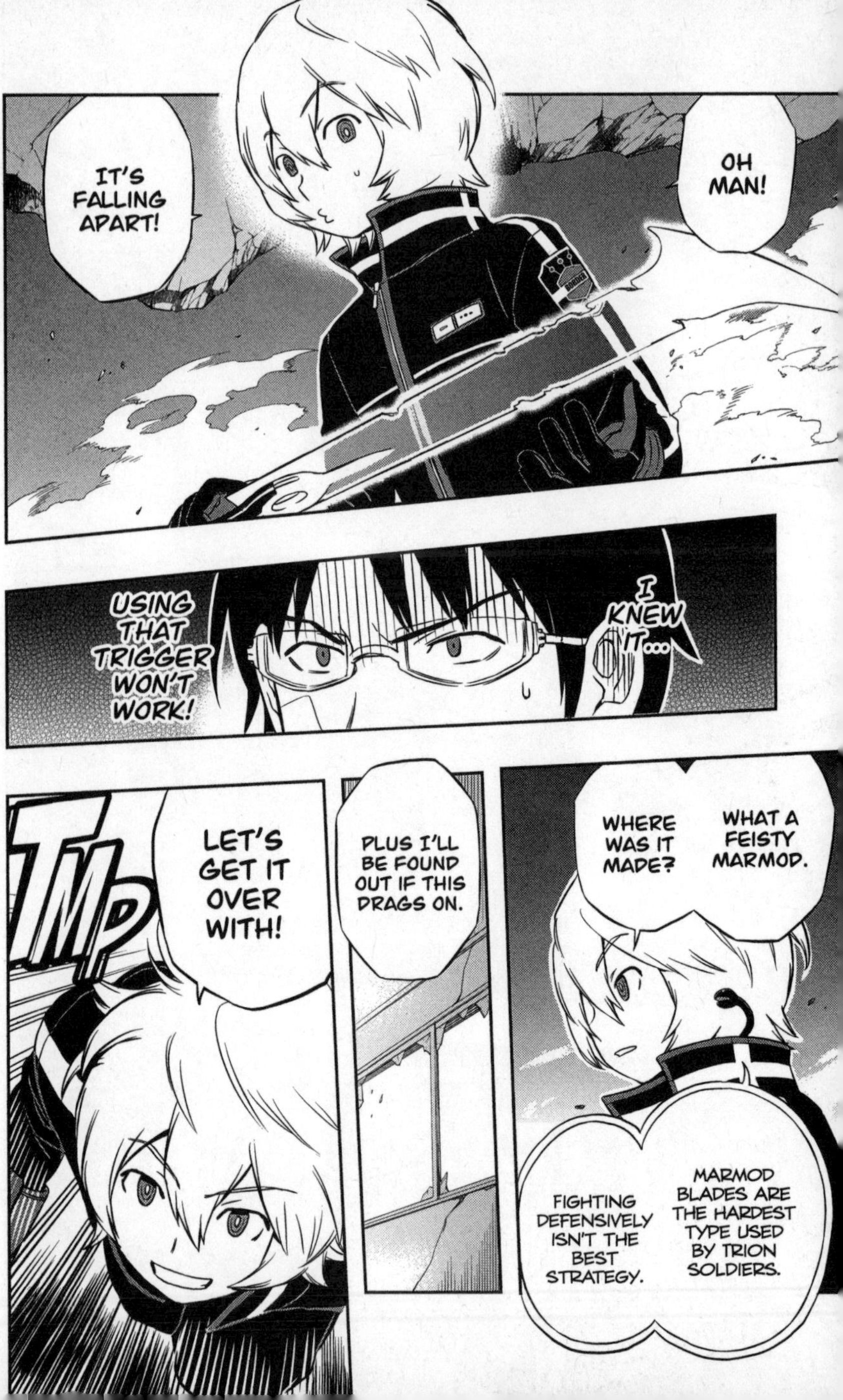
OH MAN!
IT'S FALLING APART!
I KNEW IT...
USING THAT TRIGGER WON'T WORK!
WHAT A FEISTY MARMOD.
WHERE WAS IT MADE?
MARMOD BLADES ARE THE HARDEST TYPE USED BY TRION SOLDIERS.
FIGHTING DEFENSIVELY ISN'T THE BEST STRATEGY.
PLUS I'LL BE FOUND OUT IF THIS DRAGS ON.
LET'S GET IT OVER WITH!

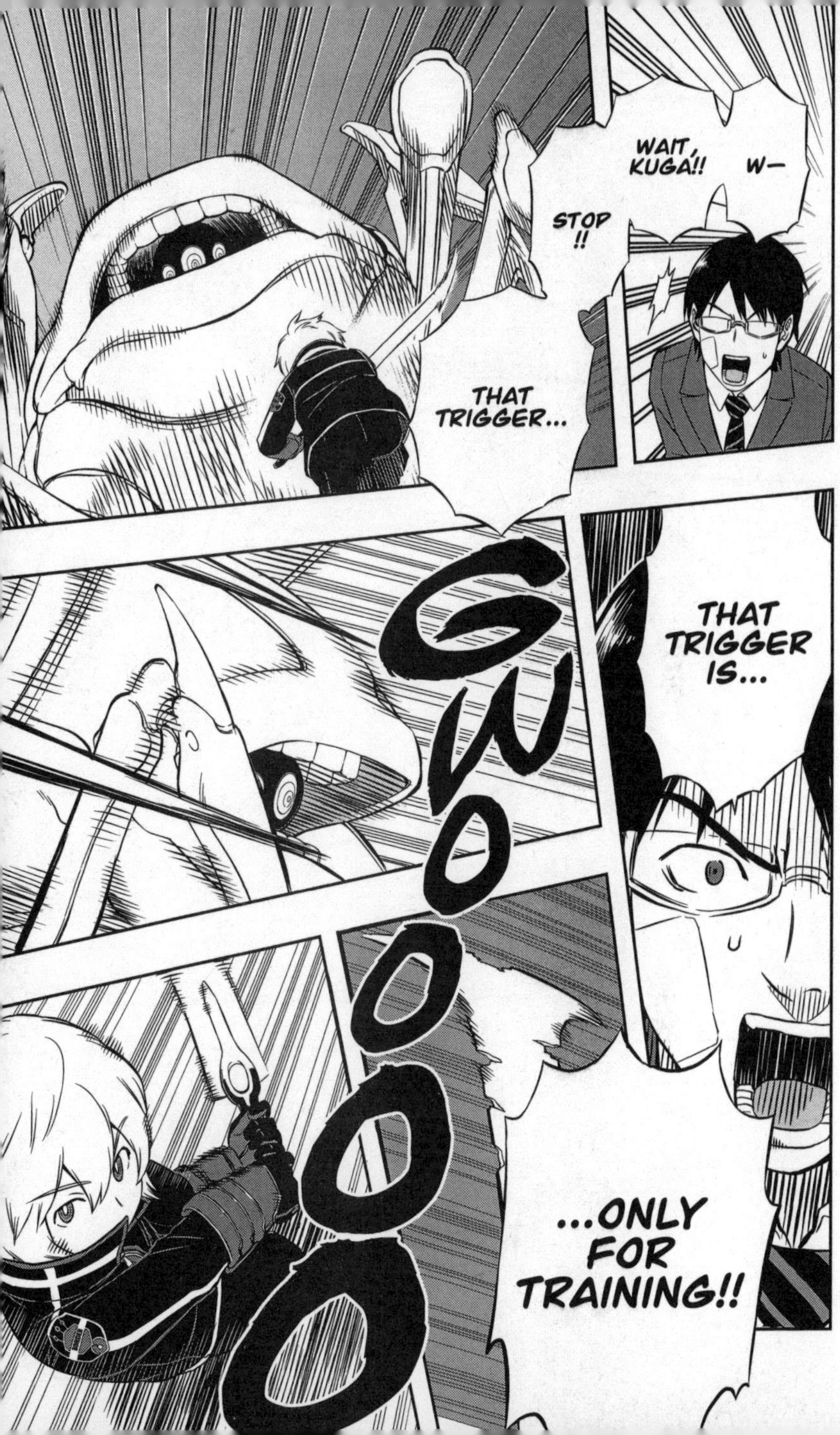
WAIT, KUGA!!
W—
STOP!!
THAT TRIGGER...
THAT TRIGGER IS...
...ONLY FOR TRAINING!!
GWOOOOO

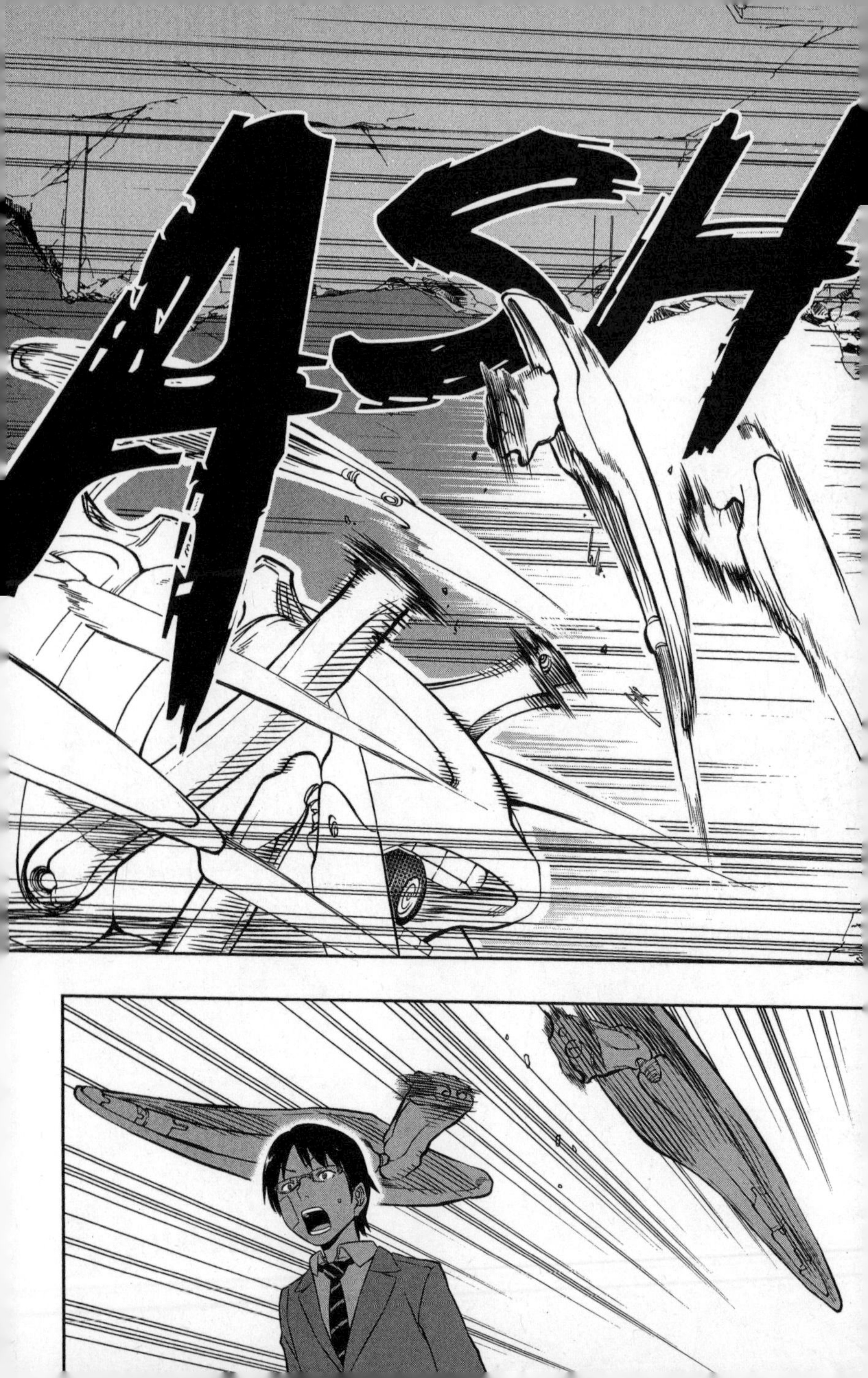
ASH

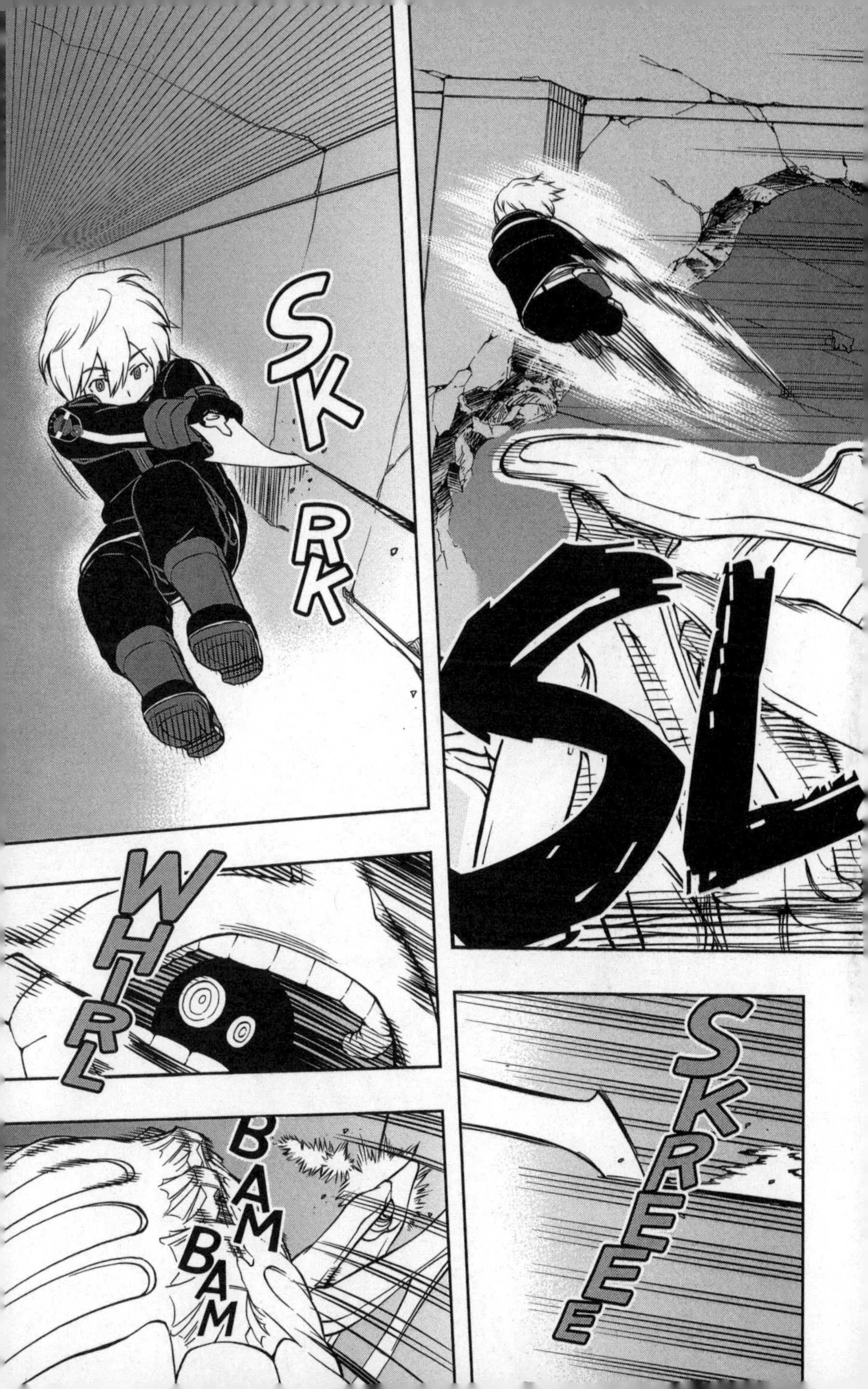
SL
SKRK
WHIRL
SKREEE
BAM BAM

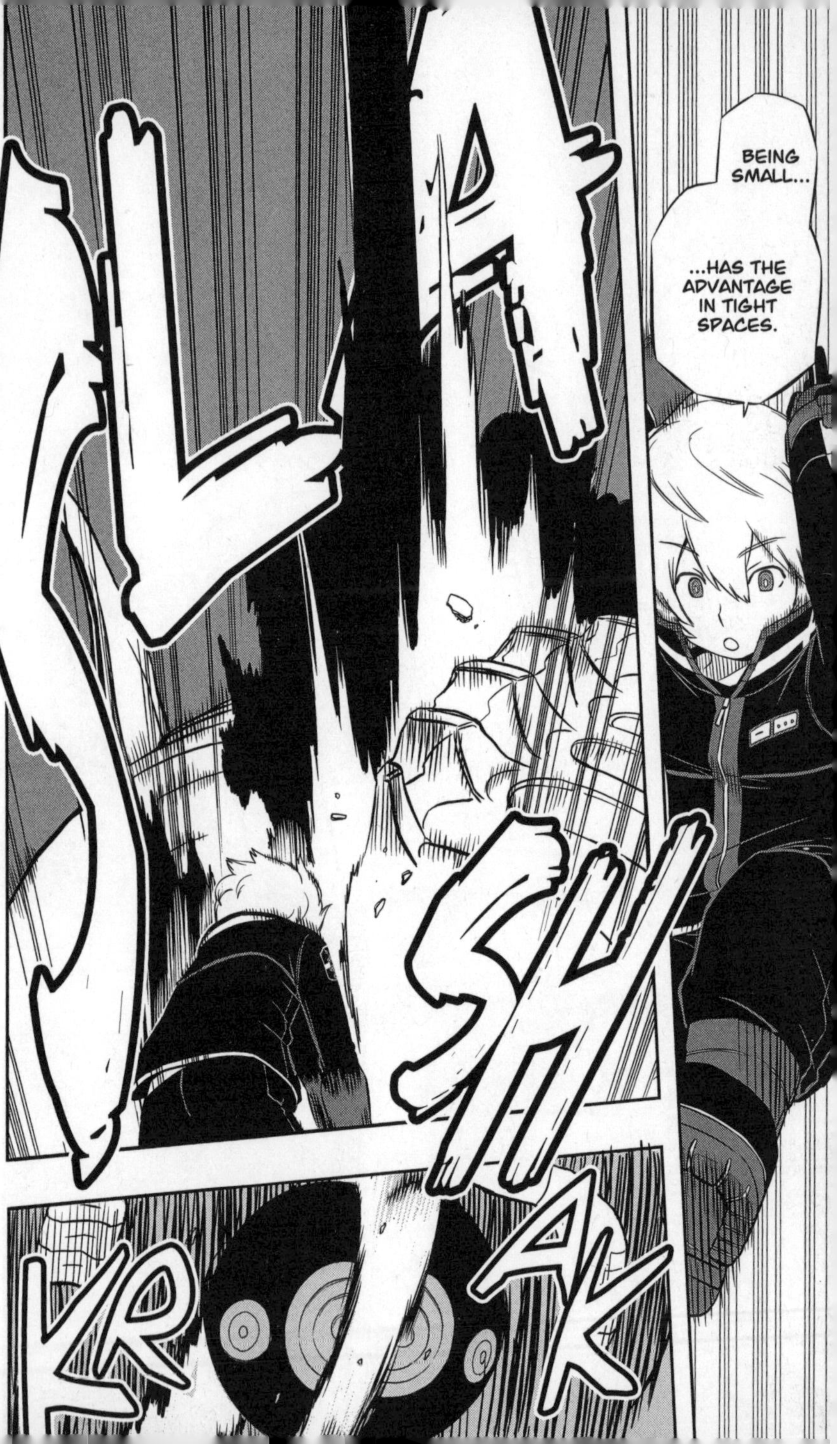
BEING SMALL...
...HAS THE ADVANTAGE IN TIGHT SPACES.

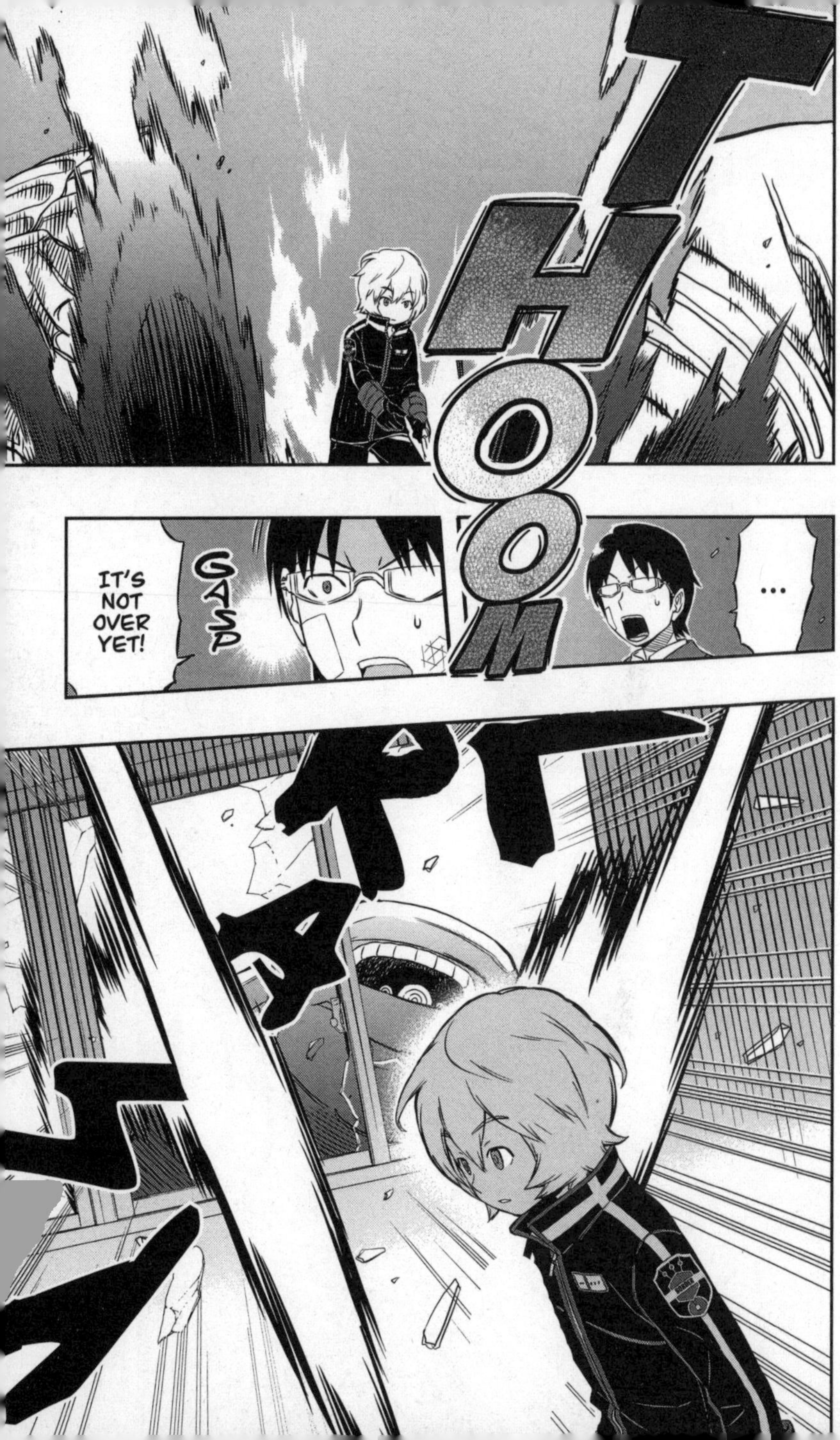
THOOM
...
GASP
IT'S NOT OVER YET!

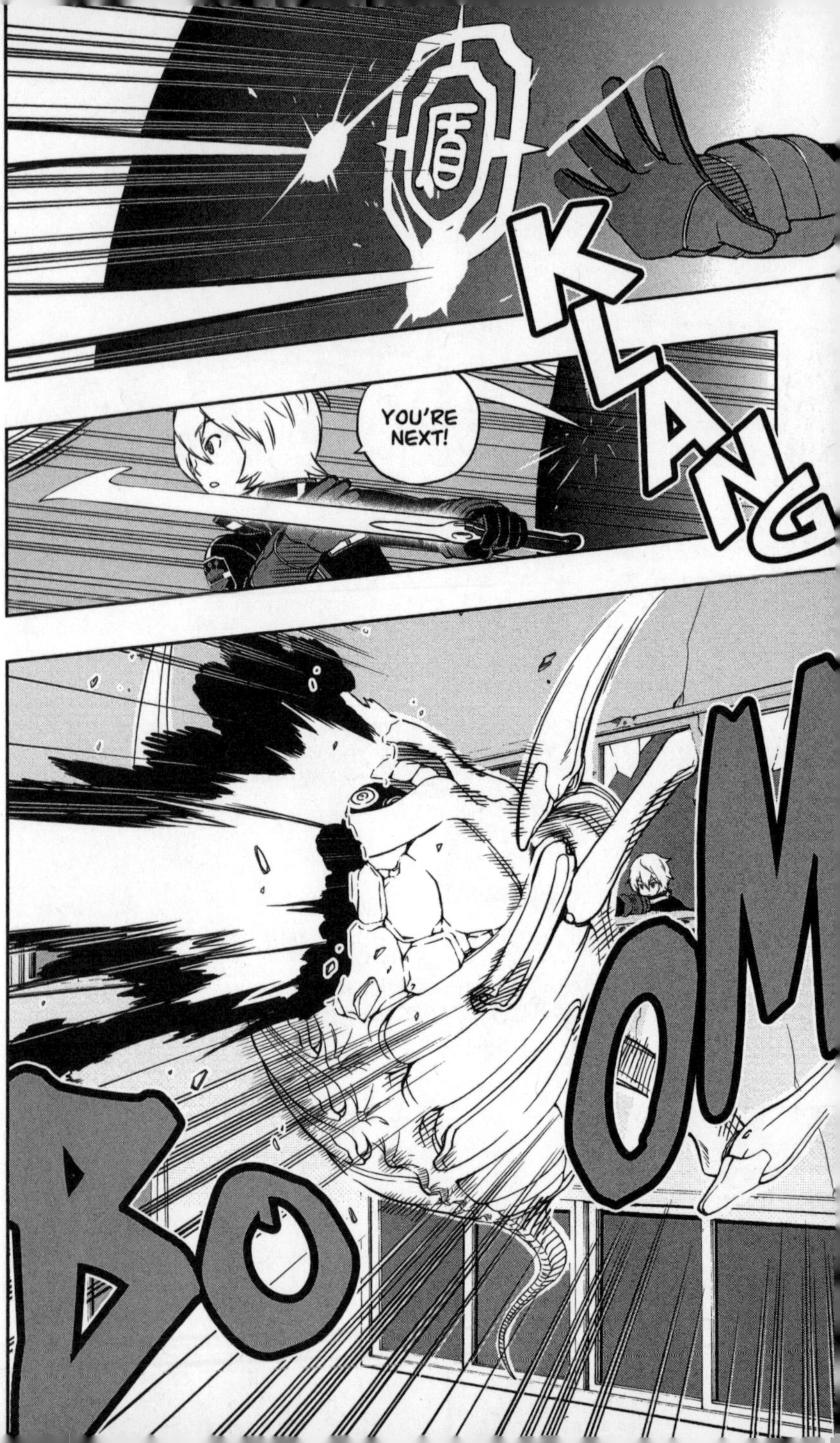
盾
KLANG
YOU'RE NEXT!
BOOM

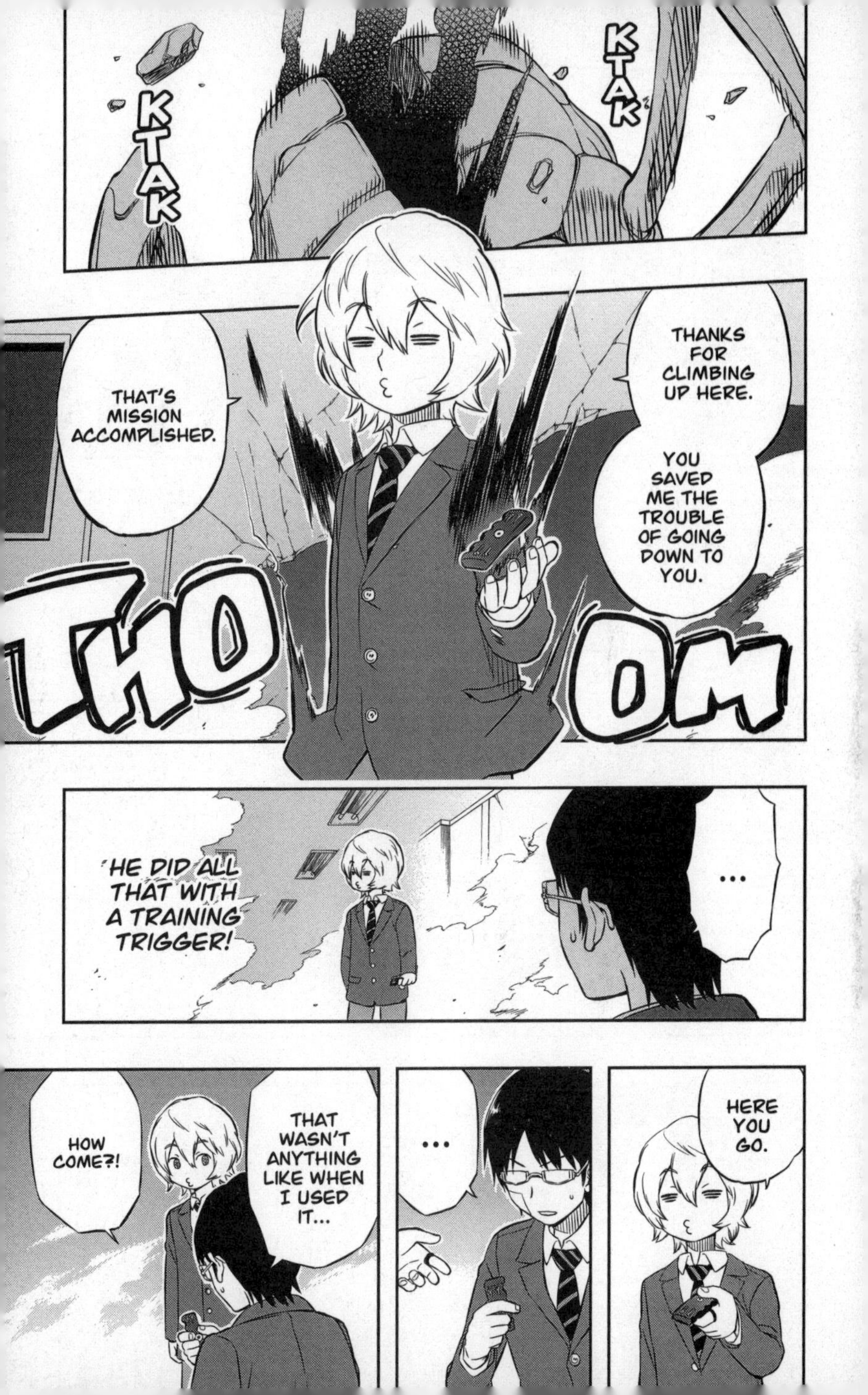
KTAK
KTAK
THANKS FOR CLIMBING UP HERE.
YOU SAVED ME THE TROUBLE OF GOING DOWN TO YOU.
THAT'S MISSION ACCOMPLISHED.
THOOM
...
HE DID ALL THAT WITH A TRAINING TRIGGER!
HERE YOU GO.
...
THAT WASN'T ANYTHING LIKE WHEN I USED IT...
HOW COME?!

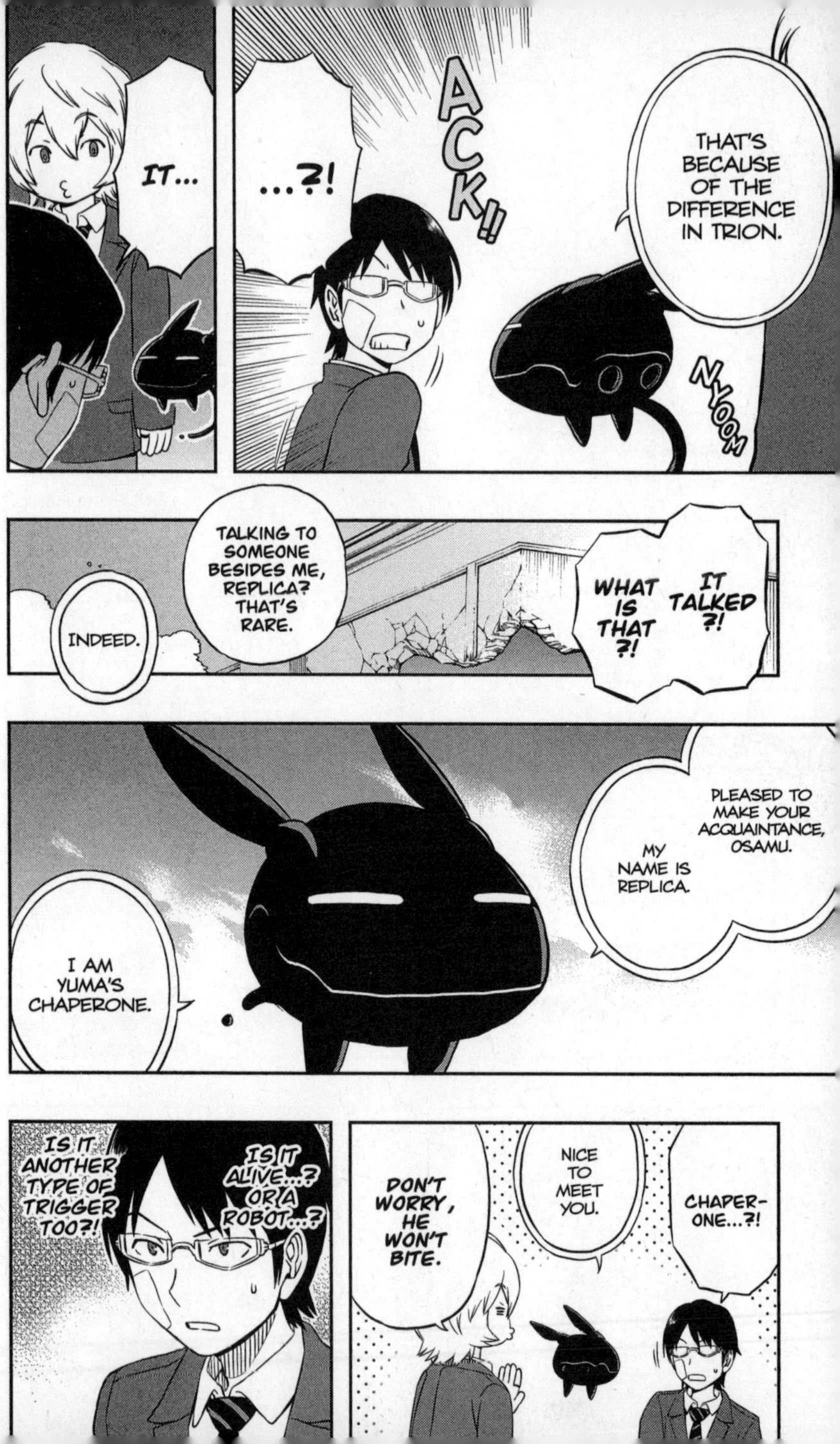
THAT'S BECAUSE OF THE DIFFERENCE IN TRION.
NYOOM
ACK!!
...?!
IT...
IT TALKED ?!
WHAT IS THAT ?!
TALKING TO SOMEONE BESIDES ME, REPLICA? THAT'S RARE.
INDEED.
PLEASED TO MAKE YOUR ACQUAINTANCE, OSAMU.
MY NAME IS REPLICA.
I AM YUMA'S CHAPERONE.
CHAPER-ONE...?!
NICE TO MEET YOU.
DON'T WORRY, HE WON'T BITE.
IS IT ALIVE...? OR A ROBOT...?
IS IT ANOTHER TYPE OF TRIGGER TOO?!

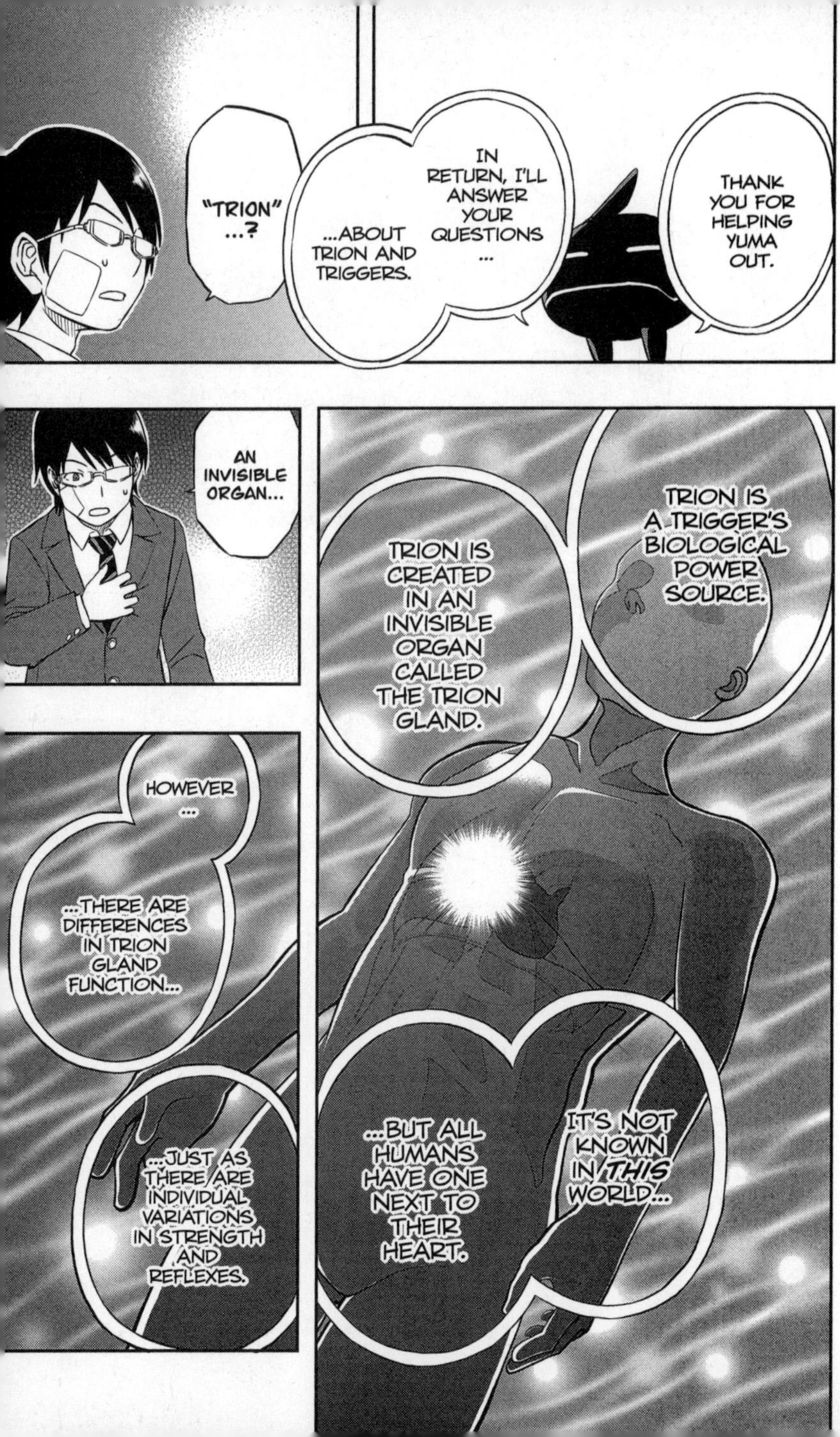
THANK YOU FOR HELPING YUMA OUT.
IN RETURN, I'LL ANSWER YOUR QUESTIONS ...
...ABOUT TRION AND TRIGGERS.
"TRION" ...?
TRION IS A TRIGGER'S BIOLOGICAL POWER SOURCE.
TRION IS CREATED IN AN INVISIBLE ORGAN CALLED THE TRION GLAND.
IT'S NOT KNOWN IN *THIS* WORLD...
...BUT ALL HUMANS HAVE ONE NEXT TO THEIR HEART.
AN INVISIBLE ORGAN...
HOWEVER ...
...THERE ARE DIFFERENCES IN TRION GLAND FUNCTION...
...JUST AS THERE ARE INDIVIDUAL VARIATIONS IN STRENGTH AND REFLEXES.

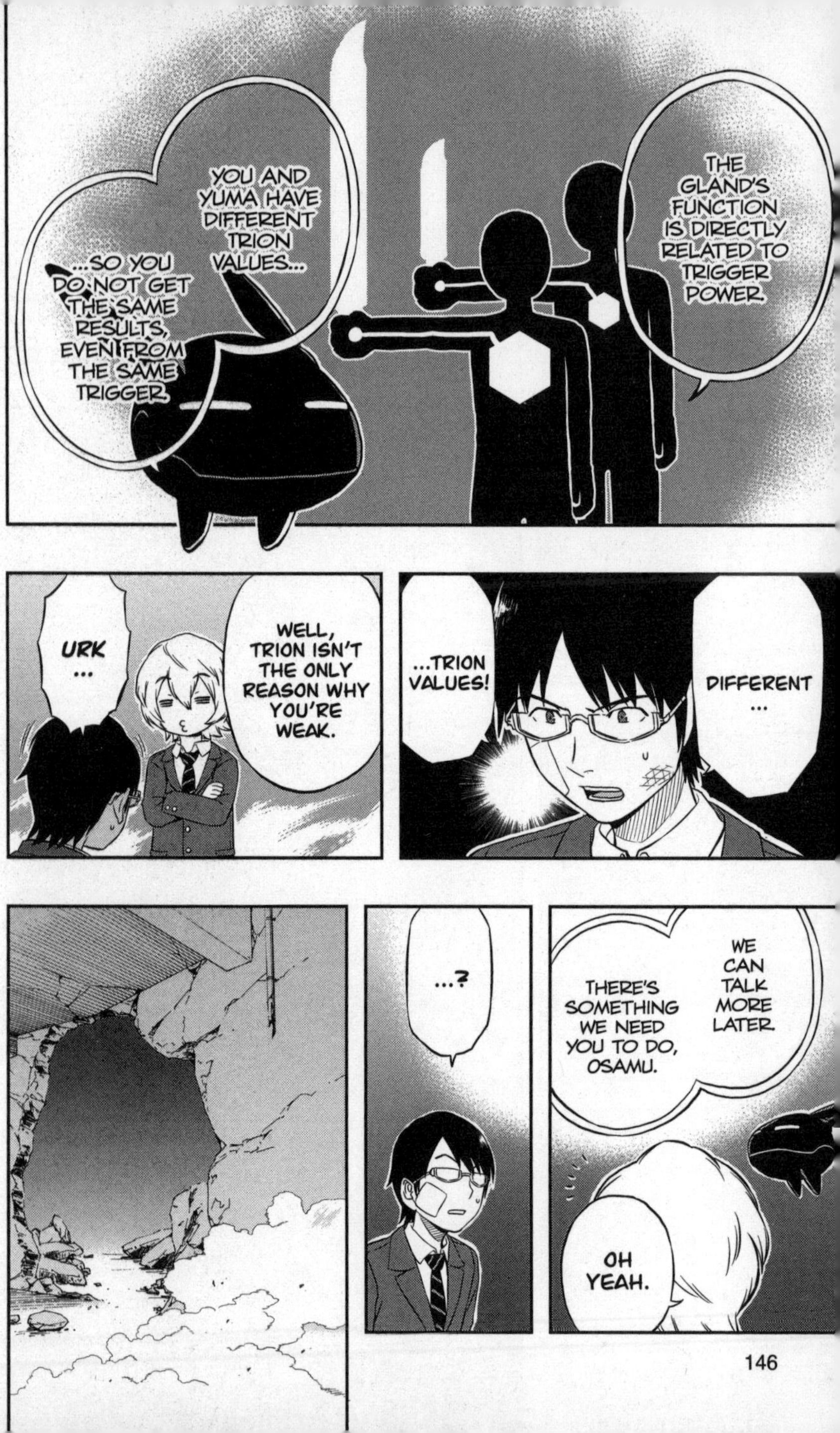
THE GLAND'S FUNCTION IS DIRECTLY RELATED TO TRIGGER POWER.
YOU AND YUMA HAVE DIFFERENT TRION VALUES...
...SO YOU DO NOT GET THE SAME RESULTS, EVEN FROM THE SAME TRIGGER.
DIFFERENT...
...TRION VALUES!
WELL, TRION ISN'T THE ONLY REASON WHY YOU'RE WEAK.
URK...
WE CAN TALK MORE LATER.
THERE'S SOMETHING WE NEED YOU TO DO, OSAMU.
OH YEAH.
...?

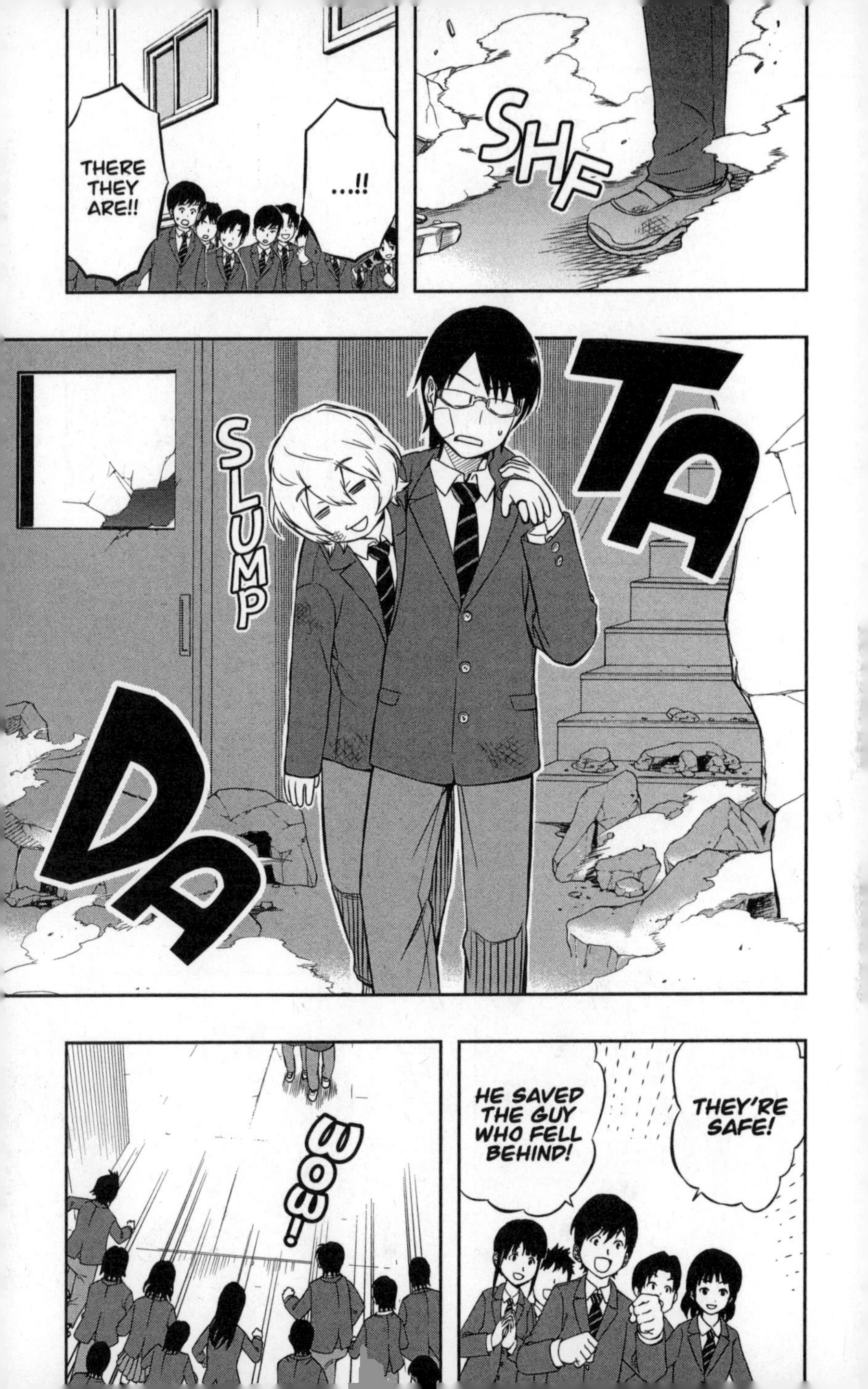
SHF
...!!
THERE THEY ARE!!
TA
SLUMP
DA
THEY'RE SAFE!
HE SAVED THE GUY WHO FELL BEHIND!
WOW!

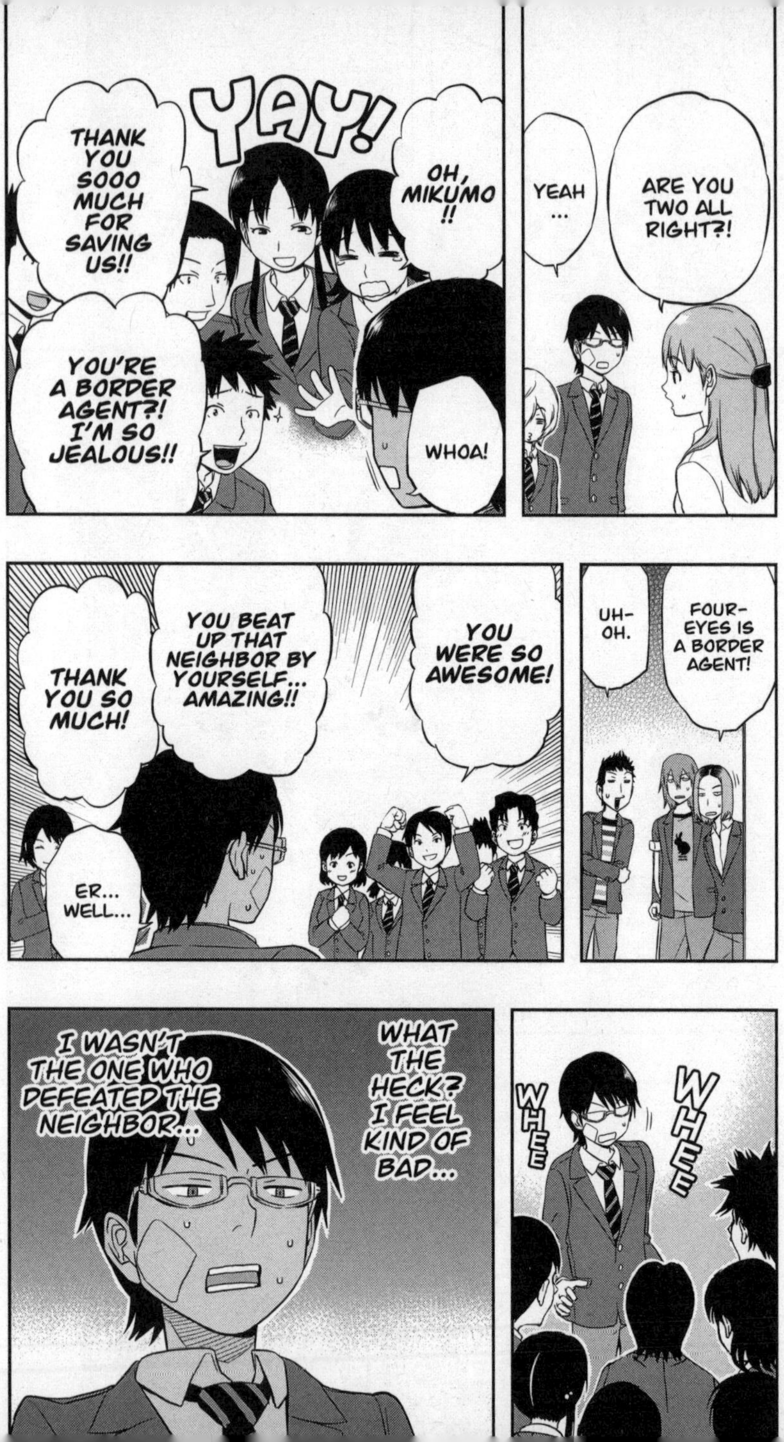
ARE YOU TWO ALL RIGHT?!
YEAH ...
YAY!
OH, MIKUMO!!
THANK YOU SOOO MUCH FOR SAVING US!!
WHOA!
YOU'RE A BORDER AGENT?! I'M SO JEALOUS!!
FOUR-EYES IS A BORDER AGENT!
UH-OH.
YOU WERE SO AWESOME!
YOU BEAT UP THAT NEIGHBOR BY YOURSELF... AMAZING!!
THANK YOU SO MUCH!
ER... WELL...
WHEE
WHEE
WHAT THE HECK? I FEEL KIND OF BAD...
I WASN'T THE ONE WHO DEFEATED THE NEIGHBOR...

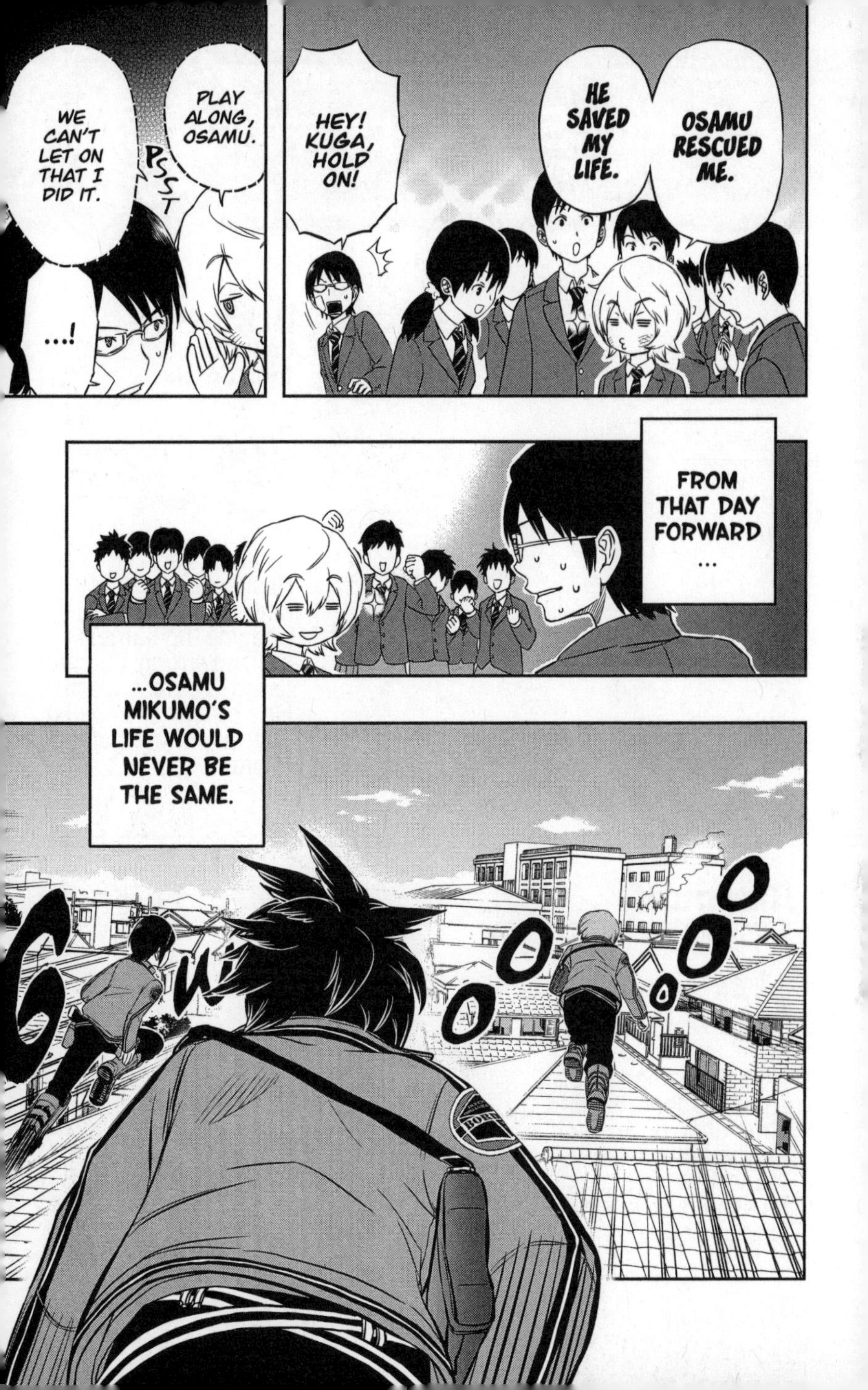

OSAMU RESCUED ME.
HE SAVED MY LIFE.
HEY! KUGA, HOLD ON!
PLAY ALONG, OSAMU.
PSST
WE CAN'T LET ON THAT I DID IT.
...!
FROM THAT DAY FORWARD ...
...OSAMU MIKUMO'S LIFE WOULD NEVER BE THE SAME.
GWi
OOOOOOOO

Trion Soldiers
Neighbor Minions

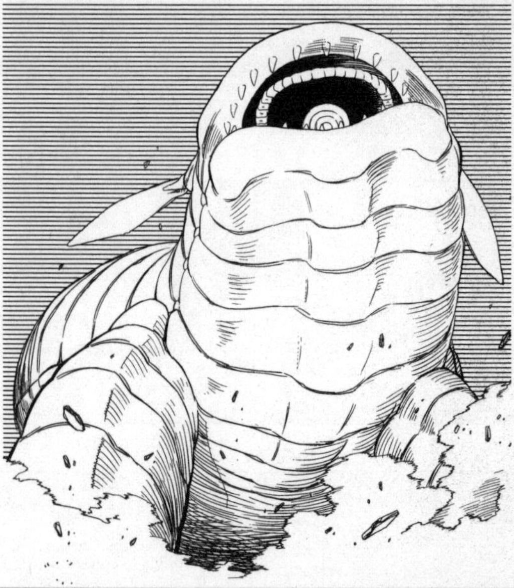

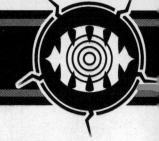

Bamster
Capturing Trion Soldier

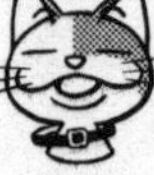

The size of a multiple-story house.

When citizens of Mikado City think of Neighbors they imagine the Bamster. Big and strong, but not tough to defeat. It's a little embarrassing that Osamu almost lost to one.

Marmod
Combat Trion Soldier

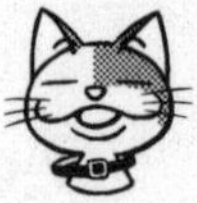

The size of a car.

I like the design, but it's a pain to draw. Yuma struck one down, but they're actually pretty tough. Osamu shouldn't be ashamed for almost losing to one.

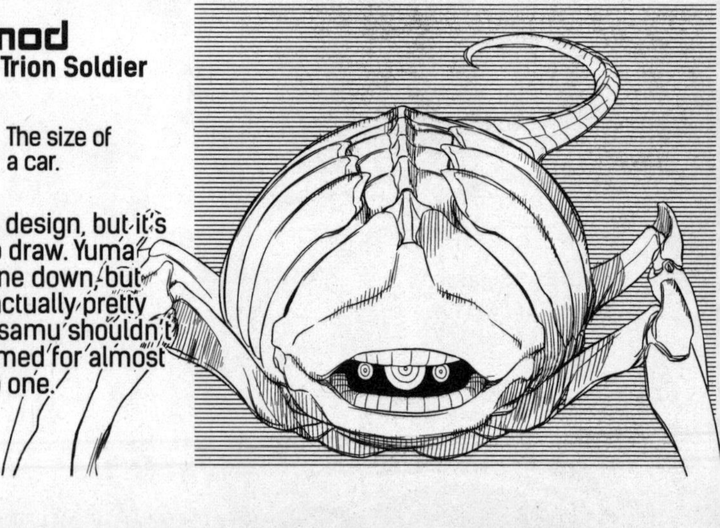

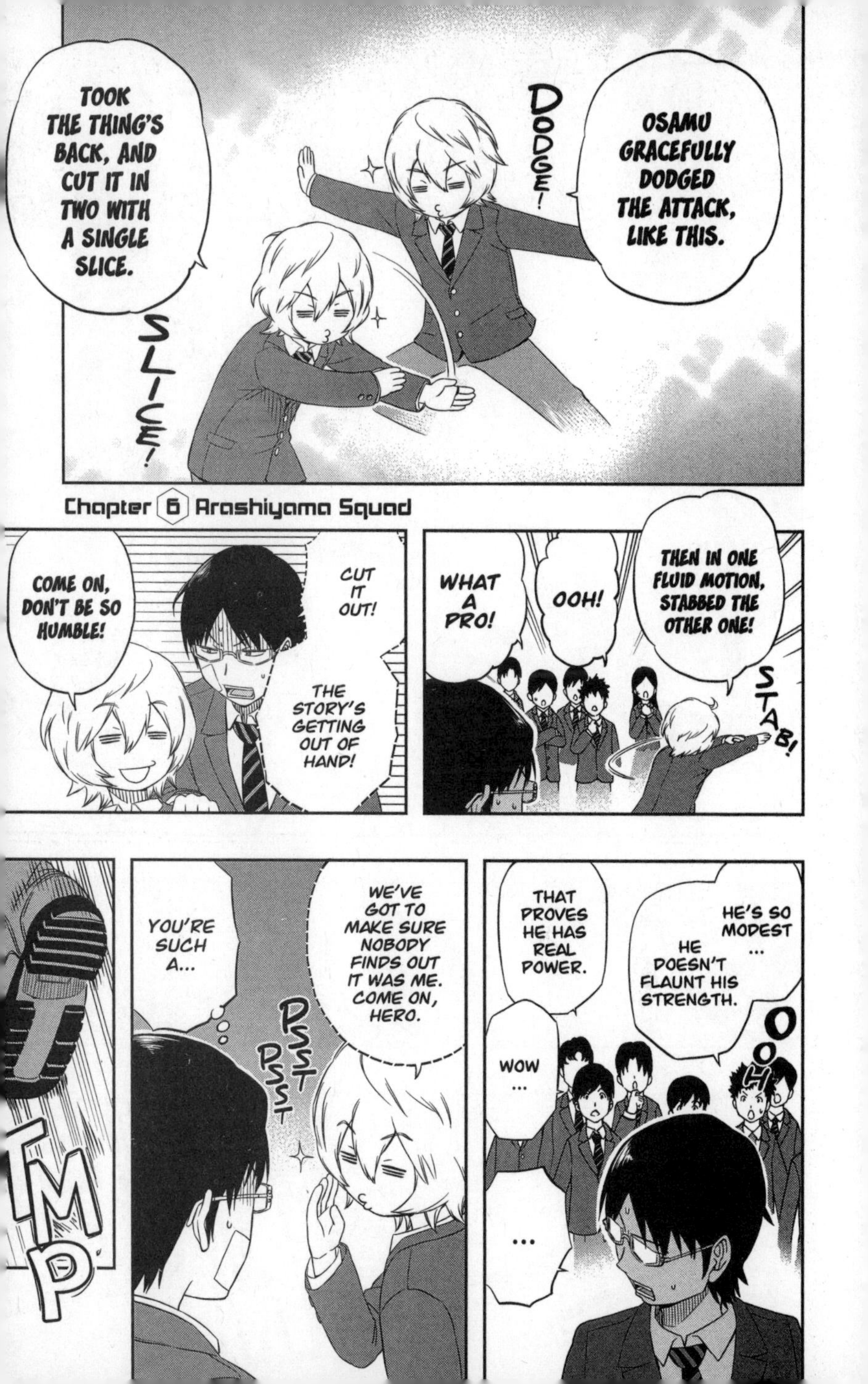
OSAMU GRACEFULLY DODGED THE ATTACK, LIKE THIS.
DODGE!
TOOK THE THING'S BACK, AND CUT IT IN TWO WITH A SINGLE SLICE.
SLICE!
THEN IN ONE FLUID MOTION, STABBED THE OTHER ONE!
STAB!
OOH!
WHAT A PRO!
CUT IT OUT!
THE STORY'S GETTING OUT OF HAND!
COME ON, DON'T BE SO HUMBLE!
HE'S SO MODEST...
HE DOESN'T FLAUNT HIS STRENGTH.
OOH
THAT PROVES HE HAS REAL POWER.
WOW...
...
WE'VE GOT TO MAKE SURE NOBODY FINDS OUT IT WAS ME. COME ON, HERO.
PSST PSST
YOU'RE SUCH A...
TMP

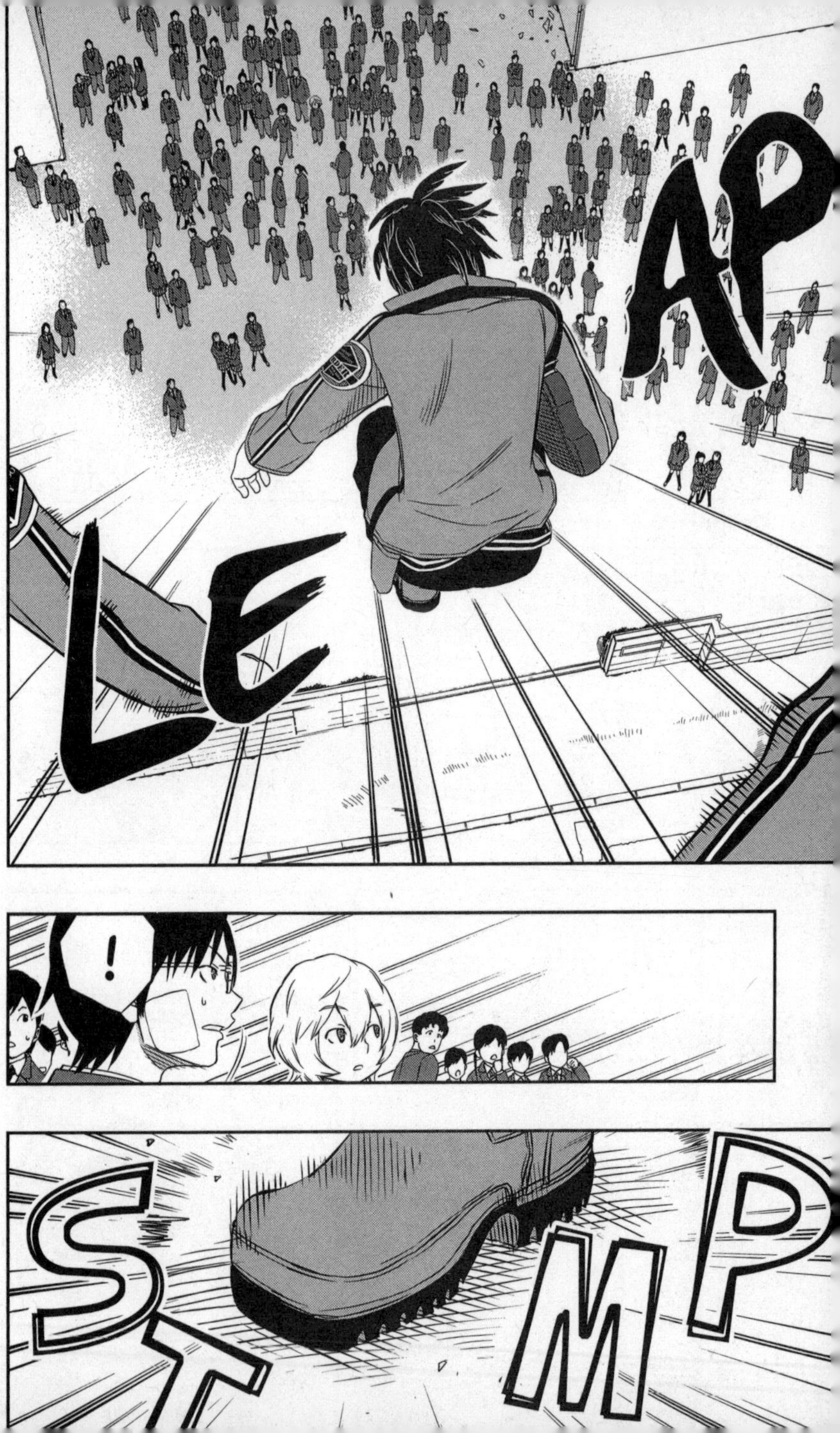
LEAP
!
ST MP

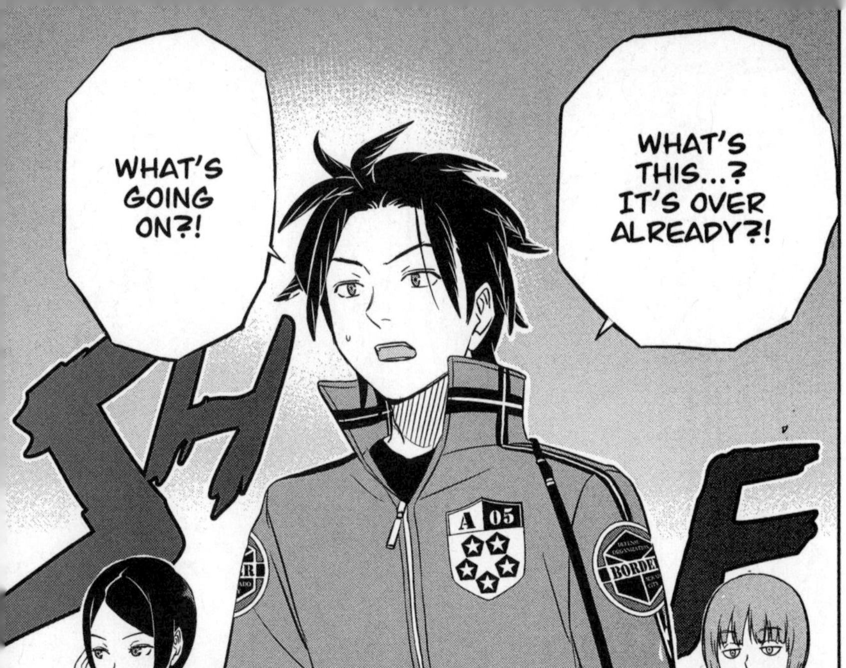
WHAT'S THIS...? IT'S OVER ALREADY?!
WHAT'S GOING ON?!
SHF
ARASHIYAMA SQUAD, REPORTING ON THE SCENE.
Chapter 6 Arashiyama Squad

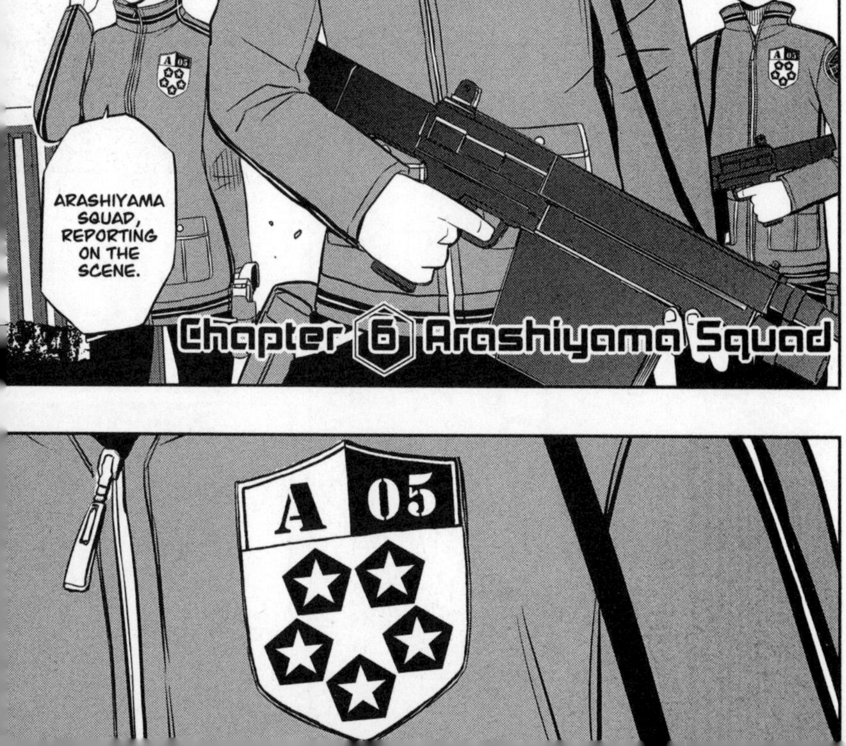
A 05

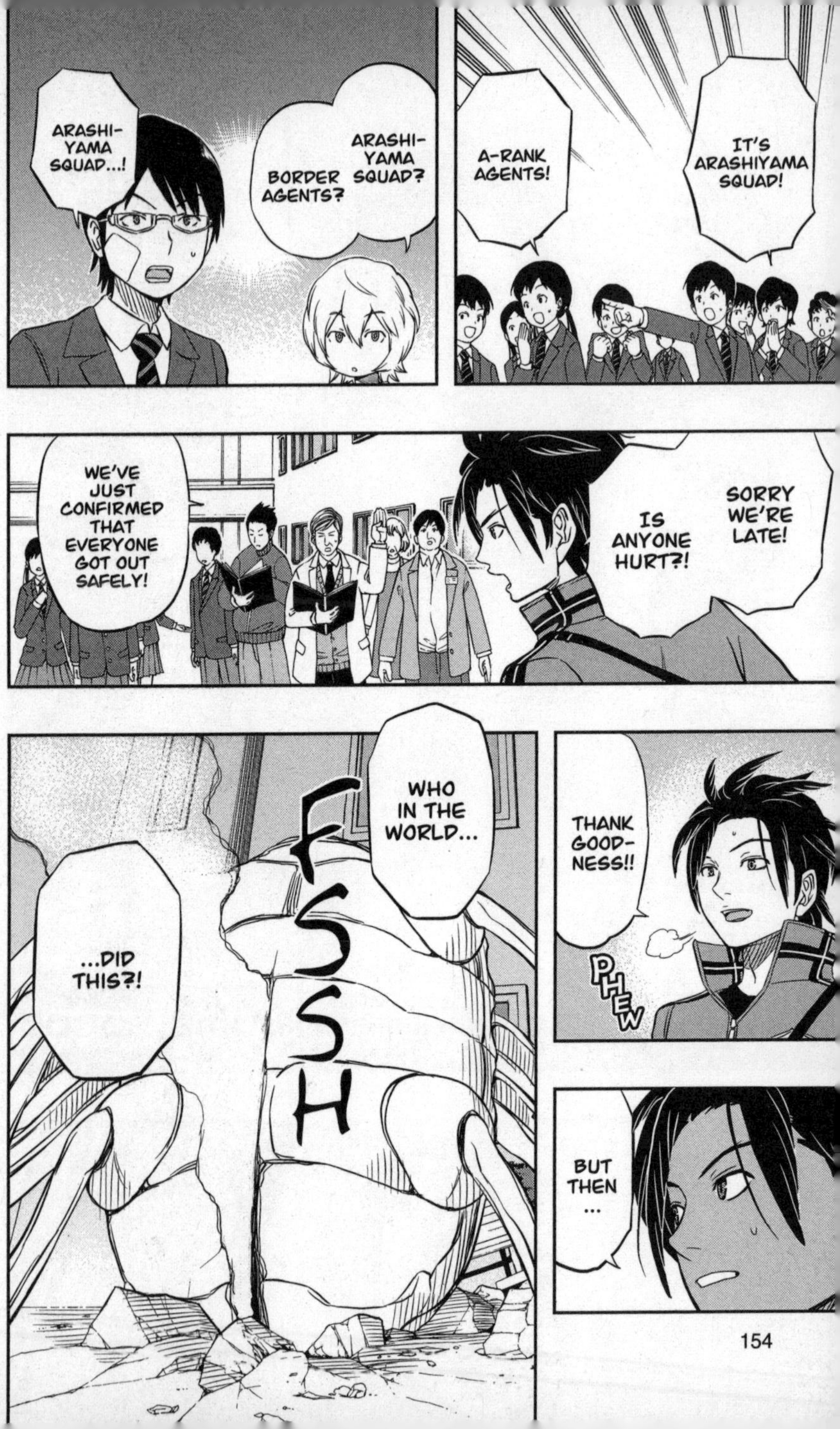
IT'S ARASHIYAMA SQUAD!
A-RANK AGENTS!
ARASHIYAMA SQUAD? BORDER AGENTS?
ARASHIYAMA SQUAD...!
SORRY WE'RE LATE!
IS ANYONE HURT?!
WE'VE JUST CONFIRMED THAT EVERYONE GOT OUT SAFELY!
THANK GOODNESS!!
PHEW
BUT THEN...
WHO IN THE WORLD...
FSSH
...DID THIS?!

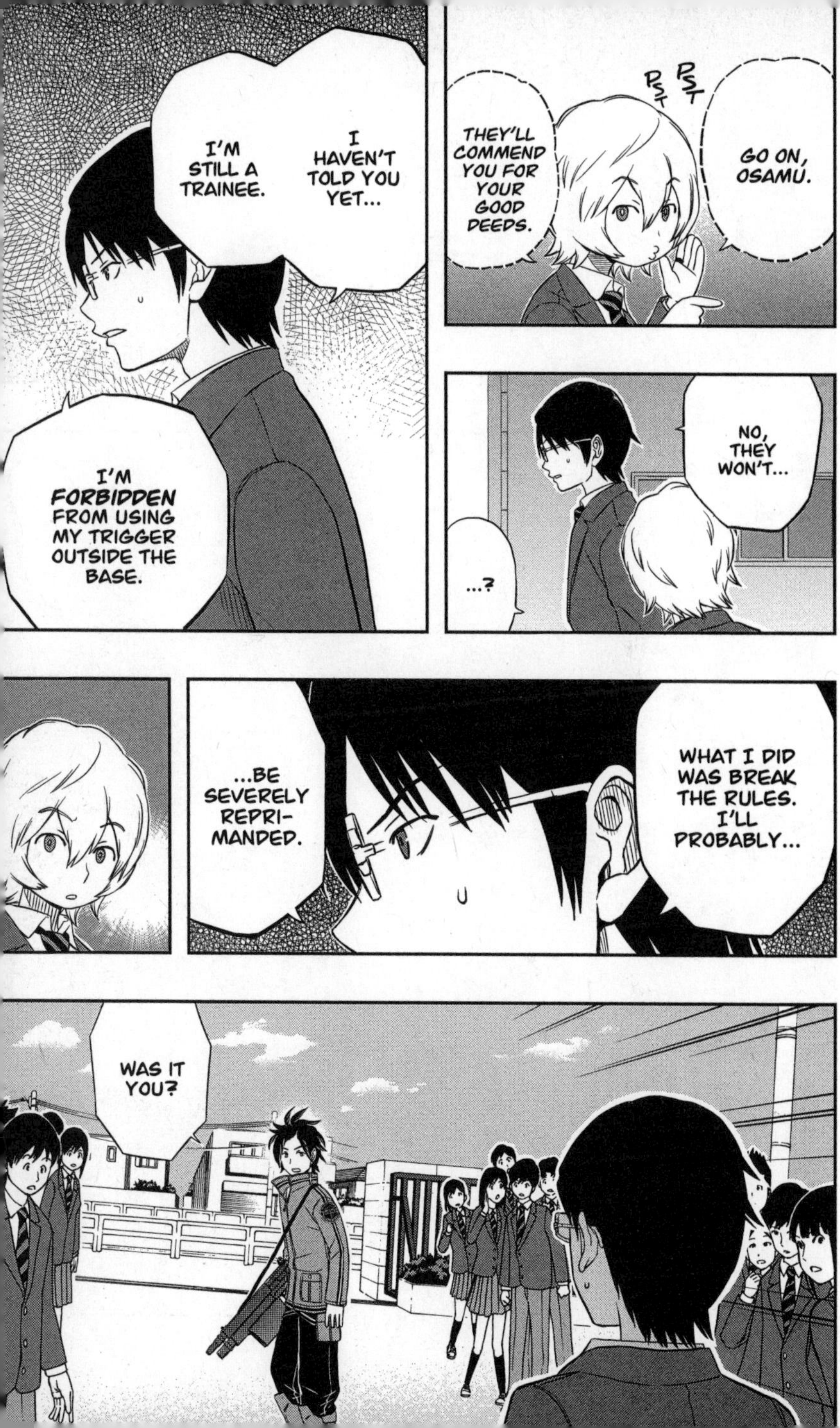
PST PST
GO ON, OSAMU.
THEY'LL COMMEND YOU FOR YOUR GOOD DEEDS.
NO, THEY WON'T...
...?
I HAVEN'T TOLD YOU YET...
I'M STILL A TRAINEE.
I'M **FORBIDDEN** FROM USING MY TRIGGER OUTSIDE THE BASE.
WHAT I DID WAS BREAK THE RULES. I'LL PROBABLY...
...BE SEVERELY REPRI-MANDED.
WAS IT YOU?

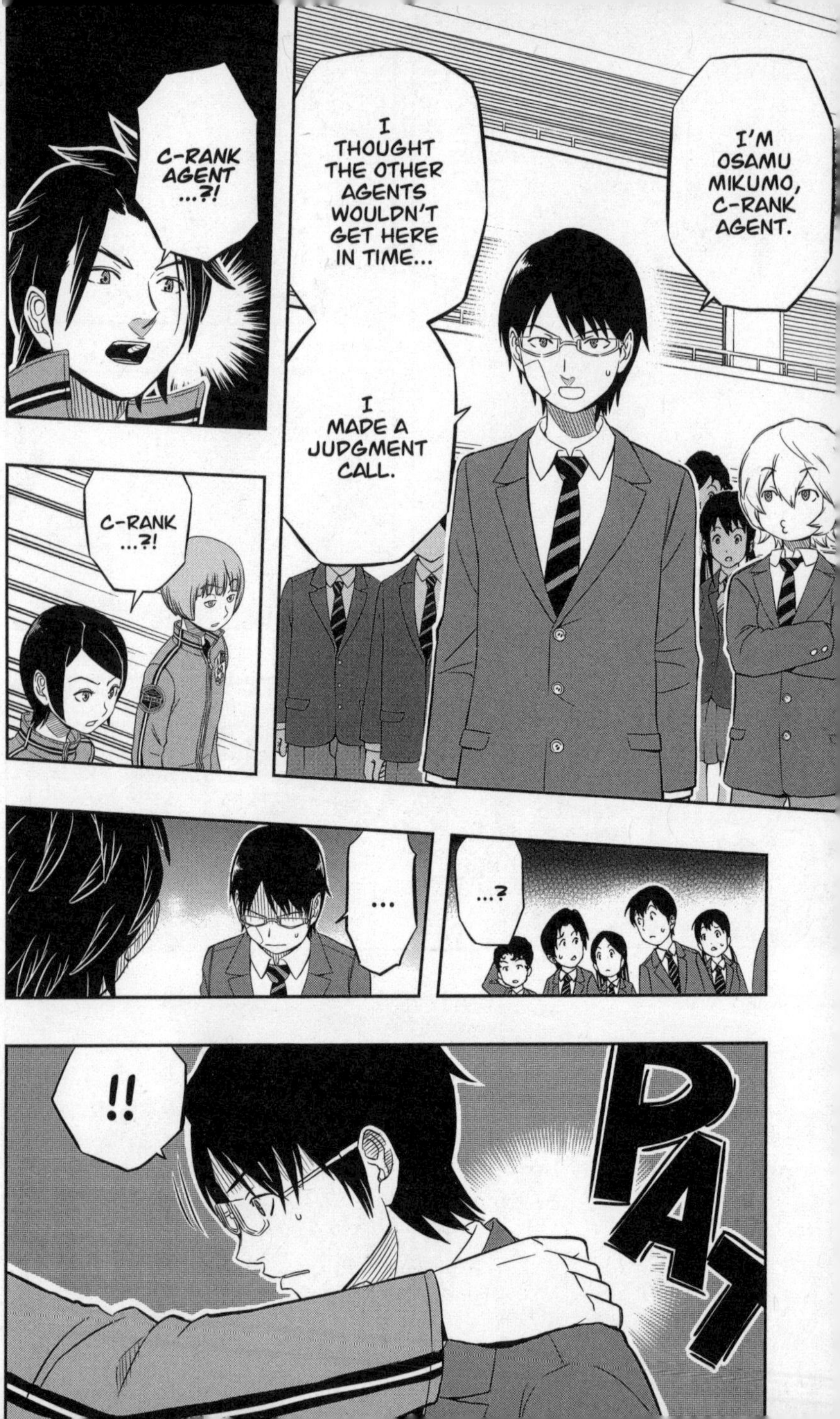
I'M OSAMU MIKUMO, C-RANK AGENT.
I THOUGHT THE OTHER AGENTS WOULDN'T GET HERE IN TIME...
I MADE A JUDGMENT CALL.
C-RANK AGENT ...?!
C-RANK ...?!
...?
...
!!
PAT

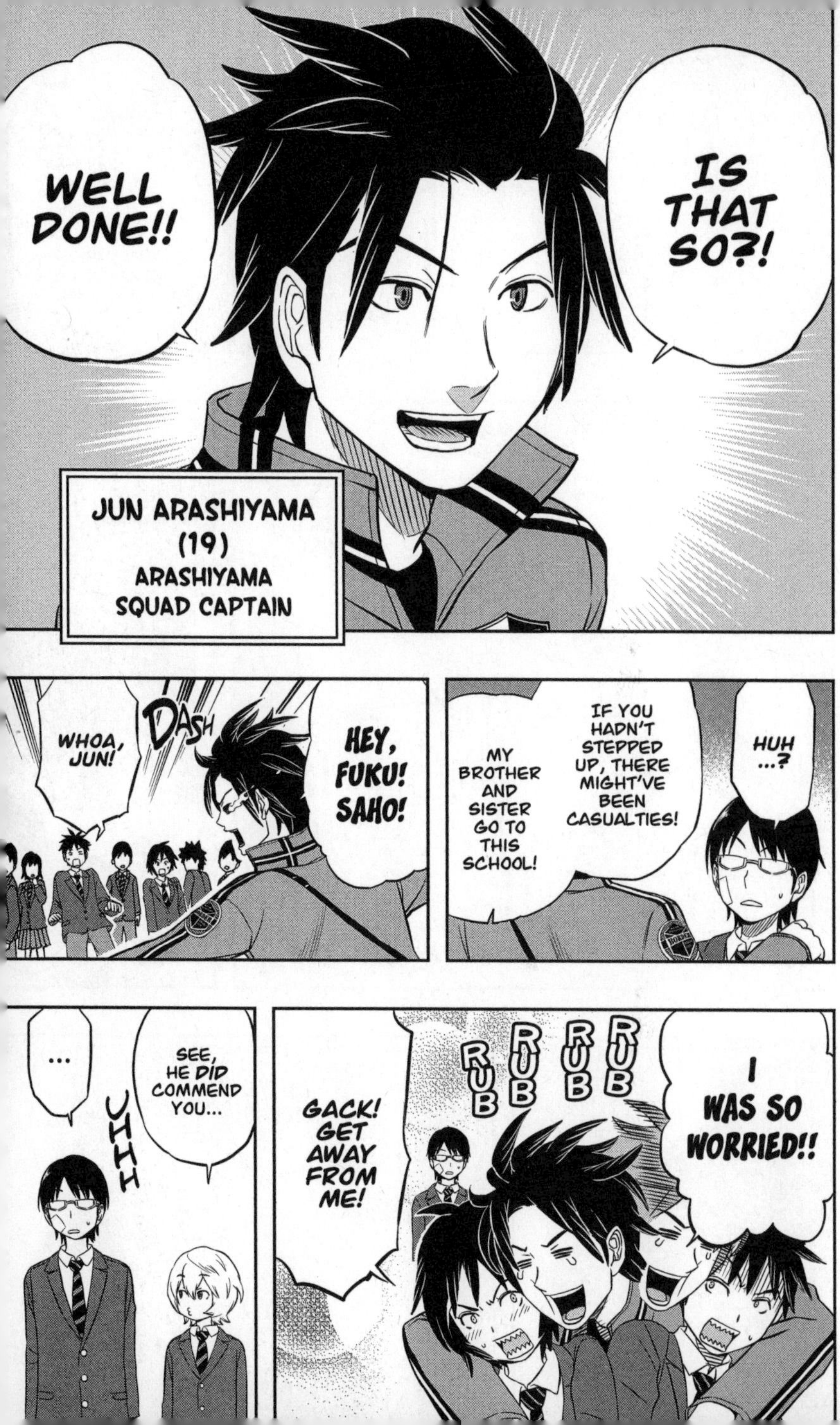
IS THAT SO?!
WELL DONE!!
JUN ARASHIYAMA (19) ARASHIYAMA SQUAD CAPTAIN
HUH ...?
IF YOU HADN'T STEPPED UP, THERE MIGHT'VE BEEN CASUALTIES!
MY BROTHER AND SISTER GO TO THIS SCHOOL!
HEY, FUKU! SAHO!
DASH
WHOA, JUN!
I WAS SO WORRIED!!
RUB RUB RUB RUB
GACK! GET AWAY FROM ME!
SEE, HE DID COMMEND YOU...
UHHH
...

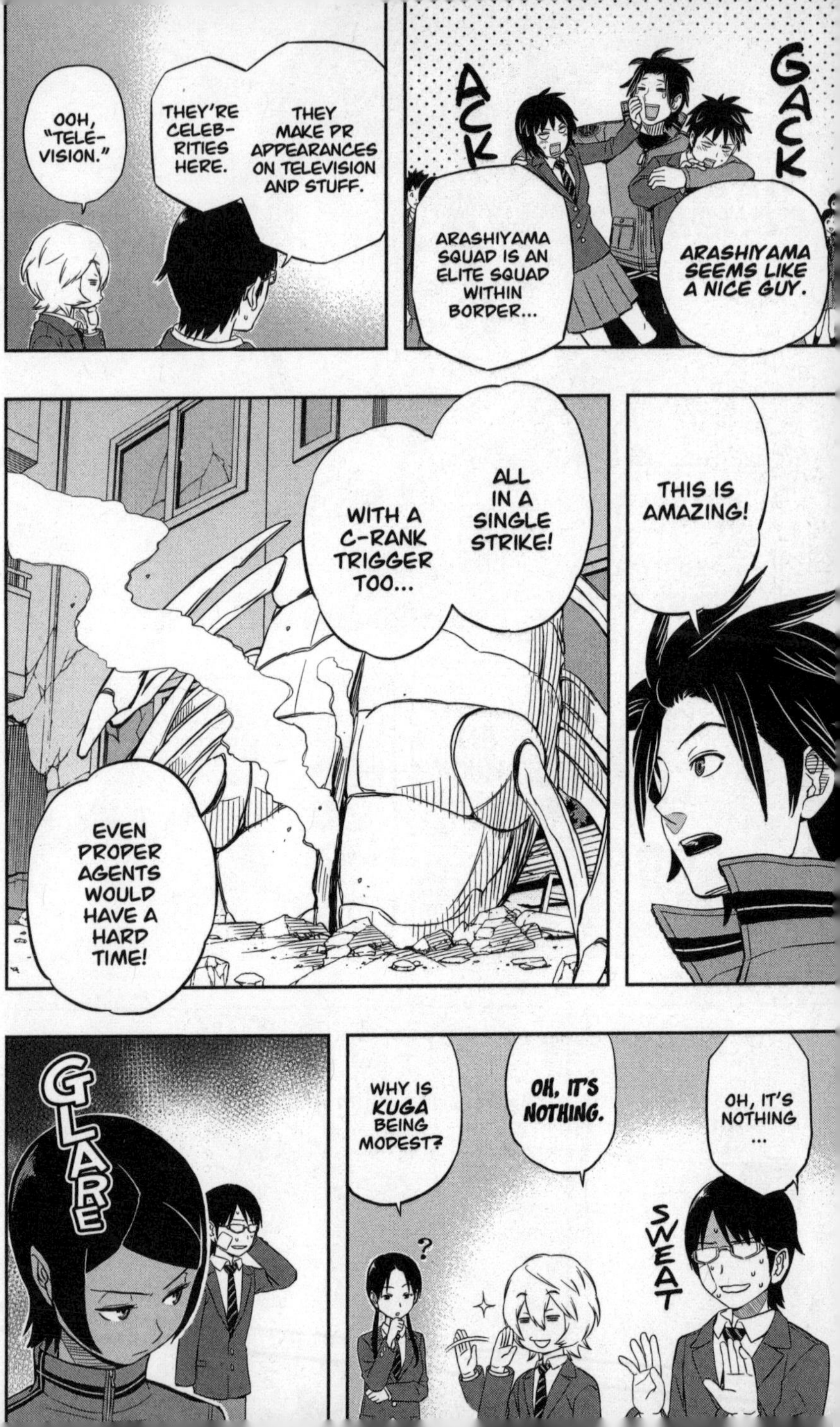
GACK
ACK
ARASHIYAMA SEEMS LIKE A NICE GUY.
ARASHIYAMA SQUAD IS AN ELITE SQUAD WITHIN BORDER...
THEY MAKE PR APPEARANCES ON TELEVISION AND STUFF.
THEY'RE CELEBRITIES HERE.
OOH, "TELEVISION."
THIS IS AMAZING!
ALL IN A SINGLE STRIKE!
WITH A C-RANK TRIGGER TOO...
EVEN PROPER AGENTS WOULD HAVE A HARD TIME!
OH, IT'S NOTHING...
SWEAT
OH, IT'S NOTHING.
WHY IS KUGA BEING MODEST?
?
GLARE

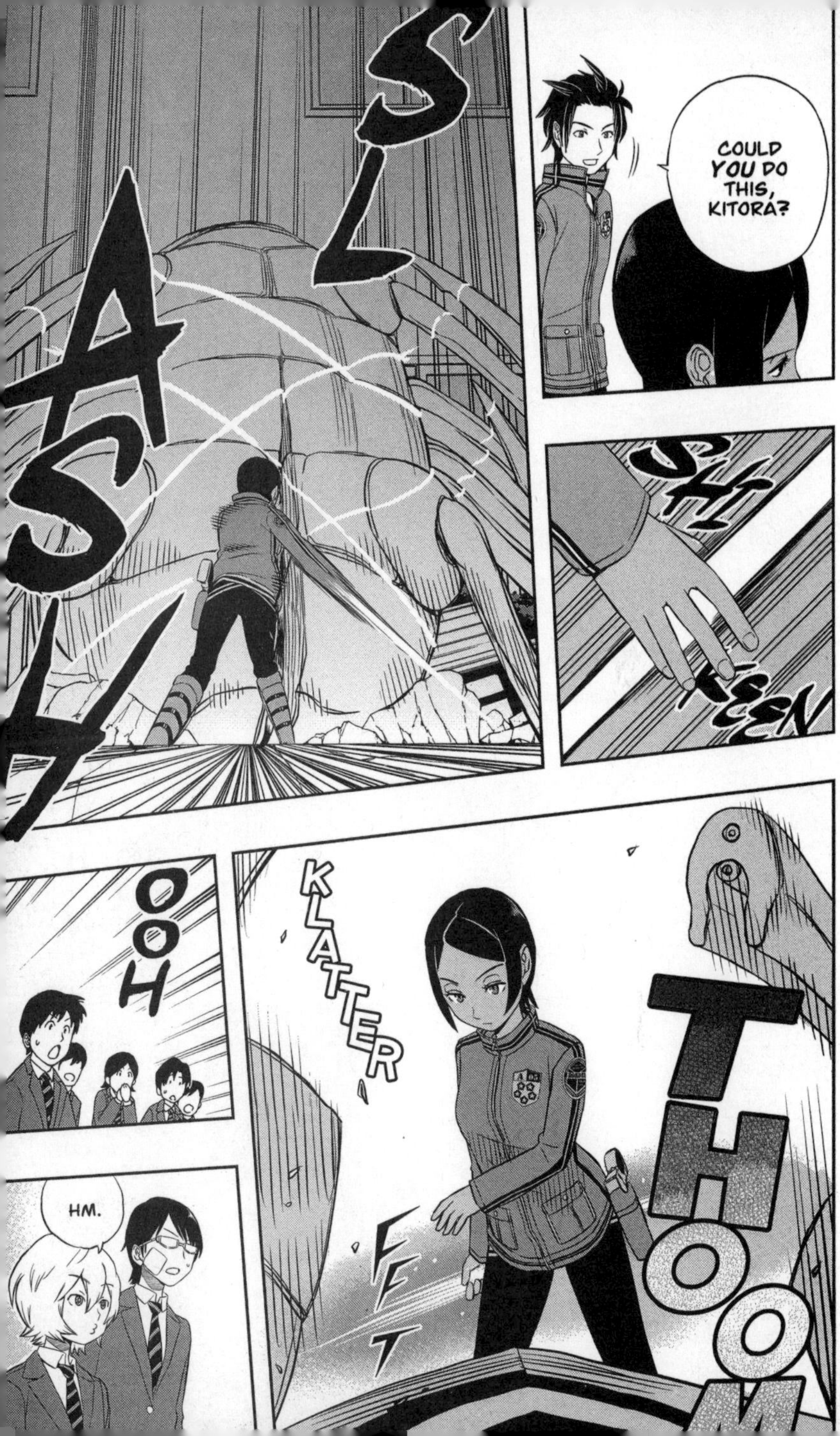
COULD YOU DO THIS, KITORA?
SHI
KEEN
SLASH
THOOOM
KLATTER
FFT
OOOH
HM.

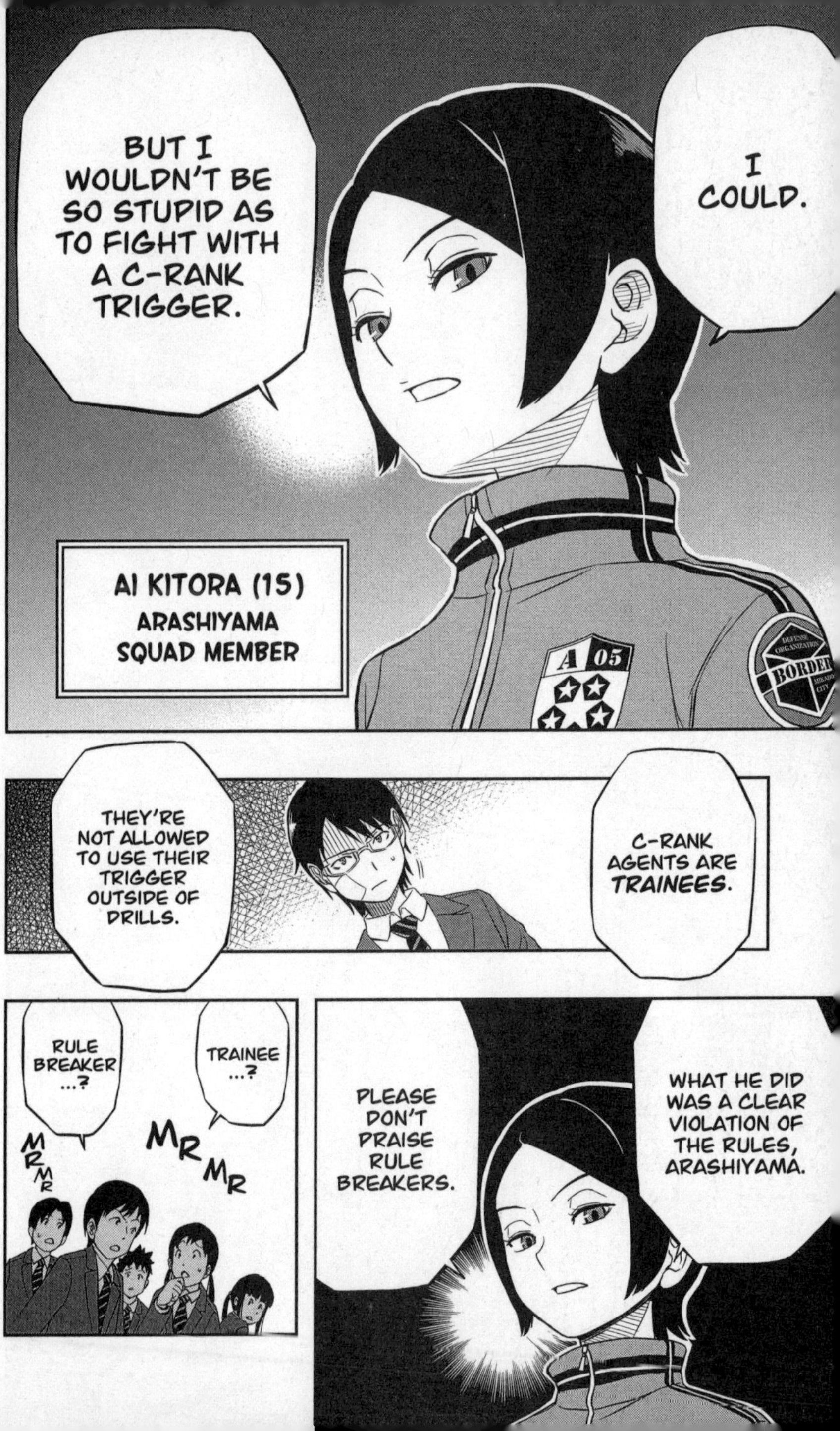
I COULD.
BUT I WOULDN'T BE SO STUPID AS TO FIGHT WITH A C-RANK TRIGGER.
AI KITORA (15)
ARASHIYAMA SQUAD MEMBER
A 05
DEFENSE ORGANIZATION BORDER
C-RANK AGENTS ARE TRAINEES.
THEY'RE NOT ALLOWED TO USE THEIR TRIGGER OUTSIDE OF DRILLS.
WHAT HE DID WAS A CLEAR VIOLATION OF THE RULES, ARASHIYAMA.
PLEASE DON'T PRAISE RULE BREAKERS.
TRAINEE ...?
RULE BREAKER ...?
MRMR
MRMR

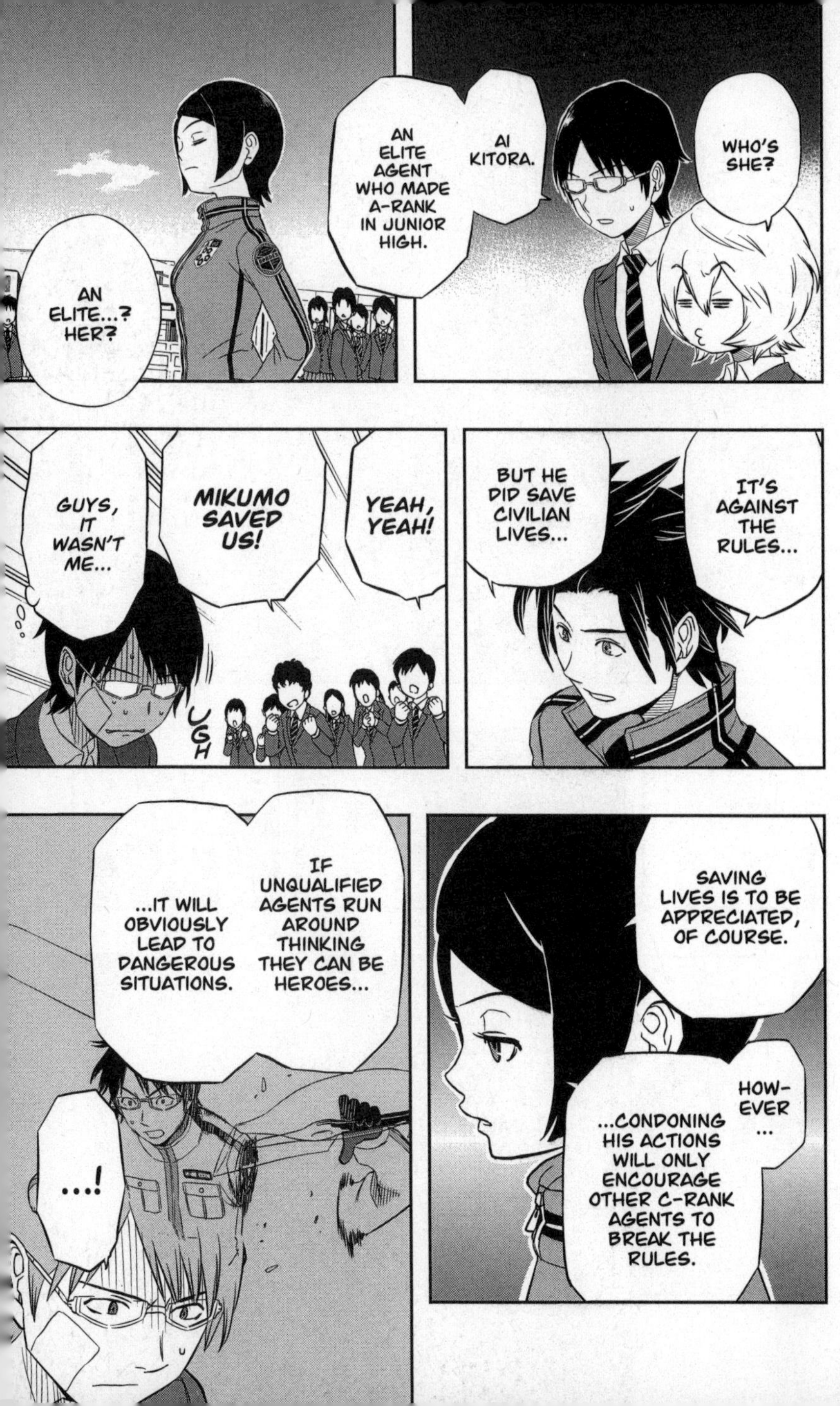
WHO'S SHE?
AI KITORA.
AN ELITE AGENT WHO MADE A-RANK IN JUNIOR HIGH.
AN ELITE...? HER?
IT'S AGAINST THE RULES...
BUT HE DID SAVE CIVILIAN LIVES...
YEAH, YEAH!
MIKUMO SAVED US!
GUYS, IT WASN'T ME...
UGH
SAVING LIVES IS TO BE APPRECIATED, OF COURSE.
HOW-EVER...
...CONDONING HIS ACTIONS WILL ONLY ENCOURAGE OTHER C-RANK AGENTS TO BREAK THE RULES.
IF UNQUALIFIED AGENTS RUN AROUND THINKING THEY CAN BE HEROES...
...IT WILL OBVIOUSLY LEAD TO DANGEROUS SITUATIONS.
...!

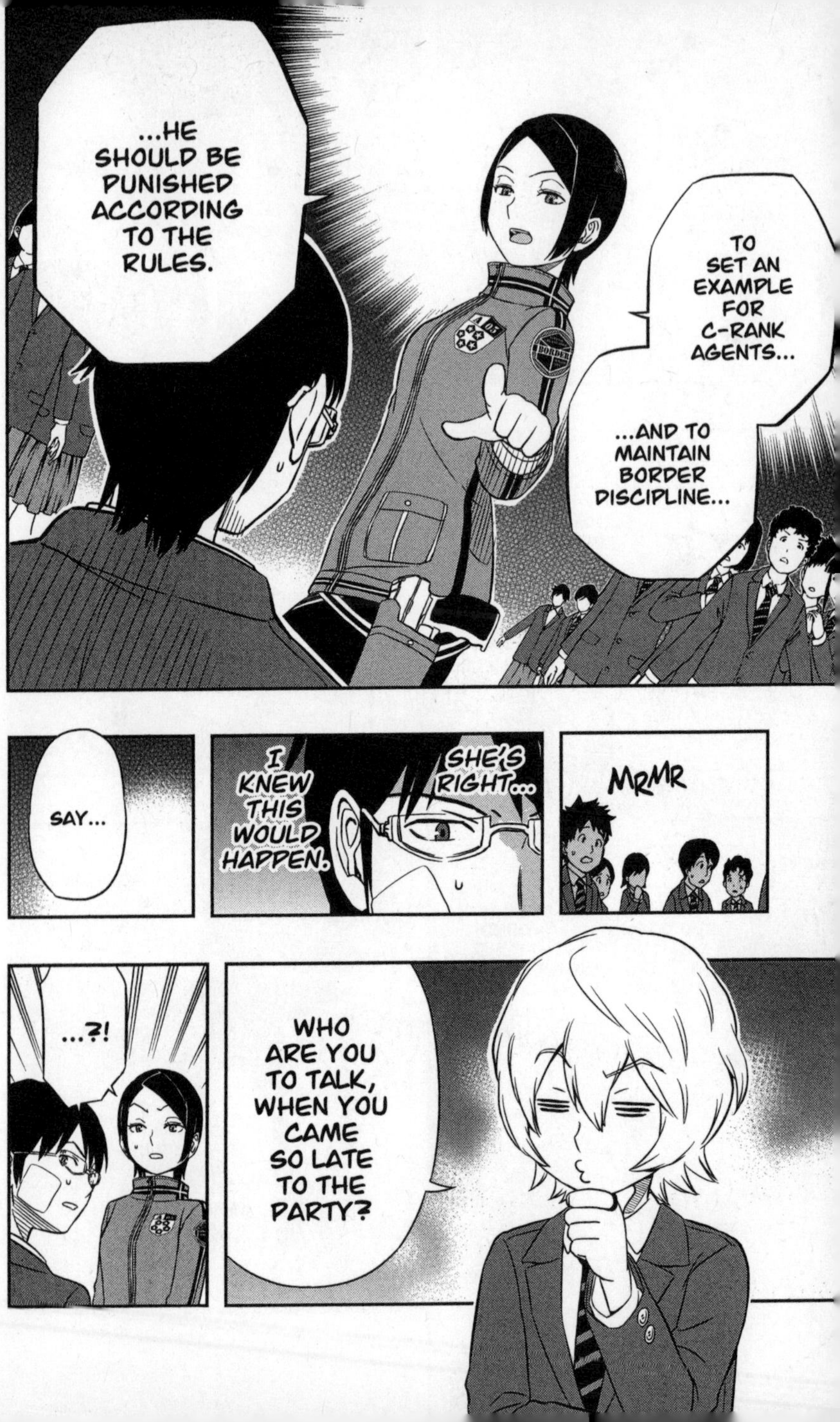
TO SET AN EXAMPLE FOR C-RANK AGENTS...
...AND TO MAINTAIN BORDER DISCIPLINE...
...HE SHOULD BE PUNISHED ACCORDING TO THE RULES.
MRMR
SHE'S RIGHT...
I KNEW THIS WOULD HAPPEN.
SAY...
WHO ARE YOU TO TALK, WHEN YOU CAME SO LATE TO THE PARTY?
...?!

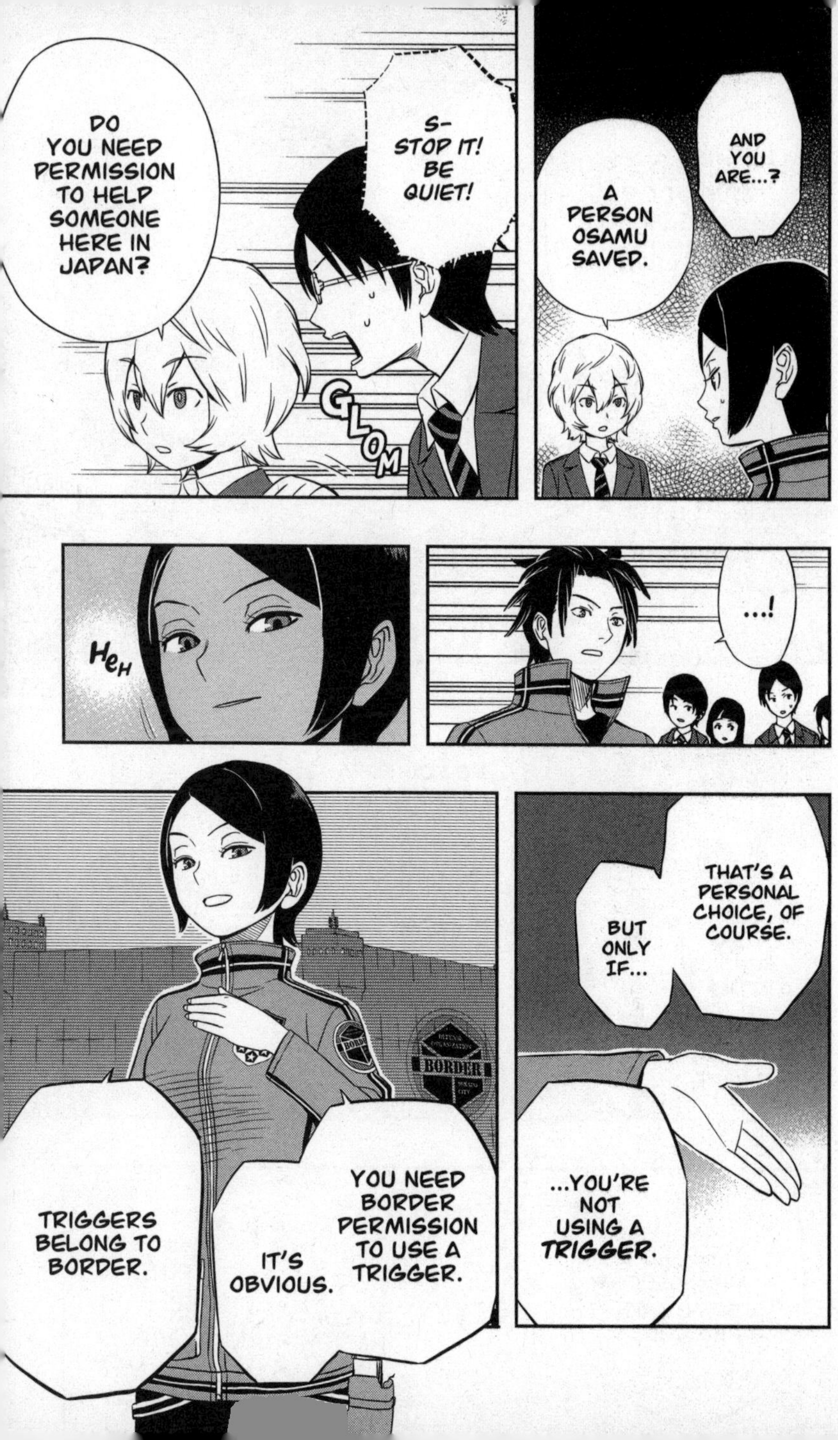
AND YOU ARE...?
A PERSON OSAMU SAVED.
DO YOU NEED PERMISSION TO HELP SOMEONE HERE IN JAPAN?
S- STOP IT! BE QUIET!
GLOM
...!
HEH
THAT'S A PERSONAL CHOICE, OF COURSE.
BUT ONLY IF...
...YOU'RE NOT USING A TRIGGER.
YOU NEED BORDER PERMISSION TO USE A TRIGGER.
IT'S OBVIOUS.
TRIGGERS BELONG TO BORDER.
BORDER

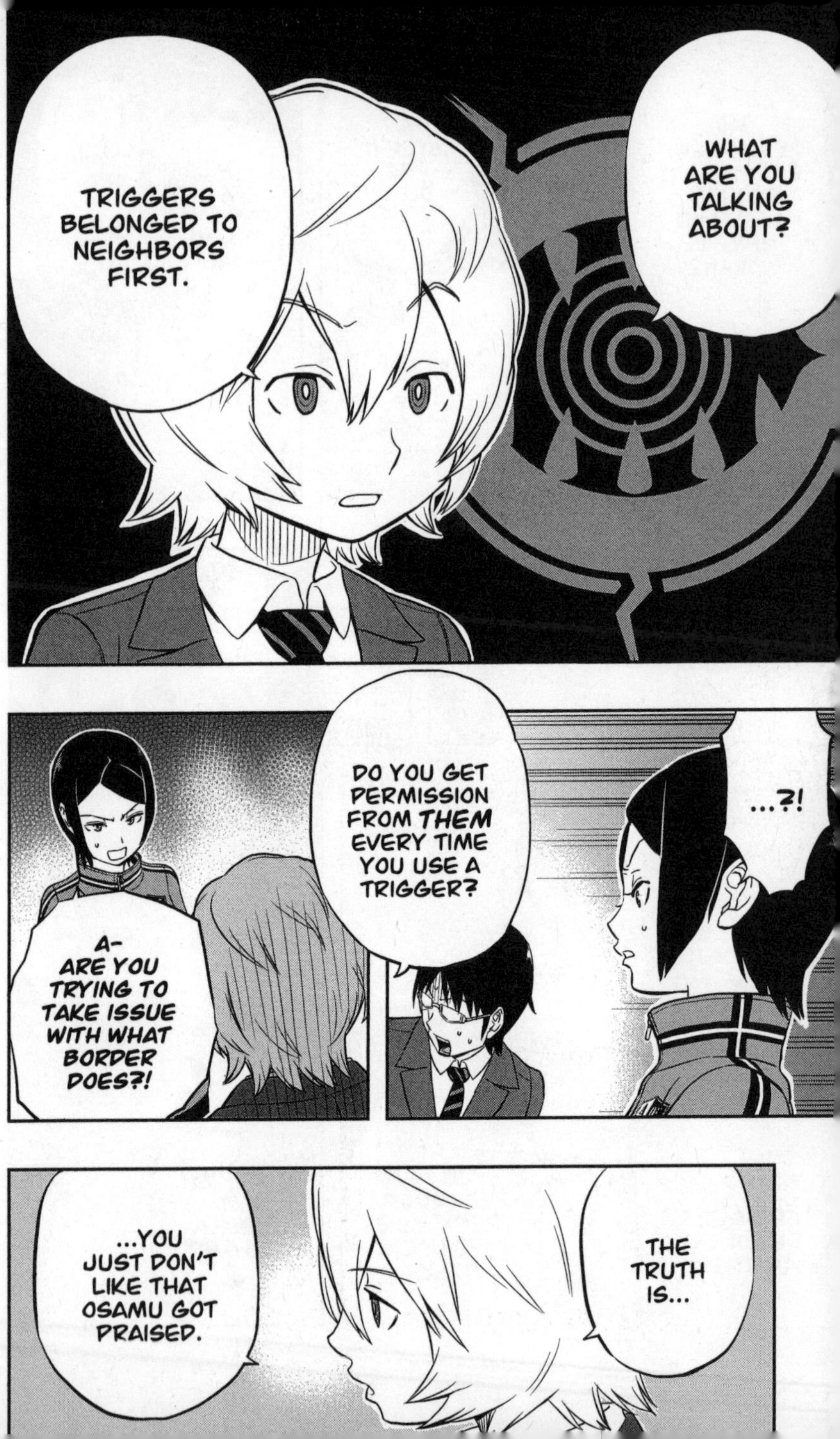
WHAT ARE YOU TALKING ABOUT?
TRIGGERS BELONGED TO NEIGHBORS FIRST.
...?!
DO YOU GET PERMISSION FROM *THEM* EVERY TIME YOU USE A TRIGGER?
A- ARE YOU TRYING TO TAKE ISSUE WITH WHAT BORDER DOES?!
THE TRUTH IS...
...YOU JUST DON'T LIKE THAT OSAMU GOT PRAISED.

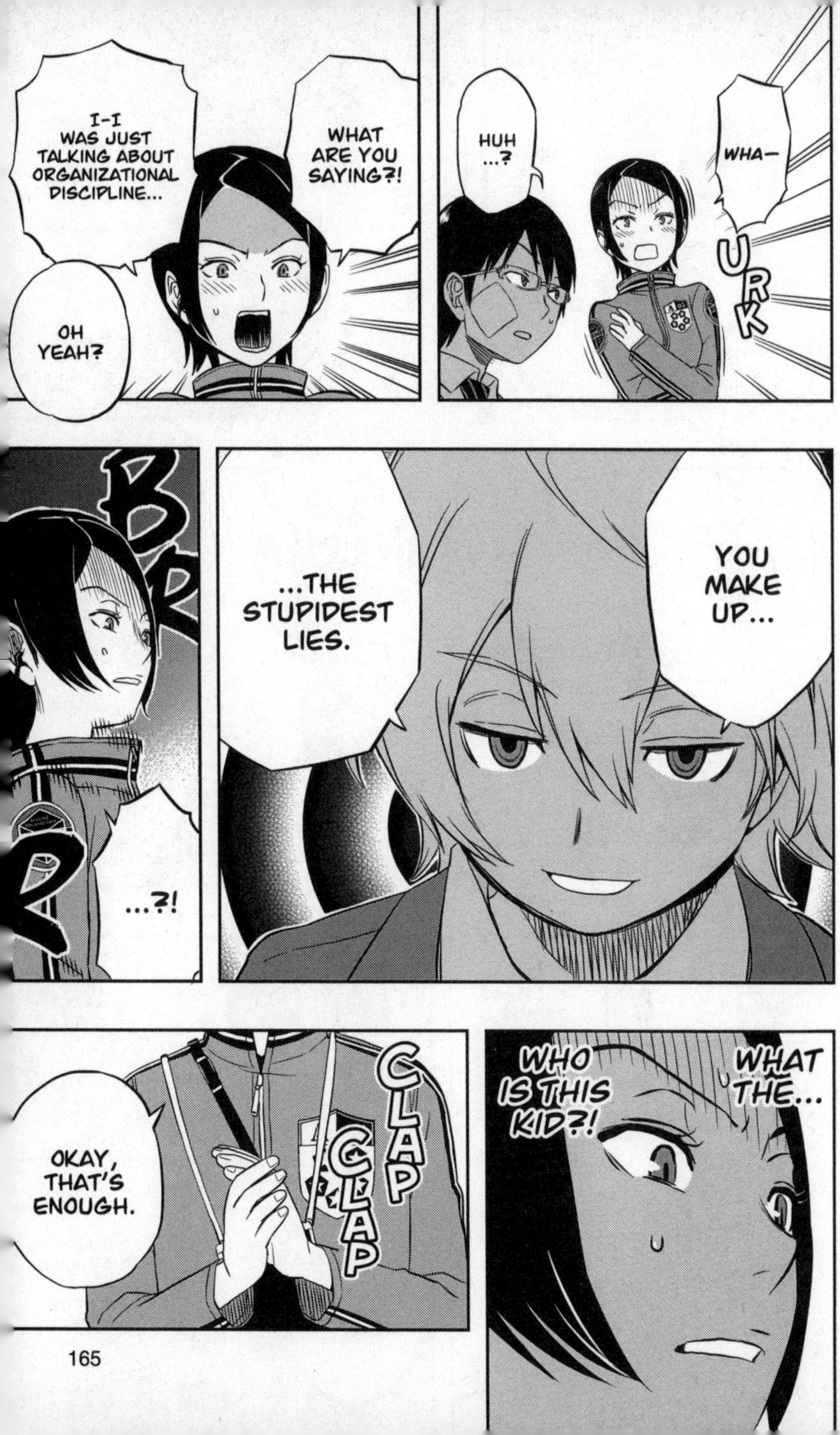
WHA—
URK
HUH ...?
WHAT ARE YOU SAYING?!
I-I WAS JUST TALKING ABOUT ORGANIZATIONAL DISCIPLINE...
OH YEAH?
YOU MAKE UP...
...THE STUPIDEST LIES.
...?!
WHAT THE...
WHO IS THIS KID?!
CLAP CLAP
OKAY, THAT'S ENOUGH.

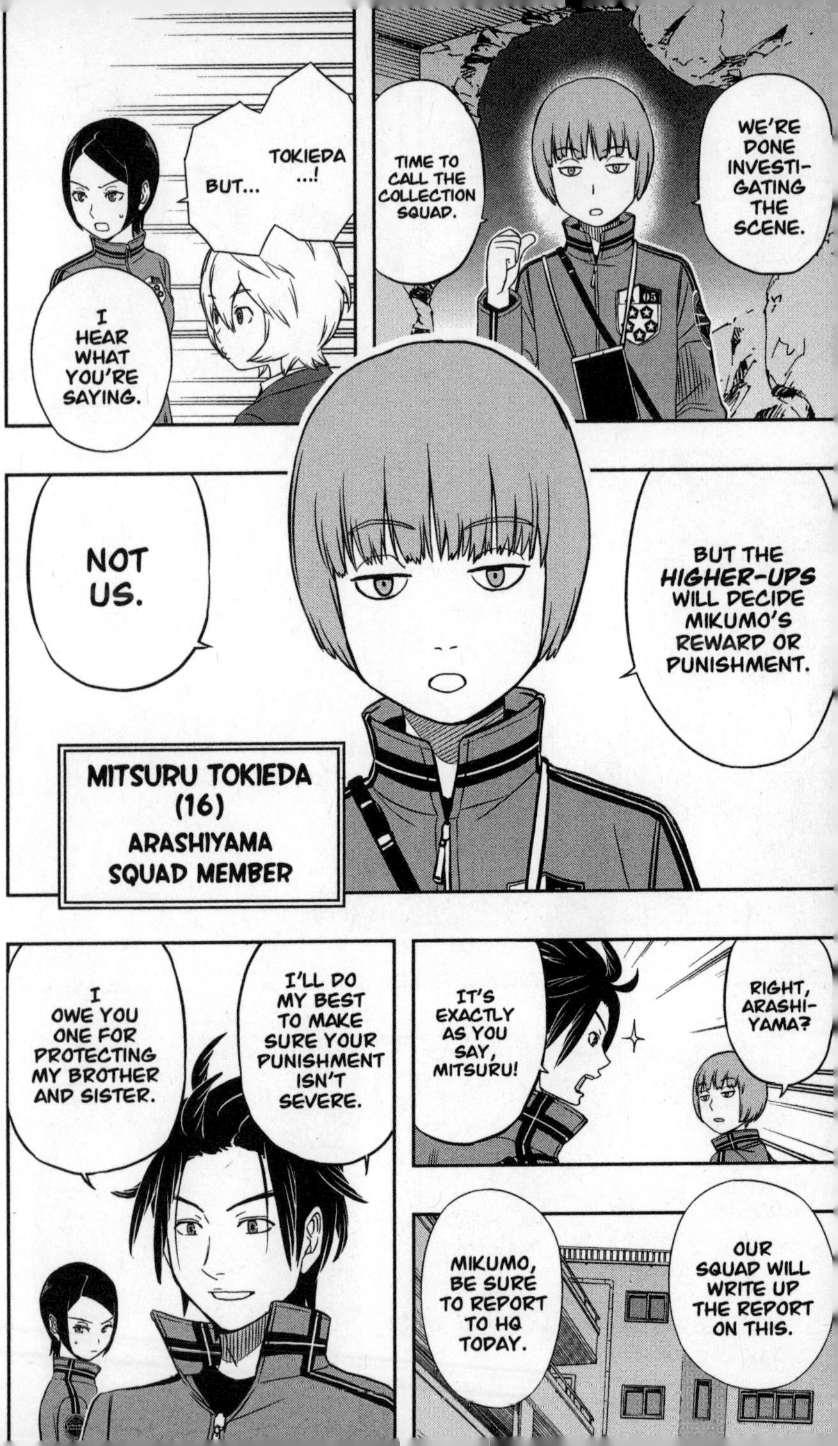
WE'RE DONE INVESTIGATING THE SCENE.
TIME TO CALL THE COLLECTION SQUAD.
TOKIEDA ...!
BUT...
I HEAR WHAT YOU'RE SAYING.
BUT THE HIGHER-UPS WILL DECIDE MIKUMO'S REWARD OR PUNISHMENT.
NOT US.
MITSURU TOKIEDA (16) ARASHIYAMA SQUAD MEMBER
RIGHT, ARASHIYAMA?
IT'S EXACTLY AS YOU SAY, MITSURU!
OUR SQUAD WILL WRITE UP THE REPORT ON THIS.
MIKUMO, BE SURE TO REPORT TO HQ TODAY.
I'LL DO MY BEST TO MAKE SURE YOUR PUNISHMENT ISN'T SEVERE.
I OWE YOU ONE FOR PROTECTING MY BROTHER AND SISTER.

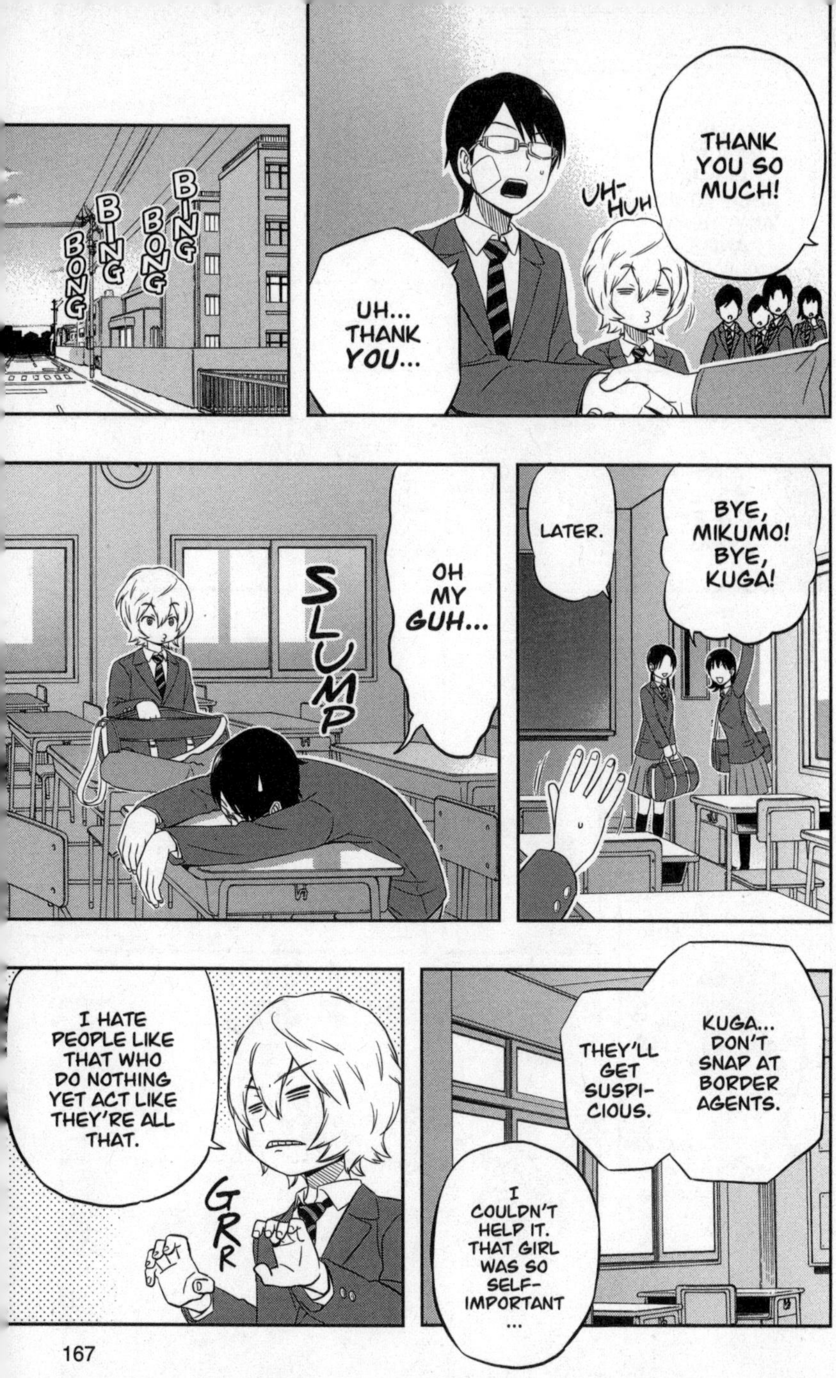
THANK YOU SO MUCH!
UH-HUH
UH... THANK YOU...
BING BONG BING BONG
BYE, MIKUMO! BYE, KUGA!
LATER.
OH MY GUH...
SLUMP
KUGA... DON'T SNAP AT BORDER AGENTS.
THEY'LL GET SUSPICIOUS.
I COULDN'T HELP IT. THAT GIRL WAS SO SELF-IMPORTANT ...
I HATE PEOPLE LIKE THAT WHO DO NOTHING YET ACT LIKE THEY'RE ALL THAT.
GRR

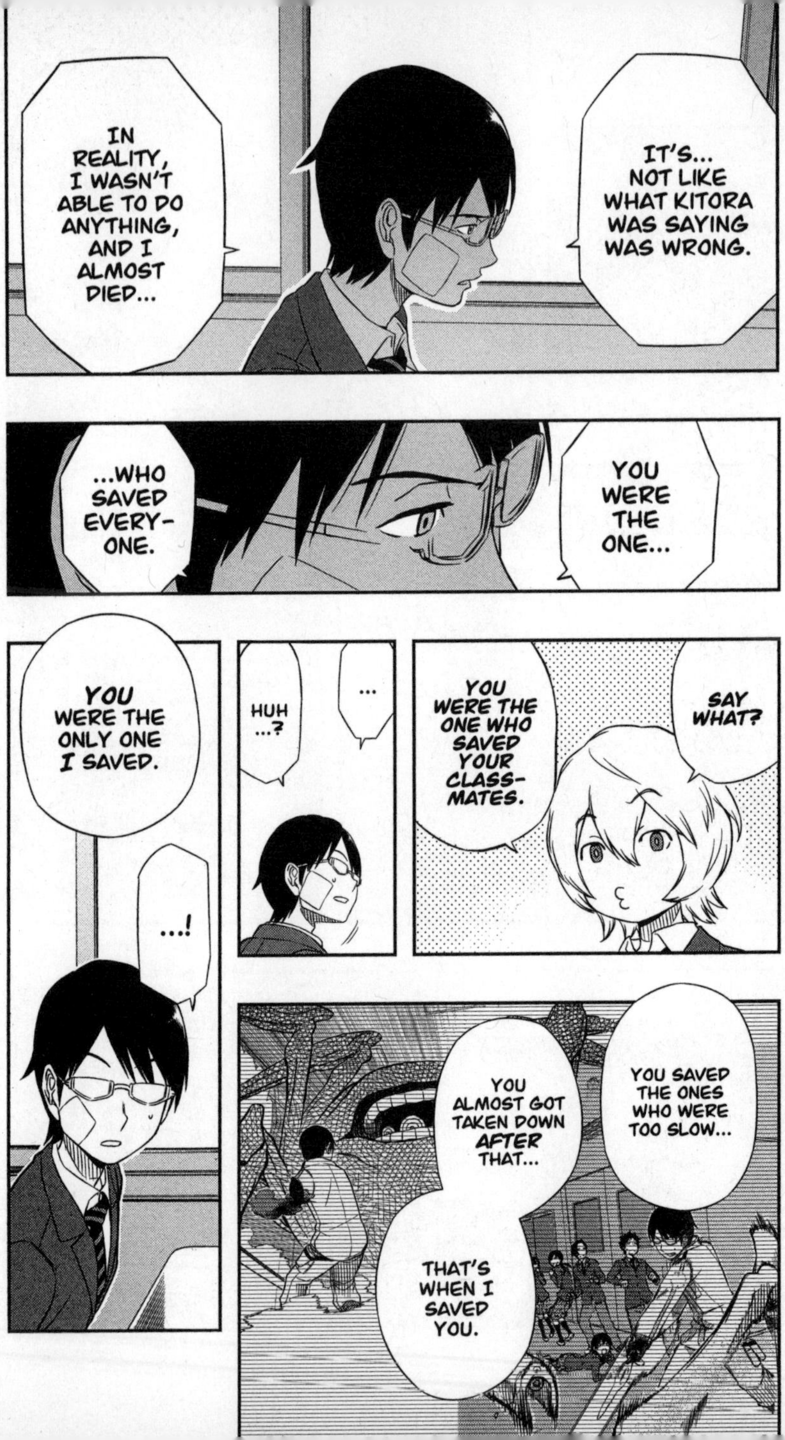
IT'S... NOT LIKE WHAT KITORA WAS SAYING WAS WRONG.
IN REALITY, I WASN'T ABLE TO DO ANYTHING, AND I ALMOST DIED...
YOU WERE THE ONE...
...WHO SAVED EVERY-ONE.
SAY WHAT?
YOU WERE THE ONE WHO SAVED YOUR CLASS-MATES.
...
HUH ...?
YOU SAVED THE ONES WHO WERE TOO SLOW...
YOU ALMOST GOT TAKEN DOWN AFTER THAT...
THAT'S WHEN I SAVED YOU.
YOU WERE THE ONLY ONE I SAVED.
...!

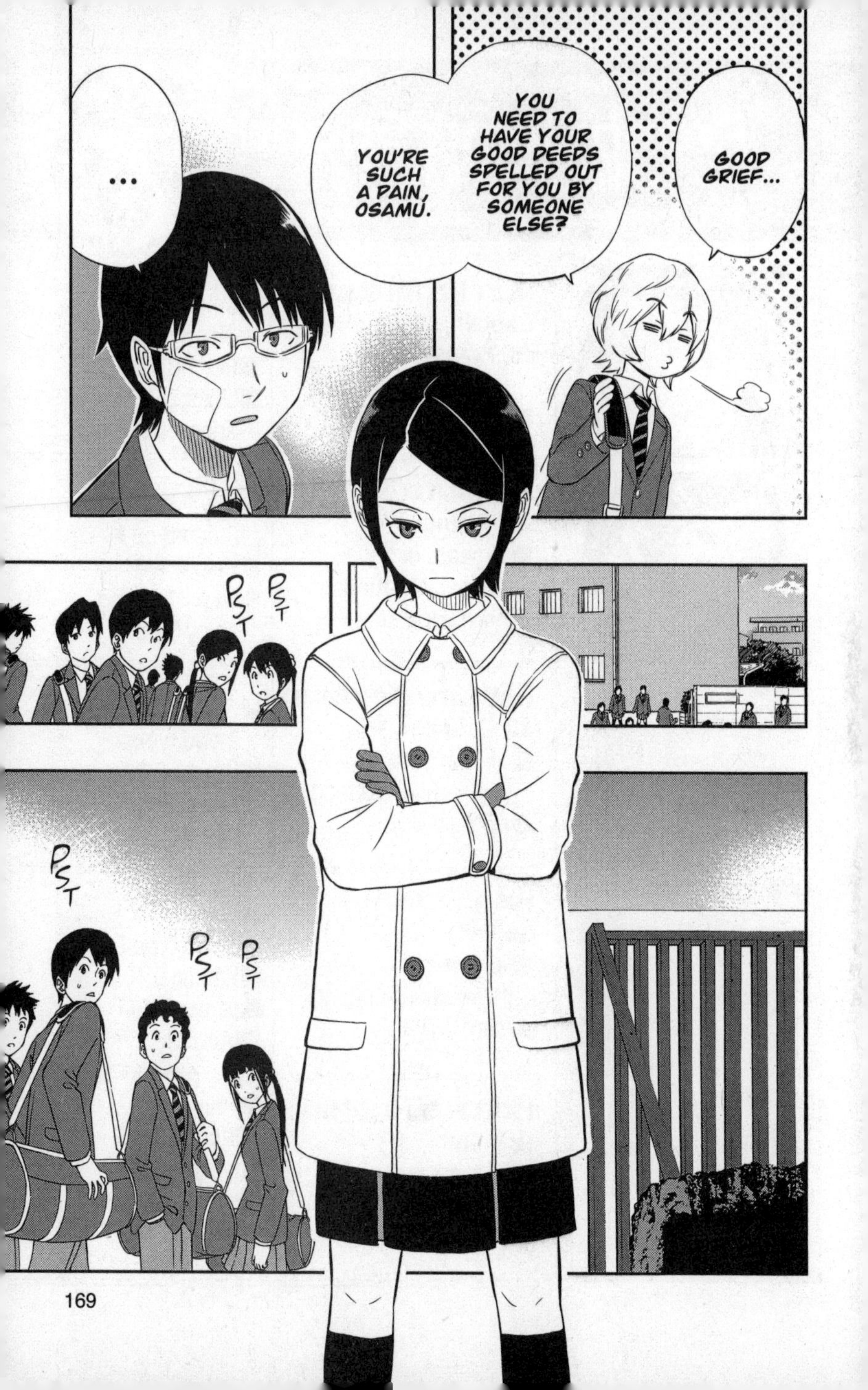
GOOD GRIEF...
YOU NEED TO HAVE YOUR GOOD DEEDS SPELLED OUT FOR YOU BY SOMEONE ELSE?
YOU'RE SUCH A PAIN, OSAMU.
...
PST PST
PST
PST PST

Arashiyama Squad

Border HQ A-Rank #5

Jun Arashiyama
Captain, All-Rounder
- 19 years old (college student)
- Born July 29

- Aptenodytes, Blood type O
- Height: 5'10"
- Likes: Siblings, dogs, seafood

Ai Kitora
All-Rounder
- 15 years old (junior high student)
- Born June 26

- Gladius, Blood type A
- Height: 5'3"
- Likes: Training, spicy food

Mitsuru Tokieda
All-Rounder
- 16 years old (high school student)
- Born April 12

- Falco, Blood type A
- Height: 5'6"
- Likes: Mochi, tangerines, cats

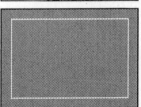

Ken Satori
Sniper
- 16 years old (high school student)
- Born July 1

- Gladius, Blood type O
- Height: 5'7"
- Likes: Girls, burgers

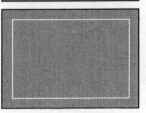

Haruka Ayatsuji
Operator
- 17 years old (high school student)
- Born May 4

- Felis, Blood type A
- Height: 5'4"
- Likes: Cleaning, reading, gummy candies

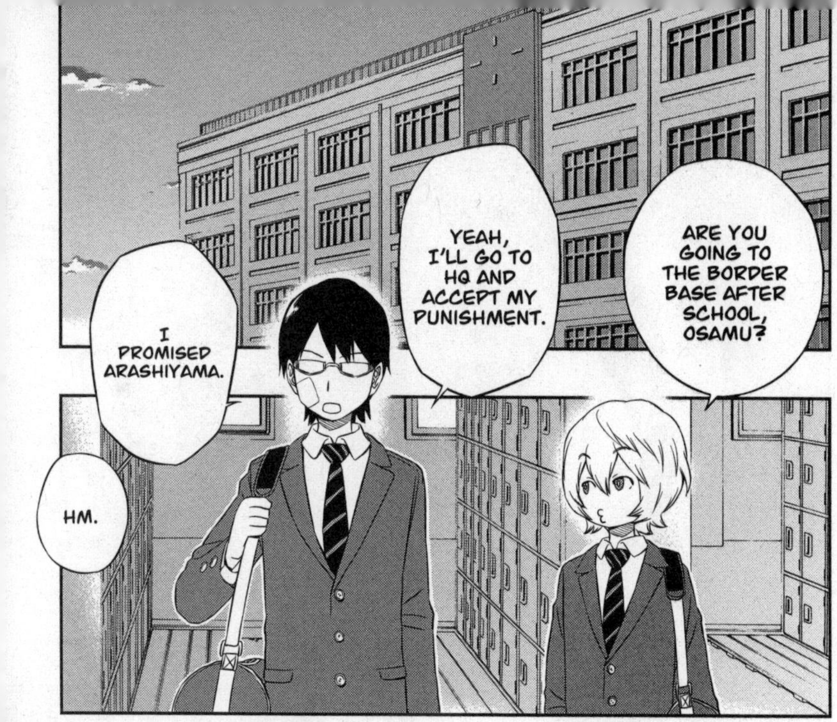
ARE YOU GOING TO THE BORDER BASE AFTER SCHOOL, OSAMU?
YEAH, I'LL GO TO HQ AND ACCEPT MY PUNISHMENT.
I PROMISED ARASHIYAMA.
HM.

Chapter 7 Ai Kitora

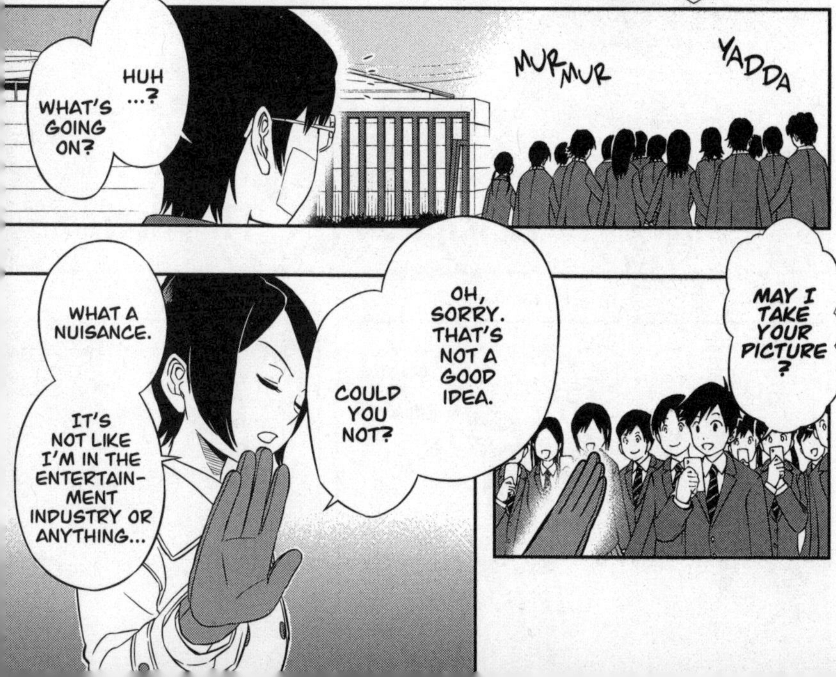
YADDA
MUR MUR
HUH...?
WHAT'S GOING ON?
MAY I TAKE YOUR PICTURE?
OH, SORRY. THAT'S NOT A GOOD IDEA.
COULD YOU NOT?
WHAT A NUISANCE.
IT'S NOT LIKE I'M IN THE ENTERTAINMENT INDUSTRY OR ANYTHING...

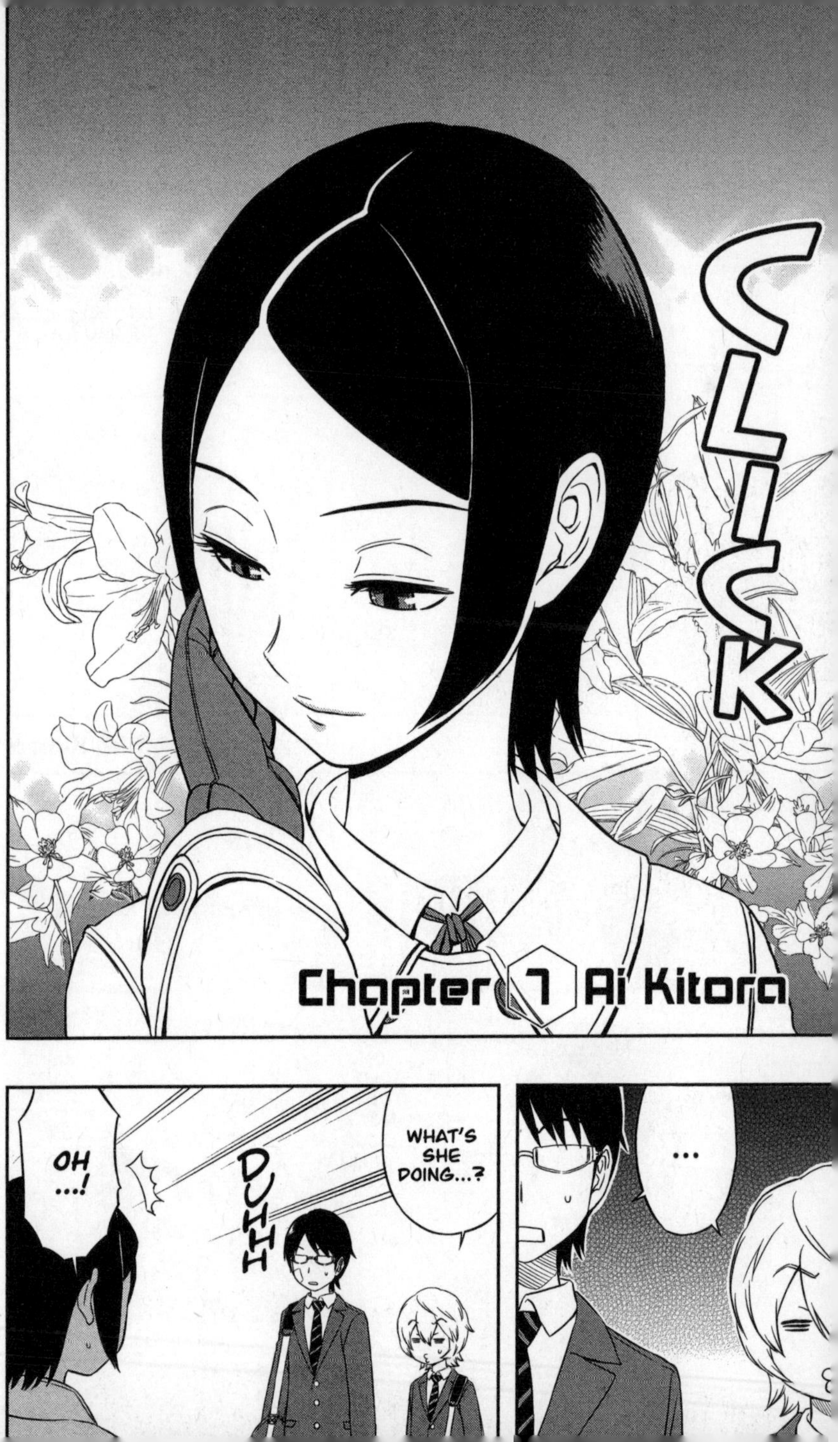
CLICK
Chapter 7 Ai Kitora
...
WHAT'S SHE DOING...?
DUHHH
OH ...!

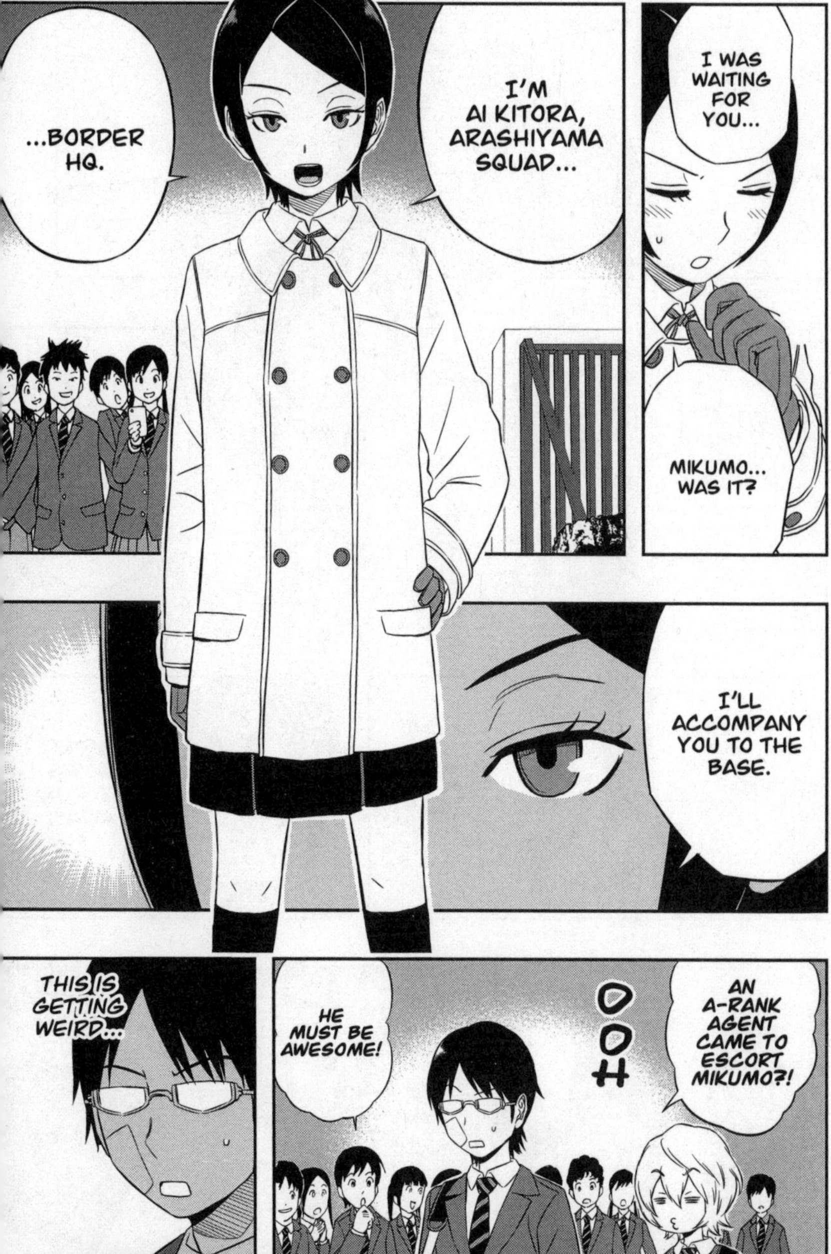
I WAS WAITING FOR YOU...
MIKUMO... WAS IT?
I'M AI KITORA, ARASHIYAMA SQUAD...
...BORDER HQ.
I'LL ACCOMPANY YOU TO THE BASE.
AN A-RANK AGENT CAME TO ESCORT MIKUMO?!
OOH
HE MUST BE AWESOME!
THIS IS GETTING WEIRD...

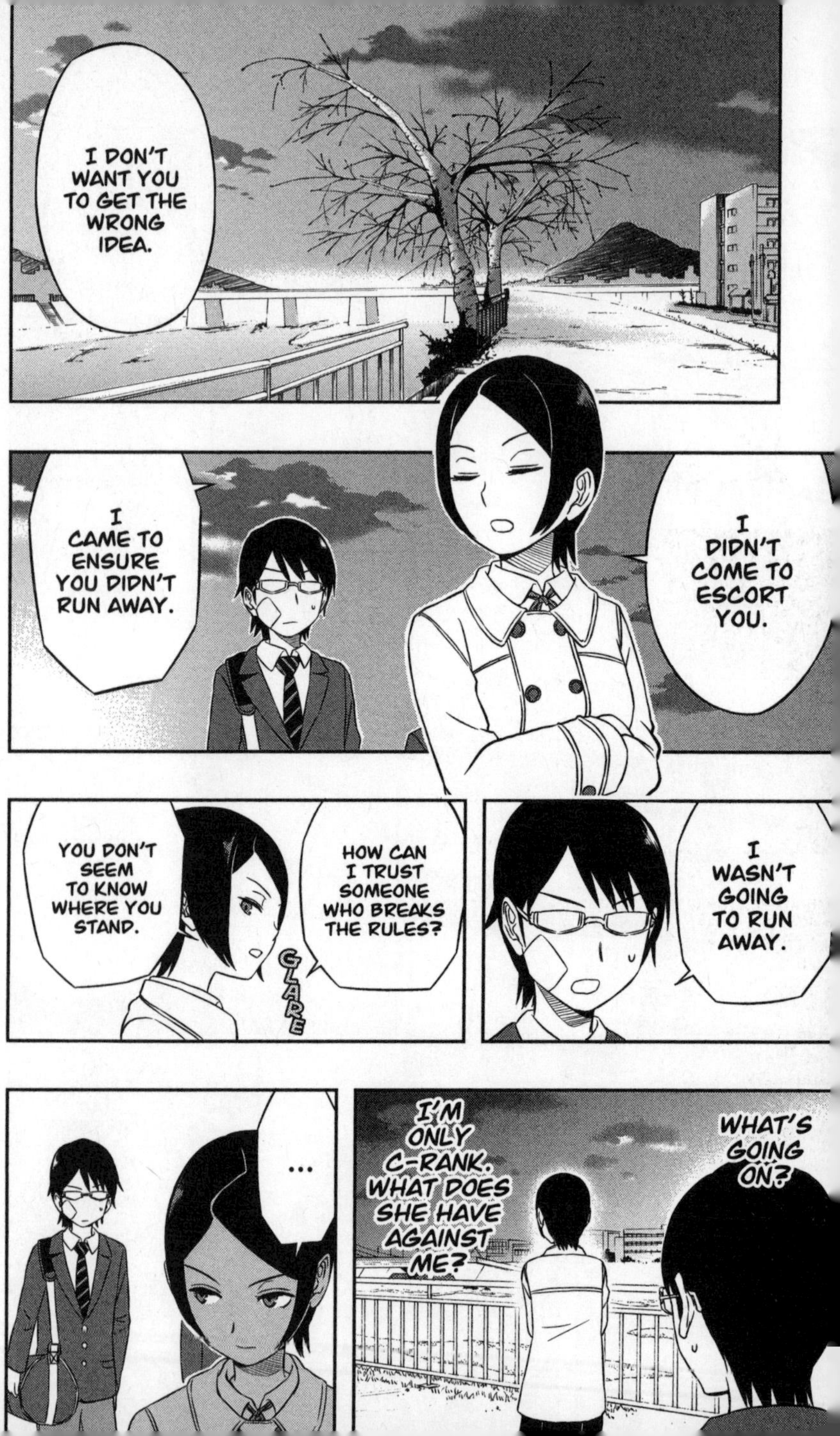
I DON'T WANT YOU TO GET THE WRONG IDEA.
I DIDN'T COME TO ESCORT YOU.
I CAME TO ENSURE YOU DIDN'T RUN AWAY.
I WASN'T GOING TO RUN AWAY.
HOW CAN I TRUST SOMEONE WHO BREAKS THE RULES?
GLARE
YOU DON'T SEEM TO KNOW WHERE YOU STAND.
WHAT'S GOING ON?
I'M ONLY C-RANK. WHAT DOES SHE HAVE AGAINST ME?
...

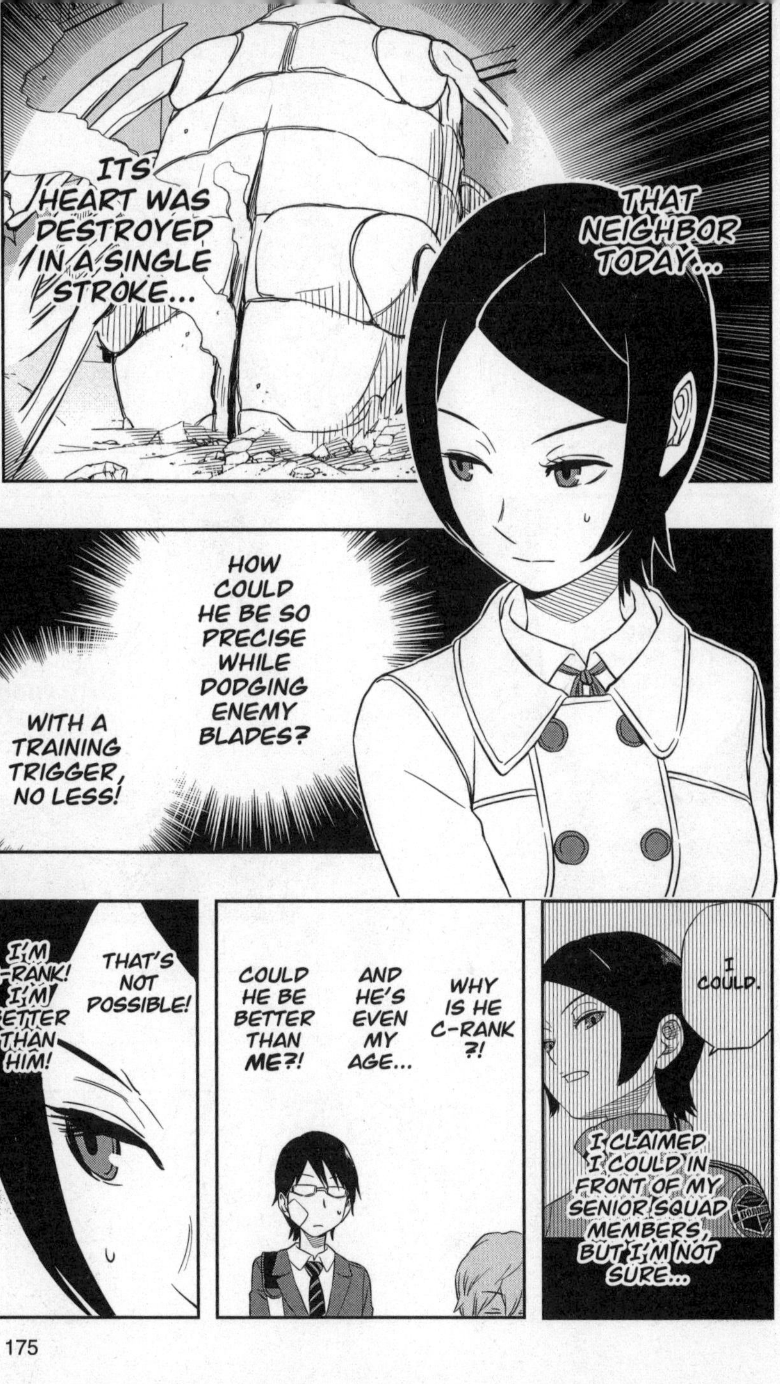
THAT NEIGHBOR TODAY...
ITS HEART WAS DESTROYED IN A SINGLE STROKE...
HOW COULD HE BE SO PRECISE WHILE DODGING ENEMY BLADES?
WITH A TRAINING TRIGGER, NO LESS!
I COULD.
I CLAIMED I COULD IN FRONT OF MY SENIOR SQUAD MEMBERS, BUT I'M NOT SURE...
WHY IS HE C-RANK?!
AND HE'S EVEN MY AGE...
COULD HE BE BETTER THAN ME?!
THAT'S NOT POSSIBLE!
I'M A-RANK! I'M BETTER THAN HIM!

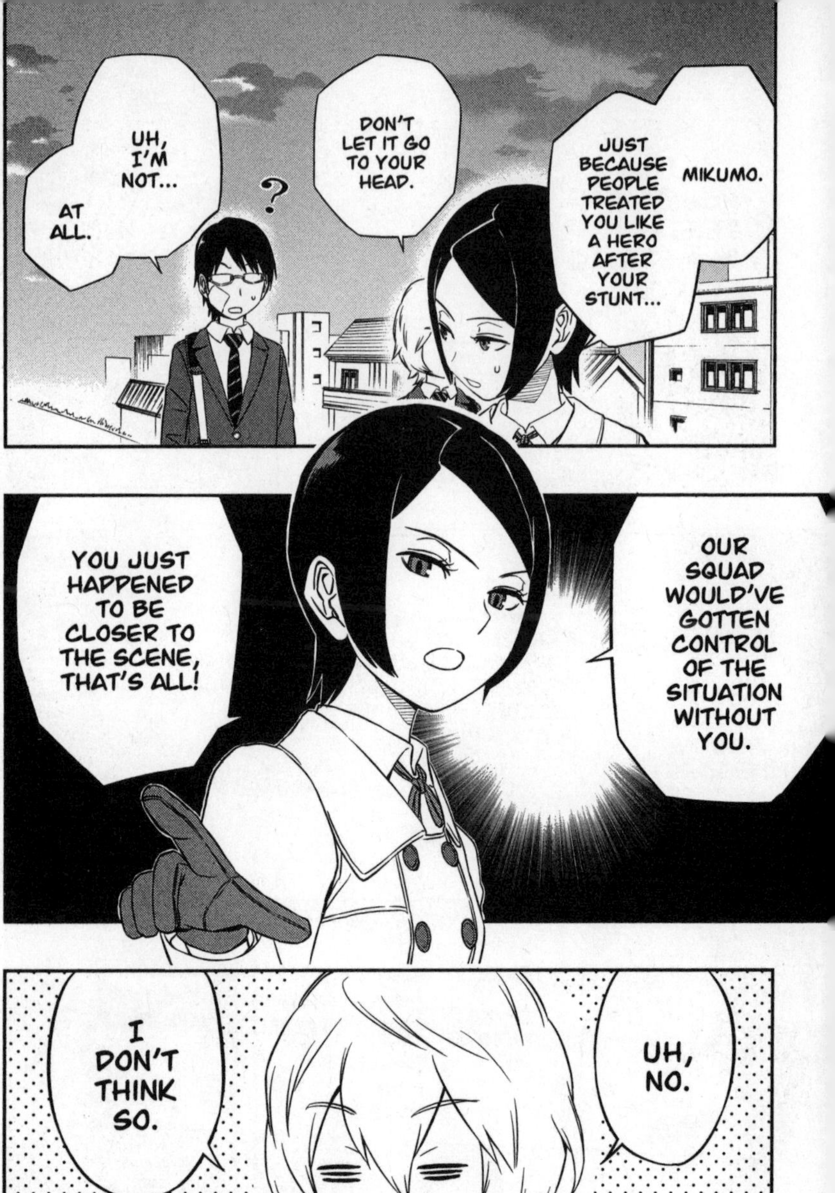
MIKUMO.
JUST BECAUSE PEOPLE TREATED YOU LIKE A HERO AFTER YOUR STUNT...
DON'T LET IT GO TO YOUR HEAD.
?
UH, I'M NOT...
AT ALL.
OUR SQUAD WOULD'VE GOTTEN CONTROL OF THE SITUATION WITHOUT YOU.
YOU JUST HAPPENED TO BE CLOSER TO THE SCENE, THAT'S ALL!
UH, NO.
I DON'T THINK SO.

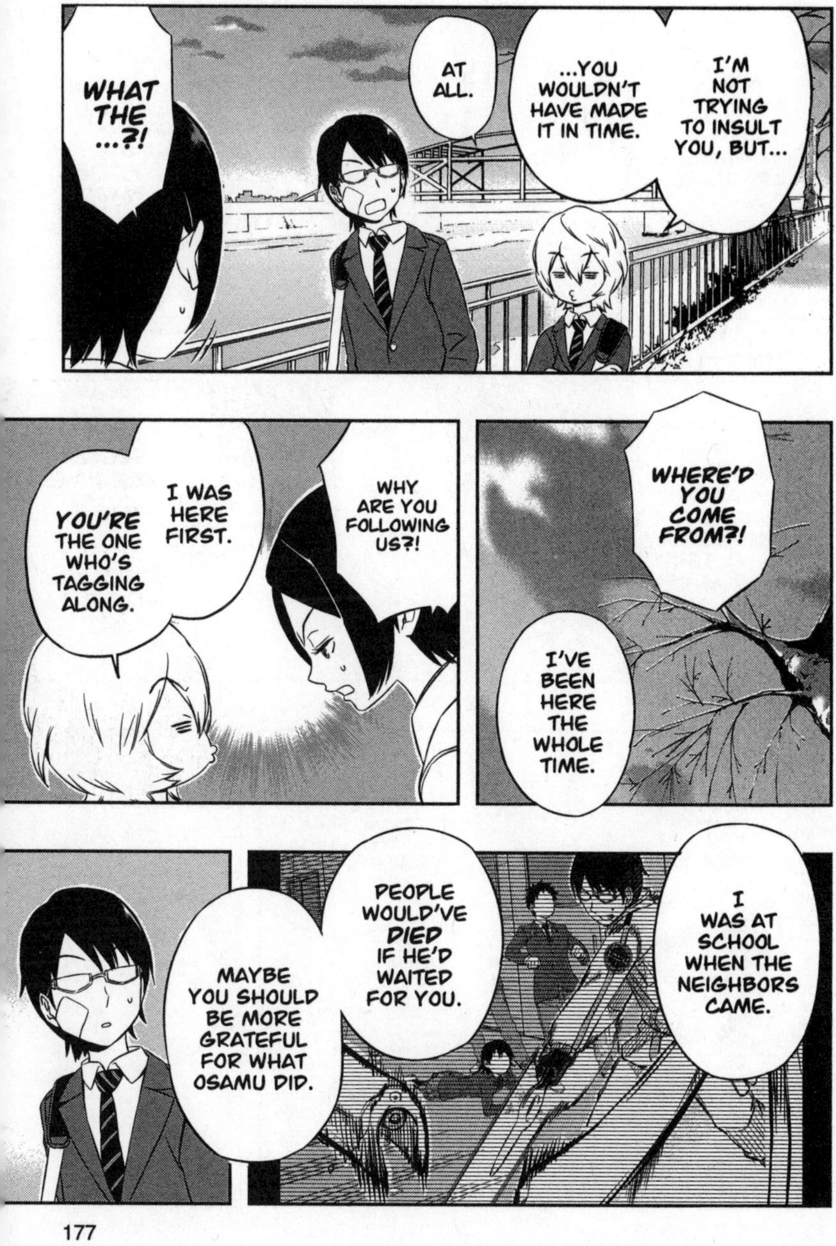
I'M NOT TRYING TO INSULT YOU, BUT...
...YOU WOULDN'T HAVE MADE IT IN TIME.
AT ALL.
WHAT THE ...?!
WHERE'D YOU COME FROM?!
I'VE BEEN HERE THE WHOLE TIME.
WHY ARE YOU FOLLOWING US?!
I WAS HERE FIRST.
YOU'RE THE ONE WHO'S TAGGING ALONG.
I WAS AT SCHOOL WHEN THE NEIGHBORS CAME.
PEOPLE WOULD'VE DIED IF HE'D WAITED FOR YOU.
MAYBE YOU SHOULD BE MORE GRATEFUL FOR WHAT OSAMU DID.

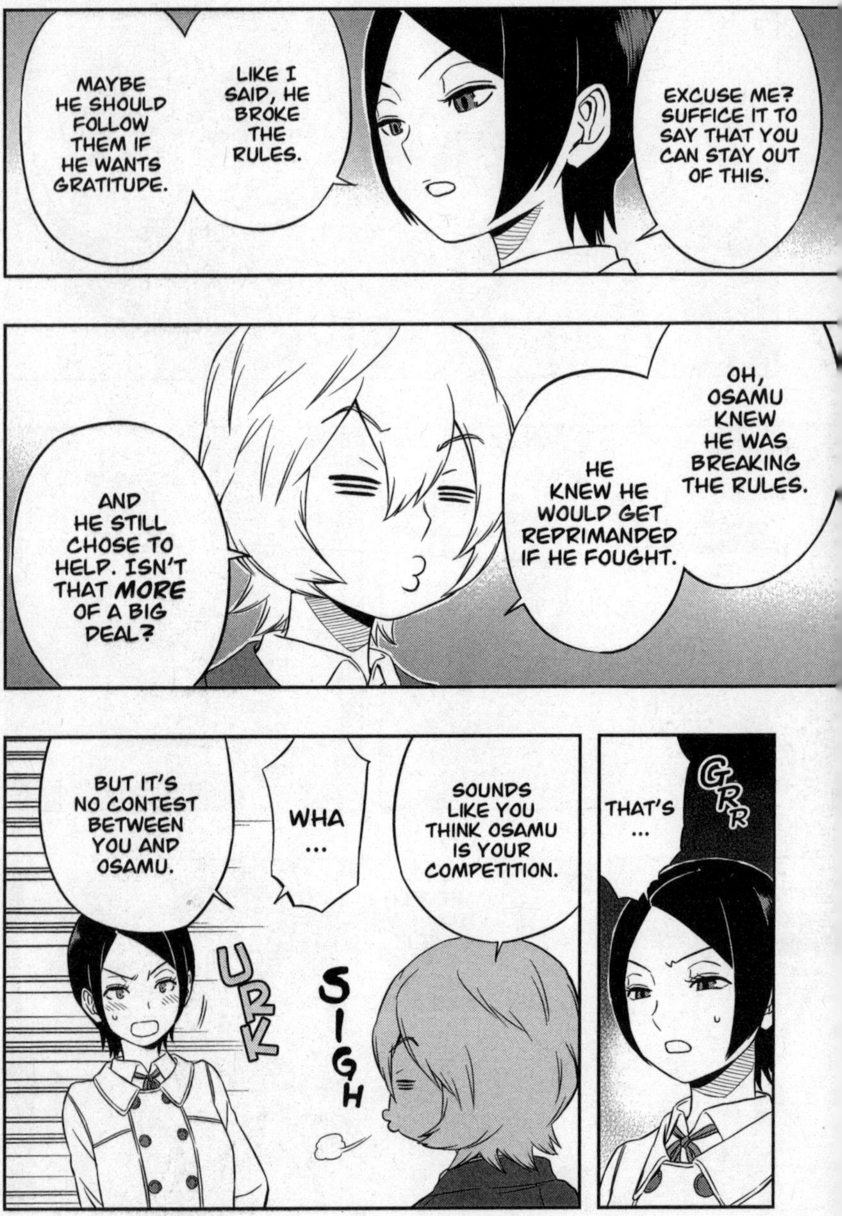
EXCUSE ME? SUFFICE IT TO SAY THAT YOU CAN STAY OUT OF THIS.
LIKE I SAID, HE BROKE THE RULES.
MAYBE HE SHOULD FOLLOW THEM IF HE WANTS GRATITUDE.
OH, OSAMU KNEW HE WAS BREAKING THE RULES.
HE KNEW HE WOULD GET REPRIMANDED IF HE FOUGHT.
AND HE STILL CHOSE TO HELP. ISN'T THAT MORE OF A BIG DEAL?
GRR
THAT'S ...
SOUNDS LIKE YOU THINK OSAMU IS YOUR COMPETITION.
WHA ...
BUT IT'S NO CONTEST BETWEEN YOU AND OSAMU.
SIGH
URK

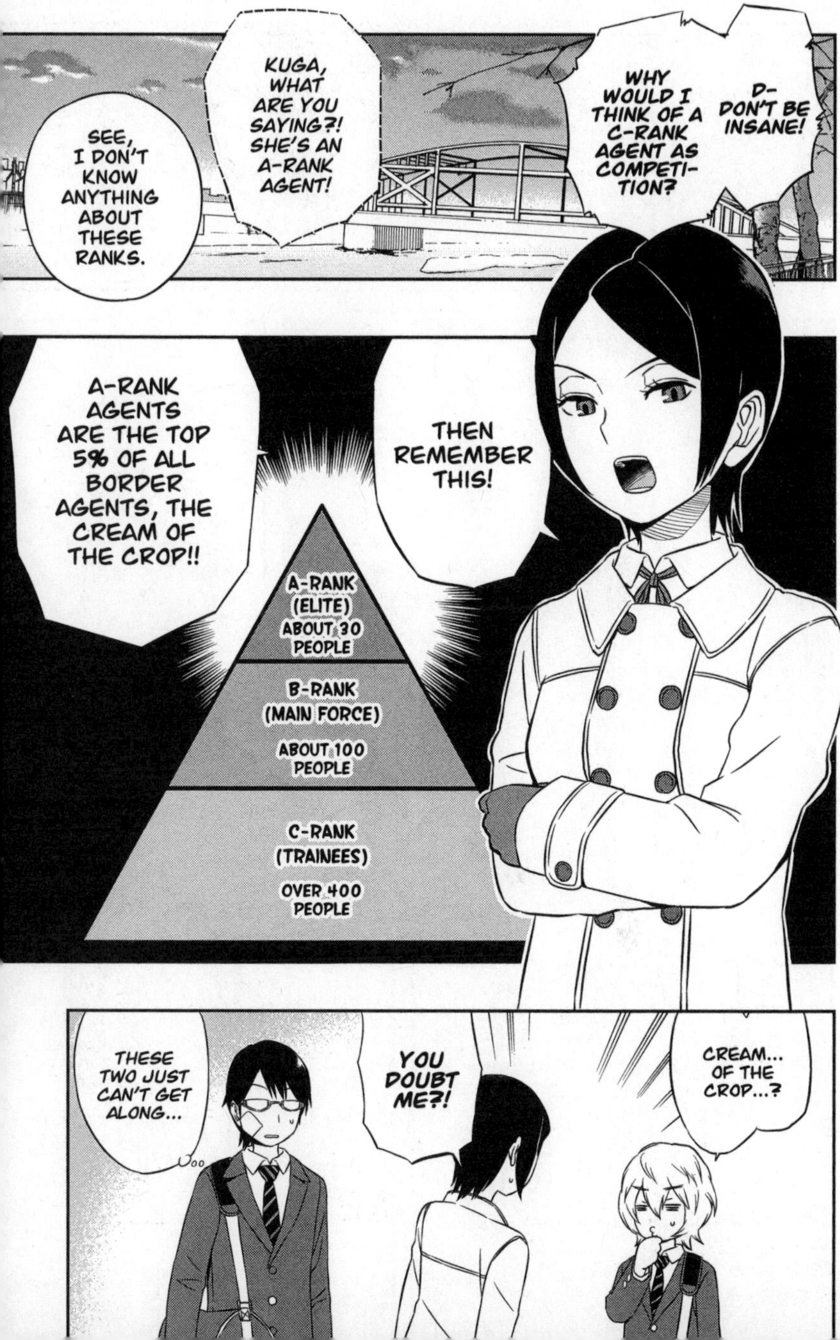
D- DON'T BE INSANE!
WHY WOULD I THINK OF A C-RANK AGENT AS COMPETITION?
KUGA, WHAT ARE YOU SAYING?! SHE'S AN A-RANK AGENT!
SEE, I DON'T KNOW ANYTHING ABOUT THESE RANKS.
THEN REMEMBER THIS!
A-RANK AGENTS ARE THE TOP 5% OF ALL BORDER AGENTS, THE CREAM OF THE CROP!!
A-RANK (ELITE) ABOUT 30 PEOPLE
B-RANK (MAIN FORCE) ABOUT 100 PEOPLE
C-RANK (TRAINEES) OVER 400 PEOPLE
CREAM... OF THE CROP...?
YOU DOUBT ME?!
THESE TWO JUST CAN'T GET ALONG...

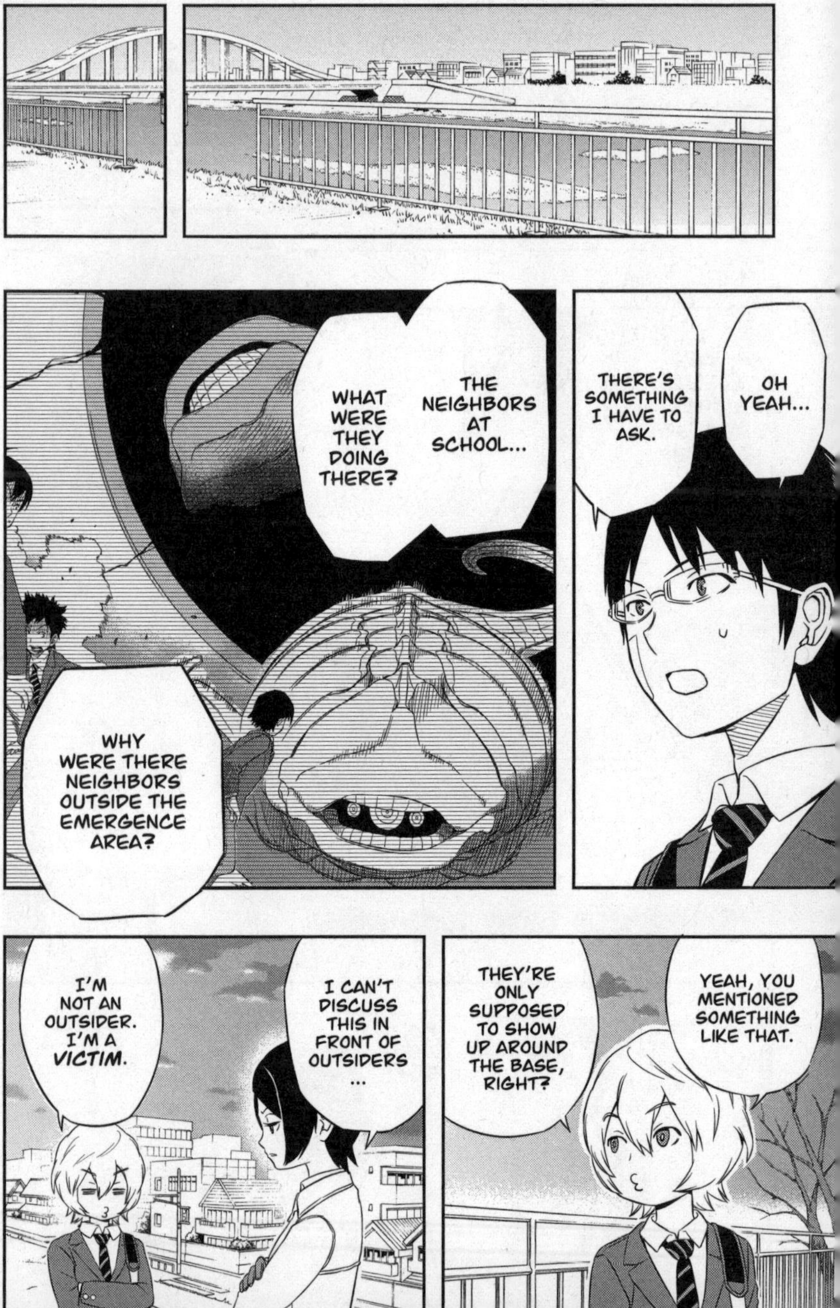
OH YEAH...
THERE'S SOMETHING I HAVE TO ASK.
THE NEIGHBORS AT SCHOOL...
WHAT WERE THEY DOING THERE?
WHY WERE THERE NEIGHBORS OUTSIDE THE EMERGENCE AREA?
YEAH, YOU MENTIONED SOMETHING LIKE THAT.
THEY'RE ONLY SUPPOSED TO SHOW UP AROUND THE BASE, RIGHT?
I CAN'T DISCUSS THIS IN FRONT OF OUTSIDERS...
I'M NOT AN OUTSIDER. I'M A *VICTIM*.

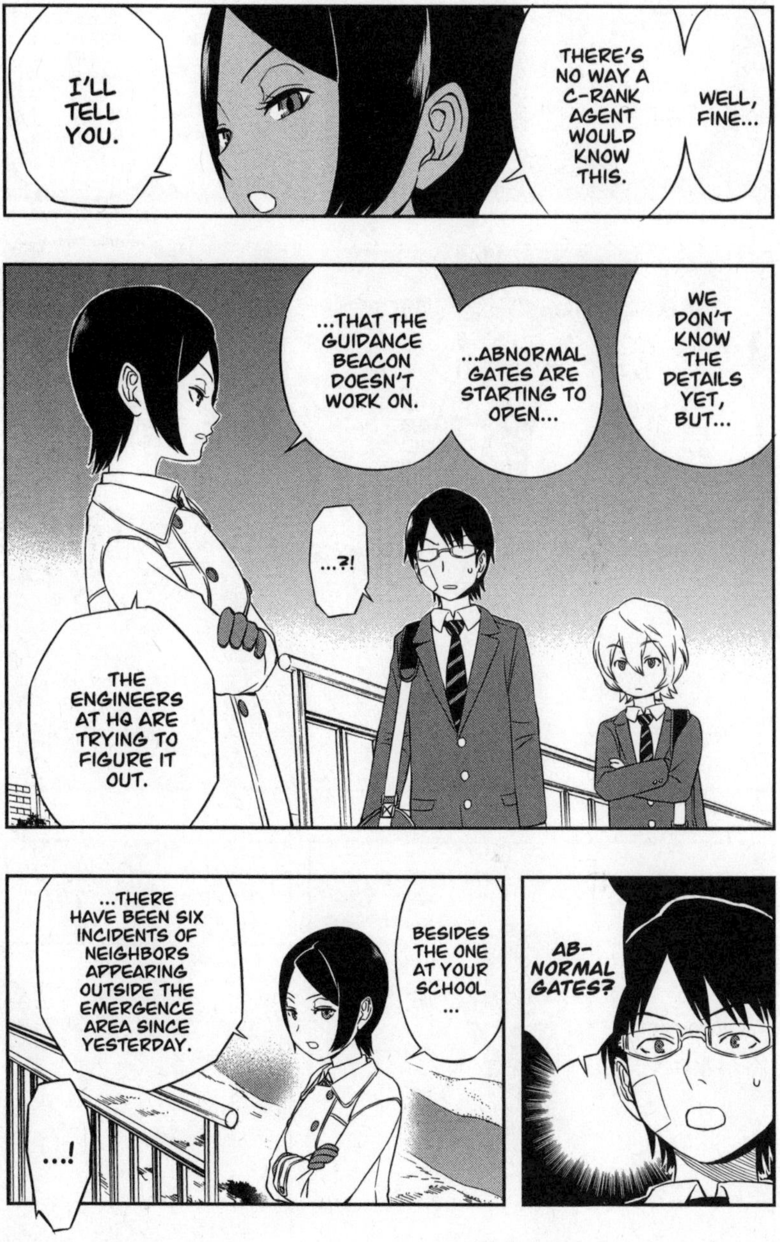
WELL, FINE...
THERE'S NO WAY A C-RANK AGENT WOULD KNOW THIS.
I'LL TELL YOU.
WE DON'T KNOW THE DETAILS YET, BUT...
...ABNORMAL GATES ARE STARTING TO OPEN...
...THAT THE GUIDANCE BEACON DOESN'T WORK ON.
...?!
THE ENGINEERS AT HQ ARE TRYING TO FIGURE IT OUT.
AB-NORMAL GATES?
BESIDES THE ONE AT YOUR SCHOOL...
...THERE HAVE BEEN SIX INCIDENTS OF NEIGHBORS APPEARING OUTSIDE THE EMERGENCE AREA SINCE YESTERDAY.
...!

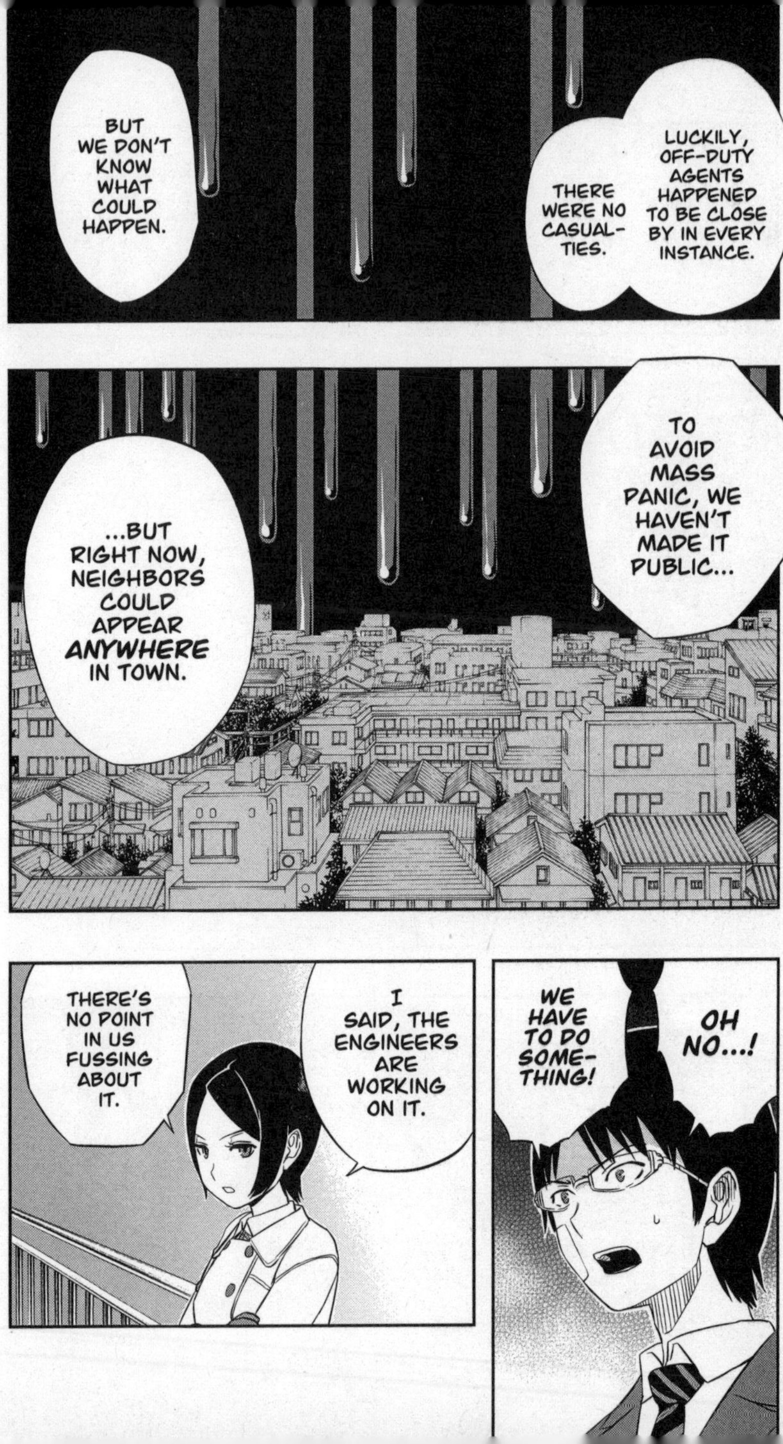
LUCKILY, OFF-DUTY AGENTS HAPPENED TO BE CLOSE BY IN EVERY INSTANCE.
THERE WERE NO CASUAL-TIES.
BUT WE DON'T KNOW WHAT COULD HAPPEN.
TO AVOID MASS PANIC, WE HAVEN'T MADE IT PUBLIC...
...BUT RIGHT NOW, NEIGHBORS COULD APPEAR ANYWHERE IN TOWN.
OH NO...!
WE HAVE TO DO SOME-THING!
I SAID, THE ENGINEERS ARE WORKING ON IT.
THERE'S NO POINT IN US FUSSING ABOUT IT.

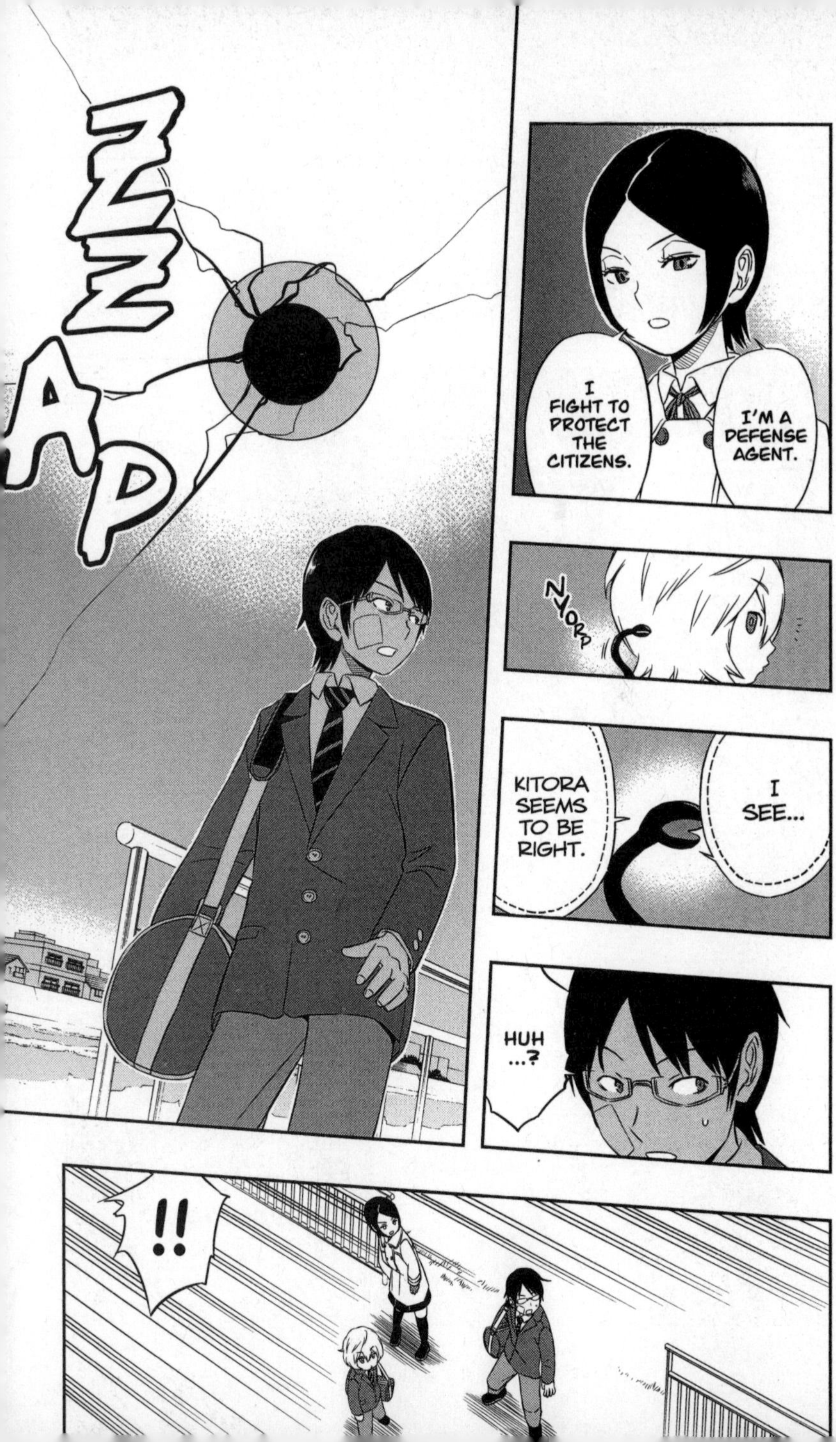
I'M A DEFENSE AGENT.
I FIGHT TO PROTECT THE CITIZENS.
NYORP
I SEE...
KITORA SEEMS TO BE RIGHT.
HUH ...?
ZZAP
!!

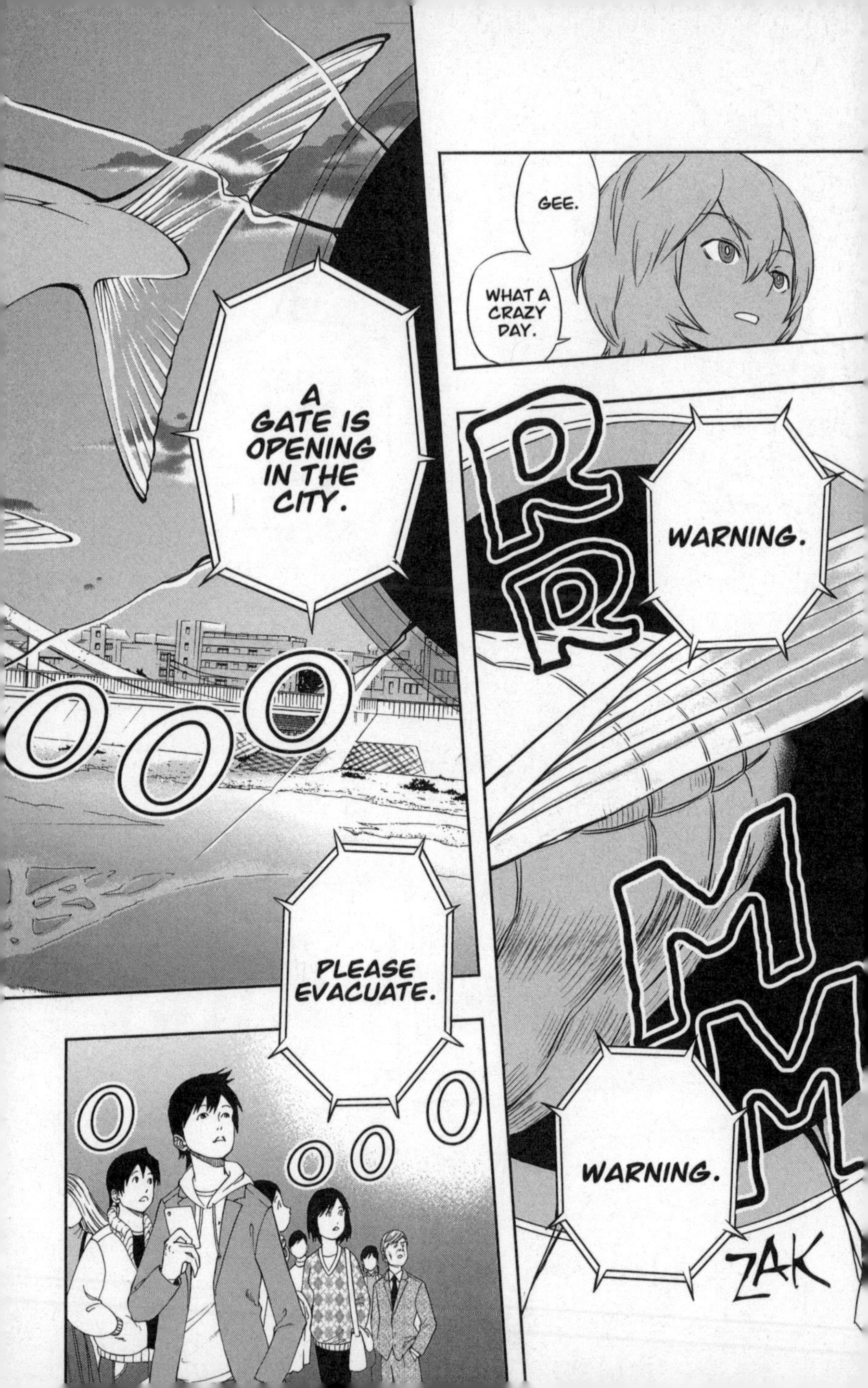
GEE.
WHAT A CRAZY DAY.
RR
WARNING.
MMM
WARNING.
ZAK
A GATE IS OPENING IN THE CITY.
OOO
PLEASE EVACUATE.
OOOO

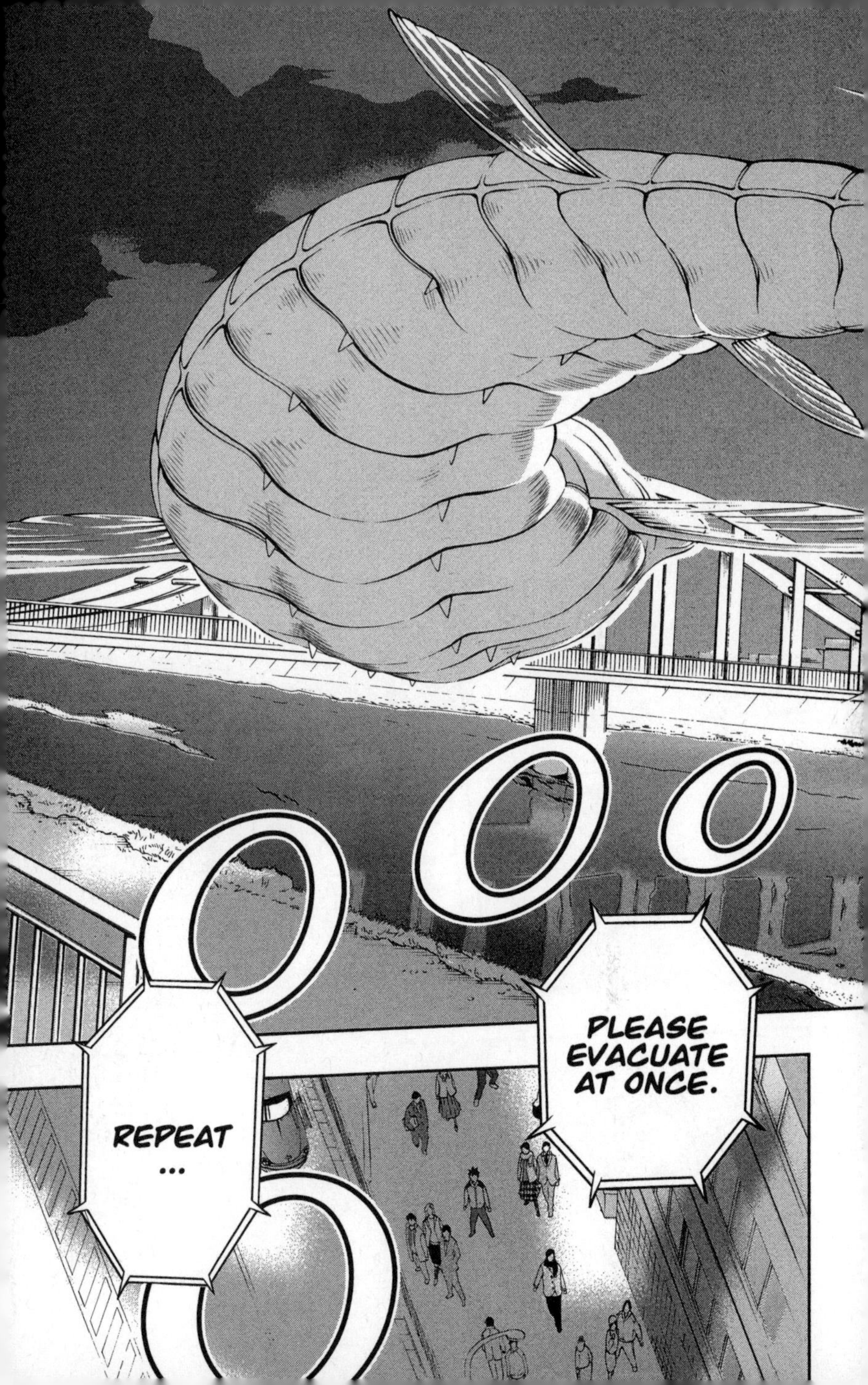
PLEASE EVACUATE AT ONCE.
REPEAT ...

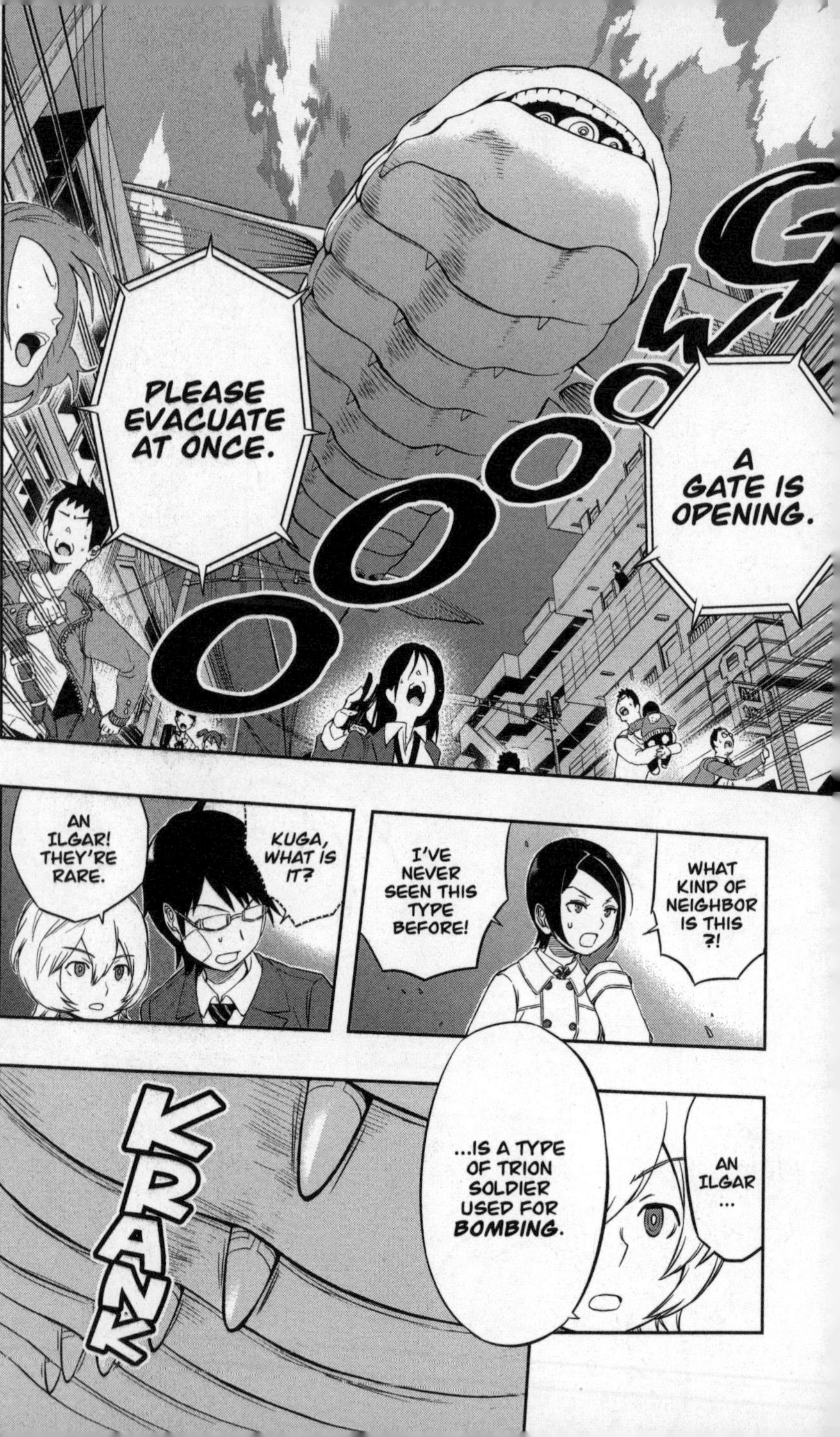
GWOOOOO
A GATE IS OPENING.
PLEASE EVACUATE AT ONCE.
WHAT KIND OF NEIGHBOR IS THIS ?!
I'VE NEVER SEEN THIS TYPE BEFORE!
KUGA, WHAT IS IT?
AN ILGAR! THEY'RE RARE.
AN ILGAR ...
...IS A TYPE OF TRION SOLDIER USED FOR BOMBING.
KRANK

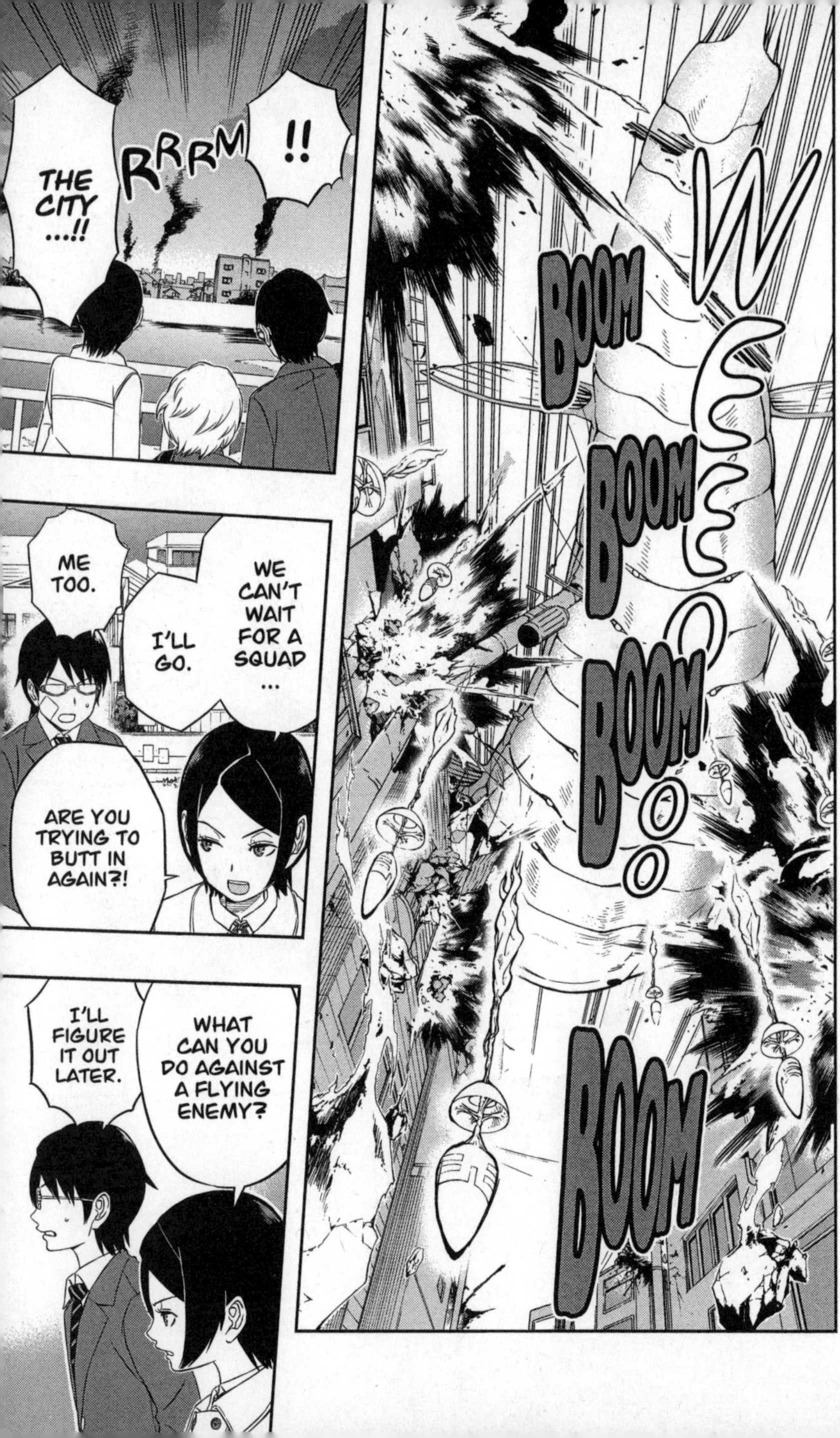
BOOM
BOOM
BOOM
BOOM
!!
RRRM
THE CITY ...!!
WE CAN'T WAIT FOR A SQUAD ...
I'LL GO.
ME TOO.
ARE YOU TRYING TO BUTT IN AGAIN?!
WHAT CAN YOU DO AGAINST A FLYING ENEMY?
I'LL FIGURE IT OUT LATER.

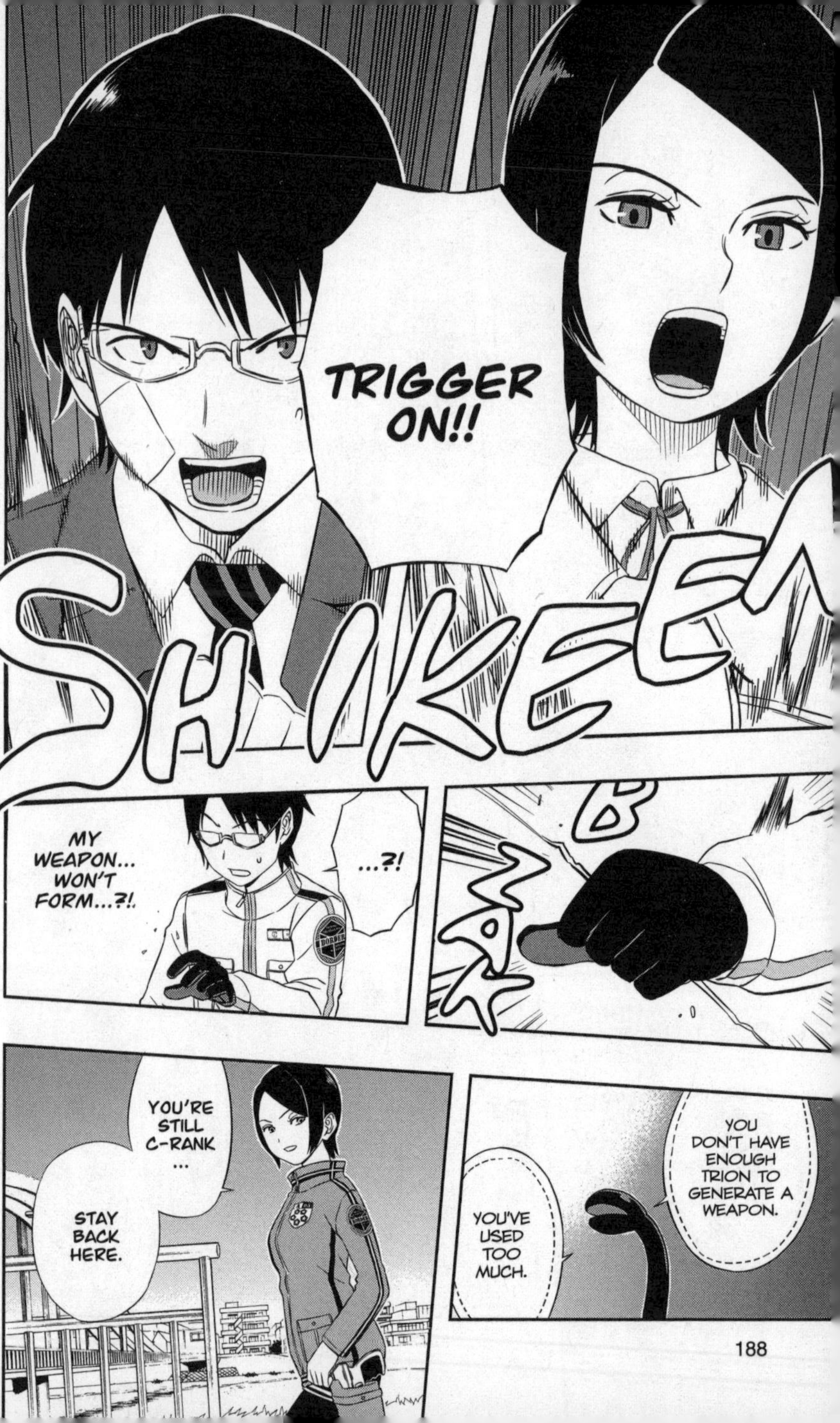
TRIGGER ON!!
...?!
MY WEAPON... WON'T FORM...?!
YOU DON'T HAVE ENOUGH TRION TO GENERATE A WEAPON.
YOU'VE USED TOO MUCH.
YOU'RE STILL C-RANK ...
STAY BACK HERE.

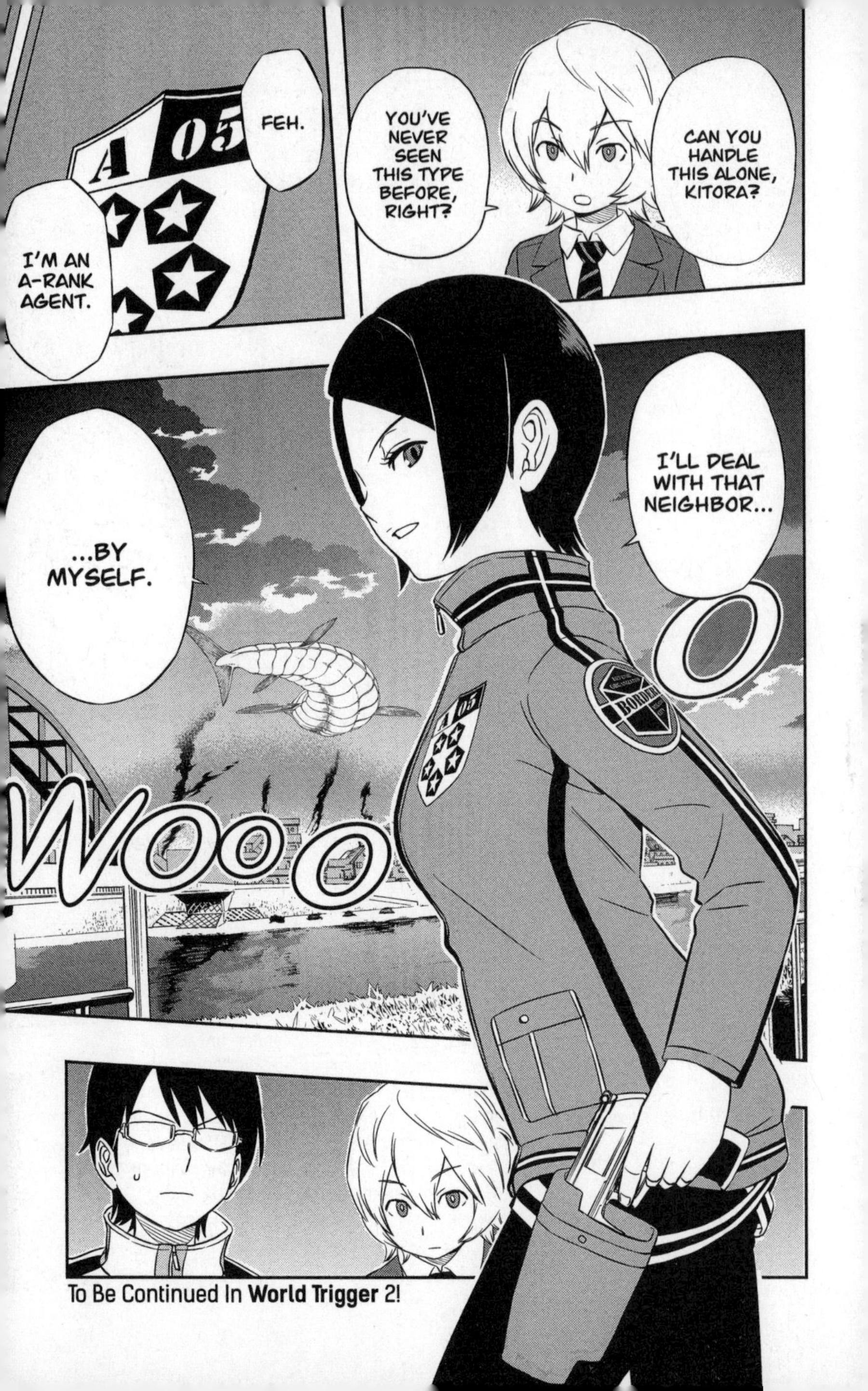
CAN YOU HANDLE THIS ALONE, KITORA?
YOU'VE NEVER SEEN THIS TYPE BEFORE, RIGHT?
FEH.
I'M AN A-RANK AGENT.
A 05
I'LL DEAL WITH THAT NEIGHBOR...
...BY MYSELF.
WOOOO
BORDER

To Be Continued In **World Trigger** 2!

WORLD TRIGGER

Bonus Character Pages

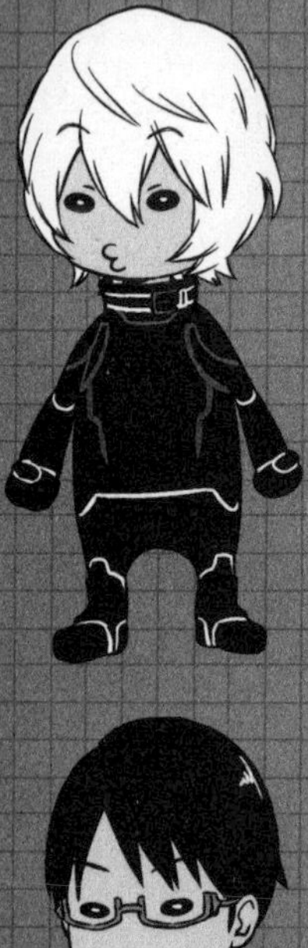

YUMA

Just Break a Leg

The true heir to the duck lips and "=" eyes. He didn't start out as a shorty, but if he'd been tall, the scene where he breaks the punk's leg would've been too controversial. So I'm glad he's a shorty. Designed after a chicken.

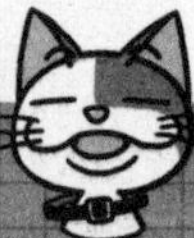

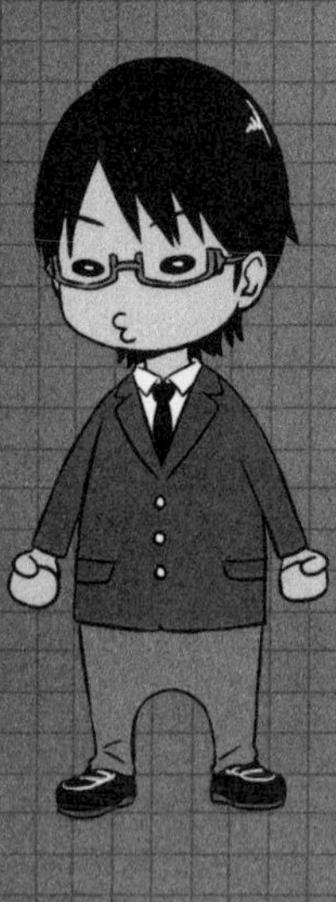

OSAMU

Four-Eyes 4Eva

A straightforward character whose only initial character description was "guy with glasses." His catchphrase is "What the...?!" At any given moment, there's a high possibility that a sweat drop is on his face. If you collect 50 Osamus without a sweat drop, you can exchange them for a chance to win one golden Osamu.

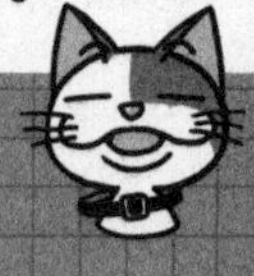

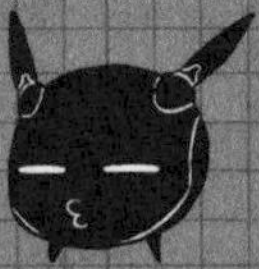

REPLICA

The Round Black Floaty Thing

Autonomous all-purpose sidekick that takes care of all exposition. Indispensable for making the story flow smoothly, and very convenient. Designed after my rice cooker.

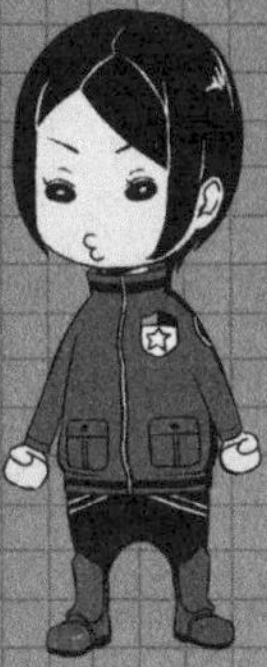

KITORA

By A-rank, for A-rank

She's skilled and proud, and that makes her vulnerable—my favorite kind of character. My editor said, "The readers might not like her personality." So her bust size was increased to counterbalance that.

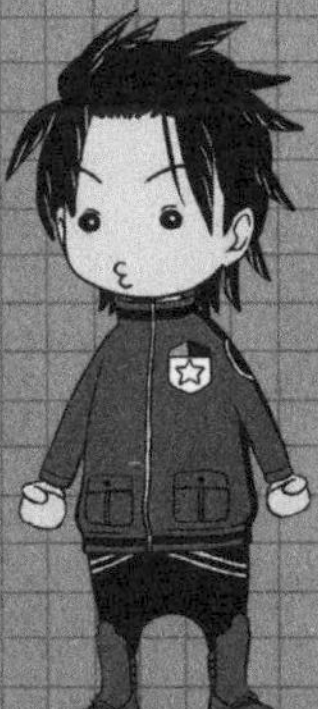

ARASHIYAMA

Brother and Sister Complex

I like this character a lot, but

DRAWING HIS HAIR IS A PAIN.

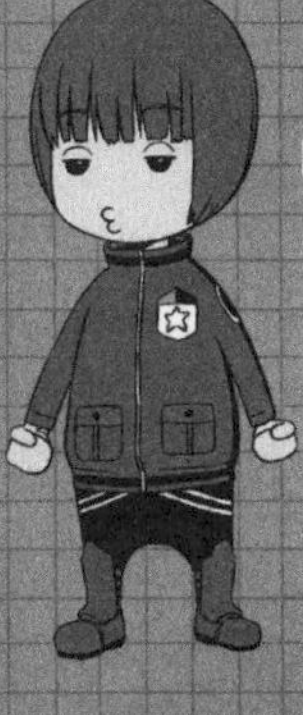

MITSURU

Right, Arashiyama?

I've always felt that characters with sleepy eyes are competent. Therefore, Mitsuru is probably competent. He was more of a pretty boy in the initial design, but his current looks are more interesting.

YOU'RE READING THE WRONG WAY!

World Trigger reads from right to left, starting in the upper-right corner. Japanese is read from right to left, meaning that action, sound effects, and word-balloon order are completely reversed from the English order.

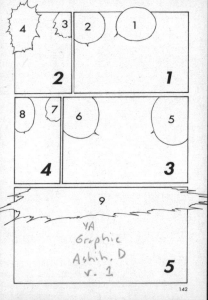